MW00612537

THE
PRECISIANIST
STRAIN

THE PRECISIANIST STRAIN

Disciplinary Religion &

Antinomian Backlash in

Puritanism to 1638

THEODORE DWIGHT BOZEMAN

Published for the
Omohundro Institute of Early American History and Culture,
Williamsburg, Virginia, by the
University of North Carolina Press,
Chapel Hill and London

The Omohundro Institute of
Early American History and Culture is sponsored
jointly by the College of William and Mary and the
Colonial Williamsburg Foundation. On November 15, 1996,
the Institute adopted its present name in honor of a
bequest from Malvern H. Omohundro, Jr.

© 2004 The University of North Carolina Press
All rights reserved
Manufactured in the United States of America

Library of Congress Cataloging-in-Publication Data
Bozeman, Theodore Dwight, 1942–
The precisianist strain : disciplinary religion and antinomian
backlash in Puritanism to 1638 / Theodore Dwight Bozeman.
p. cm.
Includes bibliographical references and index.
ISBN 0-8078-2850-5 (alk. paper)
1. Puritans—England. 2. Antinomianism—England—
History of doctrines—17th century. 3. Puritans—Massachusetts.
4. Antinomianism—Massachusetts—History of doctrines—
17th century. I. Omohundro Institute of Early American
History & Culture. II. Title.
BX9334.3 .B69   2004
285′.9—dc21   2003012950

The paper in this book meets the guidelines for permanence and
durability of the Committee on Production Guidelines for Book
Longevity of the Council on Library Resources.

This volume received indirect support from an unrestricted book
publications grant awarded to the Institute by the L. J. Skaggs and
Mary C. Skaggs Foundation of Oakland, California.

08 07 06 05 04   5 4 3 2 1

For Hannelore, always

ACKNOWLEDGMENTS

Numerous friends and colleagues contributed to the writing and revision of this book. Many thanks are due to the staffs of the American Antiquarian Society, Worcester, Massachusetts; the Massachusetts Historical Society, Boston; the Boston Public Library; the Genealogical Society of Utah, Salt Lake City; the Folger Shakespeare Library, Washington, D.C.; the Institute of Historical Research, London; and the manuscript divisions of the British Library, London, and the Bodleian Library at Oxford University. Dave Hudson and Jim Julich of the University of Iowa's Main Library assisted in the acquisition of rare tracts and microfilm copies of needed materials, and Sargent Bush, Jr., helped me obtain a rare tract by John Traske. University of Iowa faculty, including the late Sydney V. James, Ralph Keen, James McCue, Mark Peterson, James Price, and Steven Wieting, generously shared ideas as the work progressed. Charles Cohen, Richard Gildrie, Ralph Keen, Mark Peterson, Baird Tipson, Dewey D. Wallace, and Michael Winship read a late draft in its entirety and supplied invaluable commentary, as did an anonymous reader for the Omohundro Institute of Early American History and Culture. Baird Tipson allowed me an advance look at portions of the edition of Samuel Stone's *Body of Divinity* he is editing, and Merja Kyoto of Uppsala University permitted me to examine a copy of her transcription of nonsermonic parts of a notebook of Robert Keayne held by the Massachusetts Historical Society. I thank the editors of the *Journal of Ecclesiastical History* for permission to use material in Chapter 10 that first appeared in the *Journal* in 1996 in "The Glory of the 'Third Time': John Eaton as Contra-Puritan." Fredrika J. Teute, editor of publications at the Institute, shepherded the manuscript through its initial phases; and Gil Kelly, managing editor, copy-edited the final manuscript with great care and skill, assisted by Emily Moore. Progress upon the study was speeded by a research fellowship from the National Endowment for the Humanities and two Faculty Development Awards from the University of Iowa.

CONTENTS

ABBREVIATIONS

AC	David D. Hall, ed., *The Antinomian Controversy, 1636–1638* (Middletown, Conn., 1968)
AG	Robert Towne, *The Assertion of Grace* . . . (London, 1644)
AR, 1–8	Thomas Hooker, *The Application of Redemption* . . . *The First Eight Books* (London, 1656)
AR, 9–10	Thomas Hooker, *The Application of Redemption* . . . *The Ninth and Tenth Books* (London, 1657)
BDR	Richard L. Greaves and Robert Zaller, eds., *Biographical Dictionary of British Radicals in the Seventeenth Century*, 3 vols. (London, 1982–1984)
BPD	[William Fulke], *A Briefe and Plaine Declaration, Concerning the Desires of All Those Faithfull Ministers, That Have and Do Seek for the Discipline and Reformation of the Church of Englande* (London, 1584)
BWWP	Ian Breward, ed., *The Work of William Perkins* (Appleford, Eng., 1970)
CA	Tobias Crisp, *Christ Alone Exalted* (London, 1643), I–II
CAC	Robert Bolton, *Instructions for a Right Comforting Afflicted Consciences* . . . (London, 1631)
CD	George Gifforde, *A Briefe Discourse of* . . . *the Countrie Divinitie* (London, 1598)
CDGM	[Robert Parsons], *A Christian Directorie Guiding Men to Their Salvation* ([Rouen], 1585)
CDW	Henry Scudder, *The Christians Daily Walke in Holy Securitie and Peace* (London, 1627)
CF	John Cotton, *Christ the Fountaine of Life* . . . (London, 1651)
CFS	John Downame, *The Conflict betweene the Flesh and the Spirit* . . . (London, 1618)
CH	*Church History*
CJC	Sargent Bush, Jr., ed., *The Correspondence of John Cotton* (Chapel Hill, N.C., 2001)
CL	[John Udall], *A Commentarie upon the Lamentations of Jeremy* (London, 1593)

CS   [John Udall], *Certaine Sermons Taken out of Severall Places of*
          Scripture (London, 1596)

CT   Rodger Br[ie]rl[e]y, *A Bundle of Soul-Convincing, Directing, and*
          Comforting Truths . . . (London, 1677)

CW   J[ohn] Downame, *The Christian Warfare* . . . , 2d ed. (London,
          1608)

CWSR   Tho[mas] Taylor, *Circumspect Walking: Describing the Severall*
          Rules, as So Many Severall Steps in the Way of Wisdome
          (London, 1631)

DNB   *Dictionary of National Biography* (Oxford, 1917–)

DS   Nicolas Bownde, *The Doctrine of the Sabbath* . . . (London, 1595)

EGJ   John Cotton, *A Practical Commentary* . . . *upon the First Epistle*
          Generall of John (London, 1656)

EPM   Patrick Collinson, *The Elizabethan Puritan Movement* (Oxford,
          1967)

ES   Keith Wrightson, *English Society, 1580–1680* (New Brunswick,
          N.J., 1982)

EWB   John Ayre, ed., *The Early Works of Thomas Becon* (Cambridge,
          1843)

FEW   William K. B. Stoever, *"A Faire and Easie Way to Heaven":*
          Covenant Theology and Antinomianism in Early Massachusetts
          (Middletown, Conn., 1978)

FN   Thomas Wilcox, *A Short, Yet a True and Faithful Narration of the*
          Fearful Fire, That Fell in the Towne of Wooburne . . . *1595*
          (London, 1595)

GD   Robert Bolton, *Some Generall Directions for a Comfortable*
          Walking with God . . . (London, 1626)

GG   John Downame, *A Guide to Godlynesse* . . . (London, 1622)

GM   John Cotton, *Gods Mercie Mixed with His Justice* . . . (London,
          1641)

GP   Thomas Shepard, *God's Plot: The Paradoxes of Puritan Piety,*
          Being the Autobiography and Journal of Thomas Shepard,
          ed. Michael McGiffert (Amherst, Mass., 1972)

GV   John Traske, *The True Gospel Vindicated, from the Reproach of a*
          New Gospel . . . (n.p., 1636)

HC   John Eaton, *The Honey-Combe of Free Justification by Christ*
          Alone (London, 1642)

HMC   Historical Manuscripts Commission

HP	P[eter] Gunter, *A Sermon Preached . . . for the Discoverie and Confutation of . . . Hereticall Positions, . . . Held . . . by a Certaine Factious Preacher [John Eaton] of Wickam Market . . .* (London, 1615)
JJW	Richard S. Dunn, James Savage, and Laetitia Yeandle, eds., *The Journal of John Winthrop, 1630–1649* (Cambridge, Mass., 1996)
JWWP	Edward Johnson, *Johnson's Wonder-Working Providence, 1628– 1651,* ed. J. Franklin Jameson (New York, 1910)
KG	Heinrich Denzinger, *Kompendium der Glaubensbekenntnisse und kirchlichen Lehrentscheidungen,* 37th ed. (Freiburg im Breisgau, 1991)
LBH	Thomas Taylor Lewis, ed., *Letters of the Lady Brilliana Harley . . . ,* Camden Society, LVIII (London, 1854)
LG	Henry Burton, *The Law and the Gospell Reconciled . . .* (London, 1631)
LJK	John Knewstub, *Lectures of John Knewstub, upon the Twentieth Chapter of Exodus, and Certain Other Places of Scripture* (London, 1577)
LL	Carl R. Trueman, *Luther's Legacy: Salvation and English Reformers, 1525–1556* (Oxford, 1994)
MCA	Cotton Mather, *Magnalia Christi Americana; or, The Ecclesiastical History of New England,* ed. Thomas Robbins (1852; rpt. New York, 1967), I
MHS	Massachusetts Historical Society
MO	N[icholas] B[y]fielde, *The Marrow of the Oracles of God . . . ,* 5th ed. (London, 1625)
MSD	Daniel Dyke, *The Mystery of Selfe-Deceiuing; or, A Discourse and Discouery of the Deceitfulnesse of Mans Heart* (London, 1633)
MW	John E. Coxe, ed., *Miscellaneous Writings and Letters of Thomas Cranmer* (Cambridge, 1846)
NEQ	*New England Quarterly*
OED	*Oxford English Dictionary* (Oxford, 1989)
PDRG	Kenneth L. Parker and Eric J. Carlson, *"Practical Divinity": The Works and Life of Revd Richard Greenham* (Aldershot, Eng., 1998)
PG	J. T. Cliffe, *The Puritan Gentry: The Great Puritan Families of Early Stuart England* (London, 1984)
"PH"	David R. Como, "Puritans and Heretics: The Emergence of an Antinomian Underground in Early Stuart England" (Ph.D. diss., Princeton University, 1999)

PM	William Hunt, *The Puritan Moment: The Coming of Revolution in an English County* (Cambridge, Mass., 1983)
POP	Lew[i]s Bayly, *The Practice of Pietie* . . . (London, 1630)
PP	Keith Wrightson and David Levine, *Poverty and Piety in an English Village: Terling, 1525–1700*, 2d ed. (Oxford, 1995)
PPPDD	Charles E. Hambrick-Stowe, *The Practice of Piety: Puritan Devotional Disciplines in Seventeenth-Century New England* (Chapel Hill, N.C., 1982)
"PS"	David Como and Peter Lake, "Puritans, Antinomians, and Laudians in Caroline London: The Strange Case of Peter Shaw and Its Contexts," *Journal of Ecclesiastical History*, L (1999), 684–715
RC	Samuel Rawson Gardiner, ed., *Reports of Cases in the Courts of Star Chamber and High Commission* (London, 1886)
RMC	Myles Coverdale, *Remains of Myles Coverdale, Bishop of Exeter* . . . , ed. George Pearson (Cambridge, 1846)
RP	Patrick Collinson, *The Religion of Protestants: The Church in English Society, 1559–1625* (Oxford, 1982)
RRR	David Underdown, *Revel, Riot, and Rebellion: Popular Politics and Culture in England, 1603–1660* (Oxford, 1985)
RV	Thomas Taylor, *Regula Vitae: The Rule of the Law under the Gospel* . . . (London, 1631)
SCV	George Gifford, *Foure Sermons upon the Seven Chiefe Vertues* . . . (London, 1582)
SE	James Orchard Halliwell, ed., *The Autobiography and Correspondence of Sir Simonds D'Ewes*, 2 vols. (London, 1845)
SF	Jean Delumeau, *Sin and Fear: The Emergence of a Western Guilt Culture, Thirteenth–Fifteenth Centuries* (New York, 1990)
SHL	George Elwes Corrie, ed., *Sermons by Hugh Latimer* (Cambridge, 1844)
SHS	Henry Smith, *The Sermons of Master Henry Smith* (London, 1628)
SPC	[Thomas Hooker], *The Soules Preparation for Christ* . . . (London, 1638)
SPS	John Cotton, *A Sermon Preached by the Reverend Mr. John Cotton Deliver'd at Salem* (Boston, 1713), in Larzer Ziff, ed., *John Cotton on the Churches of New England* (Cambridge, Mass., 1968), 39–68
SSP	George G[i]ff[o]rd, *Foure Sermons upon Severall Partes of Scripture* (London, 1598)
ST	Richard Rogers, *Seven Treatises* . . . (London, 1603)

STC	A. W. Pollard and G. R. Redgrave, comps., *A Short-Title Catalogue of Books Printed in England . . . 1475–1640*, 2d ed., 3 vols. (London, 1976–1991); Donald Wing, comp., *Short-Title Catalogue of Books Printed in England . . . 1640–1700*, 2d ed., 3 vols. (New York, 1982–1994)
TCG	John Cotton, *A Treatise of the Covenant of Grace . . .* (London, 1671)
TCR	T[homas] C[artwright], *A Treatise of Christian Religion . . .* (London, 1616)
TR	John Udall, *The True Remedie against Famine and Warres* (London, [1588])
WCC	John Cotton, *The Way of the Congregational Churches Cleared* (1648), in Larzer Ziff, ed., *John Cotton on the Churches of New England* (Cambridge, Mass., 1968), 167–364
WJB	Aubrey Townsend, ed., *The Writings of John Bradford*, 2 vols. (Cambridge, 1848)
WL	John Cotton, *The Way of Life . . .* (London, 1641)
WMC	George Pearson, ed., *Writings and Translations of Myles Coverdale* (Cambridge, 1844)
WMQ	*William and Mary Quarterly*
WP	Samuel Eliot Morison et al., eds., *The Winthrop Papers* (Boston, 1929–)
WPEP	Thomas F. Merrill, ed., *William Perkins, 1556–1602, English Puritanist* (The Hague, 1966)
WRG	H[enry] H[olland], ed., *The Workes of . . . Richard Greenham*, 3d ed. (London, 1601)
WRS	Alexander B. Grosart, ed., *Works of Richard Sibbes*, 7 vols. (Edinburgh, 1973)
WTS	*The Works of Thomas Shepard*, 3 vols. (Boston, 1853)
WW	Paul S. Seaver, *Wallington's World: A Puritan Artisan in Seventeenth-Century London* (Stanford, Calif., 1985)
WWP	*The Workes of . . . William Perkins*, 3 vols. (London, 1616–1618)
WWT	G. E. Duffield, ed., *The Work of William Tyndale* (Philadelphia, 1965)

THE
PRECISIANIST
STRAIN

INTRODUCTION

In late Tudor and early Stuart England many were gripped by the belief that the Elizabethan Settlement of 1559 had arrested the English Reformation at an immature stage. With much disagreement on details, they still shared a desire to resume and complete the process. In time some came to judge the national church irreformable and made a Separatist schism, but a majority improvised ways to live with present imperfections, to adjust as well to ever-changing political and cultural circumstances, and yet to continue the witness for further reformation. This study examines one facet of their witness: Christianity, whatever else it may be, is a sternly regulatory system.

Today, as four hundred years ago, "Puritan" is the prevailing name for them, their outlooks, their propaganda, and their practical undertakings for reform. But now as then the term's meaning and descriptive value are under debate, and now as then the debate is not resolved and probably is incapable of resolution. Guided by two decades of research in sixteenth- and seventeenth-century materials, I nevertheless join those who argue that the term should be retained. It depicts accurately a substantive and often obsessive trait of the quest for further reformation: a hunger for purity. Purity in this context had reference to two distinct but linked concerns: primitivist and moral. First, it signified the unalloyed excellence of the original, or primitive, order of things narrated in sacred Scripture. Since that order had been corrupted in post-apostolic times by human tampering and addition and many impurities remained after 1559, a puritan (that is, purifying) strategy of cleansing and recovery was required. Of this "primitivist dimension" I offered a reading in an earlier work.[1]

The present study turns to the second concern of the quest for purity, "purenesse through sanctification." At times this too was framed in terms of loss and recovery; it was Adamic purity regained. Yet unlike, say, the apostolic order of church government, pureness of thought and deed could not simply be reinstated during the earthly course. Puritan moral canons were severe and, in a sense, unearthly. After the end of history the saints above would embrace

---

1. Theodore Dwight Bozeman, *To Live Ancient Lives: The Primitivist Dimension in Puritanism* (Chapel Hill, N.C., 1988).

them with ease, but in the present and fallen order they met with repulse. At best, among the regenerate, their realization was partial and inconstant; and always it was a matter in part of force and control. Puritans believed and spoke the language of *sola fides* ("faith alone"), of course, and often enough they affirmed the freely flowing goodness of the converted heart. At the same time, and in unacknowledged league with centuries of Catholic teaching and practice, they constructed Christianity as a disciplinary system both severe and punctilious.[2]

Among the multitude of Christian faiths, disciplined goodness had been for centuries a standard objective. Puritan creeds and ways, however, embraced the most intensive and largest-scale ascetic project in early modern Protestantism. Addressed to a lay constituency, they were studiedly elite. They arose from dissatisfaction with the average, and they could tend to extremes. This much can be inferred from the stock labels that hostile contemporaries applied to the godly and that some of those so libeled later happily co-opted: *puritan* and *precise*. The former was of broader scope. In addition to its primitivist resonances, it bore a range of meanings from insubordination and democratic disorder to a rigidly biblical literalism, to an irritating sanctimony, to a disciplinary ethos so strict as to suggest association with historical perfectionist heresies.

Running through all was a penchant for excess, for straining the limits of human capacity and endurance. That was the quality most commonly invoked by the terms "precise" and "precisian." Often simple synonyms for "Puritan" or "Puritanism," they also tended to a smaller focus. They denoted a range of qualities from exactness (as in "the precise halfe of his circumference") to accuracy (as of a measuring instrument), to strictness and care. Yet the emphasis could deepen, pointing then to the *over*exact, the excessively scrupulous, the stiffly correct, and hence to hyperbolic demand; and such were their primary senses in anti-Puritan speech. Precisianists were those who dictated a single form and degree of religious practice for all; and always, as in presbyterian advocacy of the "precise form" of apostolic church order, it was a scheme of stiff demands and observances. Wanting in sane regard for human frailty, the precise required too much; and, if their exactions proved "beyond the ability of mortalls to performe," they could only pour out rebuke. Critics who complained of "formall preciseness," or who denounced "the strictest, and most precise exactors of the *Sundayes* rest" or the "precise fellowes" who condemn village recreations targeted just this quality of maddening, carping

2. *SCV,* sig. B7.

excess, as did the nobleman who deplored the "preciseness" of an employee who had criticized his use of recreations—hawks and hounds—because they were not expressly sanctioned by Scripture.[3]

Nor did known Puritans, as they pressed their case for *"precise walking,"* a "precisenes, in following Gods word in al points," flinch from the implication. Many of their great issues were defined along a spectrum of "strictnesse or Loosenesse of Life." A primary attribute of the deity they served, "exact precise severitie" was equally a habit and credential of his people. "Walke precisely, or exactly, or strictly in all things," enjoined John Preston in a sermon, "Exact Walking," preached at court in the 1620s and published posthumously in 1630. To *"walk exactly,"* this eminent preacher and college head explained, is to "goe to the extremity." It is "so to keepe the commandements . . . that a man goes to the utmost of them, . . . lookeing to every particle of them." Later in the decade, with Preston's sermon probably before him, John Ball in an obscure curacy in Staffordshire hailed "Exactnesse, Accuratnesse, [a] . . . strict walking" aligned with Scripture "in every thing great and small." In such "preciseness in keeping Gods Commandements" he saw a cardinal "Property of a godly life"; and those who had it went "to the utmost," rendering obedience "in the least things" and "in the extremity thereof."[4]

This pattern, this zest for regulation that goes to an extremity, is named here the precisianist strain. Understandably, in the voluntary lay religion of the godly, the ideal was realized imperfectly. Well acquainted with the intran-

---

3. *OED*, s.v. "precise" ("precise halfe"), "preciseness" ("formall preciseness"); Stephen Brachlow, *The Communion of Saints: Radical Puritan and Separatist Ecclesiology, 1570–1625* (Oxford, 1988), 22 ("precise form"); Christopher Dow, *A Discourse of the Sabbath and the Lords Day* . . . , 2d ed. (London, 1636), 49 ("exactors"), 73 ("mortalls"); *CD*, 4 ("precise fellowes"); HMC, *Ninth Report, Calendar of the Manuscripts of the Most Honourable the Marquess of Salisbury* . . . , pt. 17 (London, 1938), 108–109 (employee's "preciseness").

4. *CAC*, sig. 8; *CS*, sig. D6; Nehemiah Wallington, "A Record of Gods Mercies, or A Thankfull Remembrance," 44 (irreg. pag.), MS 204, Guildhall Library, London, copy in the Genealogical Society of Utah, Salt Lake City ("Loosenesse"); T[homas] H[ooker], *The Soules Exaltation* . . . (London, 1638), 241 ("severitie"); John Preston, *Sermons Preached before His Maiestie* . . . (London, 1630), 108–109; John Ball, *The Power of Godlines* . . . (London, 1657), 29, 65. In a Latin disputation of 1643, which cited William Perkins, John Preston, Paul Baynes, Robert Bolton, Cornelius Burges, and other English Puritan notables, the Dutch Reformed theologian Gisbertus Voetius (1589–1676) defined *praecisitas* as "the exact or complete fit of human acts to the law prescribed by God" ("exacta seu perfecta actionum humanarum cum lege Dei convenientia a Deo praescripta"). Voetius, *De praecisitate ad illustrationem quaest. catechet. XCIV, CXIII, CXV* (1643), in *Selectarum disputationum theologicarum* . . . (Utrecht, 1648–1669), III, 59, 61.

sigent Old Man within the saints, Preston and those for whom he spoke acknowledged that the demand for preciseness could only be "kept Evangelically," with frequent failure and repentance. Yet the divine demand stands unabated. When the saints fall short, painful consequences follow. "If we be not exact in all, it puts us into a state of separation from God," requiring more agonies of repentance. Therefore, Preston concluded, we "must endevour to the utmost of our power" to fulfill the demand and "strive with all our might."[5]

The Deity's demand was honored when a godly minority in Richard Rogers's parish at Wethersfield in 1588 adopted an elaborate disciplinary program to drive out "the smallest even of our evill lustes," or when Rogers himself in a daily self-analysis rued that he and his wife on a recent trip were "wandringe by litle and litle in needlesse speach." It was honored in William Perkins's argument against dancing in the 1590s: "If we must give an account of every idle word, then also of every idle gesture and pace: and what account can be given of these paces backward and forward, of caperings, jumps, gambols, turning, with many other frisks" of uncontained movement? Preston's contemporary, Robert Bolton, spoke of God's demand too, urging his hearers to "weigh well . . . all circumstances, concurrents, company, probabilitie of events, and consequents," before deciding to "enter out of thy doores, upon any occasion," and formulated seven criteria by which to judge the good or evil of the venture proposed. Preston himself provided a telling epitome in a Cambridge fast day sermon of 1625. A truly regenerate person, he urged, is "afraid of every sin, . . . afraid of vaine thoughts, [afraid] to be vaine in his speeches and to give way to the least wickednesse, afraid of every inordinate affection, . . . afraid how hee spent the time from morning till night, and how to give an account thereof, afraid of recreations, least he should sleepe too much, or sleepe too little, eate too much, or eate too little," and the like. Finically "afraid" and careful of every word or gesture: at least in the ideal, that was the precise saint to a *T*.[6]

Saints so scrupulous instinctively took license to rebuke the unsevere. And, if most spurned the rebuke and cried the godly down "as too precise," they but lent their accusers strength. Exposing their reluctance to check themselves and to do good, they added documentation to the case for a tighter ordering of

---

5. Preston, *Sermons before His Maiestie*, 114, 116.

6. *ST*, 477–492 (the quote is at 480); M. M. Knappen, ed., *Two Elizabethan Puritan Diaries, by Richard Rogers and Samuel Ward* (Chicago, 1933), 58; William Perkins, *A Discourse of Conscience* (Cambridge, 1596), in *WPEP*, 46; *GD*, 185 and, for the seven criteria, 149–154; John Preston, *The Golden Scepter Held Forth to the Humble* . . . (London, 1638), 7–8. The Wethersfield group would avoid "unnecessary and idle talke." *ST*, 489.

English life. But, even more consequentially, their anger drove the saints closer together and helped them better to know and esteem themselves. By learning to interpret opposition as a mark of sainthood, precise walkers "gather[ed] vigour . . . from the very oppositions of the wicked" and so made themselves "invincible," and this they could accomplish in part by co-opting the language of preciseness. Such a one was Richard Greenham, pastor at Dry Drayton during the 1570s and 1580s, who insisted that, through his scrupulous avoidance of all forms of idolatry, the biblical king *"David* was a precisian." And Robert Bolton of Broughton in Northamptonshire, one of many conforming Puritan clerics of the early seventeenth century who had mastered the art of preciseness, also spoke for those who had recast "those nick-names of Puritan, [and] Precisian" into "honourable badges." Once simply endured, now such names had become aspects of a partially separate and heroically ascetic identity that fed upon contrast—and sometimes confrontation—with the slack and impure. Understood this way, the saints' preciseness was a crux of their singularity.[7]

Understandably, average people found the precisianist way too daunting, and some made haste to ignore or denounce it. But what if appreciable numbers of men and women already recruited by Puritan evangelism found the struggle too hard and the compensations too few? Exactly that was the ground of the first wave of "antinomian" troubles that began to arise in the mid-1610s and sparked initial controversies in London around 1630 and in New England in 1636–1638. By the century's second decade the level of disciplinary demand had risen so high as to generate a virtual counter-Puritanism, not merely a set of gripes against strictness, but a distinctive redraft of the Christian redemption. From John Eaton to Anne Hutchinson, its formative theorists imagined a way of life far less encumbered, far more gratifying, and notably more feminine and "yielding" than the Puritan precisianist way.

7. *CAC,* 45 ("too precise"), 334 ("nick-names"); *GD,* 29 ("vigour," "invincible"); Richard Greenham, *The Workes of . . . M. Richard Greenham . . .* , 5th ed., ed. H[enry] H[olland] (London, 1612), 321 (David). In *GM,* 57, John Cotton marked the reinforcing impact of opposition upon the saints' identity and discipline. In *PM,* 231, William Hunt remarks the unifying effect of opposition upon the Puritan community.

I

BACKGROUNDS OF DISCIPLINARY RELIGION

CHAPTER I
DISCIPLINARY THEMES IN THE ENGLISH REFORMATION

The first decades of Elizabeth's reign were a polarizing time. Reflecting the temperate aims of the religious settlement of 1559, the outlook of, say, John Whitgift, Richard Field, or Richard Hooker was measurably less personal and exacting than that of the presbyterian militants who came to the fore in the 1570s and 1580s. Nowhere was the contrast sharper than in disciplinary issues. All defenders of the arrangements of 1559 emphasized law and moral reformation, but within a context of moderation and conformity. Favoring more and more the liturgical religion of the Book of Common Prayer, seeking quiet and collective consent to the authorized forms, they rebuffed calls for an apostolically reorganized and tightened church discipline. In their eyes, the presbyterian clamor for firmer regulation seemed a virtually Catharist extreme. Contrary to the spirit of the settlement, its advocates were driven by a sectarian will "to purge the earth of all manner evil."[1]

A radical minority well to the left within the Puritan spectrum in their time, early English presbyterians were an importunate breed. This is evident most readily in their disciplinary proposals, but it is apparent too in many other ways, as in their growing revulsion against festivities and recreations of the older communal culture, practices more easily tolerated in Lutheran Germany or Scandinavia and in earlier Protestant England. In such patterns one finds an early expression of the drive toward harder regulation that evoked the epithets "puritan" and "precise." The objective of this study is to analyze this venture and provide a partial chart of its course and effects. Specifically, we trace it in the presbyterian propaganda, next through the Puritan practical theology and practice of piety of later Elizabethan and early Stuart times, and then into earliest New England. Finally, we view it in the mirror of its antino-

---

1. Richard Hooker, *Of the Laws of Ecclesiastical Polity* (London, 1907), I, 133.

mian antithesis, which arose in the mid-1610s and became an insurrectionary movement in Massachusetts two decades later.[2]

To understand the surge of moral demand that arose in mid-Elizabethan times and not only persisted but intensified after the presbyterian defeats of the 1580s, we first should attempt to estimate at least some of the forces that underlay it well into the following century. The matter is far too complex to permit a neatly causal account, let alone one that would connect English developments to similar cycles of disciplinary fervor in Switzerland, France, the Netherlands, the Palatinate, and elsewhere in the middle and later seventeenth century; but we can identify a number of probable influences. Socioeconomic changes and worries as well as the experience of resistance and persecution played a part and are addressed in Chapter 3. Chapters 1 and 2 sketch a background in religious history, a long arc of Protestant disciplinary emphasis traceable back to Henrician times. Aligned with patterns in Reformed Protestant lands, it was also in some respects distinctively English.

Initial Sources and Backgrounds

Presbyterian debts to the earlier English Reformation are sure but difficult to reckon. Thomas Cartwright and his associates cited Continental Reformed contemporaries like Theodore Beza or Franciscus Junius more readily than they did their pre-Marian forebears, yet they belonged to a national tradition that from the beginning had accented legal and ascetic elements of the faith. Although a small minority in the land, England's earliest Protestants had espoused a forthright solifidian—"faith alone"—belief and the pessimistic estimate of human nature that it presupposed. They therefore were evangelicals in the Reformation sense. Yet, if their theologies were solifidian, they were also disciplinary in fundamental intent. This can be shown by comparison with Martin Luther's teachings, many of which were "highly idiosyncratic and individual to Luther himself." In varying degrees, the English shared Luther's belief in unconditional pardon and his denial that personal exertions and merits are a hinge of human destiny; and, like him but to a more limited

---

2. Reformed attitudes to popular culture are discussed in Peter Burke, *Popular Culture in Early Modern Europe* (New York, 1978), 216–219; Bob Scribner, "A Comparative Overview," in Bob Scribner, Roy Porter, and Mikuláš Teich, eds., *The Reformation in National Context* (Cambridge, 1994), 221–222, and Kaspar von Greyerz, "Switzerland," 42. Tessa Watt finds that "the first generation of Protestant reformers in England made no sharp break with pre-Reformation attitudes to traditional recreations," in *Cheap Print and Popular Piety, 1550–1640* (Cambridge, 1991), 41.

extent, they defined a humbler place for law and duty within the Christian life. Few, however, embraced with full force Luther's view that sola fides contradicts the native human sense of good and evil, his sometimes starkly drawn and dialectical distinctions between gospel and law, his relegation of the law's disciplinary purposes to a secondary category below its penitential function, his affirmation of a rare but real situational liberty to transcend positive law, his conception of Christian obedience as an unconstrained overflow, his softening of the traditional ascetic ideal, his conception of the Bible as a *Trostbuch* (book of consolation) and not a lawbook, his rejection of belief that Christ and Moses were lawgivers for Christians, his exclusion of the secular commonwealth from the realm of Christian renewal, or his dismissal of the covenantal and Deuteronomic theology of the Old Testament.[3]

Since views like these seemed to dilute morality, they had limited appeal in the island kingdom. There the Reformation emerged in a period of deeply felt concern about social order. Memory of the widespread disruptions of the midfifteenth century remained vivid in the sixteenth. For generations after the cessation of hostilities, ruling classes who dreaded a reversion to anarchy were preoccupied with issues of social unity and obedience, and by the 1530s they were troubled as well by a changing economic pattern that increased poverty and social tension. The Reformation itself was destabilizing. Shaped and restrained by the king's religious conservatism and his scrupulous attention to the forms of legitimacy, it nonetheless entailed sweeping institutional and ideological changes that must have been anomic for many citizens. Throughout the body of religious legislation and admonition emanating from king and Parliament, and in much additional commentary by both clerical and secular leaders, advocacy of reformation was conditioned by a fear of disorder. The fear was reinforced by anti-Protestant rebellions in 1536 and 1549, which disrupted ordinary life in large regions of the country and posed alarming problems for both national and local government. By accentuating concerns about social discipline, these intertwined backgrounds helped to temper the charm of a pure solifidianism and to encourage correlation of "fayeth, dutie and obedience."[4]

---

3. Euan Cameron, "The Search for Luther's Place in the Reformation," *Journal of Ecclesiastical History*, XLV (1994), 475. A modern study of the theology of William Tyndale, Robert Barnes, John Frith, John Hooper, and John Bradford concludes that all "considerably modified" Luther's soteriology along practical and ethical lines (*LL*, 5).

4. *The Primer, Set Furth by the Kinges Maiestie and His Clergie* . . . (London, 1546), preface. See also *SHL*, 28–29, a text from 1536 equating "righteousness" with morality and

They also might have bolstered the appeal of ethically laden theological sources. Prominent English evangelicals affirmed continuities between their own movement and the Wycliffite-Lollard line of dissent and appear to have recognized—or acknowledged—no sharp break between Wyclif's or Lollard concepts of redemption and their own. The Wycliffite heritage might have served them more as a broadly congenial native antecedent than as a substantive influence upon their theory of redemption, but their unqualified praise for a tradition whose theory of redemption focused on law and obedience attests that their notions of "faith only" were less categoric than Luther's and less sharply sundered from the past.[5]

Additional support for this conclusion appears when we turn to the most obvious inheritance of all: the Catholic heritage in all its cumulative weight. In England as in other Protestant lands, medieval patterns of thought persisted. The strongly ethical emphases of Robert Barnes, Myles Coverdale, John Hooper, and John Bale, for instance, echo their early monastic training. Catholic Christian humanism, not a monolithic doctrine, but a widely shared set of intellectual values, also greatly influenced the founding figures of the English Reformation. Most emerged from a humanistically flavored educational background, and their new, ardently contra-Catholic theologies all continued, albeit in differing ways and degrees, to reflect humanist concerns. Like Wyclif and the Lollards, humanists focused their theories of redemption, not upon guilt and insecurity, but upon moral weakness and corruption. They venerated patristic theology and drew without question upon the Fathers' construction of the gospel as a new law. Luther had drawn the line hard against such doctrine, but many English evangelicals took a strikingly different attitude. "Notes on Justification," gathered by Archbishop Thomas Cranmer, placed Desiderius Erasmus, the foremost Christian humanist, among historic au-

---

making pointed reference to the rebellious "men in the North country." Mid-Tudor Protestants frequently noted and deplored increasing vagrancy and associated it with disorder and the menace of rebellion. Whitney R. D. Jones, *The Tudor Commonwealth, 1529–1559: A Study of the Impact of Social and Economic Developments of Mid-Tudor England upon Contemporary Concepts of the Nature and Duties of the Commonwealth* (London, 1970), 9, 41, 47, 55–56, 108–132.

5. For examples, see *WWT,* 94; N. T. Wright, ed., *The Work of John Frith* (Oxford, 1978), 344; Henry Christmas, ed., *Select Works of John Bale* (Cambridge, 1849), 171, 391, 394 (and see 351). William Roy (or possibly William Barlowe, or the two men in collaboration), for example, modified two Lollard tracts for inclusion in *A Proper Dyaloge betwene a Gentill-man and a Husbandman . . .* (Antwerp, 1530). No reader of this work would find reason to suspect that Lollard doctrine stopped short of Protestantism at any essential point.

thorities who had excluded from justification "the merit and dignity of all works and virtues"; and George Joye stated outright that "Erasmus . . . affirm[s] onely faith to iustifye." Others prepared editions of Catholic humanist texts, and a royal injunction of 1547 required that a translation of Erasmus's *Paraphrases* on the four Gospels and Acts be placed in every parish church; all clergy beneath the rank of bachelor of divinity were ordered to obtain and study a personal copy. Clearly the Reformation that English Protestants envisaged was one in which humanist writings and ideas, with little if any modification, held an honored place.[6]

In other ways, too, Christian humanism crossed doctrinal boundaries between the old faith and the new and brought with it a moralizing flavor. The solifidian element in evangelical teaching was joined to, and inevitably qualified by, a zeal to recover primitive ways. *Quod primum verum* ("that which is first is true"), a basic premise of medieval Catholic reform movements (including Lollardy) and certainly of Christian humanism, remained structural to Protestant thinking. Evangelicals shared humanist beliefs that the apostolic order—"the first, original, and most perfect church of the apostles"—was normative for the Christian movement in all periods and places and that the early church and its theologians had remained faithful to the norm for some five centuries after Christ. Since the Christian movement thereafter had veered from the original, the Reformation must reinstate the "primitive church, and [the time] nigh therunto when the church was most purest" as the Christian movement's regulative guide. Finding a prescriptive model at the apostolic Scripture's core, and venting their ire as much upon inherited forms and practices lacking original warrant as upon fallacious theories of redemption, evangelicals further magnified legal demand.[7]

6. *MW*, 207; George Joye, *The Refutation of the Byshop of Winchesters Derke Declaration* . . . (n.p., 1546), lvii–lviii. The humanist backgrounds of Tyndale, Frith, Barnes, and Hooper are discussed in *LL*, 44–53. A 1533 rendering of Erasmus's *Enchiridion militis christiani*, the most popular statement of his Platonizing *philosophia Christi*, is attributed to Tyndale, and Myles Coverdale prepared an abridgment of the work in 1545. [Desiderius] Erasmus, *A Booke Called in Latyn Enchiridion Militis Christiani, and in Englysshe the Manuell of the Christen Knyght* . . . , trans. William Tyndale(?) (n.p., 1533); Erasmus, *A Shorte Recapitulacion; or, Abrigement of Erasmus Enchiridion* . . . , trans. M[yles] Coverdale (n.p., [1545]). The royal injunction is in Edward Cardwell, ed., *Documentary Annals of the Reformed Church of England*, new ed. (Oxford, 1844), I, 9, 13.

7. *MW*, 351 (and see 226–227, 528). Primitive ways: Theodore Dwight Bozeman, *To Live Ancient Lives: The Primitivist Dimension in Puritanism* (Chapel Hill, N.C., 1988), 19–25, 52–56.

Humanist literature and its summons *ad fontes* (to the ancient sources) also promoted direct and extensive reading of the patristic theologians and an appreciation of their heavily ethical and legal orientation.[8] It was thus at least partly responsible for the evangelicals' frequently doubled appeal to "scriptures and of the ancient fathers." The theological impact of this linkage is registered most revealingly in the widespread (and wholly anachronistic) conviction that many of the Fathers propounded a doctrine of justification in a solifidian sense. This was a great point with Cranmer, who in his "Notes on Justification" as well as his *Homily of Salvation* prepared for the 1547 book of homilies, confidently marshaled citations from "divers ancient authors," including Augustine, Chrysostom, Jerome, Origen, and Ambrose, to prove their doctrine of justification "the *same*" as that of the apostle Paul. Likewise regarding the patristic era as a loyal extension of the Christian primordium, Coverdale and Joye found in Protestant teaching "the *same* article of justification . . . maintained by the [patristic] doctors . . . specially by St Augustine [but also by] Cyril, Ambrose, Origen, Hilary, . . . [and] Athanasius, with other more." In stark contrast with Luther's view that the Fathers "one and all disregarded the supremely plain and clear teaching of Paul" on the subject of grace, these judgments further display the English tendency to merge solifidian belief with a strongly disciplinary conception of Christian existence.[9]

If evangelicals nurtured a sense of positive continuity with Lollard, patristic, and humanist concepts of redemption, it is easier to understand why, long

8. See, for example, Richard Taverner's 1540 collection of sermons upon New Testament texts, in which Erasmus is the only modern authority cited, but hundreds of citations manifest "the mynde and sentence [opinion] of the auncient doctours." Taverner, who regarded patristic thought as a needed antidote to the common confusion of Protestant teaching with "lawles libertie," dedicated roughly half of that volume to ethical exhortation and included one unbroken series of twenty sermons whose themes—faith working through love, struggle against concupiscence, and heavenly reward—were drawn almost exclusively from patristic sources with virtually no "Protestant" admixture (*Postils on the Epistles and Gospels*, ed. Edward Cardwell [Oxford, 1841], 228). Taverner composed an indeterminate number of the sermons, collecting the rest from unidentified sources. For the twenty sermons, see 460–509.

9. *EWB*, 6; *MW*, 130–131, 208 (and see the entire text of the "Notes" on 202–211); *RMC*, 340; Martin Luther, *On the Bondage of the Will: A New Translation of De Servo Arbitrio (1525)*, trans. and ed. J. I. Packer and O. R. Johnston (London, 1957), 294–295. Luther also noted: "How little it helps a man to rely on the ancient fathers . . . ! Were they not all equally blind to . . . Paul's clearest and plainest words [about grace and works]?" (247, 294). In Joye's view, "all the olde holy doctours" taught that "only faith iustifieth" (*Refutation*, cxliiii [and see lviii, lxxiii]).

before the rise of Puritanism, they had come to identify by and large with the emergent Reformed branch of the Reformation. English theology at midcentury defies tidy labels, but it exhibited a far closer kinship with developments at Strasbourg, Zurich, and other Reformed centers than with those at Wittenberg. In this study the term "Reformed" calls attention to two specific and interrelated features of soteriological thought: a relatively conservative, "eminently ethical" understanding of individual redemption together with an emphasis upon organized ecclesiastical discipline and, second, inclusion of the civil community within the realm of religious and moral reformation.[10]

Both tendencies are exemplified in the career and thought of Martin Bucer, leader of the Reformation in Strasbourg until he was forced from the city in 1549. Appointed then to the Regius chair of Divinity at the University of Cambridge, he took an active part in the intensified phase of the English Reformation under Edward VI (1549–1553). Both in Strasbourg and Cambridge Bucer exhibited the tendencies in Reformed thinking that proved congenial to the English. With particular dependence upon Augustine and Erasmus, he was more concerned with moral corruption than with the problem of an afflicted conscience and propounded "a strongly ethical conception of justification." Indeed, he explicitly "implicate[d] human moral action under the aegis of justification." He understood Scripture as law and was comfortable with phrases like "the law of Christ." With other reformers bred theologically in cities of the German Rhineland, he saw the course of individual redemption taking place within a larger, intensely corporate, Christian civil community duty-bound to obey the Lord's law under pain of temporal punishment. At Cambridge, he "crie[d] incessantly . . . that [the English] should practice penitence, . . . and constrain [them]selves by some sort of discipline" and outlined a program for national religious and moral reform in a book dedicated to the young king, *De regno Christi*.[11]

10. Hans Walter Frei, "Johannes Oekolampads Versuch, Kirchenzucht durch den Bann zu üben," *Zwingliana*, VII, no. 8 (1942), 494. Noting that the Reformation in the Rhineland "differed from the Lutheran Reformation . . . in the greater importance it attributed to the 'sanctification' of the individual member of a church and of the parish community as a whole," Kaspar von Greyerz remarks also upon its "particular emphasis on church discipline . . . and moral control," in "Switzerland," in Scribner, Porter, and Teich, eds., *The Reformation in National Context*, 38. See also *LL*, 78.

11. Alister McGrath, *The Intellectual Origins of the European Reformation* (Oxford, 1987), 53, 35 (and see 34); Martin Greschat, *Martin Bucer: Ein Reformator und seine Zeit* (Munich, 1990), 218; Constantin Hopf, *Martin Bucer and the English Reformation* (Oxford, 1946), 21, 103. "The origins of Bucer's theology," says McGrath, "are not to be sought in . . .

Bucer's vision of reformation both meshed with and promoted a trend already well in evidence by the reign of Edward VI. The great published collection of letters from the Zurich archives relative to the English Reformation reveals an extensive network of associations with Reformed leaders. Protestants of advanced views who fled to the Continent in the wake of the conservative Six Articles Act of 1539 tended to establish Reformed associations, and they returned after Henry's death to participate in the Edwardian reformation as "radical Protestants, principally of Zwinglian persuasion"; and the form of worship and church polity of the "Strangers' Churches" that emerged in London in the early 1550s, and were an element of Cranmer's strategy for hastening reform of the English church, were drawn largely from the models of Strasbourg, Zurich, and Geneva. Such observations suggest that, well before the rise of a Puritan opposition in the reign of Elizabeth, English evangelicals were party to variations upon Protestant faith in which disciplinary interests stood to the fore.[12]

A Theological Ellipse:
Faith and Behavior in English Reformation Thought

How, more specifically, did evangelicals reformulate the Christian redemption? For a few, like John Frith (1503–1533) and Sir Richard Tracy (d. 1569), sola fides was the definitive and absorbing issue, but for others it was less deter-

---

the agonizing over man's status *coram Deo*" evident in the early Luther (*Intellectual Origins,* 53). Law and gospel: Friedhelm Krüger, *Bucer und Erasmus* (Wiesbaden, 1970), 70–71. Bucer applied the doctrine of temporal punishment to England in *De Regno Christi,* in Wilhelm Pauck, ed., *Melanchthon and Bucer* (Philadelphia, 1969), 271, 279–280. Among Continental theologians, he stands as one of the two or three largest individual influences upon English theology during the earlier seventeenth century. A "great . . . number of English writings of that [Henrician and Edwardian] period [quote] Bucer's works . . . as authority," and his funeral in 1551 was "a great event" with some three thousand people present (Hopf, *Martin Bucer,* xi, 29).

12. W. K. Jordan, *Edward VI: The Young King; The Protectorship of the Duke of Somerset* (Cambridge, Mass., 1968), 26; Andrew Pettegree, *Foreign Protestant Communities in Sixteenth-Century London* (Oxford, 1986), 25–35, 68–74. For the Zurich letters, see Hastings Robinson, ed. and trans., *The Zurich Letters,* 3 vols. (Cambridge, 1842–1846); Robinson, ed. and trans., *Original Letters Relative to the English Reformation,* 2 vols. (Cambridge, 1846–1848).

On the Six Articles Act, which upheld clerical celibacy, auricular confession, and other traditional practices, see A. G. Dickens, *The English Reformation,* 2d ed. (London, 1989), 201.

minative. William Tyndale (1494?–1536), George Joye (d. 1553), Thomas Cranmer (1489–1556), John Bradford (1510–1555), John Hooper (d. 1555), Thomas Becon (1512–1567), John Bale (1495–1563), Hugh Latimer (1485–1555), Nicholas Ridley (1500–1555), and many others cited in this chapter so correlated faith and behavior as to move distinctly to the right of Frith and Tracy. They occupied a wide range of stations within the reforming movement. Their doctrinal positions varied in many ways and degrees, and some, like Tyndale, displayed notable shifts in emphasis with the passing years.[13]

Nevertheless, they appear collectively to have espoused a doctrine of justification in which man was not only declared but also "made righteous *by fayth onely*." All deemed free pardon the most important article of faith, but, with a few exceptions, their outlooks did not center upon the afflicted conscience and its search for a gracious God. They saw the human predicament as much or more in terms of moral corruption as of unresolved guilt. For them the experience of pardon was seldom as central as for Luther, and both its meaning and practical consequences were assessed relative to other and profoundly held priorities.[14]

13. Frith's theology is surveyed in *LL*, 121–155. For Tracy's views, see Richarde Tracy, *The Profe and Declaration of Thys Proposition: Fayth Only Iustifieth* (n.p., 1543?).

14. Alister McGrath, *Iustitia Dei: A History of the Christian Doctrine of Justification* (Cambridge, 1986), II, 101; *RMC*, 232, and see *WMC*, 6–11; Dewey D. Wallace, Jr., *Puritans and Predestination: Grace in English Protestant Theology, 1525–1695* (Chapel Hill, N.C., 1982), 7, and see 9–10. Righteousness by faith: Cranmer's homilies on "salvation" and "faith," prepared for the official book of homilies of 1547 (Thomas Cranmer et al., *Certayne Sermons or Homilies* . . . [London, 1547]), provide an example. Both accent solifidian themes, but the thesis that "out of . . . faith springeth good works" is stressed equally in the former and structures the latter. This is the more noteworthy, since a homily "of good works" also was included in that volume, also probably written by Cranmer (*MW*, 130 [and see the full texts on 128–149]). Compare his concepts of justification as a patristic doctrine and the Bible as a law book, as noted above (n. 6, and text; and see below, n. 17, and text).

Afflicted conscience: for examples, see *LL*, 84–88, 239–241.

Human predicament: an example is Coverdale's *Fruitful Lessons upon the Passion, Burial, Resurrection, Ascension, and of the Sending of the Holy Ghost,* reprinted in *WMC*, 195–421. Adapted from an earlier work by Zwingli and employing themes from medieval spirituality (including the Passion of Christ as a curative "medicine" for sin), this work assesses the human condition largely in terms of personal and social "wickedness and iniquity" and gives far more play to the self's moral reconstruction and empowerment than to pardon and comfort. For the themes cited, see, for example, 201, 207, 233, 264, 279, 309, 312, 357.

Many found it hard to believe that, if consciences were consoled and re-oriented through the grant of forgiveness, spontaneous love and gratitude would take over and morality in effect would take care of itself. No complaint appears more often in their writing than the manifest failure of Protestant preaching and instruction to curb lusts and order lives. After years of evangeli-cal preaching and polemic, little "amendment of life, but . . . all kind of shameless sinning" was abroad. So most devoted the greater part of their attention to moral castigation and counsel. In context of the Swiss and south German doctrine of predestination to which the English in general sub-scribed, some argued, in a fashion "foreign to Luther's outlook," that sancti-fication was the principal earthly objective of divine election. No fewer than six saw organized discipline as a crucial mark of the church, and Cranmer, responding as archbishop of Canterbury to Parliament's mandate of 1550 for a revision of English ecclesiastical law, proposed an explicit disciplinary pro-cedure that partly anticipates Elizabethan presbyterian schemes. Bradford and Becon became part of the prehistory of a tradition of English pietist devotion, centered upon introspective self-regimentation, that was to rise to its zenith in Puritan circles around the turn of the seventeenth century.[15]

English penitential teaching expressly echoed and bolstered moral pri-orities. In contrast, again, to Luther, whose penitential teaching stressed the rueful sinner's attainment of peace through acknowledgment of fault and trust in unconditional pardon, several of the English included a moment of moral renewal. In harmony with Reformed tendencies on the Continent and in

15. Sin and amendment: Becon, for example, prepared tracts on the art of prayer and the gospel's "consolacion and comfort" accompanied by prefaces that emphasize "the [cor-rupt] manners of men" and the "destruction almost of all godly living" in England as the primary context defining consideration of the gospel (*EWB*, 36–37, 43). For the prefaces, see *EWB*, 37–44, 125–129.

Church discipline: John Ponet, *A Short Catechisme*, in T. H. L. Parker, ed., *English Reformers* (Philadelphia, 1966), 171–174; Henry Christmas, ed., *The Works of Nicholas Ridley* (Cambridge, 1843), 123; Charles Nevinson, ed., *Later Writings of Bishop [John] Hooper* (Cambridge, 1852), 43, 51–52, 126–127 (but cf. 87); John Ayre, ed., *The Catechism of Thomas Becon* (Cambridge, 1844), 42 (and see *EWB*, 7); *WWT*, 114; William Tyndale, *Expositions and Notes on Sundry Portions of the Holy Scriptures, Together with the Practice of Prelates*, ed. Henry Walter (Cambridge, 1849), 252; and Edmond Al[l]en, *A Cathechisme, That Is to Say, a Christen Instruccion of the Principall Pointes of Christes Religion . . .* (London, 1551), sig. Avi–Bii. For Cranmer's scheme, see James C. Spalding, "The Refor-matio Legum Ecclesiasticarum of 1552 and the Furthering of Discipline in England," *CH*, XXXIX (1970), 162–171. Bradford and Becon: the relevant texts are collected in *WJB*, I; *EWB*; and Ayre, ed., *Catechism of Becon*.

unmistakable continuity with historic Catholic doctrine that tied "contrition, by definition, to the intention to amend," they required an actual change in the penitent. For them, a renewal of moral resolve was integral to the penitential experience, and a few included the manifest alteration of behavior. They agreed that moral will or effort cannot merit forgiveness, yet rang variations on the theme that repentance is "an inward . . . sorrow . . . whereunto is also added a . . . desire . . . to frame our life in all points according to the holy will of God expressed in the divine scriptures." However qualified by reference to the divine initiative and by denial of efficacy to human works, such teaching underscored moral responsibility; it also adumbrated Puritan penitential and preparationist teaching of later decades.[16]

Evangelicals keen for amendment also were concerned as much for the common weal as for the individual's quest for a gracious God. Blending Christian humanist ideals of civic reform with belief that the corporate and contractual theology of the Old Testament codetermines the Christian dispensation, they embraced the moral welfare and reform of society within their conception of what redemption was about. In a particularly telling example, the corporate interest dominated most of the prefatory matter attached to the first complete, published English translations of the Bible. This is the more notable, since the dissemination of these Bibles, intended for a popular audience without a reading knowledge of Latin, Greek, or Hebrew, was a supreme event of the English Reformation and probably "fell into a more important category than the [translated] theological writings of the [Continental] Reformers." As if in concert, the dedications and prologues of the Coverdale Bible of 1535 and the Matthew Bible of 1537 (edited and translated by John

---

16. Thomas Tentler, *Sin and Confession on the Eve of the Reformation* (Princeton, N.J., 1977), 237, and see 105, 238; Ayre, ed., *Catechism of Becon*, 10. Luther affirmed "two elements in true repentance: recognition of sin and recognition of grace; or, . . . the fear of God and trust in mercy" (Jaroslav Pelikan, ed., *Luther's Works* [Saint Louis, 1955–1986], XII, 305; and see Theodore G. Tappert, ed. and trans., *The Book of Concord: The Confessions of the Evangelical Lutheran Church* [Philadelphia, 1959], 34–35). He desired chiefly that "simple faith in . . . unmerited forgiveness . . . go before [repentance] and remain in command" (*Luther's Works*, XXXV, 15). Bradford found amendment "no part of penance indeed, but a plain effect . . . of true penance," but Tyndale identified "the very [biblical] sense and signification" of "this word REPENTANCE" as "to be converted and to turn to God . . . , to know his will, and to live according to his laws; and to be cured of our corrupt nature" (*WJB*, I, 45, and see 51; *WWT*, 113). See also Myles Coverdale, "A Prologe," to Coverdale, ed. and trans., *Biblia: The Bible: That Is, the Holy Scrypture of the Olde and New Testament, Faythfully and Truly Translated out of Douche and Latyne in to Englishe* (n.p., 1535), unpag.

Rogers) concentrated upon the Pentateuchal presentation of divine law and assigned it a national purpose. Thus the official issuance of Holy Writ in English became an imitation of the acts of biblical monarchs charged with "the ryght and iust administracyon of the lawes that God gave unto Moses." Since clearly the king "coulde not but will his subiectes to reade and folowe all the poyntes of that lawe," its promulgation in the vernacular was fraught with ethical consequences for the whole community. In the words of Coverdale's dedication to the king, Holy Writ "maketh children of obedience, breuely [briefly], it teacheth all estates their office and duety. . . . [and] setleth every thyng in frame." Again, Cranmer's famous "Prologue or Preface," first attached to the 1540 edition of the Great Bible (a revision by Coverdale of the Matthew Bible), presented that work as the divine rules for Christian living in all spheres of life: "Herein may princes learn how to govern their subjects; subjects obedience, . . . to their princes: husbands, how they should behave them unto their wives," and so on. These and a legion of similar statements construed Sacred Writ as a book of law, which bound not only the church but also the civil community. Indisputably, Coverdale, Rogers, and Cranmer beheld and celebrated individual, solifidian dimensions in Holy Writ as well. But what reader of their prefaces reasonably could infer that justification by faith only is its definitive message?[17]

Doubtless the prefaces reflected the balance of theological forces in the

17. E. G. Rupp, *Studies in the Making of the English Protestant Tradition* (Cambridge, 1966), 48; Coverdale, ed. and trans., *Biblia: The Bible*, sigs. *ii, *iiii; "To the Moost Noble and Gracyous . . . Henry the Eyght," in John Rogers [pseud. Thomas Matthew], ed., *The Byble, Which Is All the Holy Scripture: In Whych Are Contayned the Olde and Newe Testament Truly and Purely Translated into Englysh by Thomas Matthew* (n.p., 1537), unpag.; Cranmer, "A Prologue or Preface," in Coverdale, ed., *The Byble in Englyshe, That Is to Saye, the Content of Al the Holy Scrypture, Bothe of the Olde and Newe Testament* (London, 1540), sig. +ii.

For the corporate ideal, see Berndt Hamm, "The Urban Reformation in the Holy Roman Empire," in Thomas A. Brady, Jr., Heiko A. Oberman, and James D. Tracy, eds., *Handbook of European History, 1400–1600: Late Middle Ages, Renaissance, and Reformation* (Grand Rapids, Mich., 1995), II, 213–214. Nicholas Ridley, Bradford, Becon, Hooper, and Thomas Lever were associated with the "Commonwealth Men," the Protestant group whose criticism of grasping landlords and advocacy of the economic welfare of common folk carried "a deep religious connotation." Dickens, *The English Reformation*, 249.

For Pentateuchal presentation, see "An Exhortacyon to the Studye of the Holy Scrypture Gathered out of the Byble," in Rogers, ed., *The Byble, Which Is All the Holy Scripture*, and in Coverdale, ed., *The Byble in Englyshe*, unpag.; "Unto . . . Kynge Henry the Eyght" and "A Prologe," in Coverdale, ed. and trans., *Biblia: The Bible*, sigs. ii–iiii, unpag.

realm at the time as well as the king's more traditional understanding of redemption, but the fact remains that they represented the Bible as the supreme compend of rules and precedents for righteous living, and so it entered the realm of law. By the same token, few if any evangelicals sympathized with Luther's denial of intrinsic authority to Mosaic law, if, indeed, they were aware of it. Latimer described the Protestant cleric expounding Old Testament precepts to his people as "sitting in Moses' chair," and Joye pictured Moses as "mayster and chefe governer of the church of Israell . . . [who] comanded the same preceptes which are now comanded to us by Christ." And clearly, in a manner consistent with Lollard, Erasmian, and patristic and broader Roman Catholic emphases, "law" in this context denoted all the saving essentials of the sacred word, including the message of Christ himself. Rogers presented his Matthew Bible of 1537 flatly and inclusively as "a translacyon of the Lordes lawe." Preparing for her execution in 1554, Lady Jane Grey gave a Greek New Testament to her sister Katherine with this gloss: "It is the book, dear sister, of the law of the Lord. . . . Desire with David, good sister, to understand the law of the Lord God." Here, explicitly, is the "biblicism containing a moral legalism" that some have found in the theology of the English Reformation. With many of their associates, these evangelicals appraised Scripture, gracious promises and all, as a legal gift.[18]

In a further disciplinary move, evangelicals also deployed the concept of covenant, understood in a limited contractual sense, as a useful vehicle of the gospel message. Given the prominence of contractual themes in the Old Testament, the great increase in biblical reading and study among Protestants might have sufficed in some instances, as very likely in the case of Tyndale, to draw new attention to them. Exposure to the ideas of Ulrich Zwingli, Heinrich Bullinger, and other early Reformed figures abroad who made use of covenant formulas probably also played a part. In any case, the first English ventures in covenant—or "federal"—theology began a trend of large significance for the future of English Protestant and, particularly, Puritan thought.

Like Luther, not all English writers took this step. A majority either ex-

18. *SHL*, 85; George Joye, *A Contrarye . . . Consultacion . . .* (Antwerp? 1549?), sig. Giii; [Rogers], "To the Moost Noble . . . Kyng Henry the Eyght," unpag. dedication of Rogers, ed., *The Byble, Which Is All the Holy Scripture;* Stephen Reed Cattley, ed., *The Acts and Monuments of John Foxe* (London, 1837–1841), VI, 422; Basil Hall, "Lutheranism in England (1520–1600)," in Derek Baker, ed., *Reform and Reformation: England and the Continent, c. 1500–c. 1750* (Oxford, 1979), 109; and see Diarmaid MacCulloch's similar formulation in *The Later Reformation in England, 1547–1603* (Houndmills, Basingstoke, Hampshire, 1990), 67.

pressed no special interest in the covenant idea or expounded it, with Bradford, in noncontractual or unilateral terms: "Thou hast made a covenant with me, which thou wilt never forget, that thou art and wilt be my Lord and my God; that is, thou wilt forgive me my sins and be wholly mine." But at least seven figures—Joye, Coverdale, Hooper, Becon, Bale, Edmond Allen, and, most prominently, Tyndale—were prepared openly to employ the idea of a reciprocal pact as an apt description of the divine and human encounter. Tyndale, who reorganized his theology around covenantal ideas as he struggled to translate and interpret the Old Testament in the 1520s and 1530s, urged the readers of his commentary on Genesis:

> Seek . . . in the scripture, . . . chiefly and above all, the covenants made between God and us; that is to say, the law and commandments which God commandeth us to do; and then the mercy promised unto all them that submit themselves unto the law. For all the [biblical] promises . . . do include a covenant: that is, God bindeth himself to fulfil that mercy unto thee only if thou wilt endeavour thyself to keep his laws.

So also George Joye, writing about 1534, and supposing that "in Substance . . . the doctrine of Moses and Cryst is al one," proclaimed the "bargyn" or "couenaunt wherby God hath promysed . . . his . . . mercyfull plesure unto us agreinge with us upon certayne condicions . . . saynge, I will be thy God . . . so that thou walke before me be perfit and pure."[19]

For these and other evangelicals, the covenant was a special type of contract

---

19. *WJB*, I, 149; *WWT*, 41; George Joye, The *Subuersion of Moris False Foundacion* . . . [Antwerp, 1534], sigs. liii, lvi (second pag.); Jens G. Møeller, "The Beginnings of Puritan Covenant Theology," *Jour. Eccl. Hist.*, XIV (1963), 52–56, notes the covenant theme in Bradford, Becon, Hooper, Tyndale, and Bale. For Hooper's theology of covenant, see *LL*, 213–214, 218–219. Tyndale considered "the general covenant" the master form of the covenant ideal: "If we meek ourselves to God, to keep all his laws, . . . then God has bound himself to us, to keep . . . all the mercies promised" (*WWT*, 106). See *LL*, 108–119, for Tyndale's concept of covenant and the scholarly controversies surrounding it. Some modern writers correct exaggerated accounts of strict contractual conditionality in Tyndale's theology but understate the degree to which legal and disciplinary interests tempered the paradoxical solifidianism he learned from Luther. See Michael McGiffert, "William Tyndale's Conception of Covenant," *Jour. Eccl. Hist.*, XXXII (1981), 167–184; Patrick Collinson, "William Tyndale and the Course of the English Reformation," *Reformation*, I (1996), 72–97. Reciprocal versions of covenant also appeared in a catechism probably written or translated from a Continental original by Bishop Edmund Allen: *A Shorte Cathechisme: A Briefe and Godly Bringinge up of Youth* . . . (Zurich, 1550), sigs. C, Dii, E, Eii, and see Kvii.

or bargain consonant with solifidian belief. Acting more as a father than a business partner, the Deity frames the pact as a gift of love and imparts power to meet its condition. Like belief that moral renewal is included in predestination, this formulation sustains the Protestant fix upon divine gratuity in the absence of human merit and capability, as does the attendant conviction that the human partner's obedience is utterly insufficient to please God and that ever-renewed repentance and pardon are required. At the same time, with its resort to the eminently human logic of reciprocal relations, imperative conditions, and law, early English covenant theology tended to portray redemption in terms at some remove from Luther's supralogical notion of sola fides and of duty unconstrained. It envisioned faith as at once independent of works and yet necessarily bound to them.

In keeping with its Hebraic origin, moreover, the contract bound to law and obedience not only the justified individual but also, upon partially different terms, the nation. By no means a Puritan invention, the conception of a covenanted, latter-day Israel subject to a Deuteronomic scheme of judgments and mercies informed the reformations in Zurich, Basel, and probably other Protestant cities from the early 1520s. Possibly in some connection with Zurich, this "Israelite paradigm" was championed by Tyndale in the early 1530s and by others in England in the next decade. A carrier of "that remarkable sense of responsibility for public affairs" characteristic of Reformed thought, it appeared in Tyndale's *Practice of Prelates* (1530) and his revised *Prologue to the Pentateuch* (1534), and his early advocacy might have contributed to its eventual popularization. Since the visiting Reformed theologians Bucer and Peter Martyr Vermigli, together with Joye, Becon, Bradford, Latimer, Hooper, Thomas Lever, and others, vigorously promoted the concept in works of the 1540s and early 1550s, the way was prepared for creation of the first English Protestant jeremiads in the 1550s, when several commentators interpreted the Protestant loss of the throne in 1553 as a covenantal judgment upon the nation for its half-hearted reception of the Protestant gospel: "Alas! England, alas! that this heavy plague of God should fall upon thee. . . . Thy faults . . . were never more plainly told . . . than . . . in King Edwards' days, but thou . . . didst amend never a whit." Bradford's *Sermon of Repentance* of 1553 was an elaborate jeremiad in this vein, pleading that God "save England, and give us repentance."[20]

20. Michael McGiffert, "God's Controversy with Jacobean England," *American Historical Review*, LXXXVIII (1983), 1153; Gottfried Wilhelm Locher, *Zwingli's Thought: New Perspectives* (Leiden, 1981), 29; Christmas, ed., *Works of Ridley*, 58, 61; *WJB*, I, 62, and

Such doctrine rested on assumptions that finely tangle the meaning of sola fides. First, a covenanted nation shares in a fashion in the Christian experience of divine wrath and punishment, repentance and ethical renewal, and reconciliation to divine favor. As from the individual, so too from the communal standpoint, the antidote to divine anger was to "repent [inclusive of moral amendment], ask mercy, pardon, and truly to turn to the Lord." Presuming an audience of baptized members of the Church of England, this appeal drew explicitly upon the resources of the Christian atonement. Second, the nation itself is subject to a Deuteronomic scheme (scorned by Luther as "nothing but a heap of blessings and cursings" that belonged to law and not gospel) presuming direct proportion between ethical behavior and divine favor and punishment. When the public weal was at stake, "To avoid this [punishment], let us amend our lives," was the dominant concern. At such times it could even appear that obedience to divine will and law was the great matter determining access to divine favor. Third, evangelical discussion of the individual's transaction with grace overlapped, at times extensively, with the Deuteronomic emphasis upon behavior and its temporal reward and punishment. Becon, for one, saw an identical redemptive process at work in the cases of the city of Nineveh, to whose citizens the prophet Jonah had preached, and Mary Magdalene, a female disciple of Jesus: Jonah threatened the Ninevites with temporal punishment "for their dissolute . . . living." "But they, [repenting] and mending their life, . . . were saved. . . . [And] Mary Magdalene . . . inasmuch as she . . . repented and bewailed her sinful living, her sins were forgiven her." Works like Bradford's *Sermon of Repentance* (1553) or Hooper's *Homilye to Be Read in the Tyme of Pestylence* (1553) likewise drew no clear distinction between the nation-in-covenant and the realm of saving grace, between individual and collective sin, repentance, and pardon. All three men, moreover, together with many of their Protestant colleagues, took for granted that the temporal punishments that figured so largely in biblical narratives were integral as well to

---

see 19–21, 38–42. Tyndale's *Prelates* and *Prologue:* William A. Clebsch, *England's Earliest Protestants, 1520–1535* (New Haven, Conn., 1964), 162, 182. Protestant cities and Deuteronomic scheme: Locher, *Zwingli's Thought*, 3, 34–35, 105, 146–147; J. Wayne Baker, *Heinrich Bullinger and the Covenant: The Other Reformed Tradition* (Athens, Ohio, 1980), 101, 104. Bucer and Vermigli: E. C. Whitaker, *Martin Bucer and the Book of Common Prayer* (Great Wakering, 1974), 136, 170; Spalding, "Reformatio Legum Ecclesiasticarum of 1552," *CH*, XXXIX (1970), 169. Works of the 1540s and 1550s: Joye, *A Contrarye Consultacion*, sigs. Aiiii–Aviii, Bv–Bvii, Fvii; *EWB*, 38–39, 238–261; *WJB*, I, 9–21; *SHL*, 91–92, 239–246; Thomas Lever, *Sermons, 1550*, ed. Edward Arber (London, 1871), 22–25, 55–58; Samuel Carr, ed., *Early Writings of John Hooper* (Cambridge, 1843), 433–558.

the Christian's earthly course: when, for example, "there is any unjust exaction laid upon thee, it is a plague and a punishment for thy sins, as all other plagues are: as are hunger, dearth, pestilence."[21]

Assuredly, early covenant theory in the English tradition had other purposes as well. Freely lavished grace was at its core, and its notion of a divinely guaranteed pact provided a firm basis for assurance. But its fuller work was to link and coordinate sola fides with rule, duty, and the Deuteronomic ideal and thus to echo and reinforce the duality that we have traced through this chapter. Without question, the determination not to "ascrybe any parte of . . . saluacion to our dedis," so familiar today, was the most novel, noteworthy, and controversial element in early evangelical teaching. It worked a permanent revolution in attitude toward Christian works, and it originated with Luther. Yet its passage into the island kingdom was a process, not of simple transmission, but of severe refraction. Its suggestion of a new Christianity preoccupied less with law and moral necessity was modified by a strong and decidedly traditional assertion of disciplinary priorities. Certainly there were many individual differences, but many among the English affiliated justification to Erasmian, patristic, Hebraic, legal, and contractual themes as well as to deep concerns for order and unity in the realm. All were vigorous anti-Catholics committed to God's gratuitous mercy without human deserving, but for them a revolutionized life was a gift no less gracious, and no less coveted, than a pacified conscience. The result was a biformity that was to prove long-lasting, a commitment to types of theological syntax that joined more heartily than they distanced Old and New Testament, faith and works, gospel and law. Since it was pardon and reformation together that manifested the divine word, will, and gratuity, the evangelical mission was frankly twofold. The citizenry must be taught that "the Gospel is glad tidings of mercy and peace, *and that* our corrupt nature shall be healed again," or that Christ "is *not onely* made our ryghtwysnes, *but* our halowyng *also,* for . . . the Lorde . . . promyseth *both* to pardon our wyckednes, *and also* to wryte hys law in our hertes."[22]

Although the exact lines of influence beyond 1558 are not clear, those earliest English Protestants embracing this bifocal pattern unwittingly laid foundations for further and more advanced undertakings in Protestant disciplinary

21. *WJB,* I, 20–21, 38–81 (Bradford) (and see *EWB,* 127, 184–185, 238–261); Pelikan, ed., *Luther's Works,* IX, 267; *SHL,* 91, 300; *EWB,* 76 (Becon); Nevinson, ed., *Later Writings of Hooper,* 159–175.

22. Joye, *Subuersion,* v; *WWT,* 112; Richard Taverner, *A Catechisme; or, Institution of the Christen Religion* (n.p., 1539), sigs. 32–33, 76, all emphases mine.

religion. After the failure of the Marian reaction, a new generation of evangelicals would open the first presbyterian chapter in their nation's history. In
line with pre-Marian belief in apostolic primacy, they sought to reform the
Church of England by biblical standards, but more than churchly restructur-
ing was at stake. A second factor was also at work, a famously unsparing
resolve to subdue sin and rule life by the divine law and covenant. Many
contemporary forces contributed to it, but it also marked one logical line of
development out of the earlier English Reformation. England's earliest reformers made the inaugural choices that shaped Protestantism in their land as
a strongly disciplinary movement, and it is improbable that those choices,
made by so large a contingent of articulate and often powerful men, did not
help to shape the later, harder quest for purity of life. As will appear in
chapters below, presbyterian and later Puritans shared with their English
forebears a dual understanding of redemption, and they shared all of the
doctrinal biases surveyed above, although of course they developed the issues
further and added others not emphasized in earlier years. Presbyterian demands were stiff, but in many ways they were familiar. The famous cry for
"further reformation" registered disappointment with the compromise of 1559,
but it also continued trends in evidence long before.[23]

23. I agree with Peter Lake, but with a different emphasis, that presbyterianism was not
"a foreign import grafted on to a native protestant tradition which was ill suited to receive
it, but . . . the product and extension of long term trends . . . within English Protestant
thought and feeling." "Presbyterianism, the Idea of a National Church, and the Argument
from Divine Right," in Lake and Maria Dowling, eds., *Protestantism and the National
Church in Sixteenth Century England* (London, 1987), 195.

CHAPTER 2

DISCIPLINARY THEMES OF THE PRESBYTERIAN MOVEMENT

Conservative defenders of the arrangements of 1559 had good reason to berate Thomas Cartwright (1535–1603) and his presbyterian peers as disciplinary extremists. Presbyterian theology, to begin with, belonged to the longer curve of development traced above. It endorsed the special commitments to moral transformation, law, and duty evident in pre-Marian theology and tended toward rigorous versions of Reformed soteriology. Sheer grace and faith only, the Lutheran core, were ever prominent but commonly paired and occasionally blended with behavioral requirements. Faith *and* works, gospel *and* law, New *and* Old Testament, individual *and* communal redemption: these and other ubiquitous pairs reproduced the forthrightly bifocal figure described earlier. Not all presbyterians, it is true, were committed to it equally. Like John Frith or Richard Tracy of an earlier generation, William Fulke (1538–1589), Josias Nichols (1555?–1639), and Thomas Wilcox (1549?–1608) tended to celebrate trust in Christ's propitiatory death as the primary factor in redemption, although they also sounded contrapuntal themes. But most of the figures we are considering, like their English forebears, were at pains not to "sever or sunder those thinges which the Lorde himselfe hath so neerely coupled," namely the extrinsic righteousness of justification and, rightly understood, the "righteousnesse inherent" of sanctification.[1]

---

1. *SCV*, sig. A7; *SSP*, 113. Knewstub's statement that "iustification, sanctification, and true holiness of life, are the free [gratuitous] works of God within us" is typical (*LJK*, 66). See also William Fulke, *A Comfortable Sermon of Faith, in Temptations and Afflictions . . .* (London, 1574); T[homas] W[ilcox], *Large Letters, Three in Number, Containing Much Necessarie Matter, for the Instruction and Comfort of Such, as Are Distressed in Conscience by Feeling of Sinne, and Feare of Gods Wrath* (London, 1589); Josias Nicholls, *Abraham's Faith: That Is, the Olde Religion . . .* (London, 1602). For contrapuntal themes, see Theodore

In keeping too with earlier patterns, presbyterians were inclined to see moral incapacity and evil as the core of the unregenerate condition, did not trust morality to pour forth uncommanded after justification, and dwelt upon sin and reformation most of the time. They spoke of Christian freedom, but usually had in mind freedom to obey, and there is no semblance of Luther's suggestions that the Christian at the highest reaches of the moral life may transcend the law, disregard Moses, or create new decalogues. They saw moral amendment as essential to repentance, matter-of-factly conceived the Bible as a book of binding rules and precedents, presumed the immediate relevance of Old Testament precedents and values within the Christian dispensation, and often posed gospel promises in a conditional mode.

Yet presbyterians did not halt there. They pushed beyond mid-Tudor precedents to harder values that here will be termed "strong Reformed." With their pledge to "walk precisely, or exactly" by biblical rules that did not sanction current liturgical vestments, the original, antivestiarian Puritans of the 1560s had pioneered this development. Presbyterians too wished to purge unbiblical usages in the Prayer Book of 1559, but they had additional, indeed vaulting ambitions. They sought to regulate the mass of citizens, who "are not so precise, but follow their owne desires." This was an increase both in scope and intensity of demand, and to that end a fuller ensemble of tactics was required. To restrain the citizenry, a particularly efficient means was at hand, the "exacte [and uniform] paterne off Discipline" displayed in the apostolic church, yet the work of elders and courts was only part of the plan. Painful sermons, pastoral counsel, edifying literature, fasts, and other private exercises together with semiseparation from ungodly neighbors and townsfolk and efforts to curb or excise elements of popular culture—all had a part. Here, in a many-pronged venture to "frame [English] lives precisely" by the biblical code, we find the stridently higher grade of demand for which "precise" and "precisian" first became popular terms of reproach.[2]

Stiffened demand is evident in a series of presbyterian theological adjustments. There was, to begin with, a renewed interest in the traditional Roman Catholic belief that "God and man must be like each other if they [a]re ever to

---

Dwight Bozeman, "Federal Theology and the 'National Covenant': An Elizabethan Case Study," *CH*, LXI (1992), 396 n. 7.

2. Antivestiarians: [Anthony Gilby], *To My Loving Brethren That Is Troublyd abowt the Popishe Apparell* . . . (n.p., [1566]), sig. Aiv. See also [Robert Crowley], *A Briefe Discourse against the Outwarde Apparell* . . . (n.p., [1566]), sig. Aviii. Presbyterians: *CS*, sigs. Gii, Hviii; [Walter Travers], *A Full and Plaine Declaration of Ecclesiasticall Discipline owt off the Word off God* (n.p., 1574), 6.

be at one with each other." A common ingredient in Catholic theories of redemption and of the ascetic life, the call to imitate divine qualities, to become more godlike in fact and thus merit divine favor stood in obvious tension with Protestant ideals of justification and seldom appeared in the theology of the English Reformation. But leading presbyterians restated belief that, if men and women "bee the children of GOD, there must be a likenes betweene him and them." Certainly, imitation and likeness must be modified to suit the evangelical context, becoming fruits and not causes or elements of justification; but thus understood they became useful and frequent aids to disciplinary exhortation. Cartwright could state bluntly, "As every one com-meth nearer unto [God] . . . in holinesse, so they are best liked and loued of him."[3]

In presbyterian circles too, kingship, law, and obedience were elemental and sometimes obsessive themes. All writers underscored them, and at times they blended into a master image of overarching divine monarchy. Its constit-uent elements, documented essentially from the Hebraic Scriptures, were God the king fiercely solicitous of his ethical glory, his all-embracing cosmic realm, the biblical "rule, . . . line [and] . . . squyre" that spell out its governing principles and statutes, and the duty of believers to reflect the divine honor and protect it from corruption by strict obedience. Within this framework, there is an oft-repeated portrayal of Christ as vice-monarch and lawgiver.[4]

One can imagine, again, the irascible Luther's reaction to Cartwright's flat statements that the "Gospell" aims to "perswade [men] to submit themselves to the kingdome of CHRIST, and to obey his laws," or to claims by John Knewstub (1544–1624) and George Gifford (1548–1600) that Christ's "life was given for the purchase of a zealous giving of our lives to the works that please

3. Steven Ozment, *The Age of Reform, 1250–1550: An Intellectual and Religious History of Late Medieval and Reformation Europe* (New Haven, Conn., 1980), 243, and see 46, 53; *TR,* 44; *TCR,* 14.

4. *TCR,* 78 (Field, Wilcox, and Fenner used virtually the same expression; Field and Wilcox quoted in Albert Peel, ed., *The Seconde Parte of a Register* . . . [Cambridge, 1915], I, 85); Dudley Fenner, *Certain Godly and Learned Treatises* . . . (Edinburgh, 1592), 80.

Ethical glory: "The end wee looke at in all of our 'dueties,'" said Knewstub, "must bee by doeing thereof to get honour and glorie to our God. . . . [Wherefore] the . . . breach of his commaundement, doth reach to the stayning and polluting of his name" (*LJK,* 48, 62, and see 74–75). Sin as corruption of the divine honor: *TR,* 54, 83–84. Christ as monarch and lawgiver: Dudley Fenner's phrasing is typical: "Christe being a King, hath prescribed Lawes for his gouernment" (*A Counter-Poyson, Modestly Written for the Time* . . . [London, 1584?], "The Author to the Reader," 9 [sep. pagin.]).

him" and that "the true worship of God hath for the ground and foundation, sincere obedience." And when we find a figure like John Udall (1560–1592), who died in prison (or immediately after his release) in 1592 for the presbyterian cause, suggesting that "Amend your lives" is "a sentence . . . containing the very substance of all religion, and the whole sum of Christianity," we may infer that advocacy of formal church discipline was but one expression of a shifting view of redemption itself.[5]

Covenant Theory and the Israelite Paradigm

Telling support for this conclusion appears in covenant theory. Elizabethan presbyterians were not covenant theologians in a strict sense, for in their thought the contract idea does not function as "the conceptual keystone of Puritan divinity," but serves as one of several figures articulating a complex worldview. All were pledged to the Israelite paradigm of pre-Marian thought. Most espoused as well the familiar union of solifidian with contractual themes, and several stood to the fore in the revision of late-century covenant divinity in which the familiar redemptive pact—now formally termed the "covenant of grace"—was clarified and reinforced through contrast with a purely legal "covenant of works." Furthermore, and contrary to a long-lived surmise that Puritan divinity embraced separate covenants of grace and nation, an individual and solifidian covenant of grace and a conditional and earthly national covenant, presbyterians sustained the earlier evangelical belief that the individual and the commonwealth partake of one and the same pact. It is at once individual and corporate, gracious and conditional. Those within it are Christian Israelites, beneficiaries of the gospel of unconditional pardon and yet pledged to a Hebraic and Deuteronomic scheme of laws, duties, rewards, and punishments. Thus was the Christian's saving faith an intriguingly dual affair: in one dimen-

5. Thomas Cartwright, *A Commentary upon the Epistle . . . to the Colossians . . .* (London, 1612), 95; John Knewstub, *A Sermon Preached at Paules Crosse . . . 1579* (London, 1579), 44–45; G[eorge] Giff[o]rd, *Eight Sermons, upon the First Foure Chapters, and Part of the Fift[h], of Ecclesiastes* (London, 1589), 126; *CS*, sig. Hiiii. Such evidence illuminates G. R. Elton's finding that in Elizabethan England Luther had become a secondary figure of little influence. See Elton, "Luther in England," in Bernd Moeller, ed., *Luther in der Neuzeit* (Gütersloh, 1983), 126–129. Cf. Jaroslav Pelikan, ed., *Luther's Works* (Saint Louis, 1955–1986), XXVI, 26: "Two words, 'grace' and 'peace,' contain a summary of all of Christianity. Grace pardons sin, and peace quiets the conscience."

sion freed from law, works, and retribution, but in a second firmly subject to them all.[6]

Within the pact, belief in "faith only" flatly ruled out *antecedent* conditions for grace and pardon. Yet, when it was affirmed that trust in Christ was the pact's sole condition, the meaning of "condition" was determined in part by the Deuteronomic scheme and the closely connected vision of sacred monarchy and its strict statutory government; it was coupled as well to a complex Christology that assigned to the Redeemer and vice-monarch a medley of special enabling, law-giving, and ruling functions. There were, as Knewstub put it, "severall commodities that come with this gifte of Jesus Christ" (he cited "wisdom, righteousnesse, sanctification, and redemption" "from all danger, affliction, and corruption"). Thus to have faith in Christ was not essentially to repose in his mercy and forgiveness. It was as well, and necessarily, to partake of his power of moral perfection, to embrace the rigors of divine government, to have and nurture an aversion to sin and a love for the law. It is true "that the Lord in mercie for Christ covereth the sinnes of his, but it is as true, that the Lorde cureth the sinnes of his." Dudley Fenner (1558?–1587) was sure that "the remedie of our sinnes . . . is Christ his death" but left his audience in no doubt that the atoning death worked as well "to give power to kill the sin, and to quicken us to obedience." With this same, dual construct in mind, Cartwright could include rule over the churchly "Kingdome" as a crucial element of Christ's role as mediator, and Gifford could acknowledge that God "hath couenanted . . . that all which beleeve in his sonne shall not be confounded" but then interpret the believer's tie to Christ, with heavy Platonic accents, in terms of power against concupiscent entanglement in the "earthly and transitorie."[7]

Picturing Christian redemption as a complex of pardon plus moral remodeling within a cosmic monarchy whose king "hath coupled the glorie of

6. David Zaret, *The Heavenly Contract: Ideology and Organization in Pre-Revolutionary Puritanism* (Chicago, 1985), 128; and see David A. Weir, *The Origins of the Federal Theology in Sixteenth-Century Reformation Thought* (Oxford, 1990), 3, 62, 118–119, 137–147. For the individual and corporate pact, see Bozeman, "Federal Theology," *CH*, LXI (1992), 394–407.

7. *LJK*, 20, 268; ("To what end," asked Gifford, "was the death of Christ? Not onely to make satisfaction for sinne, but also to destroy . . . sinne. . . . Christ died to slay sinne" [*SSP*, 38]); Fenner, *Certain Treatises*, 86 (and see 100, 115, 155, 178). For other examples of the bifocal pattern, see Fenner, *Sacra theologia, sive veritas quae est secundum pietatem* (Geneva, 1589), bk. 4, chap. 6, 47–48; George G[i]ff[o]rd, *Fifteene Sermons, upon the Song of Salomon* (London, 1598), 108, and see 95–113 for the Platonizing context.

his name . . . to the doeing of his wil," and certain that "those who minde his commaundementes to doe them, are they to whome onlie his mercies are promised," presbyterians thus underwrote and indeed mandated *consequent* conditions in the pact. It was the Deity's role to forgive sin and to supply regenerative will and power, and it was "our parte, to declare that we are [Christ's], . . . by dying unto sinne, and living unto righteousnesse." As Stephen Egerton (1555?–1621?) phrased it for his congregation at Saint Anne's, Blackfriars, in London, the pact that carried favor also imposed a "condition of our dutie in the behalfe of our selves."[8]

Reflecting its history of associations with the Old Testament, possibly with medieval modernism in the tradition of William of Ockham, and likely with the covenant formulas of William Tyndale, Heinrich Bullinger, Caspar Olevianus, and other Reformed theologians, the contract notion thus was ideally suited to express a vision of new righteousness no less actual than imputed. Construed as a gracious work, a pact forged by a deity who both imposed and fulfilled the conditions, it cohered with the concept of justification by faith alone. At the same time, its reciprocal, ethical theme harmonized with a vision of life within a rigorous monarchy ordered in every significant detail by the sacred Book. And certainly, as a concept rooted first and foremost in the Old Testament, it offered a way to sustain continuity with the Israelite church and its conviction, as John Field encapsulated it, that "onely they shall be preserved that walke with God, to beleeve his promises, and to feare his iudgements: . . . and be careful to walke in al dutifull obedience." Faced with this array of moralizing implications, Fulke or Nichols well might take pause, but passionate disciplinarians like Field and Knewstub saw in the covenant an ideal instrument for their purposes.[9]

In roughly the last quarter of the sixteenth century, among English theologians attracted to the contract idea, interest in the Israelite paradigm appears

8. *LJK*, 19, 49, 313; [Stephen] Egerton, *An Ordinary Lecture, Preached at the Blackefriers* (London, 1589), sig. Av. The invocation of "the covenant [of grace] made with *Abraham*" in Gifford's *SSP,* 80, blends effortlessly with that work's striking, relentless emphasis upon mortification and discipline. The spotlight falls less upon Abraham's trustful faith as the covenant-founding deed than upon his obedience to divine command. For other unequivocally conditional statements, see *LJK,* 49, 122, 346–347; Egerton, *An Ordinary Lecture,* sig. A5.

9. John Field, *A Godly Exhortation, by Occasion of the Late Iudgement of God, Shewed at Parris-garden . . .* (London, 1583), sig. A8. Knewstub explained that the Lord "hath entred covenant with us to be our God, in causing us to walke in his wayes, that he thereby may be magnified." *LJK,* 48 (see also 67, 122).

to have expanded. In tracts like John Field's *Godly Exhortation, by Occasion of the Late Iudgement of God, Shewed at Parris-garden* (1583) and Thomas Wilcox's *Short, Yet a True and Faithful Narration of the Fearful Fire, That Fell in the Towne of Wooburne . . . 1595,* it became the basis for an increasingly detailed analysis of current adversities. In the same period, it began with some regularity to find collective ritual expression. During the later 1570s, the public fast day emerged as an eminent expression of English and, especially, of Puritan piety; and at least two presbyterians, Cartwright and Udall, were prominent theoreticians of the device. By providing a ritually charged and, by the next decade, frequent mode of communal response to the Lord's "grievous chastisement," fast days provided a most useful means to dramatize and propagate Deuteronomic doctrine. For the term of a fast (Cartwright recommended "at the least . . . a whole day") participants now would be immersed in an affecting work of corporate asceticism and reflection whose root was moral failure, whose substance was contrition ("humiliation") and ethical reform ("amendment"), and whose rationale was openly Deuteronomic.[10]

By the mid-Elizabethan years advanced Protestants had learned to portray with a particular intensity their nation's temporal weal and woe in terms of the Israelite paradigm. The tactic was especially serviceable to presbyterians, who could depict the arrest of religious reformation and the government's rejection of apostolic polity and discipline as a dangerous flirtation with divine wrath. But, more to the point, here was another spur to moral reformation. Since plague, flood, dearth, fire, war, and countless lesser afflictions were direct results of sin, opportunities ever were on hand to review and arraign disorderly behavior (including village sports and festivities), to magnify an audience's sense of the gravity surrounding moral duty and self-control, and to call the authorities to firmer control of public morals.[11]

10. T[homas] C[artwright], *A Reply to an Answere Made of M. Doctor Whitgifte . . .* (n.p., 1573), 138–139; Albert Peel and Leland H. Carlson, eds., *Cartwrightiana* (London, 1951), 139. On rising interest in the paradigm: Michael McGiffert, "God's Controversy with Jacobean England," *American Historical Review,* LXXXVIII (1983), 1164. Providential interpretation of adversities in contemporary England is surveyed and contextualized in Alexandra Walsham, *Providence in Early Modern England* (Oxford, 1999), 116–166. The fast day: Cartwright was the probable author of William Wilkinson, *A Very Godly and Learned Treatise, of the Exercise of Fastyng . . .* (London, 1580), and discussed the ordinance also in his *TCR,* 247–250. For his authorship, see Peel and Carlson, eds., *Cartwrightiana,* 118–120. Udall explained the duty of corporate "solemn fasting" in *TR,* 88.

11. For flirtation with divine wrath, see [John Field and Thomas Wilcox], *An Admonition to the Parliament* (1572), in W. H. Frere and C. E. Douglas, eds., *Puritan Manifestoes: A*

Thomas Wilcox, coauthor of the *Admonition to Parliament* of 1572 and a leading presbyterian agitator and divine, epitomized the paradigm's regulatory uses in his *Narration of the Fearful Fire*. There we are able to see a mind steeped in Israelite ways engaged in detailed analysis of an actual local calamity. In the summer of 1595, a fire broke out in a thatched cottage, spread rapidly, and engulfed half or more of Woburn. No life was lost, but hundreds of men, women, and children were left homeless and without provision against the coming winter. In this simple, local occurrence, Wilcox saw a poignant saga in which the very forces of nature were arrayed against sin. If sparks remained hidden in the ashes of a hearth in which a simple old woman carelessly had discarded her bedding straw, if a wind sprang up at just the right moment, if the town's thatched houses and storage sheds had been rendered dry as tinder by weeks of drought, and if leading townsmen who might have doused the fire at an early stage were at work in outlying fields at the crucial time—these were not acts of "fortune and secondary causes," but providentially interlaced effects designed to call an erring community to account. With much invocation of Old Testament precedents ("Ah people laden with iniquitie, . . . they have . . . provoked the holy one of Israell"), Wilcox showed how a country village met its temporal fate according to the rules of a divine and ethical monarchy with whose "majestie" and "glory" "there can dwell no manner of wickednes." Thus did Woburn's fire, an unforgettable hour in which precise Protestants could see "the hande of God punishing the sinnes of men," dramatize the temporal wages of sin.[12]

Since, then, "transgressions [are] as it were gable ropes to ha[u]le downe iudgements," Wilcox's reflections upon the event turned at the end to a scathing review of immoralities of the day, first in Woburn and then in the nation as a whole. Idleness, new fashions and luxuries, usury, fornication, Sabbath breaking, "wicked recreations," and the other normal items of Puritan complaint were included in the indictment, and Wilcox also maintained that large stocks of foodstuffs and drink specifically had been targeted for destruction in order to put the townspeople "in mind how they have offended . . . in abusing these blessings to gourmandise, and drunkenness." He paid specific attention to lower-class disorders, to the widespread "idleness and carelessnes" that he

---

Study in the Origins of the Puritan Revolt (New York, 1972), 12; John Udall, *A Demonstration of the Truth of That Discipline, Which Christ Hath Prescribed in His Word* . . . (1588), ed. Edward Arber (London, 1880), 6–7.

12. *FN*, 21, 25–26, 31, 36–37 (and see 28–29, 58). For divine glory and majesty, see *FN*, 20–21, 30–31, 43.

associated with "great and grievous povertie," to problems with alehouses, to the desultory work and bad behavior of "day labourers and men of manuall occupations," and to parents who allowed their children to "swarme in [the] streetes, and . . . runne up and downe daily in mire and dirt. . . . and some of them . . . pilfering, breaking . . . hedges, learning to lie, sweare," and the like.[13]

The *Narration of the Fearful Fire*, in short, is a full-scale Puritan jeremiad, probably one of the earliest, yet already a full realization of the type. And in it we see how Deuteronomic interpretation of a current calamity bred opportunities to arraign unlawful behavior. With its central image of a majestically angry deity assaulting an earthly community, it suggested the inadequacy of existing procedures of church discipline; but, more, it was a potent means to magnify an audience's sense of the gravity surrounding moral duty and self-control. Personal behavior, quite aside from its role in Christian regeneration, now was a matter of basic corporate welfare and survival. In the hands of Wilcox and dozens like him, the theologically positive use of ever-present adversities and the warning of others to come would become a virtuosic aid to the Puritan campaign for a more precisely governed life.

Unquestionably, then, the covenant ideal, with its vision of earthly penalties and now buttressed by the fast day, was a heaven-sent auxiliary to an ethically strenuous program. But to restrict its application to the corporate, temporal realm would at once have abridged the plain biblical deliverance that "all miseries are the punishements of GOD for sinne" and curtailed its great potential for ordering and sanctifying a people. And in simple fact, the curses-and-favors formula was also a normal—indeed, vital—aspect of the Lord's nurture and regimentation of his individual saints. That he "dooth nowe and then sende uppon whole nations some punishment or other" was but half the message of Scripture and experience, for it was equally necessary to grasp that "every one of us" separately and with some frequency "shall find the Lordes rodde uppon him." In this way as in many others, the covenant proved both corporate and personal, national and gracious, for it applied as readily to "euerye priuate man," certainly to every regenerate saint, as to their English commonweal.[14]

Belief that the Deity inflicts earthly punishments for sin was scarcely an Elizabethan invention and had been an occasional motif in pre-Marian evangelical teaching. It bore, too, an intriguing resemblance to Catholic views,

13. *FN,* 21, 58, 71, 68–69.

14. *TR,* 52, 19, 87. For additional elaboration and documentation, see Bozeman, "Federal Theology," *CH,* LXI (1992), 403.

recently reaffirmed at the Council of Trent, of the necessity of a temporal punishment of sin that played so important a role in the rite of penance and underlay the doctrine of purgatory. But now, in conjunction with the paradigm's ascending popularity in the 1570s and beyond, penal afflictions were drawn wholesale into the covenant. Since the aim was to reform and reconcile and not, as in the covenant of works, to overwhelm and destroy, punishments were strokes of grace. In his survey of Woburn's fire, Wilcox positively rejoiced at how the disaster had "scoured" the saints from "corruption" endangering their salvation, recalled them to basic Christian values, evoked healing contrition, and given an opportunity for the elect to fulfill the biblical requirement that those who would reign with Christ after the Resurrection must suffer with him in this life. At times the punishment itself might be softened by special favors, as when a collapsing gallery at Parris-Garden in London in the early 1580s killed and injured many yet spared others equally guilty and thus also manifested the divine mercy. Normally, however, the Lord sent unmitigated "calamities and troubles." Extending to the severest personal disasters, they made known "the anger of God . . . hot against sinne." Moreover, as at least Udall and Cartwright insisted, their severity was proportioned directly to the severity of the offense.[15]

And so there came into play, square in the realm of individual experience, and—for the elect—square in the realm of covenanted grace, the exacting quid pro quo of Israelite principle. Now the doctrine of personal deliverance through a ransoming atonement was openly tied to belief in a systematic, causal connection between moral fault and temporal adversity. Now more than ever, sin, repentance, and reconciliation would continue to be the structuring realities of Christian personal existence defined by the covenant, but the experience of those realities was framed in part by an explicit moral calculus of faults and penalties. If in the long run the divine revenge was annulled, it had a more essential place in the daily practice of life. In point of fact, those who trust in Christ are most painfully subject to it, since in return for their boon of

---

15. *FN*, 22, and see 24–25, 43–46, and [William Fulke], *A Godly and Learned Sermon* . . . [London, 1580], 31 ("Even the rod by whiche [God] scourgeth . . . [is] a demonstration of his mercie"); *TR*, 19; *CL*, 38. On pre-Marian teaching: John Frith, *The Whole Workes of W. Tyndall, John Frith, and Doct. Barnes* (London, 1573), 5; *WWT*, 112. For Tyndale's particular interest in Deuteronomic rewards and punishments, see William A. Clebsch, *England's Earliest Protestants, 1520–1535* (New Haven, Conn., 1964), 189–190. Special favors: Field, *A Godly Exhortation*, sig. Ciii; *CL*, 24, 27, 95; *TCR*, 72.

grace the Lord holds them to a higher standard: conformity in thought and deed, as Wilcox put it, to Scripture's "exact perfection."[16]

Exact perfection—that was the nub of the matter. Elizabethan presbyterians were committed apostles of a solifidian creed, but, as we will see, concerns about disorder and laxity stirred them as much as hostility to Catholic works-righteousness. They were preoccupied with the government of behavior, and their notion of government was notably severe. Not fearing to require too much, they accented strictness and exactitude, and so wove a *precisianist strain* into Protestant faith. Yet, strenuous as they were, they did not yet reach the pinnacle of Puritan moral demand. That was attained in the next, even more strenuous phase of development (traced in Chapters 4–9).

16. *The Works of . . . Thomas Wilcocks . . .* , 2d ed. (London, 1624), 38. For the saints' special vulnerability to punishment, see Cartwright, *Colossians,* 177, and *CL,* 95.

CHAPTER 3

DISCIPLINE
AS STABILIZER
IN SHIFTING
TIMES

I n presbyterian visions of reformation, the theological ellipse of pre-Marian days still held firmly in place. Yet its disciplinary pole, buttressed by calls for strictness and exactitude and by the canons of Deuteronomy, now stood more prominent. To prepare for later discussion of the Puritan pietist phase, we must try to give a fuller account of this development. Presbyterian ideals were related to earlier phases of the English and Continental Reformations, but they reflected too a variety of contemporary cares and opportunities. Presbyterians were harsh critics of the Roman church, and their struggle for moral reform met a need to counter persistent Catholic accusations, now set forward in the reinvigorated spirit of the Counter Reformation, that Protestant teaching about justification undercut morality. Continuing identification with international Reformed Protestantism also was a factor. From 1550 to 1553 and again after 1559 the London "stranger churches" had provided models of a church revamped and disciplined along Reformed lines, and there is ample evidence that the presbyterian leaders knew and envied them. Some had spent time in Continental Reformed communities during the Marian reaction, and all esteemed the disciplinary achievements of churches in Scotland, France, the northern Netherlands, and the German-Swiss Rhineland. Presbyterian interest in the Genevan discipline is well known, and it is remarkable how closely the English push for a "further reformation" echoed the contemporary cycles of reform, in formerly Lutheran territories, that now are called the "Second Reformation." There as in England aggressive Reformed elites, against the opposition of popular majorities, aimed to radicalize a conservative Protestant establishment, to make a cleaner sweep of Catholic liturgical elements, and to introduce apostolic discipline.[1]

1. Stranger churches: Andrew Pettegree, *Foreign Protestant Communities in Sixteenth-*

The Reformation of Manners

Modern students of Elizabethan and early Stuart England relate Puritan disciplinary ventures to a troublesome set of socioeconomic changes. As noted in Chapter 1, Protestant ethical emphasis in mid-Tudor times reflected a dread of disorder. Deepened by periodic episodes of unrest and rebellion, that dread was reinforced later in the century by the long-range effects of accelerated population growth, arguably the "underlying force in English life [from the early 1500s] until the Civil Wars." Those able to capitalize upon increased demand for goods and services improved their income and standard of living; they also labored to distance themselves from their poorer neighbors through distinctive interests in religion, education, and manners and a more critical attitude toward traditional festivities and other elements of popular culture. Yet the same forces that brought prosperity to some worked to impoverish others. Affected, for example, by rising prices, falling levels of real wages, or by a growing pressure of population upon limited supplies of land, many joined the swelling ranks of struggling subsistence farmers or wholly landless citizens in the fluctuating labor market or on the tramp. They, in turn, became more vulnerable to the periodic effects of dearth or economic depression. In the century before the Civil War, most dramatically during the terrible agrarian and trade crises of the 1580s and 1620s, these trends joined to produce a large-scale increase in destitution, vagrancy, and dependence upon local programs of poor relief. They also sharpened cultural differences, as the poor clung to traditional village enjoyments and as alehouses tended to become centers of lower-class drinking, sociability, games, and, often enough, of gambling, carousing behavior, illicit sex, and crime. Faced with these dangers and with a growing host of vagrants, mounting crime, rising poor rates, and all the spiraling effects of a demographic and economic crisis that "seemed almost on the point of overwhelming the Elizabethan and early Stuart community," respectable society had reason for grave concern.[2]

Century London (Oxford, 1986), 272–273. Second Reformation: Heinz Schilling, *Religion, Political Culture, and the Emergence of Early Modern Society* (Leiden, 1992), 247–301. The first and pace-setting Second Reformation was introduced in the German Palatinate beginning in the later 1560s, the eve of Thomas Cartwright's inaugural push for a presbyterian reformation in 1570.

2. J. A. Sharpe, *Crime in Early Modern England, 1550–1750* (London, 1984), 16; Peter Clark, *English Provincial Society from the Reformation to the Revolution: Religion, Politics, and Society in Kent, 1500–1640* (Hassocks, 1977), 186. For the "panic-stricken" concern about order in this period, see also Sharpe, *Crime in Early Modern England*, 183, and see 17,

Within this portrait of a poverty-ridden, polarized, and fearful society in the sixteenth and early seventeenth century, Puritanism appears as a timely and eminently functional force. Understood as a disciplinary agent called into play by fears of disorder, it is assigned a role in the process of readjustment through which the rising classes both redefined their place in society and, more particularly, sought to contain and control the poor and often to ameliorate their distress. Those in city, town, and county communities who struggled to contain the poverty crisis tended to be members of the Dissenting minority within the national church desirous of further reformation. With some frequency, organized and vigorous programs to relieve want and control misbehavior were the work of local notables in partnership with a Puritan clergyman and perhaps backed by the county magistrates. Committed to godly discipline, to work, and to the monogamous and patriarchal family, such figures naturally shared the social anxieties of their time, and they strove for practical solutions. When they were able to achieve power or at least substantial influence within a local setting, they spearheaded an ambitious "reformation of manners." Forming a "vanguard in the growing use of poor-relief as a means of social control," they made full use of the popular remedies of the day, like the strict policing of vagrants, the establishment of workhouses, or the taxing power to collect money for the poor. They sought more strictly to police tippling, fornication, and other common sins and to curb the expressive festivities and recreations of traditional communal culture that contrasted so sharply with the newer standards of "godliness" and self-control.[3]

Such, in brief, is the thesis of a Puritan reformation of manners in later Elizabethan and early Stuart England. Stated in baldest form, the Puritan factor becomes a "cultural wedge" distancing a privileged few from the depressed multitude; more pointedly, it is an "ideology of discipline" or "culture of discipline" deployed by local alliances of rising, solid, and godly citizens to order the lower classes. Sensitive in most cases to the dangers of oversimple

---

167; A. L. Beier, *Masterless Men: The Vagrancy Problem in England, 1560–1640* (London, 1985), 6–10. For polarization, see *ES*, 194–199, 220–226; Peter Clark, *The English Alehouse: A Social History, 1200–1830* (London, 1983), 151–157. In *English Alehouse*, 145 (and see 124–132, 157–158), Clark argues that alehouses increasingly appeared to respectable citizens as "strongholds of a populist world which aimed to overthrow established respectable society."

3. Paul Slack, "Poverty and Social Regulation in Elizabethan England," in Christopher Haigh, ed., *The Reign of Elizabeth I* (Athens, Ga., 1985), 238. The "reformation of manners" thesis is formulated in detail in *PM*; David Underdown, *Fire from Heaven: Life in an English Town in the Seventeenth Century* (New Haven, Conn., 1992); *PP*.

class analysis, advocates of this approach yet see an undeniable trend associating Puritan moral reform with respectable and often upwardly mobile parish notables and their perception of an endangered society.[4]

Entering the mainstream of scholarship in the late 1970s, the thesis meanwhile has been a fruitful subject of debate. In particular, it has proven difficult to document a widespread, clear-cut polarization of popular and respectable society. Rarely if ever did local situations reflect a clean division between a rising, respectable, disciplinarian group and a disadvantaged world of poverty and alehouses. Drink, dancing, gambling, playgoing, bearbaiting, sports, May festivities, and other recreational activities were no special preserve of the poor, and perhaps the association between alehouses and poverty has been overdrawn. Even in so-called Puritan towns, the disciplinarians probably were a minority most if not all of the time, leaving a majority—or at least a sizable fraction—of the upper and middle ranks indifferent, ambivalent, or hostile to their reformation and its assault upon older and pleasureful traditions. Elizabethan and Stuart Puritans tended to belong to the middling and upper ranks of society, but not all prospered or were upwardly mobile. They had no monopoly of concern about poverty, vagrancy, and disorder. Many county and village officers zealous for sobriety and orderliness were hostile to Puritan religious objectives, and not all local reformations of the period were the work of godly coalitions. At a more general level, the proposal of a distinctively English reformation of manners tends to inflate the importance of the decades around 1600 and to neglect long-range rhythms of moral regulation over several centuries. Finally, some formulations of the thesis tend to make class interest and social control primary defining terms of a profoundly religious movement. The net effect of such criticism is to qualify, although hardly to set aside, the perception that Puritan disciplinary concerns were related to changing socioeconomic patterns and a rising tide of poverty and its dangers.[5]

4. *PP*, 162; *PM*, x; Barry Reay, ed., *Popular Culture in Seventeenth-Century England* (London, 1985), 12–13.

5. Clearcut polarization: *RP*, 189–241; Eamon Duffy, "The Godly and the Multitude in Stuart England," *Seventeenth Century*, I (1986), 35–37; Tessa Watt, *Cheap Print and Popular Piety, 1550–1640* (Cambridge, 1991), 71, 73, 326. A study of a Puritan artisan in the early Stuart period finds that "sense of conflict between social strata" was "virtually absent" from his thought; see Paul S. Seaver, *Wallington's World: A Puritan Artisan in Seventeenth-Century London* (Stanford, Calif., 1985), 223. Clean division: Patrick Collinson, *The Birth-pangs of Protestant England: Religious and Cultural Change in the Sixteenth and Seventeenth Centuries* (New York, 1988), 153; *PP*, 136. Resistant majority: *RP*, 190–191, 200–202, 256–257; Joan Kent, *The English Village Constable, 1580–1642: A Social and Administrative Study*

Presbyterians React to the Crisis of Poverty

In ways limited but substantial, that perception coheres with Elizabethan presbyterian teaching. Thomas Cartwright, John Knewstub, John Udall, and other leading publicists of the 1570s and 1580s championed a scheme of church discipline enforced by an apostolic eldership and a hierarchy of courts. Cartwright set forth the first systematic plan in a series of lectures delivered at Cambridge University in 1570 and thus began an era of widespread agitation for reform that ended only with the creation, discovery, and suppression of an underground organization of presbyterian classes in the 1570s and 1580s. Both the apostolic scheme itself and the larger theological project that grounded it reveal connections between the desire to control behavior and worries about poverty and disorder.

To begin with, virtually all of the presbyterians whose views are a matter of record belonged to the respectable ranks. Most stemmed from families of the middling sort, were part of the university-trained elite, and often enjoyed the support of sympathetic gentry and nobility. Ecclesiastical radicals intending root-and-branch reform of the church, they were social conservatives with no wish to disrupt the existing social or gender hierarchy. Excluding women from roles of authority, they expected the leading men of the parish to staff the lay presbytery in charge of formal discipline and affirmed the "mutuality of magistracy and ministry" in the work of religious and moral reformation. Foes of Separatism, they taught their charges "to seek the peace of the common wealth . . . and not to rebel against or revile the governours thereof." They called for substantial changes, to be sure, and certainly their ideals harbored a potential beyond conscious intent for changing the structures of authority in society. Yet the hoped-for social world of the future, as in the doctrine of the mid-Tudor Commonwealthmen, was to be largely continuous with the present, one of familiar station, hierarchy, dutiful work, and withal "a peaceable and quiet life in all godlinesse and honesty . . . under a christian Prince."

(Oxford, 1986), 294–295. Not prospering: *PM*, 125. Concern about vagrancy: see the case study of Keevil in Martin Ingram, "The Reform of Popular Culture? Sex and Marriage in Early Modern England," in Reay, ed., *Popular Culture*, 158–160; and see Buchanan Sharp, *In Contempt of All Authority: Rural Artisans and Riot in the West of England, 1586–1660* (Berkeley, Calif., 1980), 305. Long-range rhythms: Martin Ingram, "Reformation of Manners in Early Modern England," in Paul Griffiths, Adam Fox, and Steve Hindle, eds., *The Experience of Authority in Early Modern England* (New York, 1996), 47–88. Social control: David Underdown, "Assessing an Artisan," *Journal of British Studies*, XXVI (1987), 262.

Identified as they were with respectable society, did articulate presbyterians register alarm about poverty and disorder?[6]

In an age-old vein of Christian exhortation, they rebuked cursing, drunkenness, and other common misbehaviors; yet with notable frequency their castigations became extreme. English sinning, so it appeared, had soared beyond familiar bounds. A conviction that "almost the whole world is drowned in sin and iniquitie," that "all wickednesse overflowe[s]" and "run[s] over almost in every place," lent edge to presbyterian utterance. Often it underlay appeals for more morally stringent preaching. "Howe," it was asked, "commes disorder in townes? . . . licence and libertie to all hauocke? . . . thefts, outrages, and misdemeanours of all sorts"? The answer was clear: "in [the] want and barrennesse of Preachers," whether occasioned by simple lack of supply or by episcopal silencing of Nonconformists. Extending the range of disorder to outrage and havoc and compounding the effect with suggestion of ecclesiastical error and mismanagement, the language expressed a sense that the social world was out of control.[7]

And that loss of control, considered in light of the Deuteronomic scheme of punishments, assumed frightful dimensions. Given the torrential flow of sin, the authorities' stubborn refusal to institute New Testament discipline

6. *RP*, 153, and see entire chapter; *CL*, 10; *BPD*, 145. Social status of Elizabethan clergy: Michael Walzer, *The Revolution of the Saints: A Study in the Origins of Radical Politics* (New York, 1969), 135; Dudley Fenner, an "heir to great possessions," was an exception (*DNB*, s.v. "Fenner, Dudley"). Conservatives: The Puritan civil lawyer William Stoughton insisted that presbyterian reform "will not draw with it any least alteration, of anie part, of . . . temporall . . . government, nor almost of anie one common statute, or customarie law" (*An Assertion for True and Christian Church-Policie* [Middelburg, 1604], 34–35). Presbyterian proposals, however, were "prejudiciall" to the system of impropriations and patronage that controlled many clerical livings and appointments ("Petition of the House of Commons to the Lords for reformation of the clergy, together with the substance of Archbishop Whitgift's answer" [1585], Tanner Manuscripts, LXXVIII, item 41, p. 91, Bodeian Library, Oxford University). On leading men: Christopher Hill, *Society and Puritanism in Pre-Revolutionary England*, 2d ed. (New York, 1967), 235–236.

7. *CS*, sig. I; *BPD*, 91; Thomas Cartwright, *The Second Replie of Thomas Cartwright: Agaynst Maister Doctor Whitgiftes Second Answer, touching the Churche Discipline* (n.p., 1575), sig. XXXiv; *A Parte of a Register* . . . (n.p., [1593]), 292 (and see the entire passage, 286–294). Such texts may register "an attempt to make up lost ground" after a mid-Tudor decline of ecclesiastical and judicial control (Ingram, "The Reform of Popular Culture?" in Reay, ed., *Popular Culture*, 140). Susan Dwyer Amussen is quoted from *An Ordered Society: Gender and Class in Early Modern England* (Oxford, 1988), 181 (and see 175).

risked calamity. A sense of danger rang clearly enough through warnings that only a recovery of apostolic discipline could "appeas[e] the fierce wrath of God." Calls for better discipline gained force from a conviction that the nation had reached a point of intolerable danger and climax, that "wonderfull heapes and piles of sinne . . . cry . . . for vengeance upon the whole realme."[8]

And which of the nation's numberless sins most jeopardized its security? Misbehaviors of the poor were included in presbyterian complaint, but they did not dominate, and generous attention was paid to faults of the middling and upper ranks. Supporting the inference that Puritan constituencies were drawn primarily, although never exclusively, from the ranks of the "sociologically competent," both the forms of address and the intellectual pitch of presbyterian rhetoric, not to mention the heavy reliance upon print communication, suggest that it was addressed to established and at least modestly educated and literate householders. Discussion of idleness, adultery, intoxication, sports, gaming, or the singing of bawdy songs much of the time referred indifferently to all social groups or clearly identified the activities of solid citizens. In the early 1580s, both Cartwright and John Field (d. 1588), the organizing genius behind the classis movement of the 1570s and 1580s, called explicitly for a "reformation of maners"; but Field's concern was with the "people of al sorts and conditions" who visited bearbaiting shows, cockfights, theaters, alehouses, taverns, and gaming and dicing bouts on the Sabbath, and Cartwright singled out too-lenient magistrates, unworthy clergy, and unreformed parishioners in general. George Gifford, the ringleader of the presbyterians in Essex, censured evenhandedly the idle lives of the nonworking poor and of pleasure-seeking rich men's sons. In line with the insistence of Walter Travers (1548–1635) that "riche and pore and all degrees and orders" were to be reached and corrected, Gifford also criticized preachers who hesitated to denounce the pride, materialism, and unjust behavior of their social superiors, including "the great Lords and Ladies," and the obtuse village traditionalist portrayed in his *Countrie Divinitie* was made to remark that some of "the best in the Parish" clung to traditional recreations and vices and scorned the precise. Not only the drinking and sporting of respectable citizens but also their

8. *BPD*, sig. 2, and see sig. 4; *CD*, sig. Aiii. The threat of a catastrophic divine punishment for failure to institute the discipline was a commonplace of presbyterian propaganda. See, for example, *TR*, 47–48, 63–64; [John Field and Thomas Wilcox], *An Admonition to the Parliament* (1572), in W. H. Frere and C. E. Douglas, eds., *Puritan Manifestoes: A Study in the Origins of the Puritan Revolt* (New York, 1972), 6, 18–19; [Walter Travers], *A Full and Plaine Declaration of Ecclesiasticall Discipline owt off the Word off God* (n.p., 1574), 2, 5.

pride, pretentious dressing, reading of amorous books, and "banquetting, [and] surfetting" were decried.[9]

Equally revealing is the roster of economic sins. Presbyterians regularly assailed usury, sharp business practices, the engrossing of land, and the like, and failure to pay servants a fair wage was as liable to censure as was the malingering and careless work of the servants themselves. And when we find "covetousnesse"—as when a man "wrest[s] and wring[s] whatsoever [he] can lay hold on" or "is not content with his estate, but thrust[s] himself into divers Trades and Occupations to enlarge himselfe"—established as a compendious term for economic misbehavior, we may suggest that the presbyterian party viewed absorption in commercial gain and the sharp dealing that often attended it as integral to the contemporary moral crisis. Cartwright suspected that "buying and selling, when men doe employ themselves so much therein, that they cannot attend to the service of God," was an augury of the Second Coming of Christ to Judgment.[10]

Yet, if their complaint of wayward behavior moved well upward through the social spectrum, presbyterians did focus with some frequency upon the poor, as in the "Orders" drawn up by the Dedham Puritans in 1588 for curbing the "naughtie disposition of [the] disordered," specifically among their "poore neighbors," or in connected denunciations of "Atheisme, profanenes, securitie, blasphemie, horrible othes, . . . neglect, yea contempt of the Sabboth day, the dishonour of all to whom honour is due, the murders, adulteries, robberies, perjuries, the swarmes of rogues and beggers." Vividly recalled scenes from the lower ranks appeared in presbyterian reproofs of idleness and a roving life, extramarital sexual activity, crimes against property, and the lowlife entertain-

---

9. Walzer, *Revolution of the Saints*, 309 (see also *PM*, 124; *RRR*, 42; *RP*, 221); Albert Peel and Leland H. Carlson, eds., *Cartwrightiana* (London, 1951), 144–145; John Field, *A Godly Exhortation, by Occasion of the Late Iudgement of God, Shewed at Parris-garden . . .* (London, 1583), sigs. B5, B8 (see also Josiah, *The Reformation of Religion* [n.p., 1590?], sig. A3; Josias Nichols, *The Plea of the Innocent . . .* [n.p., 1602], 225); [Travers], *Full and Plaine Declaration*, 141; *CS*, sig. L7; *SSP*, 4–6; *CD*, 3. All social groups: *CD*, 2, 5, 13, 26, 29, 70, 73; John Field, *Godly Prayers and Meditations . . .* (London, 1601), 170. Gifford's censures: G[eorge] Giff[o]rd, *Eight Sermons, upon the First Foure Chapters, and Part of the Fift[h] of Ecclesiastes* (London, 1589), 110–114.

10. Thomas Cartwright, *A Commentary upon . . . the Epistle to the Colossians . . .* (London, 1612), 174; *TCR*, 333. On servants and masters, see *LJK*, 87–88. Criticism of predatory economic behavior, joined to a vigorous advocacy of the "just price," is fundamental to the moral commentary of John Knewstub. See *LJK*, 16, 98, 125, 137–140, 148–156, 158–159; John Knewstub, *A Sermon Preached at Paules Crosse . . . 1579* (London, 1579), 19, 26–31.

ments of alehouses. Prominent marks for a disciplinary reform were "day labourers and men of manuall occupations . . . haunt[ing] . . . alehouses," wasting time, neglecting their calling, and contributing to "great and grievous poverty." It is also worthy of note that, in the preaching of the leading presbyterian, the lower-class criminal itinerant became a very metaphor of evil. Seeking an image to convey the full baseness of unregenerate humanity, Cartwright could term them only "vagabonds and rogues from the common wealth of God." Even sinful Christians, he thought, contrite for sin and coming to beg mercy from the great God, are "all beggars, and worse. nay *worse* than the vilest *rogues* and *vagabounds*."[11]

To Protestants alarmed at mounting disorder, current agencies of control seemed increasingly impotent. Since sinning, not restricted to but common in the lower orders, threatened to overflow the "bankes . . . [of] the ordinary justice of the land," more efficient measures were required. And so William Fulke, warning that "where this Discipline is not, [it is] no marvell if all wickednesse overflowe," advertised apostolic elders and courts expressly as the needed stricter agency of control; and Sir Francis Walsingham, a moderate Puritan who found the apostolic scheme too democratic, complained of those who "put it into the people's heads, that if the discipline were planted, there would be no vagabonds or beggars." The program of elders and courts, if only the authorities should agree to adopt it, would correct disorders in every social group and certainly the ways of beggars and rogues. Those who pressed this argument obviously were addressing themselves to constituencies who perceived, or could be persuaded to perceive, a trend toward "unbridled licence" in their society and who associated it in part with disorders among the poor.[12]

11. Roland G. Usher, ed., *The Presbyterian Movement in the Reign of Queen Elizabeth as Illustrated by the Minute Book of the Dedham Classis, 1582–1589* (London, 1905), 99–100; [Walter Travers], *A Defence of the Ecclesiastical Discipline Ordayned of God to Be Used in His Church, against a Replie of Maister Bridges* (n.p., 1588), 64–65 (the context of Travers's statement suggests that he was speaking of poverty-related offenses); *FN*, 68; Cartwright, *Colossians*, 78, 187. Gifford blasted "shamefull beggerie" together with "ragged roges, . . . ruffians, and theeves," ascribing much of the problem to idleness. Giff[o]rd, *Eight Sermons*, 111–112.

12. *The Unlawful Practises of Prelates against Godly Ministers* . . . (n.p., 1584?), sig. B7; *BPD*, 91, 13; Gilbert Burnet, *The History of the Reformation of the Church of England*, ed. Nicholas Pocock, 2d ed. (Oxford, 1865), VI, 665. Peter Lake describes the presbyterian scheme as "a sort of cross between a secret police force and a system of social control" ("Presbyterianism, the Idea of a National Church, and the Argument from Divine Right,"

Yet, again in accord with the "reformation of manners," presbyterians made no claim that compulsory measures alone could contain the crisis. The imposition of discipline must go hand in hand with expanded charitable assistance. Continuous with the social criticism of the older Christian Humanists and the mid-Tudor Commonwealth writers, through presbyterian rhetoric ran strains of special sympathy with the poor and remarking upon the unheeding spirit of the affluent and powerful. The exploitative and uncharitable attitudes of wealthier citizens were partly responsible for poverty and thus were open to rebuke and, by implication, to church discipline after a presbyterian reformation. Such analysis could be part of a larger critique of the religious establishment's evangelistic complacency, as in Walter Travers's call for apostolic catechists who would attend "especially [to] the rude and ignorant" or in his report of the poor folk "dying in the fieldes under hedges, and in Townes and Cities, [begging] at the Dores," doomed to spiritual death by the want of evangelical preaching. But far commoner were efforts to sensitize the consciences of the affluent both to their complicity in material poverty and to their charitable responsibilities. Finding "the streetes . . . full of the cries of the poore," Dudley Fenner suggested that "fulnesse of meate and unmercifulnesse" among more privileged citizens was a root of the problem: "No man remem[bers] Joseph." John Udall thought that the wish to obtain more means to relieve poor neighbors should stand high among Christian motives for vocational diligence, and he identified callous attitudes toward those in need as a cause of recent covenantal punishments: "GOD hath straightned his hand among us, partly to see howe wee of more wealth will open ours to them that neede, . . . and not . . . make the dearest times serve our turns beste, and seeke to grow rich by the miseries of manie." Such admonitions made it plain that Christian response to the poverty crisis must include not merely the correction of sin but also the better mobilization of charity.[13]

At the center of presbyterian polity stood the pastoral and lay elders, whose

---

in Lake and Maria Dowling, eds., *Protestantism and the National Church in Sixteenth Century England* [London, 1987], 193–224, esp. 202). For more evidence of presbyterian belief that existing laws and agencies were incapable of managing the social crisis, see *BPD*, 104–105; *Parte of a Register*, 291, 309; [Dudley Fenner], *A Defense of the Godlie Ministers* . . . (London, 1587), 130.

13. [Travers], *Full and Plaine Declaration*, 139; [Travers], *A Defence of the Ecclesiastical Discipline*, 65; [Dudley Fenner], *A Counter-Poyson, Modestly Written for the Time* . . . (London, 1584?), sigs. 3, 4; *TR*, 69; and see Udall, *Obedience to the Gospell* (London, 1584), sigs. F3, F5.

division of labor supplied the needed evangelical and disciplinary care in each congregation. Bound to serve all parishioners alike, these ministries had no specialized responsibility for the poor, but beside the elder stood another figure: the deacon. Bearing little resemblance to the catechist, preacher, and liturgical assistant who bore the name within the official church, his defining duty was to the poor. Like the fast day or the Sabbath, the diaconate was not a presbyterian creation. Included in mid-Tudor English proposals for church reform and implemented in the Reformed exile churches in London and elsewhere, the office of deacon had been a popular element of Reformed ecclesiology for decades and became a particular mark of the churches drawing inspiration from the Genevan reformation. With slight variations, the deacon was charged with relief and care of the local parish poor. Often there was provision as well for a "widow," an aging female member of the congregation who functioned as an assistant deacon.[14]

The first English sketches of the new polity uniformly designate deacons as essential New Testament "Ministers of the poor," providing spiritual comfort as well as material aid. There is the familiar division between male deacon and the widow, with the deacon to "attend upon the poore, collecting for them, and distributing unto them," and making certain that no aid is squandered upon the able-bodied. Subordinate to the deacon, the widow was to assist the deacon in service to the "sicke and impotent among the poore," washing clothes and bedding and meeting other personal needs. Deacons were to make regular reports to the local presbytery or consistory upon welfare finances and the general condition of recipients.[15]

14. Mid-Tudor proposals: William Tyndale, *Expositions and Notes on Sundry Portions of the Holy Scriptures, Together with The Practice of Prelates,* ed. Henry Walter (Cambridge, 1849), 253; Martin Bucer, *De regno Christi,* in Wilhelm Pauck, ed., *Melanchthon and Bucer* (Philadelphia, 1969), 306–313. Exile churches: for the exile churches, see Andrew Spicer, "Poor Relief and the Exile Communities," in Beat A. Kümin, *Reformations Old and New: Essays on the Socio-Economic Impact of Religious Change, c. 1470–1630* (Aldershot, 1996), 237–255; John a Lasco, *Forma et ratio tota ecclesiastici ministerii, in peregrinorum, potissimum vero Germanorum ecclesia: instituta Londini* (Frankfurt, 1555?), 5–13, 51–57. Reformed eccle-siology: Calvin's influential formulation included "two distinct grades" of deacon, a supe-rior male officer in charge of distributing alms and otherwise "administering the affairs" of the needy, and a female officer, usually a widow, in charge of personal services to the sick and impotent. John Calvin, *Institutes of the Christian Religion,* ed. John T. McNeill (Phila-delphia, 1960), II, bk. 4, chap. 3, sect. 9, 1061–1062, 1062 n. 11, bk. 4, chap. 13, sect. 19, 1274.

15. Thomas Cartwright, *The Rest of the Second Replie of Thomas Cartwri[gh]t . . .* (n.p., 1577), 109; *TCR,* 307–308; *BPD,* 103, and see 104. Restriction of aid to the legitimate poor:

Diaconal ministry, in short, was a vital part of a church rightly reformed; and that ministry, though imitative of ancient apostolic forms, was intensely relevant to a society facing a landslide of poverty. It provided, first, a sorely needed additional means to decrease suffering. Given the large numbers of poor in every parish, and these insufficiently provided for, "the use of this office . . . is manifest." But its curative potential extended beyond mere welfare. It would be, in fact, a crucial adjunct of reformatory preaching and the disciplining eldership, a third salient in the drive to aid and order the poor. "Wheroff cometh it," Cartwright asked, "that [with] so many excellent lawes provided against roges and beggers: there are yet . . . such nombers. Is it not heroff, that the office off [the] Deacons which god had ordeined for that purpose. . . is abolished"? Fulke, too, called his audiences to "see, for want of these [diaconal] offices, what great inconveniences are among us, concerning the poore." "For, although ther be very good politike laws made for provision of the poore," yet by reason of ineffectual enforcement and other abuses "smal reliefe cometh thereby to the poore indeed." So beggars multiply, and those that "walke disorderlye . . . doe even overflowe" the counties and endanger the public peace. Such statements indicate no intention to displace existing almshouses, hospitals, police, and court agencies or the provisions of current poor legislation, but they reiterate presbyterian belief that poverty stood high among present disorders that cried out for redress, that existing institutions and procedures were unable to contain it, that the apostolic church provided exactly the right set of remedies, and that the campaign for further reformation must give them an honored and urgent place.[16]

Clearly, then, a set of concerns related to population growth, expanding poverty, and dread of disorder in the later seventeenth century were ingredient to the presbyterian quest for disciplinary reform; but they cannot explain the venture as a whole. Other probable contributing factors included a peculiar history of failure and frustration in religious reformation and a variety of psychic discomforts accompanying social change.

[Field and Wilcox], *Admonition to the Parliament*, in Frere and Douglas, eds., *Puritan Manifestoes*, 15, and *BPD*, 105. Regular reports: *A Second Admonition to the Parliament*, in Frere and Douglas, eds., *Puritan Manifestoes*, 121–124. The author also proposed that, if local resources should suffice, appeal could be made to the higher "councell provinciall" for a supplementary levy upon area churches. *Second Admonition*, 122–124.

16. Cartwright, *Rest of the Second Replie*, 113; Cartwright, *Second Replie*, sig. XXXiv; *BPD*, 104–105. In *BPD*, 105, Fulke also complained that "neither by politique, nor by ecclesiasticall Lawe," are poor, idle, and disorderly persons "broughte into order."

Embattlement Stiffens Demand

Arrested far short of the substantial redesign planned by advanced reformers in the reign of Edward VI, the Protestant establishment that had taken form under Elizabeth represented a stubbornly ambiguous realization of Reformed ideals. It arrested and indeed reversed in some details the Edwardian Reformation as of 1553, and it quickly became clear that the queen regarded the arrangements of 1559 for the most part as permanent, did not view the Swiss and other Reformed churches abroad as models for her church, and would allow no further structural changes. Naturally, she and her episcopal commissioners (with some exceptions early in the reign) viewed refusal to accept and support the religious settlement as an act of disorder and defiance. It is likely that the rising curve of Puritan ethical militance registered the frustrations that arose under these circumstances.

Certainly, the presbyterian story under Elizabeth was a saga of disappointments. Behind Cartwright's pathbreaking lectures of 1570 already lay a decade and more of rebuffs. Memories were fresh of the rejection of reform in the Convocation of 1563, of the vestiarian defeats of 1565–1566, of many acts of episcopal repression; and the reaction to Cartwright's challenge of 1570 was swift and severe. A host of like-minded Dissenters appeared in his wake during the following two decades; but, when they struggled to open the church to real disciplinary reform, they were constrained and often prosecuted by authorities who deemed their proposals obsessively "precise" and blind to the requirements of a truly comprehensive church. Presbyterian efforts not only failed to accomplish significant change; they also firmed the resolve of those sympathetic to the prescribed forms to defend and entrench them. Under these circumstances, advocates of a disciplinary reformation who at first foresaw only passing skirmishes in a time of transition beyond the compromises of 1559 were caught up in a seemingly interminable struggle. Through the following decades, the bolder spirits continued the drive to alter the balance of forces within the church, but they were harassed and punished, and at least in some cases such experiences had a hardening effect. They contributed to yet harsher assessments of episcopal government, to the extreme propaganda of the Marprelate tracts, and occasionally to outright separation from the national church and to exile abroad.[17]

Yet in other ways, too, the experience of dissent and opposition could

17. On the defeat of radical proposals at the Convocation of 1563, the vestiarian controversy of 1565–1566, and the Marprelate tracts, see Patrick Collinson, *The Elizabethan Puritan Movement* (Oxford, 1967), 34, 55–56, 71–91, 391–396.

toughen attitudes. Presbyterian leaders were nationalistic, nonseparating Dissenters who associated their nation with biblical Israel and upheld the ideal of an inclusive religious establishment. Yet theirs was a more stringent value system than that of apologists for the settlement, and their vision of church reformation embraced pronouncedly sectarian features. Scornful of the undisciplined majority, their teaching documents the thesis that a principal "meaning of puritanism is . . . a social situation: the partly self-inflicted isolation of the godly." In the belief that the justification of Christians before God is concealed by the ambiguity of their sin, Luther had opposed attempts to separate true believers from the rest of the congregation. Yet presbyterian clergy, like Udall in Kingston on Thames in Surrey, or Gifford in Maldon, Essex, explicitly urged their followers to draw themselves apart in local enclaves and to keep aloof from ungodly neighbors and townsfolk. Calling one another, or being called in derision, "the brethren" (although in some cases a majority might have been women), in good sectarian fashion the godly chose and indeed accented and savored a minority status within their church and town. How better to affirm their singularity and unify their subculture than to reckon them, as their clergy did, a "very smal" presence, "a smal, poore, . . . flocke" amid the hostile multitude?[18]

And, if such flocks were poor in worldly esteem, they were rich in skills of restraint. Forbearance and control were more their hallmarks than trust in pardon or a freely flowing Christian liberty, let alone a taste for boisterous village rites. In a pattern that their pietist successors were to carry forward with a will, presbyterians formulated an ideal of godliness in studied contrast to the religion of ceremonies and common prayer. In the saintly coteries within their parishes, Knewstub and Stephen Egerton saw the "peculiar people, zealous of good works" portrayed in Titus 2:14. They were called to a stricter grade of behavior, and good works in this context tended to be acts of

---

18. *RP,* 230 (and see Peter Lake, "William Bradshaw, Antichrist, and the Community of the Godly," *Journal of Ecclesiastical History,* XXXVI [1985], 589: "The whole thrust of the puritan [ideology] was towards the division of existing communities . . . between the godly and the ungodly"); *SCV,* sig. D6; Thomas Wilcox, "Epistle Dedicatorie" to Iohn Calvin, *Three Propositions or Speeches . . .* , trans. T[homas] W[ilcox] (London, 1580), 4; John Udall, *Amendment of Life . . .* (London, 1588), sig. A3. Luther: David C. Steinmetz, *Reformers in the Wings* (Philadephia, 1971), 86. Udall and Gifford: Udall urged his followers in Kingston on Thames to keep separate from impure townsfolk, "shak[ing] off the familiaritie of that kind of people" (*CS,* sigs. D5, F8; *CL,* 8). W. J. Petchey identifies a "distinct group" of devout Puritans gathered around Gifford for private religious practices at Maldon in the 1580s and 1590s (*A Prospect of Maldon, 1500–1689* [Chelmsford, 1991], 219).

subjection and refrainment. By about 1580, although well aware that they spoke of a seldom-attained ideal, presbyterian leaders regularly portrayed the Lord's true people in these terms. They were "The holy," the minority who bowed to the "iron rod" of Christ's rule, the few who *wrestle and strive* with [them] selves to the obedience of Gods will," who "debarre themselves from sinfull pleasures," who work unceasingly "to bridle appetite." Continuous with ancient monastic ideals, this portrait projected a semisectarian social world at variance with popular Christianity, its relatively unintensive styles, and its frequently permissive attitude toward seasonal customs and alehouse enjoyments.[19]

Self-inflicted isolation, of course, was but one part of a larger project. A true and national recovery of apostolic controls remained a distant goal, but preliminary steps were taken in parishes supplied with reform-minded preachers and a converted laity ready to do their censuring part. There the rugged code of conduct, the summary call to a "depriv[ation] of . . . commodities, and abandon[ment] . . . of . . . pleasures," could be extended in some part to the community at large. But the broader citizenry resisted. Confronted with novel and rigorous demands and sometimes finding their clergyman in league with local magistrates to reform public behavior, conservative parishioners—like their counterparts in European Reformed centers—set up a long-lived litany of complaint: "It was never merrie since men . . . have medled with the Scriptures." Valuing their right to "ma[k]e merrie together" without interference, they rallied to defend a traditional way of life that included "good neighbourhood," conviviality, and sport. They resented the reformers' reproving rhetoric and manner and "rage[d] against the instruments [that is, "painful" clergy] that God useth to correct them." In presbyterian report, this was the context in which the terms "Puritan" and "precise" were becoming current. Resentful parishioners used them to portray the manner and presumption of the "busie controller," "alwaies chiding," "checking every man," and generally

19. Knewstub, *Sermon Preached at Paules Crosse*, 44; Stephen Egerton, *A Briefe Methode of Catechizing* (London, 1610), 8–9; *SCV,* sig. B2 ("the Holy"); John Udall, *A Demonstration of the Truth of that Discipline, Which Christ Hath Prescribed in His Word . . .* (1588), ed. Edward Arber (London, 1880), 11 ("iron rod"); Cartwright, *Colossians,* 42 *("wrestle"),* George G[i]ff[o]rd, *Fifteene Sermons, upon the Song of Salomon* (London, 1598), 100 ("debarre"); *The Works of . . . Thomas Wilcocks . . . ,* 2d ed. (London, 1624), 112. For the "unintensive" religion of "parish anglicans," see Christopher Haigh, *English Reformations: Religion, Politics, and Society under the Tudors* (Oxford, 1993), 291, and the larger discussion at 285–295.

abridging pleasure. These and countless similar protests reflect a determination to preserve cherished freedoms and enjoyments against meddling agents of restriction.[20]

And often enough conservative villagers acted out their resentments. From this period and beyond there is abundant evidence of conflict between Puritans and their opponents in towns and parishes, and this certainly was the case when presbyterian clergy were present, as in Fenner's Cranbrook, Kent, of the mid-1580s or in Gifford's Maldon, Essex, or Josias Nichols's Eastwell, Kent, in the 1580s and 1590s. Likewise, reports of the "ungodly, deriding and scoffing at the just" became ubiquitous in presbyterian expression from the 1580s, if not earlier. Having in mind both this context of local history and broader conflicts with episcopal and governmental authorities, we better understand the sense of embattlement, of standing "like a besieged Citie" amid the nominally religious masses that flavored Puritan rhetoric in the later Elizabethan and early Stuart decades; and here is a correlate in social experience of the sharply polarized universe of Puritan predestinarian doctrine. But, when we consider the often adversarial character of Puritan experience in local communities, there is reason to suspect that the push for reform had been drawn into a dialectical process. Subject, of course, to many variations and fluctuations, the demand for restraint and control bred a defiant opposition that might in turn have stiffened the demand.[21]

20. *TR*, 65; *CD*, 6, 27 (litany); *CL*, 18 (resentment); *CS*, sigs. H8 (preciseness; and see *CD*, 4, 26). Knewstub and Egerton explicitly urged the godly to censure the sins of others (*LJK*, 170–174; George Gifford, *A Godlie . . . Sermon upon . . . Saint James* [London, 1582], sig. Dvi). For merriment, see also W. J. Sheils, *The Puritans in the Diocese of Peterborough, 1558–1610* (Northampton, 1979), 45; *PM*, 149, 151. Puritan rigor contrasted sharply with an easygoing village culture and religion, which valued spontaneity and was relatively tolerant of disorder. See J. G. R. Parry, *A Protestant Vision: William Harrison and the Reformation of Elizabethan England* (Cambridge, 1987), 277; Peter Burke, *Popular Culture in Early Modern Europe* (New York, 1978), 213. Note also Patrick Collinson's judgment that "a religious system so daunting in its . . . ethical demands was unlikely to appeal to the masses, especially since it set its face against so much of the traditional way of life." *RP*, 231, and see 201, 268.

21. *Works of Wilcocks*, 26; Wilcox, "Epistle Dedicatorie" to Calvin, *Three Propositions*, trans W[ilcox], 4; and see *RRR*, 33, 41. For examples of conflict in towns, see *PM*, 147–155; Patrick Collinson, "Cranbrook and the Fletchers: Popular and Unpopular Religion in the Kentish Weald," in Collinson, *Godly People: Essays on English Protestantism and Puritanism* (London, 1983), 417–419. A group of citizens in Maldon aided by the local vicar, Robert Palmer, led resistance to the reformation of manners promoted by George Gifford

This suggestion accords with the view that conflicted social experience and stiffened morality tend to concur. The strenuous moral attitudes common to social movements—including religious movements—and to religious sects reflect their sense of friction with the larger society. Indeed, the experience of opposition and strain may itself become a force that tightens the protesting community's value commitments. It is possible, too, that the godly, or some of them, were ambivalent about the pleasures they denied, and needed a sharpened sense of difference and opposition to counter their attraction.[22]

Discipline and Social Change

Nor is this all, for sects and social movements tend to emerge in times of rapid social change. A basic function of these groups, it would seem, is "psychological reorganization," the remaking of personal identity blurred by social flux. Again, they are said to readjust or "revitalize" a society whose changing cultural patterns have moved out of phase with prevailing values. Again, the fit with emergent Puritanism seems close.[23] Against the background of the Mar-

----

and his allies in the town government in the 1580s and 1590s. Gifford had been disbeneficed in 1584 but was licensed by his bishop and continued his ministry as an unbeneficed preacher. Petchey, *Prospect of Maldon*, 210, 216–217, 223–228.

22. See, for example, Kurt Lang and Gladys Engel Lang, *Collective Dynamics* (New York, 1961), 497–499; Bryan R. Wilson, *Magic and the Millennium: A Sociological Study of Religious Movements of Protest among Tribal and Third-World Peoples* (New York, 1973), 498–502; William Sims Bainbridge and Rodney Stark, "Sectarian Tension," *Review of Religious Research*, XII (1980), 105–124; Milton J. Yinger, *Countercultures: The Promise and the Peril of a World Turned Upside Down* (New York. 1982), 76, 187. C. John Sommerville interprets nonseparating Puritanism as a social movement, in "Interpreting Seventeenth-Century English Religion as Social Movements," *CH*, LXIX (2000), 749–769. Ritchie D. Kendall, *The Drama of Dissent: The Radical Poetics of Nonconformity, 1380–1590* (Chapel Hill, N.C., 1986), 6, discusses the Puritan Nonconformist "pursuit of identity through a ritual combat with an ambivalently regarded nemesis."

23. Popular in the 1960s and 1970s, the emphasis upon social change and consequent psychic strain as a factor in the emergence of social movements has been eclipsed since then by theories of resource mobilization and rational choice. These offer useful approaches to movement emergence but fail to show that change and stress do not contribute, and tend "inadequately [to] address the problem of individual participation." See Myra Marx Ferree and Frederick D. Miller, "Mobilization and Meaning: Toward an Integration of Social Psychological and Resource Perspectives on Social Movements," *Sociological Inquiry*, LV (1985), 39. In *Religion in Sociological Perspective* (Oxford, 1982), 122, Bryan Wilson argues that new religious movements seek "to address human anxiety

ian persecutions and of all the recent and wrenching turns in official religious policy, Elizabethan and early Stuart England was gripped by the forces of polarization and disorder discussed above, and for the most part they began to reach crisis in the first decades of the Puritan century. It is evident, for example, that "the effects of population growth, inflation, agrarian change and industrial expansion first became clearly apparent" in "the mid-sixteenth century decades" and became acute thereafter; that "it was in the later sixteenth and early seventeenth century that [the poverty crisis] reached its most menacing proportions"; or that "the great age of social mobility precisely coincide[d] with the great age of Puritanism." In these and related trends some also see another fundamental shift, the "onset of [a] new [acquisitive] order," the emergence of a "fiercely competitive" society . . . permeated by the ethos of agrarian and commercial capitalism." Clearly, the decades around 1600 were at once a time of Puritan vigor and influence and a stressful era in which age-old standards and customs were undermined, newer ways of life began to emerge, and "society was, and felt itself to be, under pressure."[24]

[which stems] directly from the changing character of social organization," as do several of the essays in James A. Beckford, ed., *New Religious Movements and Rapid Social Change* (London, 1986). For sects and change, see *International Encyclopedia of the Social Sciences* (New York, 1972), XIV, 132; Bryan R. Wilson, ed., *Patterns of Sectarianism: Organisation and Ideology in Social and Religious Movements* (London, 1967), 31.

On revitalizing society: Hans Toch, *The Social Psychology of Social Movements* (Indianapolis, Ind., 1965), 125. See also the connections drawn between social change, the disturbance of "moral obligations," and the emergence of new ideological forms in Robert Wuthnow, *Meaning and Moral Order: Explorations in Cultural Analysis* (Berkeley, Calif., 1987), 154–158. I draw upon the concept of revitalization as formulated by William G. McLoughlin, *Revivals, Awakening, and Reform: An Essay on Religion and Social Change in America, 1607–1977* (Chicago, 1978), xiii, 8, 10–18.

24. On approaching crisis: C. G. A. Clay, *Economic Expansion and Social Change: England, 1500–1700* (Cambridge, 1984), II, 224; Beier, *Masterless Men*, 18; Lawrence Stone, "Social Mobility in England, 1500–1700," *Past and Present*, no. 33 (April 1966), 44. See also Marjorie Keniston McIntosh, *Controlling Misbehavior in England, 1370–1600* (Cambridge, 1998), 3–4, 14. Patrick Collinson marks about 1580 as a "moral and cultural watershed" in England inaugurating a period of "creeping ascetic totalitarianism." *From Iconoclasm to Iconophobia: The Cultural Impact of the Second English Reformation* (Reading, 1986), 8, 25.

On fundamental shift: *ES*, 223; *RRR*, 42, and see the entire section 9–43; Sharpe, *Crime in Early Modern England*, 183. Alan Everitt, *Change in the Provinces: The Seventeenth Century* (Leicester, 1969), 30 (and see 33); *RRR*, 9; and Michael Zuckerman, "The Fabrication of Identity in Early America," *WMQ*, 3d Ser., XXXIV (1977), 185, 192, see an

Thinking it more than coincident that extraordinary preoccupations with sin and control arose just in this time, some historians view Puritan zeal for discipline as an adjustment to social change. It was the work of an emergent middle class "fumbl[ing] for a new ethos" appropriate to its new and early capitalist world of self-control and work; or a response to the "anxiety" and "acute fear of disorder and 'wickedness'" typical of early modernization; or a reaction to the erosion of identity in an increasingly Protestant, commercial, and individualistic culture; or, most specifically, a "natural and perhaps inevitable reaction" to the problem of the poor and consequent fears of disorder. Susan Amussen finds it a part of "a desperate struggle to contain events" that seemed rapidly to outstrip available measures of control. While these analyses differ at many points, all see the Puritan zest for regulation as an adjustment to changing social experience. In Derek Hirst's phrase, in a period of flux the Puritan "desire for discipline" became "an attractive tool for stabilizing the world."[25] This suggestion, it might be added, finds support in the work of social psychologists who hold that persons disturbed by change tend to define those of different interests or viewpoints as moral adversaries, to display "egocentric self-righteousness and the moral condemnation of others," or to "extend their need for order . . . to the society at large [and demand] rigid control."[26]

If men and women who became Puritans, drawn most often from middling and sociologically competent levels of society, relatively literate and possessed of a heightened sense of individual worth, were involved in a major readjustment of their society, they presumably were subject in high degree to the stress of change. They might feel an "anxiety about status" generated by social polarization and mobility. Again, like the entrepreneurial worrier that George

---

exceptional level of psychic strain in the period. See also the analysis of "ethical anxiety" in Clay, *Economic Expansion and Social Change,* II, 225, and *PM,* 125.

25. Hill, *Society and Puritanism,* 221–222; Walzer, *Revolution of the Saints,* 303; Zuckerman, "Fabrication of Identity," *WMQ,* 3d Ser., XXXIV (1977), 193; Paul Slack, "Poverty and Politics in Salisbury, 1597–1666," in Peter Clark and Paul Slack, eds., *Crisis and Order in English Towns, 1500–1700: Essays in Urban History* (London, 1972), 185; Amussen, *An Ordered Society,* 175–176; Derek Hirst, *Authority and Conflict: England, 1603–1658* (London, 1986), 75. Similar connections are drawn in *RRR,* 41, and *PP,* 209–211.

26. Zuckerman, "Fabrication of Identity," *WMQ,* 3d Ser., XXXIV (1977), 193, and the sources cited there; Herbert McClosky and John H. Schaar, "Psychological Dimensions of Anomy," *American Sociological Review,* XXX (1965), 28. See also Angela A. Aidala, "Social Change, Gender Roles, and New Religious Movements," *Sociological Analysis,* XLVI (1985), 292.

Gifford sketched in living detail for his Maldon congregation about 1588, one might "labour to gather riches, . . . [but] have such hindrances and losses, and meete with so many crosse matters, that it vexeth and disquie[te]th my heart." "I have such care to increase and keepe that which I have, that my hart resteth not in the night. . . . I cannot sleepe quietly. . . . My heart, when I lie in my bed, is either upon my goods in the fields, or devising where I may light upon some good bargaine." Such a person might be susceptible to a doctrine of purity and control, and exactly this was Gifford's larger message, expressly advanced as therapy for social ills. For business cares, commercial sharp dealing, oppression of the poor, wanton dancing, and increasing idleness, mendicity, and roguery there was only one cure: religious "rebirth"; and rebirth meant a disciplinary makeover. It required submission to God the "king and law-maker," identification with the small flock of the ascetic godly, strenuous containment of "lusts and concupiscences," and assiduous "travail . . . in [one's] vocation."[27]

Gifford's reflexive, trusting call to an ordered life may help explain why for so many contemporaries a rhetoric of sin, restraint, and purity could arise so spontaneously, elicit voluntary assent, touch the quick, change perspective, imbue with a sense of purpose, and breed desires to censure and separate from the unregenerate. In addition to their more manifest purposes, Puritan ideas about "separating, purifying, demarcating and punishing transgressions" symbolized and aspired to resolve psychosocial discontents. They allowed new senses of identity to be created on a basis of stringent self-control and aversion to impurity. To beneficiaries of social change, they supplied both a flattering redefinition of their place in society and a means to affirm their distance from the disorderly poor. And, by redefining relationships, by valuing the comradeship and exclusiveness brought by membership in an intensive subculture, they provided a new basis for interpersonal trust and community.[28]

What made a path of strong denial and control a plausible option for a significant minority of the Elizabethan English—and their early Stuart successors? No full and certain answer is possible, of course, but more was in play than infectious ideas and examples from Reformed centers abroad. The chan-

27. *RRR*, 29, and see *PM*, 125; Giff[o]rd, *Eight Sermons*, 66–67 (and see 68–74, 115), 69 (sharp dealing), 79 (dancing), 105 (oppression of poor), 110–112 (idleness, mendicity, roguery), 128 (new birth, lusts), 130 (God as king and lawmaker).

28. Mary Douglas, *Purity and Danger: An Analysis of the Concepts of Pollution and Taboo* (New York, 1966), 4. Puritanism's "passionate re-emphasis of the traditional Christian call for amendment of life presented . . . opportunities for a redefinition of selfhood, a new and deeply comforting sense of identity." *PP*, 210.

nels of actual influence are unclear, but the imperious spirit damned as Puritan and precise was not an Elizabethan invention. It stood logically in descent from initial choices made and concepts forged by earlier English reformers already in dialogue with the Continental Reformed, and the clamor for "further" reformation had reference to a process begun before 1553. The present chapter suggests that contemporary social experience also was at work. By the last decades of the sixteenth century a dynamic fraction of the population, not under state regulation but voluntarily, moved to steady themselves and their society by selecting a life more exactly defined and ordered and "embrac[ing] identities defined primarily by their aversion to iniquity." And often enough those identities were etched more sharply through friction with the ungodly in dozens of towns and parishes, at least for limited periods. The reconstruction of identity through purity, conflict, and antithesis seems logical and likely enough, given the power of ascetic ideals in historic Western Christianity, given the important function that "the adversary" served in the age, and given as well the known tendency of early modern Europeans, especially those involved in religious controversy, to see unbridgeable contrariety as a basic principle of reality. To find strenuous battle with sin and sinners a stabilizer in shifting times was to expand upon an eminently available option.[29]

It also helped to deepen the hold of disciplinary ideals of a peculiarly strict kind upon nonseparating Puritanism. All the forces described above conduced to the belief that a properly restored Christianity, whatever more it might be, was an exacting regulatory system. Undeniably, those who framed the Elizabethan Settlement and adjusted it to the challenges of late- and post-Elizabethan times were also concerned with order and discipline, but prophets of further reformation made the ordering mission of the apostolic church and faith a definite and central axiom of the faith. As events were to prove, the presbyterians' consistorial scheme was readily disposable, for it was but one expression of a worldview with a will to transform and control at its core. The defeat of structural reform about 1590 was, not the ruin of disciplinary religion, but its occasion to pause and then assume new forms; and indeed its greatest age still lay ahead.

29. Zuckerman, "Fabrication of Identity," *WMQ*, 3d Ser., XXXIV (1977), 193; *RP,* 182, and see Stephen Greenblatt, *Renaissance Self-Fashioning: From More to Shakespeare* (Chicago, 1980), 9. Kendall, *Drama of Dissent,* 6, argues that Puritan "nonconformists . . . define[d] themselves by negation." For themes of contrariety in the period, see Stuart Clark, "Inversion, Misrule, and the Meaning of Witchcraft," *Past and Present,* no. 87 (May 1980), 105.

II

THE PIETIST
TURN AND ITS
DISCOMFORTS

CHAPTER 4

RICHARD GREENHAM
AND THE
FIRST PROTESTANT
PIETISM

D espondency aptly describes Puritanism after 1590:

> The early Elizabethan Puritans were the first wave of the
> [Puritan] movement. . . . [Their phase] ended about 1590
> with the ignominious collapse of the presbyterian classis
> movement and the Marprelate scandal. Once more after
> 1640, Puritans and parliamentarians . . . took the initiative. . . . But for
> the period between 1590 and 1640—the middle span of Puritanism—the
> story was different. . . . This half-century was Puritanism's slough of
> despondency.

The term, indeed, encapsulates the nonseparatists' sense of grudging resignation to a church they had failed to reform. The larger characterization, however, suggesting an overall lack of positive energy and creativity, is challenged
by a re-visioning that presents the modified Puritanism of the middle span as
a dynamic and in many ways successful force. Certainly the personal and
interior religion of those years, together with the vast literary outpouring
that articulated and nurtured it, was a scene of substantial, even spectacular
achievement. This, in fact, was the very time in which dissatisfied reformers,
overcoming despondency, redirected an unabated appetite for discipline into
the first great pietist venture in Protestant history.[1]

By the early 1590s English Puritans were being compelled into an era of
soul-searching and altered expectations. From the defeat of the antivestiarian
agitation of 1565–1566 to the death of powerful patrons and friends at court
(especially of the earls of Leicester and Warwick in 1588) and to the involve-

---

1. Keith L. Sprunger, *The Learned Doctor William Ames: Dutch Backgrounds of English
and American Puritanism* (Urbana, Ill., 1972), 4–5. Cf. the positive depiction of "middle-
period Puritanism" in Stephen Foster, *The Long Argument: English Puritanism and the
Shaping of New England Culture, 1570–1700* (Chapel Hill, N.C., 1991), 65–107.

ment of two unstable Puritan gentlemen in a scheme to replace Elizabeth with a new "Messiah" in 1591, the list of failures and setbacks under Elizabeth's government had grown onerously long. As the reign neared its end, little prospect remained for an apostolic makeover of the church. By the early 1590s, with the presbyterian classis leaders being worn down in lengthy proceedings first before the Court of High Commission and then in the Star Chamber, Archbishop John Whitgift and his anti-Puritan allies had emerged in clear command of church affairs. What they did not suspect, however, was that, even as they savored victory, a creative rechanneling of the quest for further reformation was under way.

The Pietist Turn

Some practical foundations of that development were laid in the 1570s and 1580s, when emerging groups of the converted and godly in London parishes and in towns and villages in the Midlands and the South and East of England were promoting private devotional meetings, special Sabbath exercises, and other expressions of a burgeoning piety not content with the resources of the Prayer Book or of currently authorized primers of private devotion. Naturally, there was official resistance, as when Whitgift in 1583 condemned as "schisme" private religious gatherings of persons not of the same family. But the will and power were lacking to eradicate them on a large scale or to squelch the emergent theology that articulated their concerns, and in short order a pietist awakening was in progress.[2]

The turn to piety answered to a variety of present interests and opportunities, to the example of resurgent Catholic spirituality, to the increasing prosperity and self-consciousness of the gentry and the middling classes, to the rise of the printed book and tract as a means of mass religious nurture, to anxieties stimulated by social change and mobility, to weariness with doctrinal controversy, and perhaps even to conditions of greater privacy in English homes. It might have included a delayed response to the vacuum left by removal of the monastic organization of prayer, devotion, and self-discipline; by the loss of religious orders, guilds, sodalities, apostolates in education or foreign missions and other agencies with their sense of membership in a spiritual elite and their convenient outlet for religious energies; and by the abolition of shrines and images, penance and confession, and the medley of traditional paraliturgical rites. But the new spiritual initiative also was an adjustment to the failure to

2. Edward Cardwell, ed., *Documentary Annals of the Reformed Church of England,* new ed. (Oxford, 1844) I, 468.

gain power, an at least partial retreat from structural reform, and a lessened trust in organization. The results could be dramatic, as in the turn to Separatism or the Martin Marprelate project, but in nonseparating circles it provoked quieter and more effectual responses. If the national church was unreformable at present, the citizenry could be reached at personal and local levels. So advanced Protestants, few of whom had tied their fortunes to dogmatic presbyterianism or were prepared to abandon the national church, found ways to go on with life in a church still fundamentally unchanged. Bracketing structural issues, they turned attention to towns, parishes, families, and individuals and to the cultivation of spirituality in those contexts.[3]

By the century's end, in dozens of local settings moderate Puritans had managed to plant a rich complex of communal and private exercises within the framework of parish and Prayer Book. Bible reading, meditation, flocking to sermons, private meetings of the saints (sometimes underwritten by a formal covenant) for worship and mutual edification, family devotions and catecheses, Sabbath and fast day exercises both individual and communal—these were but a few of the indexes and carriers of an evolving Protestant spirituality. A prime instance of the resurgence of ritual in the international late Reformation, it was the most remarkable product of conforming Puritanism in its middle span. Students of the sermonic and other theological works of known Puritans in the late sixteenth and early seventeenth century note a striking shift of interest, "a new internal dynamic," even "a new Puritanism." While the new Puritanism is variously described, its most noted characteristic is "a move toward an inward, introspective piety." By far the most dynamic and influential movement within the Church of England in the period, within about two decades it evolved into a luxuriant spirituality without precedent or peer elsewhere in the Protestant world.[4]

3. The extent of the shift from structural reform should not be exaggerated. See Nicholas Tyacke, "The 'Rise of Puritanism' and the Legalizing of Dissent, 1571–1719," in Ole Peter Grell, Jonathan I. Israel, and Nicholas Tyacke, eds., *From Persecution to Toleration: The Glorious Revolution and Religion in England* (Oxford, 1991), 24; Foster, *Long Argument*, 66–68, 115–119.

4. Peter Clark, *English Provincial Society from the Reformation to the Revolution: Religion, Politics, and Society in Kent, 1500–1640* (Hassocks, 1977), 166; Christopher Hill, *Society and Puritanism in Pre-Revolutionary England*, 2d ed. (New York, 1967), 501–502; E. Brooks Holifield, *The Covenant Sealed: The Development of Puritan Sacramental Theology in New England, 1570–1720* (New Haven, Conn., 1974), 38. See also Elizabeth K. Hudson, "The *Plaine Mans* Pastor: Arthur Dent and the Cultivation of Popular Piety in Early Seventeenth-Century England," *Albion*, XXV (1993), 23. Initial exercises: Patrick

Hence the paradox that "the miscarriage of the . . . [presbyterian] reformation coincided with the birth of the great age of puritan religious experience," coincided, that is, with a turn to more personal, interior arts of further reformation. The emergent spirituality expanded upon the "pietistic, personal core," continuous with the evangelical religion of William Tyndale or Thomas Cranmer, which had informed the Puritan impulse from the start; and presbyterians made initial contributions to it. In particular, the spiritual writings of John Bradford (d. 1555) and Thomas Becon (d. 1567) anticipated the penitential cast and other elements of the later pietist synthesis, and Edward Dering undertook a personal and "comfortable" ministry to those with "heaviness of spirite" well before his death in 1576. Thomas Cartwright, Thomas Wilcox, George Gifford, John Udall, and other ranking presbyterians also took steps in the 1580s and 1590s toward a more interior religion. In his *Discourse touching the Doctrine of Doubting* (1598) and other late works, Wilcox addressed problems of assurance and pioneered in the art of spiritual counsel that was to loom large in pastoral theory and care in the following period. The first great pietist manual—Richard Rogers's *Seven Treatises* (1603)—was inspired in part by discussions within an East Anglian presbyterian classis in 1587, and in his preface Rogers reported "twentie years and more" of prior engagement with the subject matter. In its presbyterian manifestations, the early deepening of piety was a complement, not an alternative, to structural reform.[5]

Collinson, "Toward a Broader Understanding of the Early Dissenting Tradition," in C. Robert Cole and Michael E. Moody, eds., *The Dissenting Tradition: Essays for Leland H. Carlson* (Athens, Ohio, 1975), 12–15. The Protestant resurgence of ritual is summarized in Alexandra Walsham, *Providence in Early Modern England* (Oxford, 1999), 149.

5. *EPM*, 433; Peter Lake, *Moderate Puritans and the Elizabethan Church* (Cambridge, 1982), 284; "A Comfortable Letter Written by Maister Ed[ward] Deringe, to a Christian Gentlewoman, in Heavines of Spirite," in Dering, *Certaine Godly and Verie Comfortable Letters, Full of Christian Consolation* ([Middelburg], 1590?), sigs. A7–B4; M. M. Knappen, ed., *Two Elizabethan Puritan Diaries, by Richard Rogers and Samuel Ward* (Chicago, 1933), 69, 71. Bradford's importance in this context is noted in Dewey D. Wallace, Jr., *Puritans and Predestination: Grace in English Protestant Theology, 1525–1695* (Chapel Hill, N.C., 1982), 53. For later Puritan uses of Bradford, see *BWWP*, 355–385, 390 n. 3; and Daniel Dyke, *Two Treatises: The One, of Repentance; The Other, of Christ's Temptation* (London, 1616), 41, 144. Becon devised an elaborate daily devotional schedule; see *EWB*, 401–403. Dering's letter was an important antecedent to the pietist specialization in cases of troubled conscience, but assurance clearly is not the central concern of his numerous works, and he stopped well short of the anxious cultivation of "signs" that soon was to emerge. For other presbyterians, see, for example, T[homas] W[ilcox], *Large Letters, Three in Number, Containing Much Necessarie Matter, for the Instruction and Comfort of Such, as Are Distressed*

Yet, excepting Rogers, none of the above figures had made the fully pietist move as defined in this study. As seen in the very conception of his six-hundred-page handbook of spiritual direction, the pietist venture moved decisively beyond theirs. More profuse yet schematic, more introspective, more troubled by issues of certitude, and more laden with ritual, it emerged in the later Elizabethan years and beyond as a distinctive and broadly popular synthesis of piety. Most of its essentials, however, were in place by the 1580s at the latest. Its primary framer was a moderate Puritan not allied to the classis movement who came to prominence in the 1570s. To his story we turn below, but first there is a preliminary issue to address.

Approaches to Puritan spirituality long have been shaped by a dubious premise: that the first maturely "Pietist" episode within mainline Protestantism was the movement associated with Philipp Jakob Spener (1635–1705) and other German Lutheran figures of the later seventeenth and the eighteenth centuries. The modern view is to acknowledge that English Puritans had developed pietist tendencies, even a distinctive Puritan pietism; but their activity, together with the Dutch turn to piety that emerged in the 1610s in partial dependence upon English Puritan sources, still tends to appear as a "Vorpietismus," a forerunner to the later, full-bodied German Pietism-with-a-capital-*P*.[6]

Such treatment misleads. It obscures both the originality and the epochal fullness of the Puritan venture in piety, not to mention the similarly full-orbed Pietism of the Scottish presbyterian awakening, which began in the 1620s and 1630s, and the Dutch Second Reformation, which peaked in the 1650s and 1660s—both heavily dependent upon the English movement. German Pietism arose later in the century as a fourth pietist variety. Without question, it diverged in notable ways from the earlier movements, but it exhibited no

---

in *Conscience by Feeling of Sinne, and Feare of Gods Wrath* (London, 1589); and Albert Peel and Leland H. Carlson, eds., *Cartwrightiana* (London, 1951), 75–107. I thank Michael Winship for helpful discussion of the early deepening of piety.

6. Carl Andresen, ed., *Handbuch der Dogmen- und Theologiegeschichte* (Göttingen, 1988), II, 328. The unique fullness of the German phase is assumed in the articles under "Pietism" in *The Encyclopedia of Religion* (New York, 1987), XI; *The Oxford Dictionary of the Christian Church*, 3d ed. (Oxford, 1997), 1286; and many other widely consulted works of reference. The assumption controls even the substantial treatments of English "Pietistic Puritanism" in F. Ernest Stoeffler, *The Rise of Evangelical Pietism* (Leiden, 1965), 24–108, esp. 48–49; and Martin Brecht, ed., *Der Pietismus vom siebzehnten bis zum frühen achtzehnten Jahrhundert* (Goettingen, 1993–), I, which devotes 42 pages to "Der englische Puritanismus" and 110 pages to Spener alone.

special fullness of type. Concerns with evangelical and popular preaching, repentance, conversion, godly life, the cultivation of heartfelt religion in voluntary conventicles leading in some cases to Separatism—these and other well-known elements of the German pattern had played a prominent role in Puritan spirituality. In some respects, German Pietism was arguably *less* original and luxuriant. Certainly it was less devoted to technique and ritual exercises, less rigorously introspective, less programmatically Sabbatarian, less energized and harried by concerns about assurance, and less enriched by scholastic theology than the strikingly efflorescent piety that had arisen on English soil nearly a century earlier. In Protestant history, the conceptual breakthrough to Pietism (capital *P*) seems to have occurred in a small English parish about five miles from Cambridge after 1570.[7]

The Seminal Pietist: Richard Greenham

Through his acclaimed career at the University of Cambridge and in the pulpit of nearby Great Saint Andrews, William Perkins (1558–1602) became Puritan pietism's greatest publicist. In some accounts he is named the "the first pietist," even the true sire of European Protestant pietism.[8] Yet, if Perkins was the greatest literary disseminator of the new spirituality, his was not the formative mind. Richard Greenham (1535–1594), a "quintessentially puritanical" man twenty-three years his senior, appears to have played the more seminal role. William Haller dubbed him "the patriarch" of English "affectionate practical" divines. He has been identified as a principal originator of the Puritan Sabbatarian movement and as the first major Puritan "spiritual director and casuist." His students and early biographers styled him "the paradigmatic godly pastor," and his parish at Dry Drayton was "the first of its kind" as a center of

7. For the Scottish pattern, see Leigh Eric Schmidt, *Holy Fairs: Scottish Communions and American Revivals in the Early Modern Period* (Princeton, N.J., 1989), 18–50; John Coffey, *Politics, Religion, and the British Revolutions: The Mind of Samuel Rutherford* (Cambridge, 1997), 82–113. Schmidt notes that before about 1690 Scottish pietists "borrowed much of their devotional literature from the likes of William Perkins, Thomas Shepard, and Lewis Bayly" (*Holy Fairs*, 45–46). Both the fullness of the Dutch development and its English dependence are underscored in Fred A. van Lieburg, "From Pure Church to Pious Culture: The Further Reformation in the Seventeenth-Century Dutch Republic," in W. Fred Graham, ed., *Later Calvinism: International Perspectives* (Kirksville, Mo., 1994), 409–429.

8. August Lang, *Puritanismus und Pietismus: Studien zu ihrer Entwicklung von M. Butzer bis zum Methodismus* (Neukirchen, 1941), 130, 101; Heiko A. Oberman, preface to Johann Arndt, *True Christianity,* trans. Peter Erb (New York, 1979), xiii n. 6.

Puritan ministry and spiritual direction within a frame of reluctant conformity to the existing church. Taken together, these judgments suggest a striking possibility: that Greenham, with his redesign of piety for the postpresbyterian age, was the foremost architect of the first great awakening of Protestant piety.[9]

Greenham's career, like Perkins's and several other early pietist leaders', illustrates the shift of emphasis from structural reform to experiential piety. Hostile to many elements of the prescribed liturgy, desirous of a "th[o]rough reformation" of the church, he yet lacked the radical temper of a Cartwright or John Knewstub. A fellow at Cambridge in 1570, he signed at least one of the petitions sent to Secretary of State William Cecil (later first Baron Burghley) in defense of Cartwright. In 1573, now in the first years of a twenty-year pastoral career at nearby Dry Drayton, he courteously but firmly explained to the bishop of Ely that he would neither wear the required clerical vestments nor subscribe to unbiblical ceremonies. Although he did not share in the presbyterian agitations, he attended sessions of a Cambridgeshire classis; and he joined Cartwright, Gifford, Knewstub, and others in a series of meetings at Saint John's College in the later 1580s at which Walter Travers's presbyterian Book of Discipline was discussed and refined.[10] In 1586 he sent Burghley a series of gentle "meditations" urging measures to restore the prophesyings, to end the disbeneficing of godly preachers, to protect the spreading practice of public fasting from official interference, to correct "unlearned and ungodly ministers," and to remove clerical pluralism and nonresidency. Never abandoning hope of reform, he yet eschewed controversy, counseled restraint and patience, and chided extremists. His statement to Burghley avoided mention

9. *RP,* 109; William Haller, *The Rise of Puritanism . . .* (Philadelphia, 1972), 26–29; Patrick Collinson, "The Beginnings of English Sabbatarianism," in C. W. Dugmore and Charles Duggan, eds., *Studies in Church History,* I (1964), 217; Norman Keith Clifford, "Casuistical Divinity in English Puritanism during the Seventeenth Century: Its Origin, Development, and Significance" (Ph.D. diss., University of London, 1957), 10 (first spiritual director); H. C. Porter, *Reformation and Reaction in Tudor Cambridge* (Cambridge, 1958), 217 (director and casuist); *PDRG,* 57. R. T. Kendall sees Greenham as "the first pastor of prominence and influence in the experimental predestinarian mould" (*Calvin and English Calvinism to 1649* [Oxford, 1979], 45). Greenham's "extraordinary contemporary reputation" is documented in *PDRG,* 3–7, 22, 68 (quote on 5).

10. *PDRG,* 250; Porter, *Reformation and Reaction,* 216–217; John H. Primus, *Richard Greenham: Portrait of an Elizabethan Pastor* (Macon, Ga., 1998), 66. The letter to Ely (Richard Cox) is in *A Parte of a Register . . .* (n.p., [1593]), 86–93. Greenham explicitly attacked those who "meddle . . . about a new Church government" and neglect the more essential business of the "new birth." He also took a tolerant position on the question of "thing[s] indifferent." *WRG,* 495, 454.

of episcopal government and urged "a mean way" between Puritan and conformist concerns "whereby the . . . practice of the primitive church [might be] observed, and [yet] nothing notoriously in the principal . . . parts of the church and commonwealth [be] altered." Within this context of moderation and compromise, he devoted himself to pastoral and literary labors, made Dry Drayton into "a model parish for the conforming Puritan," celebrated the "blessed calme and peace" of Elizabeth's reign in a time of European turmoil, became a principal shaper both of the "distinctively Puritan style" of doctrine and piety and of the casuistical mode of divinity that reached maturity after his death, and developed a national reputation for spiritual counseling.[11]

Greenham's clerical labors in Dry Drayton were great, but he also extended his ministry into the wider world. He made occasional preaching visits to Cambridge and other nearby towns and participated in at least one combination lecture, but his greater work was to make the rectory at Dry Drayton a famed center of pastoral inspiration and education for two decades. Through force of personality, timeliness of idea, and a strategic Cambridge connection, he turned his country manse into a pioneer household seminary, in which theological students resided for periods of study with a man already known as a master of spiritual guidance. Arthur Hildersam lived with Greenham for a time, as did Henry Smith, an Oxford man. Richard Rogers, whom Stephen Egerton later would celebrate as "another *Greenham*," also was a frequent visitor, accompanied by Ezekiel Culverwell (pastor to John Winthrop's family in the later 1610s) on at least one occasion. Related to Greenham by marriage, John Dod rode from his parish at Hanwell, Oxfordshire, to seek advice about "crosses and hard usages" in his pastoral career. These men were, or would become, frontline Puritan clergy. Many lesser figures whom Greenham trained or counseled carried something of his vision into their pastoral and literary ministries. Just when the time was ripe for a fresh departure, Greenham thus

11. HMC, *Ninth Report, Calendar of the Manuscripts of the Most Hon. the Marquis of Salisbury* . . . , pt. 13 (London, 1915), 313–314; Porter, *Reformation and Reaction*, 216–217 (model parish); Henry Holland, "The Preface to the Reader," in *WRG*, sig. A5 (blessed peace); Peter Lake, "Defining Puritanism—Again?" in Francis J. Bremer, ed., *Puritanism: Transatlantic Perspectives on a Seventeenth-Century Anglo-American Faith* (Boston, 1993), 6. The statement to Burghley also reiterated several standard Puritan complaints and recommended that John Knewstub, the militant presbyterian, be included with more moderate figures on a government committee to debate the issues and recommend a compromise to the government. In unpublished sermons and writings Greenham also advocated church discipline and criticized "obstinate enemies of Discipline" (*WRG*, 416, and see 135, 399). Greenham's casuistical role is noted in *PDRG*, 85.

became adviser to "a kind of school" whose members would disseminate pietist spirituality well beyond the turn of the century.[12]

In a scene reminiscent of Luther's parsonage, some of the students at Dry Drayton took notes on Greenham's sermons, table talk, and pastoral counsel. Upon such figures he clearly exercised a personal magic, but it was charisma joined to an opportune program that made him a pivotal force in English religion, and that program he set forth in a large corpus of written work, which eventually was to make him "one of the most . . . respected theologians of early seventeenth-century England." With the exception of a short tract on the education of children, his numerous writings remained in manuscript until his death in 1594. *A Most Sweete and Assured Comfort for All Afflicted in Conscience* (1595) and a few other items appeared shortly thereafter; a first, incomplete collection of *The Workes of Richard Greenham* appeared in 1599, and several fuller editions followed. These included selections of the table talk, gathered from scattered copies already in circulation and edited to reflect and address the needs of the godly community around the turn of the century. None of the constituent pieces is dated, yet most certainly stem from the years at Dry Drayton (1570–1591). Here there are no obviously early works; all abundantly evidence the author's distinctive ambition to survey, enrich, and manage the interior life. Hence, to take up his work at the proper point in the Elizabethan sequence (and many of the items almost certainly predate Perkins's appointment at Cambridge in 1584 and indeed his conversion to godly religion earlier in the decade) is to realize that a corner has been turned.[13]

Continuous at most points with earlier Protestant faith and practice, Greenham's spirituality attained a new level of organization, scope, and popularity. His was not merely an active piety but an overarching practice of piety,

12. Egerton, "To the Christian Reader," in *ST,* sig. A3; S[amuel] Clarke, *A Generall Martyrologie* . . . (London, 1651), 406 (Dod married Greenham's daughter-in-law, Ann, in 1585; see Primus, *Richard Greenham,* 26); Haller, *Rise of Puritanism,* 28. Kenneth L. Parker and Eric J. Carlson suggest that, through the agency of clergy trained at Dry Drayton, "literally thousands of English lay people were, by the 1620s, in some sense the flock of Richard Greenham" (*PDRG,* 22). Preaching in Cambridge and the combination lecture: *PDRG,* 22, 63 (for "combination lecture," see Patrick Collinson, "Lectures by Combination: Sketches and Characteristics of Church Life in Seventeenth Century England," *Bulletin of the Institute of Historical Research,* XLVIII [1975], 182–213). Seminary: *PDRG,* 21. Hildersam, Rogers, and Smith: *PDRG,* 46, 95. Culverwell and Rogers: Knappen, ed., *Puritan Diaries,* 59. For Culverwell and Winthrop, see *WP,* I, 89, 155.

13. *PDRG,* 34–35, and see 52. Greenham's publications: *PDRG,* 41–57. A guide to the published works is in *PDRG,* 357–366.

an extensively theorized and practically implemented plan of life rooted in highly programmed introversion, bathed in abject emotion, and effectively transmitted to a corps of followers. Relative to the issues we are pursuing, its defining elements are two, spelled out for the most part with typical Reformed accents: (1) *an elaborate preoccupation with the self and its conflicted passage through a lifelong, often anxious venture of transformation, self-reproach and -control,* and (2) *employing methodical self-analysis and other "exercises" both private and social designed to purify and regulate behavior and to provide religious assurance.* When this program became a widely subscribed movement around the turn of the century, the first Protestant pietism was in place. In scope, intensity, and cultural power it was fully the equal of the later German variant.

Henry Holland, London pastor, long-standing associate of Greenham's and an editor of his posthumous *Workes,* offered a first account of Greenham's career in an insightful preface to that volume. There he portrayed the rector of Dry Drayton as the inaugurator of a new era in Protestant spirituality and described the forces spurring him to this achievement. Drawing upon personal recollection as well as detailed acquaintance with the written corpus, Holland recounted his friend's consuming interest in cases of "afflictions." These were, not the temporal punishments of Deuteronomic theory, but the fears and insecurities about personal redemption that seemed increasingly to abound in the last decades of the century. To place Greenham's work in perspective, Holland reminded his readers that Protestant theology hitherto had provided scant guidance for spiritually troubled saints and their pastoral advisers. Many earlier figures—Holland cited Martin Luther (1483–1546), Urbanus Rhegius (1489–1541), Jean Taffin (1528–1602), and Theodore Beza (1519–1605)—had addressed the cure of anxious souls, but none were specialists or effective systematizers in the field. Since they had not expounded fully the causes and cures of spiritual disorder, Protestant counseling remained crude and improvisatory. Clergymen, and certainly the laity themselves, had been unable in that vital area "to proceede by any certaine rule of art, and well grounded practise," and there was Greenham's point of contact with the story. Consciously entering a region in which "precepts are wanting," he had aspired to develop an adequate propaedeutic of spiritual direction. Out of the myriad of cases he encountered, and in consultation with other pastors who had similar experiences to report, he would extract the necessary "rules of direction" and bring them to "some forme of method and art."[14]

14. All quotes in this and the following two paragraphs are from *WRG*, sigs. A3–A5. Primus, *Richard Greenham*, 39–40, offers a similar account of Greenham's concern with

This, at least, was the promise of Greenham's career: he was a potentially major figure, "as fit, and as willing as any in our age" to create the first organized science of Protestant spiritual counseling. At the same time, however, Holland acknowledged candidly that Greenham had failed to complete his mission. This "man . . . of great hope, [who] could have given best rules" for spiritual science, had committed himself in effect to two careers and proved unable to master both. Greenham the spiritual researcher had accomplished much. He had analyzed numerous cases, enlarged his grasp of Christian psychology, devised therapeutic procedures, and enunciated them in a substantial number of written works. But Greenham the pastor was so involved at a practical level, so absorbed in the pain and drama of his cases and in the labor-intensive work of comfort that he neither produced a completed system nor brought his many works to final, publishable form. And this failure, Holland might have added, was Perkins's opportunity. Gripped by a religious conversion a decade or more after Greenham had assumed his post at Dry Drayton and making the most of his university position and his lectureship at Great Saint Andrews in Cambridge, Perkins began in the later 1580s to develop a fuller literary presentation of spiritual practice than the older man was able to supply.[15]

Yet Holland's Greenham, for all his shortcomings, remained an inaugural force, the first adequately equipped "spirituall Phisition" of his day. Emanating from his unpublished manuscripts in circulation, his intermittent preaching at Cambridge and elsewhere, and his household seminary, his ideas marked a new era of expanded interest and studied technique in the care and cure of souls. Granted that his writings contained but a rough draft of the promised "rules," they nonetheless embodied a major advance, and one too long withheld from the public. His science of counsel met a clear and present need of the English church, and it spoke to the church's place in the larger Protestant world. By directing more resources to the nurture of piety, it also established a bulwark, sorely needed in a half-reformed England, against the Counter Reformation. Evoking all the passion of the continuing struggle, Holland described how Catholic propagandists, quick to exploit the Protestant disadvantage in spiritual science, had begun to produce a literature of

---

afflicted consciences. For Catholic parallels with the concept of spiritual direction as an "art" with its own coherence and method, see John R. Roberts, *A Critical Anthology of English Recusant Devotional Prose, 1558–1603* (Pittsburgh, 1966), 15–16.

15. *WRG*, sig. G. "Such were his travels [travails] in his life time in preaching and comforting the afflicted, that he could not possibl[y] leave these workes as he desired." *WRG*, sig. A5–A6.

pious instruction calculated to attract and sway Protestant audiences. Since Italian authors, in Holland's view, were in the forefront of this aggression, "men [are] in danger . . . to be Italianated"; and in the now assembled *Workes* he saw a veritable arsenal of means to match and repel the challenge. They offered at once an antidote to Catholic error and a way to regain lost initiative in the "diet and cure of souls."

Holland's analysis identifies cardinal themes of Greenham's career and illuminates his influence upon the broader Puritan movement. At the same time, narrowed by confessional purposes, it requires substantial supplementing if it adequately is to disclose the secrets of Greenham's appeal. His influence upon contemporaries flowed, indeed, from an exceptional facility in the arts of practical piety. That facility, however, was neither confined to the treatment of spiritual disorders nor divorced from the vast and still vital tradition of Catholic spirituality.

Discipline and Devotion: A Shared Heritage with the Catholic Foe

Greenham in fact was the most seminal early Puritan exponent of the trans-confessional "devotional revival" that swept both Catholic and Protestant Europe in the late sixteenth and the seventeenth centuries. Integral to the Counter Reformation, the accent upon devotion—linked everywhere to ascetic personal discipline—also became ingredient to a veritable "second age of the Reformation" in some Reformed and Lutheran areas. As evidenced by the central role of meditative prayer in the Society of Jesus (founded 1540), Catholics took an early lead in the renascence of piety. Throughout the century new layers of devotional literature, much of it incorporating the emphasis upon technique promoted by the Modern Devotion in the late fourteenth and fifteenth centuries, were added to the already large cumulations stemming from medieval monastic and mendicant experience and from movements of lay piety. Now, moreover, in keeping with the purposes of Catholic counterinsurgency, the world of devotion was expanding beyond the realm of professional spirituality in the religious orders. Aiming to capture or recapture the allegiance of the laity, many of the newer treatises and handbooks, as in the French Catholic devotional movement of the late sixteenth and early seventeenth centuries, presented simplified approaches to the spiritual life. They were written or translated into the vernacular, and some were directed particularly at English audiences.[16]

16. *PPPDD*, 23; Eric Lund, "Second Age of the Reformation: Lutheran and Reformed

As the English Jesuit Robert Parsons knew, taunting his Protestant countrymen in 1582 with "the greate want of spirituall bookes in Englande, for the direction of men to pietie and devotion," a major result of the English Reformation had been to disconnect devotion not only from the religious order but also from much of the vast Catholic body of penitential and mystical instruction. As indicated, for example, by the unending stream of English translations of Thomas à Kempis's *Imitation of Christ* through the Reformation years, the disconnection was never complete.[17] Yet devotion in a Protestant context was a much simplified affair centered upon Bible reading, collections of prayers for private devotion, and the English primer. As Edmund Bunny noted in a retort to Parsons, there were also the earlier devotional works of John Bradford and Thomas Becon as well as Edward Dering's pioneering treatments of the "afflicted conscience." Yet it well could be said that the Protestant movement by about 1580 possessed embarrassingly scant resources (outside the formal routines of the Prayer Book and primers) for spiritual edification and discipline. Nor had the theologians of the presbyterian movement as a whole, occupied with institutional reform, made the recasting and nurture of spirituality their priority. It is not therefore surprising that those who did so drew both inspiration and material from Catholic tradition.[18]

From about 1580, in rough coincidence with Greenham's emergence as a pioneering spiritual director, the circulation of Catholic devotional books within England rapidly increased. Clandestine recusant presses in England, Continental centers of recusant activity, and authorized London publishers produced a growing array of both classic and contemporary Catholic works

Spirituality, 1550–1700," in Louis Dupré and Don E. Saliers, eds., *Christian Spirituality*, III, *Post-Reformation and Modern* (New York, 1989), 213. For the Catholic devotional movement, see Terence C. Cave, *Devotional Poetry in France, c. 1570–1613* (Cambridge, 1969), 1–57. For the Modern Devotion, see R. R. Post, *The Modern Devotion: Confrontation with Reformation and Humanism* (Leiden, 1968).

17. [Robert Parsons], *The First Booke of the Christian Exercise, Appertayning to Resolution* . . . ([Rouen], 1582), 1. Parsons reiterated the point in *CDGM*, 9–10. For a similar complaint by Sir Edwin Sandys about 1605, see Helen C. White, *English Devotional Literature (Prose), 1600–1640* (Madison, Wis., 1931), 64. *STC* lists eighteen Elizabethan editions of the *Imitation*.

18. Bunny's retort: White, *English Devotional Literature*, 66–67. Presbyterians: Heinz Schilling, *Religion, Political Culture, and the Emergence of Early Modern Society: Essays in German and Dutch History* (Leiden, 1992), 273–275, argues that Reformed theologians of the disciplinary Second Reformation in Germany and the Protestant Netherlands likewise were concerned with changing institutions and paid relatively little attention to issues of spirituality.

written or translated into English. *The Exercise of a Christian Life* (1579), a recusant translation from an Italian original by Gaspar Loarte (presumably an object of Holland's complaint about "Italianat[e]" propaganda), offers an early instance; but the incoming flow of Continental literature was dominated by a large selection of works from the sixteenth-century Spanish devotional awakening. Luis de Granada was the most popular Spanish author, with at least twenty editions of various works appearing in English between 1580 and 1634. Among authors writing in English, probably the most important was Robert Parsons (an admirer of Loarte, Granada, and Ignatius of Loyola), whose *First Booke of the Christian Exercise* (1582) was issued in a recast and enlarged edition as *A Christian Directorie* in 1585. Giving strong evidence of renewed English interest in Catholic spirituality, conservative Protestants too contributed to the devotional revival with expurgated editions of Catholic works. Thomas Rogers prepared a Protestantized edition of Thomas à Kempis's *Imitation of Christ*, for instance, which was reprinted sixteen times between 1580 and 1640; Frances Meres's translation of Luis de Granada's *Sinners Guyde* went through two London editions; and Edmund Bunny's sanitized version of Parsons's *Christian Exercise* enjoyed a run of thirty-two editions between 1584 and 1639.[19]

In keeping with both the evangelizing strategies and the reinvigorated spirituality of the Counter Reformation, recusant translators and editors intended their works to serve English Catholics both in England and in exile communities abroad, but they also hoped to influence Protestants. By making available a relatively noncontroversial and impressively rich literature steeped in Catholic religious ideals, they aimed to contribute to the reconversion of the English people. To this end they made relatively little use of strictly monastic literature, turning instead to work from the newer, noncloistered and service-oriented religious orders that strove to connect the emotional power of tradi-

---

19. Loarte's *Exercise:* there were five English editions of this work before 1640, one Protestantized. For translations of additional tracts by the same author in the period, see *STC*, s.v. "Loarte, Gaspar." Loarte was Spanish but spent most of his career in Italy and composed much of his work in Italian. A recusant translation of his *Godly Garden of Gethsemani* was published as early as 1576. Parsons's use of Loyola, Loarte, and Granada: Victor Houliston, ed., *Robert Persons, S.J.: The Christian Directory (1582)* . . . (Leiden, 1998), xxiii–xxxviii. Sanitized version: R[obert] P[arsons], *A Booke of Christian Exercise, Appertaining to Resolution* . . . , ed. Edm[und] Bunny (London, 1584). Bunny cited Rogers's altered edition of the *Imitation* as a model for his own endeavor (*Christian Exercise*, sig. *4). For other examples of Protestant bowdlerization, see Maria Hagedorn, *Reformation und spanische Andachtsliteratur: Luis de Granada in England* (Leipzig, 1934), 41–44, 104.

tional devotion to the realm of worldly vocation. It was no coincidence that Luis de Granada was a Dominican, or that his work embodied one of the earliest attempts "to formulate a method of prayer intended for those living in the world," or that Loarte and Parsons were members of the Society of Jesus, or that virtually all contemporary devotionalists whose works circulated in England had been influenced by Ignatius of Loyola's *Spiritual Exercises* and its particularly insistent linkage of meditation to work and action in the world.[20]

Yet the currency of such books in Elizabethan and early Stuart times, together with the dismal failure of the Counter Reformation in England, suggests that their primary effect was to strengthen Protestant resources. With specific reference to works by Parsons, Granada, and Loarte, the Puritan editors of Rogers's *Seven Treatises* and the author himself saw the work as inspired in part by the dangers of Catholic spiritual literature. Richard Baxter's encounter with Bunny's revision of Parsons's *Christian Exercise* was a landmark in his spiritual development. And certainly the remarkable series of Puritan directories from *Seven Treatises* (1603) to Baxter's own *Christian Directory* (1673) are continuous at many points with the monastic genre of "Directories" that supplied an obvious model for Parsons's work. At all events, by the time of Greenham's coming of age, at the very time when he and others were groping toward a new departure in English religion, the works of Parsons and others were carrying the powerful stimulus and challenge of Catholic spirituality into Protestant quarters.[21]

To what extent did Greenham mine Catholic literature new or old? No definite answer is possible. His citation of extrabiblical sources is sparse and decidedly selective. A rough canvass of the some 880 pages of the fullest edition of his *Workes* (1612) yields a small set of references. Patristic sources

20. Pierre Pourrat, *Christian Spirituality* (Westminster, Md., 1953–1955), III, 96. For the novelty of this program, see 96 n. 2, 280, 286–287. Roberts, *Recusant Devotional Prose*, 22–29, discusses the Ignatian influence. Reconversion: Richard Hopkins, for example, devoted his translation of L[uis] de Granada, *Of Prayer and Meditation* . . . (Paris, 1582), to "the gayninge of Christian sowles in our countrie [that is, England] from Schisme, and Heresie" (sig. avii, and see White, *English Devotional Literature*, 140, 134).

21. *ST,* sigs. A3, A4, A6 (quote at sig. A3); Richard Baxter, *Reliquiae Baxterianae* . . . (London, 1696), 3. In the preface to his *Christian Exercise,* sig. *2, Bunny complained that "divers" Protestants were reading Parsons's original "for the perswasion that it hath to godlines of life." Richard Rogers, Stephen Egerton, and Ezekiel Culverwell all saw Rogers's *Seven Treatises* as a "counterpoyson" to current Catholic spiritual writings, including those of Parsons and *"Frier* Granatensis" (*ST,* sig. A3, and see A4, B). For the Catholic "directory," see Pourrat, *Christian Spirituality,* III, 12, 16, 18 n. 2.

predominate, although a few Greek and Roman classics and contemporary Reformed texts appear. Bernard of Clairvaux is the only favored medieval author, and a single reference reveals wide acquaintance with the works of John Bradford (d. 1555). Yet it would be rash to conclude that this one-time fellow at Cambridge, holder of the bachelor's and master's degrees, passionate exponent of the Protestant cause in a time of brisk interconfessional controversy and specialist in the arts of piety, knew little of the voluminous postpatristic Catholic theological and spiritual literature available in Latin and, increasingly after about 1580, in English original or translation.[22]

In point of fact, Greenham's teaching exhibits as many "points of overlap with, as departures from, the moral and devotional emphases" of medieval and Counter Reformation Catholicism. Registering the "syncretism between pre- and post-Reformation forms" that Alexandra Walsham has documented, his writings and recorded utterances are shot through with patent Catholic motifs. They include an emphasis on meditation, interest in the Passion as a prime object of meditation, a preoccupation with technique (as in the formulation of "Rules for meditation"), the image of the saint as a "pilgrim" (the traditional *homo viator,* or *peregrinus*) journeying toward heaven through the transient and wicked world, the lifelong "spirituall battaile" against flesh, world, and devil, the attainment of detailed self-knowledge through regular and searching introspection, the use of the Decalogue as a basis of self-inspection, the analysis of sins according to "circumstances," the ceaseless "watch" over dangerous motions of the soul, a "labour for the contrary vertue" in the fight against sinful tendencies, the practice of "judging" oneself so that "God will acquite us from the fearefull iudgement to come," the distinction between an inferior repentance based upon fear of punishment ("attrition") and repentance based upon a true love of God and hatred of sin ("contrition"), a preoccupation with "afflictions," a pervasive emphasis upon penitential sorrow—and, in Greenham's aspiration to methodize pastoral counseling and in his own self-image as "Spiritual Phisition," a remarkable adaptation to a Protestant constituency of the venerable science of "spiritual direction" under the guidance of a clerical spiritual director. In accord with monastic ideals, moreover, all of the ele-

22. The great majority of citations are in "A Treatise of Hypocrisy" and the collection of short pieces titled "Godly Instructions for the Due Examining and Direction of All Men," in Richard Greenham, *The Workes of . . . M. Richard Greenham . . .* , 5th ed., ed. H[enry] H[olland] (London, 1612), 200–203, 629–831. Bradford is cited at 549; Bernard at 676–677, 750. Many citations, however, appear in marginal notes that might have been added or modified by the editors.

ments above carried implications of sustained effort, care, and strain. Self-examination and the other spiritual exercises must be performed "pricisely"; in turn, the ungodly would attack them as onerously "precise."[23]

Greenham did not reinvent this array of unmistakably traditional motifs. Like the generations of Puritan pietists who would follow in his steps, he drew upon common currents of spirituality flowing from Christian antiquity into the contemporary devotional renewal. No mainstream Protestant condemned the Catholic heritage in its entirety. In the realm of spirituality, much—saying the rosary, for example—was, indeed, hopelessly tied to superstition and heresy, but many wholesome concepts and usages remained. Greenham's work, moderating the earlier Protestant impulse to dissociate from the errant Roman church, was to reconnect with a large additional selection of traditional resources. This vast reservoir derived from patristic, medieval, and Christian Humanist texts, together with the work of contemporaries like Parsons and Protestant authors like Bradford, Dering, and the French Calvinist devotionalists, who themselves borrowed and adapted traditional motifs of spirituality both ancient and recent. All such materials were cleansed of Pelagian, mystical, or other heretical implications, removed from association with sacred places, objects, and unscriptural rites, linked to biblical teaching, and

23. Walsham, *Providence in Early Modern England*, 5, 329. Meditation: *WRG*, 22–24, 204. The Passion: *WRG*, 95. "Rules for meditation": *WRG*, 22–24 (cf. Cave's remarks on the "systematization of devotion" in Counter Reformation French Catholicism, in *Devotional Poetry in France*, 24–25 n. 38). "Pilgrim": *WRG*, 141, 146. "Spirituall battaile": *WRG*, 243, and see 229. Introspection: *WRG*, 2, 5, 8, 31, 87. Decalogue: *WRG*, 477. "Circumstances": *WRG*, 258. "Watch": *WRG*, 83, 138–139. "Contrary vertue": *WRG*, 31 (for the method of "contraries, common since patristic times," see John T. McNeill, *A History of the Cure of Souls* [New York, 1951], 114, 157). "Iudgement to come": *WRG*, 94–95, 130, 298. Types of repentance: *WRG*, 94, 104. Spiritual director: *New Catholic Encyclopedia* (New York, 1967–), IV, s.v. "Direction, Spiritual." "Precise": *WRG*, 160, 477.

Concerning "circumstances," the standard confessors' manual at the English recusant college in Douai in the late sixteenth century reviewed the circumstances "quis, quid, ubi, per quos, quoties, cur, quomodo, quando . . . [and] quibus auxiliis." Martin Azpilcueta, *Enchiridion sive manuale confessariorum . . .* , in *Operum Martini ab Azpilcueta . . . tomus secundus* (Rome, 1590), 686. For its use at Douai, see J. C. H. Aveling, "The English Clergy, Catholic and Protestant . . . ," in Aveling, ed., *Rome and the Anglicans: Historical and Doctrinal Aspects of Anglican–Roman Catholic Relations* (Berlin, 1982), 101.

Concerning Greenham, Primus misreads the mood of his "theology . . . [and] the Christian life based thereon" as essentially "upbeat, joyful, and positive in tone" (*Richard Greenham*, 179).

then spliced into the framework of evangelical and Puritan teaching. The result was to mask the true extent to which Greenham, with many other Protestants of the time, partook of a common heritage with the Catholic foe.[24]

But what, then, was the basis of appeal? An answer emerges if we return to the challenge posed to Elizabethan Protestants by the contemporary Catholic awakening. To what extent Greenham knew and used the works of Parsons and like figures cannot be determined, but his devotional program shared much more with theirs than students of Puritanism unfamiliar with Catholic backgrounds might suspect. With Parsons, Granada, and Loarte, he believed that reverential states of mind were inherently valuable and worthy of cultivation; but he concurred with them too in a more fundamental design: a wish to conscript reverence for a program of self-control. Accordingly, his pattern of borrowing from the old church discloses a profound elective affinity with three fundamental theses of the Catholic spiritual renaissance, each resonant with the ancient summons to ascetic life: first, that authentic religion is a strenuously disciplinary venture; second, that popular Christianity has declined into a nominal and morally apathetic affair with little redemptive power; and third, that specialized appeals and techniques are needed both to reawaken zeal for self-control and to guide it along desired lines. In his belief that tightened personal discipline was a prime need of the times and that a program of spirituality was its ideal delivery and support system, the rector of Dry Drayton silently appropriated pre-Protestant ideals.

Parsons's *Christian Exercise* and *Christian Directorie,* the many recusant translations of Continental books, and the bowdlerized productions of figures like Thomas Rogers and Frances Meres shared a candidly pragmatic orientation within a framework of life conceived as journey and combat; and its affinities with the new piety arising on the Protestant side, many and basic, transcend pure coincidence. Eschewing for the most part the lofty regions of

---

24. Parker and Carlson note that Greenham "excised, altered and adapted [traditional] practices . . . to wean his parishioners from . . . popery" (*PDRG,* 84). Charles E. Hambrick-Stowe describes the relationships of Puritan to Catholic spirituality along an axis from parallelism to kinship to broad continuity to direct and substantial borrowing (*PPPDD,* 23–39; and see Peter Iver Kaufman, *Prayer, Despair, and Drama: Elizabethan Introspection* [Urbana, Ill., 1996], 17). Louis L. Martz, *The Poetry of Meditation: A Study in English Religious Literature of the Seventeenth Century* (New Haven, Conn., 1954), 123, and the article on "piety" in *The Oxford Encyclopedia of the Reformation,* III, 270, find Puritan spiritual techniques strikingly similar to Catholic precedents. For the early modern "interpenetration of Catholicism and Protestantism" in a European context, see *SF,* 505–506. For French Calvinists, see Cave, *Devotional Poetry in France,* 18–23.

mystical contemplation, Catholic texts yet spoke the language of a religious elite. Like Protestant predestinarians of precise and evangelical leaning, their authors viewed the great mass of baptized citizens in Christendom as hopelessly complacent, inauthentic, and hell-bound. They knew that their literature of devotion would attract only the religious athlete ("of thousandes, skarse one," said Parsons) who had been, or might yet be, moved to enter the hard regimen of authentic religion. Aided by a spiritual director, this rare spirit must begin with a painful examen of conscience, generate a "holie hatred of . . . selfe," be brought thereby to a personal conversion understood above all as an ethical transformation, and serve the honor and majesty of the divine monarch through ceaseless effort and combat against self. Accordingly, they focused on the lower ranges of the devotional tradition, on ascetic and meditative practices designed both to produce conversion and to tighten self-control; and these they framed according to the conventions of method and regular schedule—for example, the daily and weekly calendars of prayer and meditation, or step-by-step instruction for the performance of each exercise—popularized by the movement of Modern Devotion.[25]

If all of this, and perhaps especially the emphasis upon continuous effort and struggle, sounds familiar to students of Puritan religious experience, so too does the pragmatic objective assigned in this context to spiritual exercises. Always a felt desire for fuller emotional nurture and expression was ingredient to them, but no less salient was their moral potentiality, their fitness to train the soul to "feare God, and directe [its] actions to the observance of his commaundementes." As Parsons made plain, his decision to concentrate upon "practique or active" exercises pertaining to "manners and [the] direction of life" rested upon the premise that "the whole service whiche God requireth . . . in this lyfe, consisteth in two thinges[,] . . . one to flye euill, and thother to doe good"; and Granada assured his readers that "the ende of meditation . . . is the feare of God, and amendment of our liffe" and that "praier is a most conve-

---

25. *CDGM*, 116–117; L[uis] de Granada, *Of Prayer and Meditation*, 153, and see 140–141, 149 (and see Granada, *The Sinners Guyde* . . . , trans. Francis Meres [London, 1598], 381, 453; and [Lorenzo Scupoli], *The Spiritual Conflict* [Rouen, 1613], sigs. B6, E11). Hell-bound masses: Parsons, *Christian Exercise*, 27, 37, 239, 267, 360; Granada, *A Breefe Treatise Exhorting Sinners to Repentance, Commonly Called, The Conversion of a Sinner* (n.p., 1580?), 65. Divine kingship, honor, and law: Granada, *Sinners Guyde*, 11, 473; Parsons, *Christian Exercise*, 83–87; *CDGM*, 379–386, 401–411. All of these themes link to "the counter-reformation doctrine of Christian struggle" with "ceaseless effort and combat against self." H. Outram Evennett, *The Spirit of the Counter-Reformation*, ed. John Bossy (Cambridge, 1968), 36–37, and see 41.

nient exercise for that man, that mindeth to reforme his maners, and [his] life." With few exceptions, the testimonials to devotion that ring through the literature flow directly from an estimate of its value in the struggle to rule the self.[26]

When someone asked Greenham how to defeat "concupiscence," an age-old concern of ascetic Christianity, he offered precisely a plan for self-rule tied to exercises:

> a continual examination of your selves by the law, a reverent and daily meditating of the word, a painful walking in our honest calling, an holy shaming of ourselves, . . . a continual temperance in diet, sleep and apparrel, a careful watching over our eies and other parts of our bodies, a zealous geolousy to avoid al occasions, . . . which might nourish concupiscence, a godly frequenting of times, persons, and places, which breed in us mortification, togither with an humbling of ourselves, with the shame of sins past, with the greefe of sins present, and with the fear of sins to come. [L]astly[,] a careful using of fasting, prier and watching . . . are means to come to mortification herin.

Self-inspection, meditation, mortification, watching, fasting—rooted in conviction that a repertoire of devotional rites is a vital agency of discipline, this is a telling sampler of Greenham's foundational project. As we shall see, it is a telling index too of the larger Puritan turn into "affectionate," "experimental," or "practical" divinity in later Elizabethan and early Stuart times. The traditionality of the pietist turn, it would seem, is as noteworthy as its newer, Protestant inclinations. They would scarcely express it so, but the first Puritan pietists chose to address the needs of the time by following a course already plotted by their confessional opposites. They did not depart so sharply from the past, or from the continuing Catholic tradition, as modern historiography of the English Reformation suggests. Making devotion auxiliary to a deeply

---

26. "Practique" and "manners": *CDGM*, 7. "Commaundementes": *CDGM*, 131. Diègo de Estella saw devotion as "a method unto mortification," the means to "leave the waie of wickednes, and treade the pathes of Gods commaundements" (*A Methode unto Mortification . . .*, ed. Thomas Rogers [London, 1586], 25). For "flye euill": Parsons, *Christian Exercise*, 32; Granada, *Prayer and Meditation*, 7, 21. Parsons's disciplinary emphasis is discussed in Brad S. Gregory, "The 'True and Zealouse Service of God': Robert Parsons, Edmund Bunny, and *The First Booke of the Christian Exercise*," *Journal of Ecclesiastical History*, XLV (1994), 252–268.

penitential via purgativa, they fostered not so much a new tradition of piety as a separate evolution of an old.[27]

To be sure, only a few of the figures who appear in the following chapters were avowed apostles of Greenham. Some had studied practical divinity at Dry Drayton, and others cited his works as a source of inspiration, but like him they shared in the larger contemporary renewal of piety and through it in age-old spiritual traditions and literatures. Yet, if Greenham's influence cannot be traced exactly, his importance in the story we seek to tell is large. With few and limited Protestant precedents to draw upon either at home or abroad, he was the first articulate Elizabethan to make a fully pietist turn in the sense defined here and to gather a substantial following around it. He was the first to develop an integral scheme of penitential self-analysis and "exercises" and disseminate it through teaching and example in a household seminary. He broadcast it too through his parish ministry, through extensive counseling services, through occasional turns in the pulpit of Great Saint Mary's in Cambridge and elsewhere, through scattered copies in manuscript of his writings and sayings, and eventually through publications. He was the first to offer a full-scale disciplinary program that could at once expand and vitalize spirituality and succeed without a presbyterian reformation. And that program was no mere preparative. It included or foreshadowed virtually all the constitutive aims and themes of the future pietist movement.

27. *PDRG,* 174.

CHAPTER 5

PIETY AND
SELF-MANAGEMENT
AFTER RICHARD
GREENHAM

Timely and cogently recast in Protestant idiom, the project of self-command through an ordered praxis of piety rapidly was adopted by the spiritual brotherhood of godly but generally moderate clergy who were coming to the fore at the turn of the sixteenth century and were to dominate Puritan theological and pastoral expression in the decades following. William Perkins (1558–1602) was chief among them in the early stage, breaking upon the scene in the late 1580s with a rapid succession of edifying treatises, many in multiple editions. With few exceptions, they were explicit media of the new spirituality. Since many appeared as well in Latin, Dutch, French, and other translations and influenced Continental developments both in Reformed and Lutheran quarters, Heiko Oberman names Perkins the father of European pietism.[1]

A moderate exponent of the scholastic turn in international Reformed theology in the later sixteenth century, Perkins promoted the devotional awakening with a schoolmasterly knack that was unmatched in Elizabethan times. His strength lay in topical analysis and lucid counsel, as in *A Direction for the Government of the Tongue* (1593), or his *Whole Treatise of the Cases of Conscience* (1606), or his ten-step "exercise" to relieve the "disquietnes" of a believer not closely bonded to Christ. Although little if any evidence remains to specify his relationship to Richard Greenham, Perkins's design for spir-

1. Continental editions: M. A. Shaaber, *Check-List of Works of British Authors Printed Abroad, in Languages Other than English, to 1641* (New York, 1975), 134–135; Cornelis W. Schoneveld, *Intertraffic of the Mind: Studies in Seventeenth-Century Anglo-Dutch Translation* (Leiden, 1983), 222–226. Heiko A. Oberman argues that "in the larger European perspective William Perkins . . . may well hold the best claim to the title 'Father of Pietism'" (Oberman, preface to Johann Arndt, *True Christianity*, trans. Peter Erb [New York, 1979], xiii n. 6). The "Spiritual Brotherhood" of Puritan clergy is discussed in William Haller, *The Rise of Puritanism . . .* (Philadelphia, 1972), 49–82, and *EPM*, 122–127.

ituality embraced the exacting inward analysis and other mainstays of the older man's spiritual science. Without exception, the legion of traditional borrowings (reviewed in the previous chapter) emerge again, often repeatedly, in Perkins's work. There were Perkinsian accents, to be sure—the adequacy of the "lowest degree of faith," the determination of "how farre a man may goe in the profession of the gospel, and yet be a . . . reprobate," and the like—yet these were refinements of an excruciating care of the soul continuous in most particulars with that roughed out in Dry Drayton in the 1570s and 1580s.[2]

The same may be said of the other leading prophets of godly piety in the years after Perkins's death (1602). Their theological positions varied in many ways and evolved with the passing years, but they accorded most of the time on most of the essentials. They had small hope for a structural reformation of the church, at least in the short run, but they held fast to the fundamental principle that stemmed from ancient and medieval times, had been reinstated with Protestant revisions by the pre-Marians, was articulated afresh by Elizabethan presbyterians, and then refracted into a full-blown practice of piety: religion, whatever else it may be, is a plan of stringent denial and control. Pietist Puritans attributed redemption finally to grace and faith alone, but they shared also the underlying dread of disorder and the Platonizing *contemptus mundi* of the pre-Marians and upheld their commitment to a forthrightly bipolar theology. Like William Tyndale or Myles Coverdale, for instance, they made repentance a dual affair of sorrow and amendment, and at virtually all points they kept faith with presbyterian priorities. In sacred Scripture they saw and underscored a gospel of pardon free and undeserved, but they saw too a compend of laws and precedents designed to govern human actions in fine detail. Denying, with John Preston, "that faith is nothing but a perswasion that our sinnes are forgiven," they insisted that "Christ conveyes his grace two wayes," through moral change and empowerment as much as justification. Within an overarching vision of divine kingship and rule, they championed covenant theology with its blend of free pardon and the Israelitic scheme of laws, duties, rewards and punishments (often proportioned to the degree of offense), its fast days, and its disciplinary imperatives for the larger society and continued to advertise the communal dangers of sin with Deuteronomic interpretations of fires, outbreaks of plague, and other calamities. Even the most solifidian among them—like John Downame—were occupied most of the time with the corruption, reform, and control of behavior; and they favored

---

2. "Exercise": *WWP,* I, 375 (misnumbered 362). Trademark emphases: *WWP,* I, 356; *BWWP,* 230.

grave and often melancholic states of mind. And to the elaboration of these elements and the potent new science and praxis of piety they built upon them, they brought an undiminished flair for strictness and exactitude.[3]

All of this had its social correlations and uses. Like the older presbyterians again, pietist clergy were identified with respectable society. They tended to presume an audience of householders of the middling sort without excluding either the worthy poor or the upper classes and assailed vices up and down the social ranks. They held Separatism in contempt, were careful to connect family and individual devotions to public ordinances in the local parish church, and upheld the existing social hierarchies of class and gender. Against a continuing background of rapid change and economic crisis, they and their lay associates in city, town, and county communities displayed "voracious appetites" for civic reformation. They were alarmed by the spectacle of "wandring beggers, a sinnefull and disordered people," but supported welfare for the worthy poor. They admonished the exploitative and uncharitable attitudes of wealthier citizens and, like Greenham, were notably charitable themselves. After 1590 as before, organized programs to relieve want and correct misbehavior often were the work of local alliances of the godly. Consistent with precedents set in towns like Northampton in the 1570s and 1580s or Dedham in the 1580s, such groups were at work in Gloucester and Terling after 1600, in Chelmsford, Stratford upon Avon, and Salisbury in the 1620s, in Dorchester in the 1620s and 1630s, and in many other places. Terling and Dorchester (Underdown calls it the "most 'puritan' place in England" of the period) provide the most fully analyzed cases in point. There, early in the century, a ruling "godly group" affiliated with a Puritan minister was the primary agent of an impressively organized and thorough program of moral reform that included new measures of poor relief and regulation.[4]

---

3. John Preston, *The Breast-plate of Faith and Love* . . . , 5th ed. (London, 1634), 205–206; T[homas] H[ooker], *The Soules Exaltation* . . . (London, 1638), 113. A representative construal of calamity is William Whately, *Sinne No More, . . . vpon Occasion of a Most Terrible Fire* . . . (London, 1628).

4. Paul Slack, *From Reformation to Improvement: Public Welfare in Early Modern England* (Oxford, 1999), 47; *WWP,* III, 4. For examples of moral reform in towns, see *PP,* 159 ("godly group"), and see 158, 177–182; David Underdown, *Fire from Heaven: Life in an English Town in the Seventeenth Century* (New Haven, Conn., 1994), ix, and see 5. In Terling, the Puritan clergy were Thomas Rust (1604–1631) and Thomas Weld (1625–1631); in Dorchester, John White (1605–1648). In a few places godly authorities devised imaginative fund-raising techniques, establishing municipal brewhouses or mills and funneling

Further, with the same strong suggestion of a link between the experience of conflict and a rigid moral attitude, they and their lay associates sustained also the semisectarian tendencies that presbyterians had pioneered: the sub-cultural gathering of a small and showily righteous elite mobilized against iniquity in themselves and their society, the belief that it is "impossible to have true peace with God and not wars with men . . . nay almost . . . with all . . . neighbours," the challenge to traditional values of community and good fel-lowship and the popular rites that periodically reaffirmed them, the "con-stantly maintained witness of social and cultural distinctiveness practised against neighbors," and the resulting struggles in towns and parishes in which "the godly were defining their own identity through contentions with the ungodly."[5]

Within this context, the premise of saintly self-image was a society divided by opposite ideals of the good: the wanton and the strict. Faced with this choice, the godly had chosen the costlier way. They aimed to abstain from popular ease and fun, take up the Lord's commands and the new ascetic drills, perform them with exquisite care, and rebuke those who resisted. Thereby they gained status in an exclusive and meritorious elite. But that was not all. Echoing dynamics of dissent in countless religious movements past and pres-ent, including the Dutch and French Reformed churches in their times of trouble under Catholic persecution, they exploited as well the resistance that their pose and demand evoked. As in presbyterian days, Puritan sermons and tracts after 1590 teemed with reports of verbal and sometimes physical abuse aimed at the godly, and from this enmity the holy crew made capital. Scorn and friction were welcome signs, as John Winthrop put it, that they were on the difficult path to heaven. With Henry Sherfield, magistrate of Salisbury, some positively "rejoic[ed] in the divisions" caused by their efforts to reform manners. Others glamorized abuse itself, adopting "Puritan," "precisian," and

---

the profits into the welfare system; see Peter Clark and Paul Slack, *English Towns in Transition, 1500–1700* (London, 1976), 123; Underdown, *Fire from Heaven*, 113–115. For Greenham's charity toward the poor, see John H. Primus, *Richard Greenham: Portrait of an Elizabethan Pastor* (Macon, Ga., 1998), 49–50.

5. Paul Slack, "The Public Conscience of Henry Sherfield," in John Morrill, Paul Slack, and Daniel Woolf, eds., *Public Duty and Private Conscience in Seventeenth-Century England: Essays Presented to G. E. Aylmer* (Oxford, 1993), 151; Patrick Collinson, "The Cohabitation of the Faithful with the Unfaithful," in Ole Peter Grell, Jonathan I. Israel, and Nicholas Tyacke, eds., *From Persecution to Toleration: The Glorious Revolution and Religion in England* (Oxford, 1991), 62; Slack, *From Reformation to Improvement*, 45.

other epithets aimed at them as illustrious titles. They made the reproof of transparent goodness honor it only more.[6]

Much of the pattern was drawn by Robert Bolton, a famous rector at Broughton, Northamptonshire (the parish church of the Saye and Sele family), from 1610 to his death in 1631. No doubt with an eye to his own experiences, he described an ideal parish in which a "Puritane-Preacher" suddenly appeared, attacked "reigning corruptions" from the pulpit, and summoned the few elect by means of a personal conversion into the "precise *way*." So were men and women of busy secular calling recruited into a semiseparate *"Sect"* of converted professors. Bonded by fasting, psalm singing, meditation, and other distinctive rituals, they were but loosely held by traditional values of neighborliness and social harmony. They relished ascetic arts deeply averse to the profanity, drunkenness, and loose sexuality commonly associated with alehouses and to a medley of popular amusements and festivities. They rebuked those who practiced them and were rebuked in turn as "too precise." Bolton, who saw numberless evils "sheltered under the wings of good fellowship" and explicitly cast the type of the *"Saint"* as a dead opposite to the *"goodfellow,"* thus saw sectarian righteousness and the ensuing discord with the unregenerate as the normal—indeed, desirable—condition of a parish blessed with such contrary folk. Nothing defined them better or ennobled them more than their "strong . . . counter-motion to the courses of the world" or their co-option of "Precisian" and other insults as "honourable badges." And, if in some respects the Broughton minister's portrait of local Puritanism is a promotional idealization, that merely increases its value as a record of the impulses to reorder

6. *WP,* I, 196; Slack, *From Reformation to Improvement,* 45. For "Mockings and Reproches" as badges of honor, see Robert Cawdray, *A Treasurie or Store-house of Similes* (London, 1600), 46, 582; Nehemiah Wallington, "A Record of Gods Mercies, or A Thankfull Remembrance," 184–185, MS 204, Guildhall Library, London, copy in the Genealogical Society of Utah, Salt Lake City, and see 49, 189. For scholarly comment on "badges of honor," see Marjorie Keniston McIntosh, *Controlling Misbehavior in England, 1370–1600* (Cambridge, 1998), 207; Peter Lake, "'A Charitable Christian Hatred': The Godly and Their Enemies in the 1630s," in Christopher Durston and Jacqueline Eales, eds., *The Culture of English Puritanism, 1560–1700* (New York, 1996), 154.

Psychological benefits of opposition in this context are discussed in Stephen Foster, *The Long Argument: English Puritanism and the Shaping of New England Culture, 1570–1700* (Chapel Hill, N.C., 1991), 12; Lake, "The Godly and Their Enemies," 156–165; Collinson, "The Cohabitation of the Faithful with the Unfaithful," in Grell, Israel, and Tyacke, eds., *From Persecution to Toleration,* 56; Slack, *From Reformation to Improvement,* 44.

behavior and to draw identity from aversion and antithesis that underlay the pietist turn.[7]

Puritan Practical Divinity: A Plan for Disciplinary Reformation

As even a hasty sampling of pietist sermons, tracts, and diaries will show, the reverent affection suggested today by the terms "devotion" and "piety" was ingredient to the movement, but seldom was it allowed to become an end in itself. Giving proof that the desire for purer religion and morality was not quelled by the defeats of the 1580s, the new breed of pietist pastor-theologians and their lay charges brought a brisk devotional élan to bear upon concrete objectives of reform. And, as they tied piety to self-management, they became extraordinarily creative. Unaware that twentieth-century historians would view religious thought in early modern England as an echo of ideas framed in Geneva, Zurich, Heidelberg, and other Continental centers, they made original and immensely influential contributions to the theology of their era. It is true that Continental writers like Girolamo Zanchi or Johannes Alsted were the Reformed masters of systematic and scholastic construction, but the science of praxis was the English métier. A corps of Elizabethan and early Stuart writers, disproportionally but not exclusively Puritan, were the principal framers of the practical theology, which by the mid-seventeenth century was to become a standard rubric of international Reformed divinity. "How have the English writers shone[!]," marveled Gisbertus Voetius, taking stock in the mid-1640s of developments in practical theology to that point. Rating William Perkins "the Homer of practical theologians," this premier spokesman of the "precisianist" movement in the Protestant Netherlands freely acknowledged English primacy in the field, noting how Dutch as well as German,

7. Ideal parish: *CAC*, 354–355. "*Sect*": *CAC*, 330. "Too precise," "*Saint*," "*goodfellow*": *CAC*, 44–45. "Wings of good-fellowship": *GD*, 200. "Counter-motion": *GD*, 29. "Honourable badges": *CAC*, 334. "Good-fellowship" was Bolton's favored epithet for the traditional way of life "drown'd in carnall loosenesse . . . and riotous excesse" and centered upon "Ale-houses, Tavernes, Brothel-houses, Play-houses, Conventicles of good-fellowship, sinfull and unseasonable sports," and the like (*GD*, 170, and see 5, 200, and *CAC*, 96, 264, 303, 416, 433). Joseph Bentham, in a treatise that Bolton read and approved before publication, also drew a portrait of the saints' subculture of piety and discipline in stark contrast to the lax and anti-Puritan society of "goodfellowes." *The Societie of the Saints* (London, 1630?), 278, and see "To the Reader," unpag.

Swiss, and other theological students on the Continent "eagerly learn English and obtain [English] practical books for themselves."[8]

Those practical books eschewed abstraction and fashioned doctrine directly to shape the belief and life of theological students, clergy, and godly laity. Accordingly, they focused upon law, conversion, faith, repentance, assurance, and other directly experiential doctrines and developed a body of practical instruction in such matters as casuistry, family values, fast days, and daily spiritual exercises. Unquestionably, Puritan practical theology stood on a bedrock of grace and faith alone, but it overlapped extensively with Catholic teaching, and its ruling emphasis was on behavior. It brought to fruition the humanistically leavened program laid out by Peter Ramus and other second-generation Reformed thinkers, incorporated in the 1580s into Dudley Fenner's first English Puritan theological system, and taken up by Greenham, Perkins, and other early members of the brotherhood: these figures now understood the enterprise of theology comprehensively as "a science aimed at *living* rightly and well." In this sense, theology now was a fresh plan for moral reformation. If classes and synods could not be formed to bind the citizenry, very well; there was another means: merge a powerfully affecting piety with a pragmatic "science of living well" in taut discipline and so tame human behavior at its source. The plan was simple enough in outline, but hugely complicating in the effect.[9]

8. Gisbertus Voetius, *De theologia practica*, in *Selectarum disputationum theologicarum* . . . (Utrecht, 1648–1669), III, 4, 11, and *De simplicitate et hypocrisi*, II, 483. Voetius put Thomas Hooker "above all others" in the treatment of penitential "desperation," admired Daniel Dyke as the "profundissimus scrutator" of hypocrisy, and acknowledged the contributions of Thomas Taylor, William Whately, Nicholas Byfield, Samuel Ward, Paul Baynes, John Downame, John Preston, and other ranking members of the Puritan spiritual brotherhood (*De praxi fidei*, II, 504; *De simplicitate et hypocrisi*, II, 489). Supported largely by godly clergy, John Dury strove in the 1630s to produce a compend of the "Practical Divinities which were more distinctly . . . delivered in these Churches of Great Brittaine, than in all the rest of the Christian world besides." Tom Webster, *Godly Clergy in Early Stuart England: The Caroline Puritan Movement, c. 1620–1643* (Cambridge, 1997), 258.

9. Dudley Fenner, *Sacra theologia, sive, veritas quae est secundum pietatem* (Geneva, 1589), bk. I, chap. 1, 1, emphasis and translation mine; Robert Bolton, *The Carnall Professor* . . . (London, 1634), 106 (echoing Perkins, *BWWP*, 177). Peter Ramus's formulation is in *Commentariourum de religione christiana, libri quatuor* (Frankfurt, 1576), bk. 1, 2: "Theologia est doctrina bene vivendi." For the background of Humanist concern to tie devotion to "activity in the world," see William J. Bouwsma, "The Spirituality of Renaissance Humanism," in Jill Raitt, ed., *Christian Spirituality*, II, *High Middle Ages and Reformation* (New York, 1988), 236–251. The disciplinary intent of Puritan spiritual exercises is empha-

Persuaded by Reformed theology's derisive estimate of the natural self, perhaps responsive as well to that "think[ing] of thy selfe as basely, as thou canst possibly" that the Catholic examen of self aimed to elicit, Puritan practical theologians built upon hard realism about human nature. One and all assumed that humanity's natural faculties and impulses are violently repugnant to the spirit of Christianity and its ethical demands. What is the heart but a "mill, ever grinding" out sinful desires and aims? Within the nonelect, checked only by a veneer of civil virtue and fear of punishment, the "body of sinne" simply reigns and damns. But it retains great potency too in the regenerate, more than Romish doctrine allows and certainly more than could be managed through the nominal care of souls provided by the official church; for in the saints "the scum thereof is almost continually boyling and wallopping . . . , foming out . . . filthy froth and stinking sauor into our minds." And as they strove to define this melee of impulse, the clergy drew upon older Platonic motifs, upon the image of self "caried of his lusts as the cart drawne by [a] wild horse," upon its vision of the mind filled with "swarming . . . vaine thoughts" and "impertinent wanderings," and upon its view of the senses as "windows to behold vanities" and "flood-gates, to let in the streames of iniquity." So profuse, in fact, are these themes and images in pietist rhetoric, and so continuous with the traditional *contemptus mundi*, that they constitute a selective Christian Platonism in early Stuart England. Focused by its radical view of human nature, it was quite distinct from the familiar Cambridge Platonism that flourished in the middle third of the seventeenth century.[10]

If a rampant libido surged within, dominant in the unregenerate personality but subversive too of the saints' commitment to a scripturally ruled life, it was apparent that the practice of virtue must be pursued "contrarie to our nature." The need to live *contrary to our nature:* here too was a family resemblance to Catholic instruction, to Robert Southwell's advice to the Catholic English that "man's nature being so corrupted that without continual violence and force it cannot attain to virtue or leave vice," or to Lorenzo Scupoli's warning in *The Spiritual Conflict* (1598) that "thou muyst use force with thy selfe" to tame wayward impulse and will. When Perkins called his large audience to "learne to force our natures" to a manner of life "to which our naturall disposition is as contrarie as fire to water," or when Robert Bolton (an

sized in *WW*, 7, 25, 35–37, 41, 67, 165.

10. L[uis] de Granada, *Of Prayer, and Meditation* . . . , trans. Richard Hopkins (Paris, 1582), 140; *WRG*, 143, 329. Platonic motifs: *ST*, 447; Paul Bayne[s], *Briefe Directions unto a Godly Life* . . . (London, 1637), 124; *GD*, 171; *POP*, 66.

admirer of Greenham and ever the exponent of *"precise walking"*) urged his charges to be "extraordinarily and exactly vigilant . . . over thy [unruly] heart," they spoke for a movement that had directed a substantially larger fraction of the resources of religion to order fractious human nature. Never before, never in Cranmer or Tyndale, Bucer or Calvin, had the emphasis fallen so hard and so programmatically upon the need for effort and struggle, upon the importance of containment and regulation. Never before had it seemed so needful to *"hold in* our lusts and imaginations as it were with bid and bridle," to have impulses *"bridled, held backe, and subdued,"* to *"rule and beare sway* even as Kings over our owne thoughts, wils, affections, over-mastering them." Never before, never in Zurich, Geneva, Heidelberg, or Scotland, had so ambitious a campaign been mounted to hammer and resculpt the natural self. That campaign began with the preparatory work of "humiliation" (discussed in the next chapter; here we consider the critical role of conversion).[11]

The centrality of conversion in Puritanism is a well-worn theme, but those who, with Greenham, stood upon "the doctrine of newe birth" had no exclusive claim to it. The experience of a changed life as embodied in Luis de Granada's *Conversion of a Sinner* (and which Robert Parsons, like any Reformed divine, described synonymously as "first conversion," "vocation," and "calling") was a favorite topic in tracts of the Counter Reformation circulating in England.[12] On the Protestant side, Reformed systematicians abroad like

11. Contrary to nature: *WRG*, 69; Robert Southwell, *Two Letters and Short Rules of a Good Life*, ed. Nancy Pollard Brown (Charlottesville, Va., 1973), 39; [Lorenzo Scupoli], *The Spiritual Conflict* ([London], 1598), sig. A8; *WWP*, I, 472; *CAC*, sig. 8; *GD*, 89. See also *WRS*, VI, 300: "We must offer violence to ourselves, to our own reason, to our own wills and affections." Containment and regulation: Bayne[s], *Briefe Directions*, 375; *WWT*, 138; *WWP*, I, 170. All emphases mine. Bolton's interest in Greenham: *PDRG*, 4 and n. 9. *CAC*, 140, 209–210, 227.

12. Greenham: *WRG*, 421. Granada and Parsons: [Robert Parsons], *The First Booke of the Christian Exercise, Appertayning to Resolution . . .* ([Rouen], 1582), 384, 399–400. See also [G]aspar Loarte, *The Exercise of a Christian Life* (n.p., [1597]), 2–4, 8, 255. As explicated by Parsons, or in Luis de Granada's *Conversion of a Sinner*, conversion embodied the traditional ideal of a deliberate break with the world to live a radically transformed life of prayer, spiritual warfare, and increasing likeness to God in a professional religious order. Above all it meant commitment to a struggle against evil within one's self and, in the case of the noncloistered orders, in the world. Conversion, accordingly, meant a "revolt from sinne." See [Luis de Granada], *A Breefe Treatise Exhorting Sinners to Repentance, Commonly Called, The Conversion of a Sinner* (n.p., 1580?), 57. For conversion as moral regeneration, see also Loarte, *Exercise of a Christian Life*, 255; [Granada], *Conversion of a Sinner*, 1,

Zacharias Ursinus (1534–1583) had made conversion a standard locus of theological discussion, and Elizabethan evangelicals like George Gifford and John Knewstub also had highlighted "the newe byrth in Christ Jesus." Yet Puritan practical divinity embodied the first concentrated attempt in Protestant England to make the "great and saving work of Conversion" a normative experience separating true from hypocritical Christianity. It so bisected the Christian's personal story that always afterward the saint would recall the "time . . . when [I was] thus and thus led," but that "when it pleased God," then conversion commenced, "and from that day to this it has been thus and so with me."[13]

Though the transit from sin to salvation was a complex event not reducible to ascetic remodeling and though Puritans differed in some details of interpretation, yet in pietist as in Reformed and Counter Reformation thought conversion meant a disciplinary transfiguration of the self. That this insistence upon change, this quest for "a heart which by regeneration is changed, . . . and so indued with another kinde of nature . . . whereby it hateth all sinne," was the predominant concern is apparent in a widespread, outright equation of the biblical idea of new birth with ethical regeneration: as when Arthur Dent, the minister at South Shoebury, Essex, assured readers of his best-selling *Plaine Mans Path-way to Heaven* (1601) that "regeneration and new birth . . . is a renuing and repairing of the corrupted . . . estate of our soules"; or when Thomas Hooker, in a sermon probably delivered in the late 1620s, observed matter-of-factly that the "change of mind" restoring "the conformity . . . betwixt Gods law, and the faculties of the reasonable creature" is "otherwise called regeneration, or new birth." This too, envisioned as a gradual increase of

---

57–63; *CDGM,* 615–617, 627–628; [Scupoli], *Spiritual Conflict,* sig. B7. Gifford and Knewstub: the quote is in George G[i]ff[o]rd, *A Treatise of True Fortitude* (London, 1594), sig. B7 (and see sigs. A6, B, and *LJK,* 66–68, 262.

13. Zacharias Ursinus, *The Commentary of Dr. Zacharias Ursinus, on the Heidelberg Catechism* (1562), trans. G. W. Williard (Columbus, Ohio, 1852), 467–476). Normative experience: preface by Thomas Goodwin and Philip Nye, in *AR, 1–8,* sig. B; *CF,* 99–100. In *CAC,* 249, Bolton spoke of "the incomparably greatest work, that ever the soule of Man [is] acquainted with in this life, I meane the *new-birth.*" "Thy change must be so great," said Preston, "that thou mayst say, *Ego non sum ego,* I am not my selfe, I am quite another man." *A Liveles Life; or, Mans Spirituall Death in Sinne* . . . (London, 1633), 22.

John S. Coolidge finds that "the analysis of conversion" occupied Puritan writers "very little in the early period, . . . but first becomes a prominent topic . . . in the work of Richard Rogers, Arthur Hildersam, William Perkins, Richard Sibbes," and other pietists. *The Pauline Renaissance in England: Puritanism and the Bible* (Oxford, 1970), 147.

likeness to God, was the meaning inscribed in William Whately's *New Birth* in 1618.[14]

As Dent, Hooker, and Whately clearly supposed, conversion is, not a single event completed in one moment, but a lifelong process. It might begin with a dramatic and sudden experience of "first conversion." Yet that is "but the beginning of all the worke of Christianitie," for conversion (or "regeneration") proper is never effected in an instant of time. That was impossible, since the "old man" remained potent and lethal during the earthly trek. The language of change applied only to the "new man," to the emergence of a new sense and power for good that would center but never wholly control the converted personality. Henceforth, in every hour of their conscious existence, even in wakeful moments during the night (if Greenham, who suffered from insomnia, had his way), converts must struggle against their contrary self. Their engagement and advance therein was their conversion, and by far the largest part of pietist instruction was devoted to inspire and guide it.[15]

Pietist directors in need of strategies for the conduct of spiritual warfare also made the most of the inherited conception of the Bible as a body of law. As in Cranmer's preface to the Great Bible of 1540, as in the Geneva Bible annotations, and as ever in Puritan discussion, sacred writ was not merely a message of mercy but a kind of Torah, a great compend of rules and archetypes by which human actions were to be measured and mended; but now, in conjunction with the widely promulgated Catholic emphasis upon methodical religious practice, arose an extraordinary passion to extract, classify, and apply the legion of scriptural rules to the lives of men and women. That "a Christian must have his rules alwayes before him" became an axiom of pietist teaching in the early Stuart years, and the very scrutiny and control of self by lists of rules emerged as a Puritan spiritual exercise, as did the devotional reading of tracts and treatises that promoted the exercises. Handbooks of spiritual direction usually included summaries of the rules for various occasions. Henry Scud-

---

14. *MSD*, 131; Arthur Dent, *The Plaine Mans Path-way to Heaven* . . . (London, 1603), 12; T[homas] H[ooker], *The Christians Two Chiefe Lessons* . . . (London, 1640), 263–264; William Whately, *The New Birth; or, A Treatise of Regeneration* . . . (London, 1618), 4, 13–14, and for likeness, see 10–11, 14. In *CW*, 593, Downame also explained that sanctification now routinely was "called regeneration [or] the new birth," as did Whately, *New Birth*, 13.

15. *ST*, 90; *WRG*, 2, 16, 27. For first conversion, see also *WRS*, I, 49; *WTS*, II, 80, 177; *EGJ*, 292. Conversion in a Puritan context is clarified in Baird Tipson, "The Routinized Piety of Thomas Shepard's Diary," *Early American Literature*, XIII (1978), 70–72; and Charles Lloyd Cohen, *God's Caress: The Psychology of Puritan Religious Experience* (New York, 1986), 4–5, 99–100.

der's *Christians Daily Walke* (1627) urged saints to compile and "carry in your head a *Catalogue* or *Table* of the principall duties" entailed by each of the Ten Commandments, while Richard Bernard's *Weekes Work; And a Work for Every Weeke* (1616) presented ten "Generall rules for the whole course of life." Rogers's *Seven Treatises* supplied separate sets of rules for preparation for the Lord's Supper, meditation, keeping a daily devotional calendar, and the like, and Thomas Taylor's *Circumspect Walking* (1619) provided "Special rules for [the use of] meate and drinke," "Rules for the right ordering of our selves in our sports," "Rules . . . concerning our apparell," and others.[16]

When, in 1626, Robert Bolton urged Christians to "acquire and acquaint themselves with Rules of holy life," that is, with books outlining the biblical rules, he had works like the *Seven Treatises* in mind, including almost certainly several of the separate treatises included by Nicholas Byfield (1579–1622) in *The Marrow of the Oracles of God* (1619). As we will note below, *The Marrow* is the fullest monument both to the pietist interest in behavioral evidences of a redeemed estate and to the compilation of "catalogues" of sin, but it was also the bluntest regulatory statement of its time. Approaching at times a cook-book mentality, the author laid down a myriad of rules in formidably exact sets: "When thou hast thus prepared thy selfe by these three resolutions, then . . . do these foure things following."[17] One treatise explained "what rules hee must observe, that would be delivered from his sinne," and another presented a full chapter of categorized "rules of directions" for "how faith may be

16. *MO*, 450; *CDW*, 33; Ric[hard] Bernard, *A Weekes Work; And a Work for Every Weeke* . . . (London, [1616]), 13–31; *ST*, 218–219, 244–245, 316–331; *CWSR*, 174, 186, 206. See also Thomas Goodwin's 159 pages of "directions" for the "deeply troubled" in conscience and George Webbe's rules governing devotions and secular calling: Goodwin, *A Childe of Light Walking in Darknes* . . . (London, 1636); [Webbe], "A Short Direction for the Daily Exercise of a Christian . . . ," in *A Garden of Spirituall Flowers, Planted by Ri[chard] Ro[gers, et al.] . . . [The First] Part*, enl. ed. (London, 1625), sigs. G–G2, G8–G9. This evidence documents the claim that Puritan pietism embodied a concept of life "regulated in its details by innumerable precepts." F. Ernest Stoeffler, *The Rise of Evangelical Pietism* (Leiden, 1965), 60–61.

17. *GD*, 27; *MO*, 17. In the contemporary Protestant Netherlands, Willem Teellinck's "innumerable rules on how to live in nearly every area and detail of life" were part of his effort "to infiltrate the Dutch scene with English-style, pietistic Puritanism" (Joel R. Beeke, *Assurance of Faith: Calvin, English Puritanism, and the Dutch Second Reformation* [New York, 1991], 119–120). Teellinck had studied in William Whateley's seminary at Banbury in 1604 and was a close friend of Thomas Gataker. Webster, *Godly Clergy*, 27; Francis J. Bremer, *Congregational Communion: Clerical Friendship in the Anglo-American Puritan Community* (Boston, 1994), 37.

gotten." Resembling a Jewish or Muslim code of law, the treatise therein entitled *The Rules of a Holy Life* presented nearly two hundred pages of precepts covering the major phases and facets of Christian endeavor. A brief sampler might include twenty-eight rules (with nine ancillary precepts under rule two) to guide preparation to a holy course of life, seven to order prayer, four for singing Psalms, four to guide conduct in company, fourteen for the use of speech, and seven to avoid evils in one's secular calling.[18]

To the anticipated objection that he sought to "burthen the lives of Christians with a multitude of unnecessary Precepts," Byfield had an answer. He replied that there are, after all, a multitude of rules in the Bible; and for those who thought it impossible to remember so many, he advised an installment plan in which a manageable few were learned and practiced at a time. The end effect, in a remarkable instance of Puritan zeal for the sacred book, was a virtual encasement of life in its rules.[19]

We cannot know how many of the godly undertook such a regimen in whole or part, but Elizabeth Gouge prepared "many divine directions for Devotions" sometime before her death in 1626. And it cannot be pure coincidence that a Puritan artisan and member of the godly community in early Stuart London—the one such figure for whom substantial evidence of spiritual praxis survives—gathered multiple lists of rules concerning family duties, sleeping in church, fast days, prayer, conduct in times of affliction and the like: then enforced them upon himself with a system of fines to be paid into his personal poor box and about 1640 wrote a large "paper book" devoted in part to "directions how to hear [sermons] and pray well and to live an holy life." However imperfectly it might have been realized by the rank and file, Byfield's regime of rules was a strikingly full expression of the precisianist ideal.[20]

As with all the spiritual exercises, however, the devotion to rules was set within larger ordering devices that were at once metaphors and master plans for human conduct. One such device, a theological and devotional com-

---

18. "Rules": *MO*, 14, 230. Holy course: *MO*, 449–469. Prayer: *MO*, 547–550. Psalms: *MO*, 554–555. Conduct: *MO*, 566–570. Speech: *MO*, 574–582. Secular calling: *MO*, 631–636.

19. *MO*, 444–445.

20. Nicolas Guy, *Pieties Pillar; or, A Sermon Preached at the Funerall of Mistresse Elizabeth Gouge* (London, 1626), 48; Nehemiah Wallington, "A Treatice Containing an Extract of Severall passages in my Life," 13–14, 16–17, 104–105, 136–137, V.a. 436, Folger Shakespeare Library, Washington, D.C. (microfilm, University of Iowa Library); Wallington, "A Record of Gods Mercies," 315; *WW*, 202. Seaver comments on the pattern in *WW*, 4. The artisan's book of 1640 is not extant.

monplace for centuries, was the image of life as journey. As in the writing of Luis de Granada or Diègo de Estella, the vision of a passage through transient earthly experience toward the celestial afterworld was a fundamental of the Puritan pietist worldview, but within that context attention fell less upon Platonic notions of the world's transience (although they too were prominent) and more upon the image of a "course" or "walke" that was both disciplinary and habitual. As in Scudder's *Daily Walke* or Taylor's *Circumspect Walking*, the image directed attention to behavior, since it was the "morall actions of mans life," which are "aptly resembled by the Metaphor of Walking"; and, self-evidently within a Puritan context, to *"walke with God"* meant "to frame your life according to the . . . word."[21] But pietist delineation of the Christian walk highlighted also its regular, habitual, "settled," "even and equall" character, its capacity to prevent the traveler from "br[eaking] out of [the] constant course" and to keep him or her "continuing in a constant course from the time of our conversion to the end of our liues." Embracing all the exercises and rules, this image of a life tightly ruled through all its seasons encapsulated much of the pietist agenda.[22]

Holding one's self in course was a lifelong work that enlisted the full repertoire of pietist techniques, but at its heart was a daily and weekly schedule. This too was a commonplace of the centuries, central to the Benedictine rule and to the routine of divine offices required alike of regular and secular clergy; as attested by the Jesuit martyr Robert Southwell's *Short Rules of a Good Life* (circa 1585), regular daily exercises of prayer, meditation, and self-examination were a staple of the Catholic devotional awakening.[23] Protestant

21. *CDW*, 4 (and see 7); and see *CWSR*, 3, and John Preston, *The New Covenant; or, The Saints Portion* . . . , 9th ed. (London, 1639), 185–211. For Richard Rogers, "our whole . . . course . . . ought to bee squared out after the heavenly patterne of the word of God" (*ST*, 312). *PPPDD*, 54, argues that pilgrimage was the "principal metaphor" of Puritan spirituality.

22. Bayne[s], *Briefe Directions*, 136; *ST*, 234, 336; *CW*, 242. Motifs of rule and containment dominate the personal primer in "daily directions" prepared by John Rogers of Dedham (d. 1636). Rogers strongly emphasized "the use of the 'daily direction,' and following strictly the rules thereof." *MCA*, I, 423–427 (quote at 425).

23. Southwell devised a "certain order in spending my time, allotting to every hour in the day some certain thing to be done in the same, . . . or at the least to have some times in the morning, evening, and afternoon certainly devoted to some good exercise" (*Short Rules*, ed. Brown, 38). See also Loarte, *Exercise of a Christian Life*, 15–20; Granada, *Prayer, and Meditation*, trans. Hopkins, 6, 34–276. For the the persistence of daily devotional schedules in lay recusant spirituality in the sixteenth and seventeenth centuries, see W. A.

teaching always had commended the use of prayers at regular hours, normally "when we arise in the morning, before we begin daily work, when we sit down to a meal, when . . . we have eaten, [and] when we are getting ready to retire"; and morning, evening, and mealtime prayers were standard elements of the English Primer. But it was not until the end of Elizabeth's reign, and specifically in reaction to the expanding popularity of Catholic spiritual literature, that the pietist brotherhood laid out a carefully Protestantized "daily direction," which explained—often in great detail—"how to begin the day, how to proceed in the severall actions of the same, and how to end it." Adumbrated in the work of Greenham and Perkins, the ideal was set forth fully in the fourth of Rogers's *Seven Treatises* and recapitulated with variations in Bernard's *Weekes Work* (1616), Baynes's *Briefe Directions unto a Godly Life* (1618), Scudder's *Daily Walke* (1627), Downame's *Guide to Godlynesse* (1622), and many similar works. About 1619, Byfield matter-of-factly listed the discipline of a daily schedule as a distinguishing mark of the Puritan saint.[24]

Marking the transition from pietist beginnings under Greenham and Perkins to the period of greatest efflorescence in the Stuart years, such works digested affectionate, practical divinity into a complete postpresbyterian plan for disciplinary reformation. Not to be confused with Catholic programs of daily exercise devised and therefore misbegotten by men, the "daily direction" was advertised in good Puritan fashion as "a gathering together of . . . rules out of Gods word, by which we may be enabled every day to live according to the will of God." It set those rules within a devotional framework, and, indeed, many were directives for devotional practice. The result was a calendar and guide to conduct both religious and secular from first arising to bedtime— documented in part in the diary of Lady Margaret Hoby (an admirer of the works of Greenham and Nicholas Bownde, friend of Perkins, patron of Byfield, and possibly "the first English woman to have kept a spiritual diary") at the turn of the century, in the commonplace book of Lady Brilliana Harley about two decades later, in William Hinde's biography of John Bruen (1560– 1625, an untitled gentleman and friend of Byfield, partial to the works of

Pantin, "Instructions for a Devout and Literate Layman," in J. J. G. Alexander and M. T. Gibson, eds., *Medieval Learning and Literature: Essays Presented to Richard William Hunt* (Oxford, 1976), 415–416.

24. John Calvin, *Institutes of the Christian Religion*, ed. John T. McNeill (Philadelphia, 1960), II, bk. 3, chap. 20, sect. 50, 917–918; *ST,* 303; *MO,* 112. *ST* was published in 1603, six years before Saint Francis de Sales's *Introduction to the Devout Life,* which is said to have "introduced" the "idea of . . . a manual for men and women in the world rather than in the cloister." *PPPDD,* 30.

Greenham and Richard Rogers), in several unpublished writings of the London artisan Nehemiah Wallington (1598–1658, well versed in the work of Greenham, Perkins, Scudder, Bolton, William Gouge, and others), and in Sir William Waller's *Divine Meditations . . . with a Dayly Directory* of uncertain date.[25]

Presuming regular attendance at parish services and in particular a devoted attention to sermons and eucharists, the daily direction defined a partially distinct and remarkably full private and family paraliturgy. Often delving into fine detail, it established a routine of morning, evening, mealtime, and intermittent prayers, of meditations, self-inspections, and other drills, and of a daily gathering of the family under the male head for worship. Model prayers and suggested topics for meditation and self-examination commonly were included. In some cases the individual transit through this regimen was prescribed in such detail as to resemble the daily observance for males in orthodox Judaism. The regimen included, too, instructions for saintly behavior in everyday affairs, in one's secular calling, in company and when alone, in recreation, and in the use of worldly goods. Predictably, the day's final duty was a cycle of prayer and meditation and a complete and penitential examen of self in context of the day's events. So to order the life of English men and women, to inscribe into their day a formal schedule of spiritual exercises that were (as the following chapters will make even clearer) of a peculiarly ascetic sort, this was the fullest way to move in course, to contain the Old Man and, into the bargain, to avoid Deuteronomic punishment.[26]

---

25. *ST,* 314 ("God," Rogers explained, "hath . . . appointed in his word how the whole day should be passed" [*ST,* 304]); Claire Cross, "The Religious Life of Women in Sixteenth-century Yorkshire," in *Studies in Church History,* XXVII, *Women in the Church,* ed. W. J. Sheils and Diana Wood (Oxford, 1990), 322. William Hinde, *A Faithfull Remonstrance of . . . John Bruen . . .* (London, 1641), probably was written shortly after Bruen's death in 1625. For the connections of Hoby and Bruen to Byfield, see *PG,* 38; Hinde, *Faithfull Remonstrance,* 135. For Hoby's links to Greenham, Bownde, and Perkins, see Dorothy M. Meads, ed., *Diary of Lady Margaret Hoby, 1599–1605* (Boston, 1930), 62, 71, 94, 153. Bruen admired "M. *Greenhams* workes, [and] M. Rogers his Seven Treatises" (Hinde, *Faithfull Remonstrance,* 142). Seaver notes Wallington's interest in Greenham and other pietist writers in *WW,* 6, 11, 79, 98, 102, 134, 211, 233.

26. Daily schedules are outlined, for example, in Bernard, *A Weekes Work,* 38–150, and [Webbe], "A Short Direction," in *A Garden of Spirituall Flowers,* sigs. F7–H8. Although scanty on details, Lady Margaret Hoby's diary records an early lay attempt to pattern the day's activities around a schedule of "sperituall exercises," including attendance at sermons, singing psalms, prayer, meditation, reading the Bible and books by Greenham, Perkins,

Conversion, rules, the ordered course, the daily rule—with this initial sampling of ideas and techniques we can begin to assess the pietist turn. Dedicated as they were to the recovery of biblical laws and ways, Greenham, Perkins, Rogers, and their colleagues did not esteem that impulse to transcend the known that defines the term "creativity" in a modern lexicon, yet in a period of exceptional change and economic crisis they responded flexibly to human need. Their answer to uncertainties about identity and right behavior that arose in that context was that of the older presbyterians: a purified, precise life that fed upon contrast with the slack and unruled. But a sharper accent upon conversion, a more avid summons to effort and concentration, a fuller enlistment of supportive emotions, and a greatly expanded appreciation of the power of ritual and technique: the pietist turn now had made available these and other improved means to enable such a life. To bring forth a new and more purposive self, to equip it both with better resources of spiritual direction and with an abundance of rules and methods to manage itself and maintain its course in the world, to set it upon a "well ordered and setled course" defined by a daily schedule (maintaining all the while a deep, constructive concern for the larger society and the national church)—what apter way could have been devised to control anxiety and restore a sense of mastery and direction in shifting times?[27]

The turn to piety also offered a means, aided by selective annexation of the old church's devotional traditions, to neutralize the attractions of the Counter Reformation, to strengthen Protestant resources, and to fulfill aspirations to make theology practical. Within a framework of conformity or semiconfor-

---

and other Puritan clergy, and a regular "Course of [self-]examination" (Meads, ed., *Diary of Lady Margaret Hoby*, 70, 83). For Lady Harley, see Jacqueline Eales, *Puritans and Roundheads: The Harleys of Brampton Bryan and the Outbreak of the English Civil War* (Cambridge, 1990), 51. Wallington's methodical spirituality is described in *WW*. Sir William Waller outlined rites for "awaking in a dark Night," "rising out of Bed, and putting on my Cloaths," and other daily events and exigencies and followed a detailed daily schedule for the "practice of piety" (*Divine Meditations upon Several Occasions: With a Dayly Directory* [London, 1680], 1, 5, 177). Lady Anne Waller, William Waller's second wife, also was *"frequent and constant in her private Devotions,* both in praying, reading and meditating at set hours" (Edm[und] Calamy, *The Happinesse of Those Who Sleep in Jesus, . . . a Sermon Preached at the Funeral of . . . the Lady Anne Waller . . .* [London, 1662], 29). Extraordinarily detailed and methodical instructions for meditation appear in John Ball, *A Treatise of Divine Meditation* (London, 1660), composed before 1640. For a model of daily bedtime self-inspection and confession, see *ST,* 403. For bedtime self-analysis by Puritan laity, see Meads, ed., *Diary of Lady Margaret Hoby,* esp. 62–84; Waller, *Divine Meditations,* 206.

27. Bayne[s], *Briefe Directions,* 223.

mity, it supplied at once a supplement to the Book of Common Prayer and an implicit denial of its adequacy. It helped assure the continuing vitality of the Reformed and Puritan impulse in a time of adversity in England and Protestant reverses abroad. And at all points it articulated a potent will to discipline. It cohered with the ethically weighted meaning of "piety" in the Reformed tradition, with, say, Calvin's definition of *pietas* as a rendering of both reverential love and ethical service to the divine honor, with the disciplinarian aims of presbyterian Dudley Fenner's treatment (in the first Puritan systematic theology) of "veritas quae est secundum pietatem," and with the definition of "pietie" as "true worshipping of God, soundnesse of doctrine and a pure life" in Thomas Wilson's *Christian Dictionarie* (1612). At once it fortified the legal, covenantal, and other regimental themes of the Puritan movement and rebutted the papist canard that Protestants "in Englande . . . presume . . . to be saved by their onelie faithe, and so . . . doe liue dissolutelie."[28]

By any Catholic logic, this all was a glaring contradiction, but the earliest Protestant pietists had built from a complex synthesis the means to bond solifidian belief to a strict and exacting program of life. Historic ascetic ideals were reflected clearly in it, and a Bernard of Clairvaux (a Greenham favorite) or Luis de Granada would have recognized its portrayal of life as wayfaring and warfaring, its fixation upon sin and morality, its severely penitential ethos, and its many drills and exercises as a distorted but recognizable version of the traditional via purgativa. But, indeed, in intriguing ways its severity was designed for a postmonastic world. Together with many other faiths in the history of world religions, Catholic Christianity recognized a variety of ways to conceive and live the religious life, running a wide gamut from a relatively undemanding laic path of decent behavior and observance of the sacraments to the harshest monastic regimes. When this range of involvement and intensity, together with all monastic foundations and even the concept of alternative choices itself, was swept away by the Reformation, an essential foundation was laid for the Puritan pietist renaissance. It was an unquestioned tenet of Puritan belief that redemption imposed a master and single template with little allowance for individual variations. As, say, in Perkins's sympathetic treatment of "weak faith," some allowance was made for the feeble or irresolute, but no separate pathways were constructed. Pietist directors mapped a higher way, to

---

28. Calvin, *Institutes,* ed. McNeill, bk. 1, chap. 2, sect. 2, 41, bk. 2, chap. 8, sect. 2, 369, bk. 3, chap. 2, sect. 26, 572; Fenner, *Sacra Theologia* (quote from title); Thomas Wilson, *A Christian Dictionarie . . .* (London, 1612), 359 (misnumbered 356); Richard Hopkins, "Dedicatorie Epistle," in Granada, *Of Prayer, and Meditation,* sig. b (and see sig. avii–aviii).

be sure, but one only, and it favored the strong. Cloisters and hair shirts had disappeared, but many hard prescriptions remained.[29]

Likewise, the documents under study drew no separate guidelines for men and women. Most of the time, they pressed the practice of piety upon all without respect to sex. Possibly in practice men and women reacted differently to the regimen of exercises and spiritual direction (the available evidence is scanty). Yet the architects of piety were men deeply committed to male superiority, and a large body of teaching upon gender, marriage, and family was part of their project in practical theology. They made male "preheminence and government of the woman" axiomatic and so laid bare gendered facets of the ideals of law, rule, and obedience that were basic to their thought. As men, they could perform the familiar "gender reversal" of monastic spirituality by envisioning themselves as submissive brides married to Christ, but they also projected values of dominance and activism that their society defined as male, and they clearly intended female participants to grasp them in gender-specific ways. "Male" elements in the piety cohered with the active and sometimes aggressive authority that women's role in household and agricultural management required (in bargaining at market, for example), but its more "female" summons to obedience prepared them better to be governed by their male heads.[30]

How these gendered lessons had an impact on godly poor women, we do not know, but the practice of piety might have been pursued disproportionally by well-to-do wives and widows "whose circumstances permitted a daily round of worship, reading and meditation rarely achieved by the most conscientous man." Within that round, the attempt of figures like Margaret Hoby or Brilliana Harley to examine and order themselves served many purposes. It constructed a private realm away from household duties and enabled them to improve their skills in reading and reflection and to focus upon concerns of their own, but it also was training in female submission. Devotional reading of the brotherhood's published works was itself a prominent spiritual exercise, which both Hoby and Harley followed. Like all the rites, it was training in the self-control and acquiescence that, gendered by the clergy as well as by cultural convention, held women in place. Mrs. Jane Ratcliffe appears to have made

29. This line of thought was suggested by Christopher Haigh, *English Reformations: Religion, Politics, and Society under the Tudors* (Oxford, 1993), 285–288.

30. "Preheminence": *WRG*, 153. Gender reversal: Webster, *Godly Clergy*, 103, 126–128. Bargaining: Susan Dwyer Amussen, *An Ordered Society: Gender and Class in Early Modern England* (Oxford, 1988), 119.

the very duty of subjection to her husband a topic of meditation. Within the experience of such women, pietist praxis was expressly an instrument of gender discipline, although it was much else as well.[31]

No casual array of prayers and inner musings, then, the new piety was a science of grimly self-subduing "battaile." Echoing monastic tradition, it linked an ideal of self-abnegation to a "conviction that one must always be active, forever striving." It mandated a set of rituals and called for laborious work, strain, and persistence in their use. In a favorite metaphor, it made the way to heaven emphatically narrow and hard. Knowing that only a soul game to "sweate and take paines" could pursue and endure the elaborately plotted round, the clergy made the "hardnesse and difficultie of the worke" itself a primary virtue and commendation of the scheme. Let all the defenders of tradition, fun, and the official religion charge that the precise had unduly "straiten[ed] the way" to heaven, they would remain unfazed. They were satisfied that the means now were in place to make the elect, at least, into citizens who could build their own subcultural networks, police themselves, fashion an exemplary sainthood, help guard their locale and nation against Deuteronomic punishment, and hold the pace through the days and years. Thus, after all, and without benefit of presbyterian elders and courts, a disciplinary reformation was in the making. Offering only a choice for or against a tightly ruled life, it defined in effect a worldly, informal monk- or nunhood of all believers.[32]

This and the foregoing chapter present a first round of evidence that the pietist merger of devotion and rule carried the precisianist strain to higher levels of demand, but there is more ground to cover before we can assert that conclusion. In early modern England, the ultimate stretch toward strictness and exactitude was achieved, not by technique, by the multiplication of rules, or

31. Wives and widows: Felicity Heal and Clive Holmes, *The Gentry in England and Wales, 1500–1700* (Stanford, Calif., 1994), 364 (Heal and Holmes calculate that Hoby devoted two-thirds of her waking hours to "religious acts"). Ratcliffe: John Ley, *A Patterne of Pietie; or, The Religious Life and Death of . . . Jane Ratcliffe . . .* (London, 1640), 132. "I must," she mused, "get his consent even for those times I set apart for religious duties." My treatment of female activism and yielding draws upon Amussen, *Ordered Society*, 41–46.

32. *WRG*, 243; John R. Knott, Jr., *The Sword of the Spirit: Puritan Responses to the Bible* (Chicago, 1980), 12; *WWP*, I, 472 ("paines"); [Thomas Hooker], *The Soules Humiliation* (London, 1637), 63 ("hardnesse"); *WRS*, VII, 12 ("straiten[ed] the way"). For comments on the "activist logic" and "ethic of striving that lies at the heart of Puritan thought," see Cohen, *God's Caress*, 111, 208. Self-abnegation ("self-abnegating selfhood") is discussed in Webster, *Godly Clergy*, 124–125.

even by the will to control every occasion manifest in the daily rule, but by the impressment of all disciplinary elements into a program of self-analysis. That, in turn, was closely related to urgent concerns about religious certitude that also molded the devotional awakening. Chapters 6–8 will explore the many, complex, sometimes counterproductive, but always "precise" uses that pietist directors and practicioners found for the ancient summons, "Know thyself."

CHAPTER 6

INTROSPECTION
AND
SELF-CONTROL

P uritans in an age of piety aspired to surpass the dull average of religious conviction and practice, and one factor nerving them to aim high was belief that an improved regimen of introspection would enhance self-control. Self-control: this theme, propounded and refined over several decades in a steady barrage of sermons, personal counsels, and books aimed at the laity, not only was central to the new pietism, but it also was to become a great precipitant of antinomianism after about 1620. Thus it must figure large in our story. Making the expanded array of devotional rites subservient to the struggle against self was a complex achievement, but it depended heavily upon a single instrumentality: a scanning of self that, at least in the ideal, was continual, methodical, and precise.

In Richard Greenham's words, a "descen[t] into our selves" for a *"true survey and examination of our selves"* was the primary maneuver of spiritual warfare, and it must be done "pricisely." For centuries the examen of self, under the guidance of a spiritual director, had been a cardinal element of Catholic piety for religious and sometimes for laity, and it remained basic to Counter Reformation piety. In modified form and with little emphasis upon the role of the director, self-examination was carried over into Reformed faith, deemed necessary to the painful conviction of sin that must precede the grant of pardoning and empowering grace and to preparation for the Eucharist. Theologians of the pre-Marian church routinely had affirmed the trial of self, and daily self-scrutiny was demanded in the Erasmian unofficial curriculum that continued through the century to occupy students at Oxford and Cambridge. But never before had a body of Protestant clergy caught so coherent and compelling a vision of its possibilities, seeing how an expanded program of self-surveillance might at once enrich devotion and roll back the tide of sin imperiling the nation. Neither pre-Marians nor Elizabethan presbyterians could have foreseen how introspection itself, its uses and its efficiency increased by the pietist turn and the reemergence of spiritual direction as a pastoral specialty, would become a frequent topic of preaching and counseling. "What a shame is it," exclaimed Richard Sibbes, "that so nimble and swift spirit as the soul is, that can mount up to heaven, and from thence come down into the earth in an instant, should, while it looks over all other things, overlook itself! that it should be . . . ignorant of the story of itself!" Since all saintly skill rests upon self-knowledge, it was time for a total assault upon the unexamined life.[1]

This aim, it was understood, could not be realized by women or men in isolation. Designed to initiate and nurture the experience of conversion, the new piety had a strongly individualizing thrust. In the last analysis, during the trek to New Jerusalem it was *"every man for himselfe,"* as Perkins bluntly observed. "Our owne [hearts and lives] are our charge, and not other mens." Yet, he added tellingly, the assertion otherwise "is most false." Final responsibility for searching the self belongs to each person alone, but to each as a partner in the rites through which the godly recognized and aided one another. Self-inspective motive and skill were to be nurtured by a steady diet of painful sermons often supplemented by private pastoral counseling, the mutual consultation the godly called "christian conference," the lending and borrowing of edifying literature, intercessory prayers, and the like; and in communal fasts the duty to inspect oneself became explicitly collective. In this setting, introspection was inescapably social.[2]

Once correctly understood, "mak[ing an] Anatomie of thy selfe" was directed to two principal ends. One (examined in Chapter 7) was to reassure saints in doubt about the reality of their conversion and of their standing before God. But the other was to enhance moral purity. From Greenham to Richard Baxter and beyond, and in the records of lay piety through the early decades of the seventeenth century, the famous praxis of piety of the Puritans was essentially a praxis of penitence. And repentance, in the pattern laid down before 1553, regularly was seen as a joint work of contrition and moral amendment. It is in this context that the ethical impulse behind self-anatomy ap-

---

1. *WRG,* 2, 37; *WRS,* I, 165. Writing in Massachusetts about 1640, Thomas Shepard marveled at the "discoveries" to be made by the self "by frequent reflecting upon its own acts . . . by observing ends, aims, motives of [its own] workings" (*WTS,* II, 580). Margo Todd discusses the unofficial curriculum in *Christian Humanism and the Puritan Social Order* (Cambridge, 1987), 31, 65–67, 194.

2. *WWP,* III, 419. See Diane Willen, " 'Communion of the Saints': Spiritual Reciprocity and the Godly Community in Early Modern England," *Albion,* XXVII (1995), 19–41, for a succinct account of godly communal practices.

pears. Surveillance of self (itself an act of compliance with biblical rules and archetypes) became "the necessariest lesson in Christianitie" in part because of an almost extravagant trust in its potential to make repentance, and therewith the reform of behavior, more exact and proficient. What made "the very word *Examine*" central to godly speech and counsel was its link to amendment and, indeed, explicitly to the judicial process of accusation, inquisition, indictment, and punitive correction. Considered as a "private arraignement, or close sessions" suffused with repentant sorrow and resolve to amend, introspection became the saint's keenest weapon against sin. The flood of pietist propaganda on its behalf, together with an expansive lay enthusiasm for the examined life, was the final twist of the disciplinary screw—and the final increase of preciseness—that evoked antinomian revolt.[3]

Contrition (defined in contrast to an inadequate "attrition"), conversion, spiritual battle, the "signs and evidences" of a gracious estate, the analysis of "carnal reason," Sabbath exercises, prayer, fasting, meditation, self-examination before the Lord's Supper, the daily devotional schedule, the dialogue with the self called "soliloquy," spiritual diaries—these and many other pietist themes and tactics testified to a conviction that self-knowledge was power and that from it would flow higher grades of skill in self-management. A complete canvass of the evidence would be vast, but several examples will disclose the basic pattern.

Preparation for Conversion

Consider, to begin with, the spiritual brotherhood's famed doctrine of "preparation for conversion." Preparation in this sense was an introspective ritual in which the subject, in a larger context of exposure to the excoriating, "painful" preaching in which the pietist clergy specialized, came fully to recognize his or her sinful and doomed condition. Often of long duration, preparative self-analysis aimed to elicit a state of dread, emptiness, weeping, passive surrender, and yearning for relief. These were ancient experiences of Christian spirituality, although they also expressed a stubbornly Protestant belief in human powerlessness and dependence upon grace. At the same time, and in a limited but substantial overlap with Catholic preparationist doctrine, an eloquent

3. *SHS*, 78 *("Examine")*, 80 ("Anatomie"), 81 ("arraignment"), 84 ("necessariest lesson"). For the anatomy metaphor, see also *ST,* 88, 122. Thomas Taylor urged saints: "Examine thy thoughts whence they come, and whither they go, and what they doe in thee. By which meanes thou shalt banish a number of idle and wandering thoughts." *CWSR,* 45.

subset of pietist counselors began to emphasize a substantial gain in self-control as a necessary stage of ascent to the final and rarefied state. Specifically, they cultivated an older image of the self as a morally contaminated space that required detoxification before the divine entry.[4]

"Wisdome will not rest in the defiled soule," Henry Smith had told his auditory at Saint Clement Danes, London, late in Elizabeth's reign, for "God will not come into the heart which is not cleansed." He did not apply this insight to the topic of preparation, and it played no prominent role in the teaching of Greenham, Perkins, Sibbes, and other leading figures; but the principle he enunciated, later rephrased by Thomas Hooker in pioneer Connecticut as the "impossib[ility] that Two Contraries should be in the same subject at the same time," became for others a postulate of preparationist teaching. Knowing, with Robert Bolton and John Cotton, that God "will not come into a cage of uncleane lusts," John Preston thus freely inferred that the heart "must be emptied of [lusts] before a man can take *Christ*."[5] So the moral end and power of self-inquiry ever was clear, as when a closely bonded group of Essex Puritan clergy including Richard Rogers, John Rogers of Dedham (Richard's nephew), Hooker, Thomas Shepard, and Adam Harsnett affirmed unanimously that "aversion from sin . . . goes before, our conversion unto God." "There can be no grace planted in the heart till the corruption that cumberd it . . . be scooted out." In Hooker's incomparably full analyses of preparation (most notably *The Soules Preparation for Christ* [1632]), it was when the soul made conscious of its vile nature "begins to renounce the power of . . . sinne, and to withdraw himselfe from under the dominion of his corruptions" that "roome is prepared, and way made for the Lord Jesus." Harsnett took an extreme position, declaring outright that the soul must be "regenerate and sanctified by the Spirit" before it believes and is justified, and that faith ac-

---

4. Norman Pettit, *The Heart Prepared: Grace and Conversion in Puritan Spiritual Life*, 2d ed. (Middletown, Conn., 1989), 17. For Tridentine teaching on preparation, see *KG*, 504, 505, 517–518. That "preparation" was a prerequisite of "conversion" was also an assumption of Counter Reformation manuals of spirituality in circulation in England. See, for example, [G]aspar Loarte, *The Exercise of a Christian Life* (n.p., [1597]), 2–5.

5. *SHS*, 454; *AR*, *1–8*, 373; John Preston, *The Breast-plate of Faith and Love . . .* , 5th ed. (London, 1634), 133. Preparation is treated by Charles Lloyd Cohen, *God's Caress: The Psychology of Puritan Religious Experience* (New York, 1986), 77–84. Bolton's doctrine is in *CAC*, 163, 175–176, 268; Cotton's in *WL*, 12, and see 103, 308–309, and below, Chapter 11, n. 3. Cotton continued to hold this position even at the height of his involvement in the Antinomian Controversy of 1636–1637. *TCG*, 14; and see Cohen, *God's Caress*, 84–84 and n. 25.

cordingly "is . . . not the fountaine of all other graces." Though their formulations varied, these spiritual directors agreed on the central point: only into a
soul already changed and disposed would Christ and his train of graces come.[6]

Preparationist teaching in this vein thus explicitly found a place in first
conversion for contributory moral exercises. In so doing it defined a strong
alternative to Luther's principle that "man cannot establish in himself a point
of contact for divine grace." In symmetry, for example, with pietist counsel
that renewed moral resolve is a necessary preliminary for participation in the
Lord's Supper, it offers a limited but striking recurrence of the age-old Catholic theological premise that likes attract and opposites repel, or more specifically that a human being must be likened to God to become acceptable to him.
Unmistakably too, it echoes the medieval requirement, especially important in
the tradition of the *via moderna* (the modernist theological movement) and
reiterated in part by the Council of Trent, that "aversion to sin" is integral to
the penitent's purging of his soul to "prepar[e it] for [the divine] inhabitation," with a particular stress upon the "prior necessity of this self-cleansing
activity."[7]

Of course, in Puritan circles there could be no ascription of causal, saving
efficacy or any problematic implication of freedom or goodness of will to the
penitent's preliminary activity. To avert misunderstanding, it must be insisted
that "preparative Acts, required for the plantation of faith" were a divine and
not a human work; nor did they earn or elicit grace. Yet they remained necessary precedents of grace—"needfull predispositions," as Bolton put it. So it
remained clear that the inner warfare against sin must begin and produce

6. *WTS*, I, 143; Thomas Shepard, "A Tryal of Regeneration" (n.d.), fol. 382, MS Add.
45675, British Library, London; *SPC*, 149; A[dam] H[arsnett], *A Touch-Stone of Grace*
(London, 1630), 127, and see 130. Hooker flatly insisted, "There is a separation of the soule
from sinne, before there [can] bee a reservation made for Christ" (*The Soules Implantation
into the Naturall Olive* [London, 1640], 36). See also *ST*, [19], 20 in irreg. pag.; John Rogers
of Dedham, *The Doctrine of Faith . . .*, 3d ed. (London, 1629), 173. In earliest New England,
Hooker and Shepard continued to teach that "before the woord woorke fayth to beleeue to
Justification, the hart must be made honest and good, in preparation" (*AR, 1–8*, 32, 145–
149, 158). The quote is Shepard's, in *WTS*, I, 328, and see 349.

7. Gordon J. Spykman, *Attrition and Contrition at the Council of Trent* (Amsterdam,
1955), 99; Heiko Augustinus Oberman, *The Harvest of Medieval Theology: Gabriel Biel and
Late Medieval Nominalism* (Cambridge, Mass., 1963), 152, 349, 356 (and see 175). For
likeness, see above, Chapter 2, n. 3. For eucharistic preparation, see *WRG*, 474–491; *ST*, 219
(and see 221); J[ohn] Dod and R[obert] Cleaver, *Ten Sermons Tending Chiefely to the
Fitting of Men for the Worthy Receiving of the Lords Supper* (London, 1610), 26; Paul
Bayne[s], *Briefe Directions unto a Godly Life . . .* (London, 1618), 216.

discernible initial result before the event of justification; and that result was, no mere good resolution, but a substantial modification of the penitent's attitude and behavior. With its call for behavioral change as a condition of access to the Atonement, this strain of preparationist doctrine clearly reveals the harder disciplinary accent of the pietist turn. It also requires some revision of the widely held notion that in Puritan theology "first came the traumatic conviction of sin, then the awakening hope of mercy, and finally the transformation of behavior."[8]

Standing Watch

However well prepared and then credentialed with a first conversion, new-minted saints cannot relax; they must enter a lifelong regimen of spiritual exercises. And as attested, say, by William Gouge's *Whole Armour of God* or John Preston's *Breast-plate of Faith and Love*, one group of commended rites was organized around biblical warrior imagery. The "Spirituall Watch," one drill of the armed and armored soldier, represents a telling instance of introspection in the service of self-management: "Guard and keepe thy heart more then any thing that is watched or guarded." This admonition of Perkins's was among the commonest pietist imperatives and was echoed widely in practice. The regimen of "watching over our selues carefully" reproduced a familiar feature of monastic devotion and one vigorously reaffirmed by spiritual writers of the Counter Reformation. When Greenham declared the saints' duty to "sit as it were in the watch-tower of their hearts, viewing to espie even their least declinings," or when Richard Rogers called for "hearts daily fenced thus with watch and ward," they expressed the belief in a rampant libido within (described earlier): the Old Adam within the human psyche is a hive of dangerous desires that must be vigilantly scanned and screened. Understandably, when about 1580 some twenty members of Rogers's parish in Wethersfield, Essex, became troubled by excessive "loosenesse and libertie" in their lives, they formed a conventicle pledged to a discipline of "watching over the heart"— and understandably, again, the move was assailed as too "precise." So again a historic gesture of professional Catholic spirituality was recycled as a Puritan spiritual exercise.[9]

8. *CAC*, 165, 170, and see 268; *PM*, 118.

9. Thomas Gataker, *The Spirituall Watch* . . . (London, 1619); *WWP*, II, 477; *ST*, 227 ("watching"), 329, [488]; *WRG*, 83. Warrior themes: John Downame's four-part summa of spiritual direction for afflicted consciences was built around the metaphor of combat. The

How did the exercise proceed? In obvious reliance upon Catholic teaching, the fraternity resolved the act of sin into a series of discrete psychological moments. Perkins's description of an initial wayward impulse maturing through stages of "conception, [and] birth, [to] perfection" represents the basic concept well enough, and it was this which determined the strategy of the watch. If temptation was a bare flicker at first, unfolding and hardening through consideration, consent, and enactment, then the moment to intervene was evident. Harmful thoughts and impulses were most vulnerable at their first entry into consciousness, when the mind was not committed but merely "tickled with some delight." Since, as Sibbes put it, "passions are but little motions at the first, but grow as rivers do," it is best to "stifle them in their birth." Admonitions to discern and snuff dangerous thoughts "at their first arising" or "in their *first motion*," to "kill [sin] in the wombe, as it were," thereupon abounded in pietist expression. To see and intercept at the earliest possible moment the arcs of impulse that continually streamed forth from the old self and sought gratification: that was the prime directive of the watch.[10]

And that directive was sweeping. With a true precisianist spin, it required saints to be "extraordinarily and exactly vigilant" over their impulses, and it extended without limit to scrutiny of all *"thoughts, words* and *actions,"* of each "idle roving of our braines," and of the "secretest and smallest provocations to evil."[11] The watch therefore was more than a broad surveillance. It was an art

---

complete edition is *The Christian Warfare against the Deuill, World, and Flesh* . . . (London, 1634). See also Joseph Bentham, *The Christian Conflict* . . . (London, 1635). The primary source of the imagery is Eph. 6:10–17. For lay examples of "watchfull[ness]," see William Hinde, *A Faithfull Remonstrance of . . . John Bruen* . . . (London, 1641), 54 (quote); *LBH*, 42, 57, 71. For Counter Reformation examples, see *CDGM*, 324, 328; L[uis de] Granada, *The Sinners Guyde* . . . , trans. Francis Meres (London, 1598), 514.

10. William Perkins, *The Whole Treatise of the Cases of Conscience* (London, 1606), in *WPEP*, 98; *WRS*, I, 166, and see 63 (see also John Dod and Robert Cleaver, *A Plaine and Familiar Exposition of the Ten Commandments* [London, 1618], 367: "First lusts are like a litle sparke of fire, lighting upon tinder . . . which if they be not quickely quenched, will grow to a great flame"); *WWP*, II, 477 ("first arising"); *POP*, 279–280 ("first motion"); Dod and Cleaver, *Ten Commandments*, 287 ("in the wombe"). William Ames spoke of three steps in the emergence of a sin: the apprehension of a sinful object, "some motion" of consent to it, and full consent (*Conscience, with the Power and Cases Thereof* . . . [n.p., 1639], bk. 3, 94–97 [irreg. pag.]). Cf. Parsons's analysis of "Suggestion, Delectation, and Consent" in *CDGM*, 326–327. For Puritan lay expressions, see *WW*, 32–33; Sir Harbottle Grimston, *A Christian New-Years Gift* (Cambridge, 1644), 107–108.

11. *GD*, 89; *POP*, 279; *MSD*, 139; M. M. Knappen, ed., *Two Elizabethan Puritan Diaries, by Richard Rogers and Samuel Ward* (Chicago, 1933), 64. John Ball worked out a

adaptable to specific functions of the self. Perkins spoke of it in this sense as "a narrow regard," as "a watch before our eyes, eares, lips, and all other parts of the body, that are in any action the instruments of the soule," and in his great survey of the Christian warfare John Downame provided for a daily inspection of the eyes, ears, taste, appetite, and speech. Restraint of the eyes and the tongue was emphasized most often. Greenham provided pointers for the "gouernement of the Eyes," and John Dod (Greenham's son-in-law) urged his hearers to "make a covenant with [your] eyes, to looke upon nothing" evil. Perkins too advocated "the gouernment of the eyes" and sought to restrain "the idle looking, or curious looking of men upon women, or women upon men." Henry Smith admired the "holie men" of the Christian movement who had placed the fear of God "at the doore of their lips, to examine euery word before it went out." Perkins's *Direction for the Government of the Tongue*, John Ball's "Treatise of the Government of the Tongue" (in *The Power of Godlines*), and Ames's discussion "Of the sins of the Mouth" gave specific directions for watching and governing that unruly organ given to "idle word[s]," cursing, boasting, lying, gossip, and many other serious aberrations. In a funeral ser- mon of 1640, John Ley held up Jane Ratcliffe (whose conversion had been sparked by the sermons of Nicholas Byfield) as an imitable pattern of sparse, deliberated speech who spoke little and only after careful consideration, main- taining "prudent silence" much of the time.[12]

Such directions sought to foster a state of mental readiness to screen thoughts and gentle desires before, if at all, permitting them expression. Christians should yield to no temptation, make no decision, embark upon no action, "untill wee have turned it every way, and tryed it by the light of Gods law, examined both ends, weighed well every circumstance, and searched

---

rigorous program for the "government of our thoughts" in *The Power of Godlines* . . . (London, 1657), 115–160 (quote at 121). For Catholic examples, see Granada, *Sinners Guyde*, trans. Meres, 455, and Robert Southwell's advice "watchfully to take heed to every thought, word, and deed." Southwell, *Two Letters and Short Rules of a Good Life*, ed. Nancy Pollard Brown (Charlottesville, Va., 1973), 62.

12. *WWP*, I, 188, III, 54, 56–57; *CFS*, 344–345; *WRG*, 300–303; Dod and Cleaver, *Ten Commandments*, 369–370; *SHS*, 81; *WP*, I, 439–452; Ball, *Power of Godlines*, 309–333; Ames, *Conscience*, bk. 3, 96–97; John Ley, *A Patterne of Pietie; or, The Religious Life and Death of . . . Jane Ratcliffe* (London, 1640), 29–39 (quote at 33). Ratcliffe's "prudent silence" echoed gender conventions, for which see Peter Lake, "Feminine Piety and Personal Potency: The 'Emancipation' of Mrs Jane Ratcliffe," *Seventeenth Century*, II (1987), 143– 165. Byfield's *Rules of a Holy Life* included fourteen rules to govern the use of speech (*MO*, 574–582).

every corner of it; that wee may have good *assurance* . . . of the lawfulnesse . . . of it, before wee venture upon the admission of it." Precision-minded saints must accept, for example, that "an idle word . . . can hardly ever proceed from deliberate reason," because reason informed by scriptural law at once perceives the folly of mere chatter; it learns that "before we speake, consideration must be used." If, again, a man or woman as a rational creature with an intelligible biblical "rule given . . . to live by," would only "reason the matter" beforehand, he or she "would never yield" to anger or other offensive "distempers." Deliberation, the necessity to "fore-thinke" or "suruey thorowly before-hand" any action in relation to the biblical norm, was a persistent motif.[13]

Keeping the Sabbath

Whether in the stage of preparation for conversion or in the daily watch and warfare of the converted, by the turn of the century self-inspection had become integral to a greatly expanded repertoire of means for ethical amendment and self-control, and a showpiece of that repertoire was the Puritan Sabbath. Sunday, the "Lord's Day" associated with rest from labor and devotion to worship and good works, was an ancient fixture of the Christian calendar taken over with some modification by the early English reformers. On the whole it remained a routine element of Protestant faith before the 1570s and 1580s, when a more rigorous approach began to emerge. Not the exclusive property of any religious party, a fervid Sabbatarianism nevertheless became in these years an increasingly frequent index of Puritan leanings.

A full, and in many respects innovative, theology of Sabbath rest and practice first was formulated in the 1580s and 1590s, and two primary actors in this development were Greenham and Nicholas Bownde, Greenham's stepson, admirer, and coagent of the pietist turn. Greenham's "Treatise of the Sabbath" might have been the first Puritan Sabbatarian work of the English sixteenth century. It remained in manuscript until 1599, but, since Greenham in all likelihood broadcast the new doctrine through his household seminary at Dry Drayton, he arguably was "the original source of the doctrine of the Christian Sabbath" that was to prevail within the brotherhood. Bownde's

13. Thomas Gataker, *Certaine Sermons* . . . (London, 1637), 72; *WWP,* I, 441 (and see 442, II, 477); *WRS,* 145; *POP,* 289 (and see 149, 298); *GD,* 149. See also *GD,* 185: "Euer before thou enter out of thy doores, upon any occasion, businesse, iourney, visitation; weigh well . . . all circumstances, concurrents, company, probabilitie of all events, and consequents." For a Catholic example, see Robert Bellarmine, *Spiritual Writings,* trans. and ed. John Patrick Donnelly and Roland J. Teske (New York, 1989), 308.

Doctrine of the Sabbath (1595), the first published, full-scale Sabbatarian state-ment, moved along lines similar to Greenham's and may reflect the older man's influence. As redefined initially by Greenham and more fully by Bownde, the Sabbath by the turn of the century "had become virtually an official—and prominent—doctrine of puritanism."[14]

Greenham and Bownde showed how to expand the conventional Lord's Day into a pietist "market day for our soules." Each called his audiences to set aside workaday cares and enter a special, uninterrupted "sacred time," a time defined both as a selective reenactment of the Israelite Sabbath and a foretaste of heaven's Sabbath rest. Since then, as at no other time, it was possible to "refresh our selves with spirituall pleasures," both men recommended repeated courses of prayer, psalm singing, biblical study, sermons, sacraments, medita-tion, self-inventory, conference with fellow and sister saints, reflection upon God's works in human affairs and in nature, and the like.[15] Clearly it is no coincidence that the first major statements of Sabbatarian doctrine appeared in the 1580s or that Greenham stood at the center of the development. Rooted in medieval and earlier Protestant traditions of concern for proper observance of the Lord's Day, the Sabbatarian vision of Greenham and Bownde neverthe-less was no simple "elaboration of received sabbatarian doctrine." Into the modest round of "rest, and godly contemplation" enjoined in the official Book of Homilies, they projected a lengthy moment of intensive preaching and family-centered activity. This was not an obvious extension of "the authorized teaching of the Church," but a vintage example of the nonseparating design to reform, and to reform substantially, from within. Heavy with spiritual rumi-nation and exercise, it was a principal carrier of the first Protestant pietism.[16]

Yet to leave the accent there, upon themes of rest and enjoyment, would

14. Patrick Collinson, "The Beginnings of English Sabbatarianism," in C. W. Dugmore and Charles Duggan, eds., *Studies in Church History*, I (1964), 217; *EPM*, 436. Bownde reported earlier correspondence on the subject with Greenham in *DS*, sigs. A3–A4.

15. *DS*, 188, and see *WRG*, 159; John H. Primus, *Holy Time: Moderate Puritanism and the Sabbath* (Macon, Ga., 1989), 179; *WRG*, 168. Available in an English translation as early as 1579, Gaspar Loarte's outline of procedure for Sunday and festival days, including exercises to prepare for worship, apply the doctrine learned to one's self, meditate often during the day, discuss religious matters with others, read religious books, and perform works of charity, markedly resembles Greenham's and Bownde's Sabbatarian instruction. Loarte, *Christian Life*, 22–30.

16. Kenneth Parker, *The English Sabbath: A Study of Doctrine and Discipline from the Reformation to the Civil War* (Cambridge, 1988), 91, 94; *Certaine Sermons or Homilies . . .* (1623; rpt. Gainesville, Fla., 1968), 128.

distort Sabbatarian purposes. In the typically antitheoretic spirit of practical theology, Greenham and Bownde had little interest in inward reflection or recreation without measurable gain in the realm of behavior. Rightly to observe this day was a way for saints to surpass the average level of religious performance, and, although one measure of their achievement was a deepened trust in the divine pardon and other benefits, progress in the struggle to do good received the greater attention. Patrick Collinson has well remarked that the growing preoccupation of Elizabethan Puritan divines with Sabbath "reflected a growing interest . . . with questions of ethics"; and ethics, as ever in this world of thought, meant service to the divine honor through precise conformity to biblical rules.[17]

It is well to recall that Luther, in yet another expression of his hostility to legalistic religion, had interpreted the fourth commandment as a part of Hebrew ceremonial law without force in the Christian dispensation. England's earliest Protestants came to no consensus on the issue. Robert Barnes and John Frith, for example, took a position similar to Luther's. But Hugh Latimer, John Hooper, and others asserted a stronger, proto-Sabbatarian view, and their approach, emphasizing law and obedience in context of the Ten Commandments, came to fruition in the 1580s and the decades following.[18]

Like a number of other Sabbatarian theorists, Bownde developed his conception of the Sabbath in the course of preaching upon the Decalogue. Keeping that day was a strict and "bounden dutie" to one of the Lord's ten primary commands, a command, moreover, spelled out more fully than the others, excepting the prohibition of graven images. Why, Bownde wondered, had the Lord dwelt at extra length upon the Sabbath command? The answer was clear: to underline its exact, binding character. This was necessary because human nature, faced with a strict demand to spend a full day weekly in religious exercises, is "rebellious and corrupt . . . here especially." Rebellion was evident enough in the tendency of many baptized Englishmen and -women both to sleep late on the Lord's Day and to misspend lengthy intervals in sport and

17. Collinson, "Beginnings of English Sabbatarianism," in Dugmore and Duggan, eds., *Studies in Church History,* I (1964), 208.

18. Theodore G. Tappert, ed. and trans., *The Book of Concord: The Confessions of the Evangelical Lutheran Church* (Philadelphia, 1959), 375–377. Proto-Sabbatarian views: *The Whole Workes of W. Tyndall, John Frith, and Doct. Barnes* (London, 1573), 96, 206; *SHL,* 471–473; Samuel Carr, ed., *Early Writings of John Hooper* (Cambridge, 1843), 337–342. Parker, *The English Sabbath,* 32–40, amends Winton U. Solberg's judgment that "the early English reformers were vigorously anti-Sabbatarian." Solberg, *Redeem the Time: The Puritan Sabbath in Early America* (Cambridge, Mass., 1977), 23.

recreation or in restful inactivity. So it was time to highlight the prescriptive character of the rite, to "beate that into our eares, which we are so unwilling to heare, and more loth to followe," to give reminder that the Jews were "severely tied" and "bound . . . most straightly" to the Sabbath, and to enlist all means (including governmental compulsion) to "enforce" and "compell" man's contrary nature to yield to the weekly discipline. To minds so admiring of law and submission, this was a necessary transvaluation of rest, as in Bownde's demonstration that the fourth commandment "doth . . . require that men should *rest*," or his insistence that "the *rest upon this* [day] must be a most *carefull, exact and precise rest*," or in his ringing call to English magistrates to institute a mandatory Sabbath rest and compel "all men . . . to stoope unto it." Spiritual pleasure, it was clear, was a function, not of Christian liberty or restful ease, but of regimented abstinence.[19]

As portrayed by these two pietist founders, the Sabbath experience incorporated a variety of activities, including relief of the poor and admiring contemplation of the physical creation, but its largest component was a stream of interior activity devoted to the continuing work of conversion. Greenham knew that the prospect of a weekly scanning and arraignment of wayward impulse seemed intolerably "precise" to average Protestants, but he knew too that it was the Sabbath's work to lift men and women to a higher standard of self-awareness and control: "How can a man lie long in the liking of sin, who embraceth this [Sabbath] doctrine in conscience" and submits to its regular schedule to "have his sinnes discovered, his conscience unripped, the iudgements of God against his sinnes threatened, whereby he might come to a loathing . . . of his sinnes daily"?[20]

In part this was a work of the two recommended public services of worship, under the ministration of a painful preacher, but in part it was to be accomplished through the pietist paraliturgy, cycles of individual self-analysis and amendment of life before and after the services. Both Greenham and Bownde required a period of concentrated preparation before each service and of stock-taking afterward. Godly parishioners must study Scripture, meditate, and pray, but in particular they must *"examine themselues, . . . how they haue spent the*

19. *DS*, 164 ("bounden dutie"), 4("rebellious" nature), 53 (precise rest), 55 ("our eares"), 59–60 ("severely tied" . . . "compel"), 63 (required rest), 276 ("stoope").

20. *WRG*, 159–160. Performance of "duties of love" to the poor, sick, and otherwise afflicted was a basic Sabbath duty. For Greenham this included rebuking misbehavior and striving to bring sinners to repentance. *WRG*, 191.

weeke past, and euery day in it, calling themselues to an account before God." After the service they were to undertake another meditative review, "occupying . . . the whole minde" with "those generall rules, which wee have heard out of Gods worde" and with the basics of faith and repentance. Bownde saw this partly as a task for small "meetings of the godlie" in mutual "conference" and discussion—the classical pietist *ecclesiola in ecclesia* (a little church within the church). Greenham also recommended a final round of analysis during the night, and again the ethical, penitential note was prominent: "We are to examine our selves, with what . . . increase of good things we have been conversant in these dueties. . . . Hath the Lords increase of mercy brought me a daies increase of holines? . . . Is sinne more grieuous unto us"? And the like.[21]

How securely Greenham and Bownde fixed the type of the Puritan Sabbath, even a cursory sampling of the later propaganda will show. Such monuments of the genre as Robert Cleaver's *Declaration of the Christian Sabbath* (1625), Richard Bernard's *Threefold Treatise of the Sabbath* (1641), Thomas Shepard's *Theses Sabbaticae* (1649), or the sections devoted to the topic in works like Dod and Cleaver's *Ten Commandments* (1603) or Bayly's *Practice of Pietie* (2d ed., 1612) were all testaments to the emergence of a Puritan pietism. All portrayed Sabbath observance as at once a festive time of biblical worship and devotion, a display of strict obedience to biblical law, and an aggressive stratagem in the war against sin employing repeated rounds of reproachful self-analysis. And, while we know little of how the theory was realized and perhaps modified in practice, it is evident that rigorous Sabbath observance had become a Puritan standard by the early 1600s. Puritan squires and their wives in early Stuart times brought "keen anticipation" to the Lord's Day, attended services at their parish church early and late in the day, and devoted the time remaining to "exercises."[22]

The Fast Day

A similarly potent mix of introspective devotion and regulatory purpose appeared in Puritan commendations of fasting. Magisterial Protestants always had recognized fasting, properly divested of Lenten works-righteousness and

21. *DS*, 198 *("examine")*, 219 ("meetings"), and see 210–222; and see *WRG*, 188–189, 191 (final round); *DS*, 203 ("occupying"); 206 ("generall rules"). In a common pietist simile, Greenham likened meditative preparation for worship to the merchant's weekly reckoning of accounts. *WRG*, 187.

22. *PG*, 40. See also Foster, *Long Argument*, 78–82.

of medieval mystical imaginings, as an aid to religious edification. Yet to read chronologically through Puritan literature of the sixteenth and early seventeenth centuries is to discover a remarkable surge of interest in this traditional ascetic practice. During the later 1570s (as noted in Chapter 3), the public "day of fast and humiliation" emerged as an eminent expression of Puritan piety, together with smaller-scale congregational, family, and private fasts. This development was incorporated wholesale into the pietist turn. Pietist preachers and spiritual counselors enthusiastically promoted both the public and private rite, bidding themselves and their lay charges to become virtual athletes of the fast. A study "Of the Doctrine of Fasting" was among Greenham's posthumously published tracts, and in 1604 Bownde contributed *The Holy Exercise of Fasting*. Instruction in the art of the fast thereafter became a staple of pietist utterance.[23]

And what so satisfied Greenham and his colleagues, as they spurred themselves and their charges into fast day routines, was their proven ability at once to nurture devotion and to "take downe the flesh." By definition the work commenced with acts of "separation and restraint," depriving the body and its urges. Denial of food and drink, curtailment of sleep, the "abstinence from . . . *musick, sweet smells, soft aparell*" were all aimed first to "subdue the . . . flesh." Yet these outward exercises subserved inward duties, beginning with the examen of self that Deuteronomic principle required. We cannot, Arthur Hildersam explained, grasp the import of the current affliction "unless every one of us enter into his own heart, and say[s], what have I done?" And, of course, the ensuing cycles of sorrow and amendment continued and expanded the self-inspective work. So and always, the rite's core element was found "in the inward . . . graces of the mind holpen forward by the bodily exercise," and principally in the "better fitting of us to the spirituall wrestling with the sinful lustes of our fleshly mindes." Here again, in a prime exhibit of practical theology, was a tactical merger of introspection and ascetic drill.[24]

Preparation for conversion, Sabbath, and fasting—Puritan ardor for such exercises brings into question a current thesis that "ethical and disciplinary"

23. *WRG,* 504–508; Nicolas Bownde, *The Holy Exercise of Fasting* . . . (Cambridge, 1604). Arth[ur] Hildersam, *The Doctrine of Fasting and Praier, and Humiliation for Sinne* . . . (London, 1633), offers a later example. Fasting was approved expressly, for example, by the Second Helvetic Confession of 1566. Arthur C. Cochrane, ed., *Reformed Confessions of the Sixteenth Century* (Philadelphia, 1966), 292.

24. Dod, *Ten Commandments,* 369–370; Hildersam, *Fasting,* 57, 58 (and see 28, 36); *WWP,* III, 156–157; Bownde, *Fasting,* 28 ("inward . . . graces"), 36 ("better fitting").

forms of religion are typically averse to ritual. On the contrary, agents of the devotional awakening greatly expanded the ritual resources available to help the saints compel themselves to purity. They made, too, the critical scan within—"ty[ing] yourself to a dayly self exemnation," as Lady Brilliana Harley put it in 1639—a primary ingredient of the devotional awakening and its most potent means to strengthen inner controls. Greater purity through stricter self-analysis and -regulation: there was the initial end and means of the first Protestant pietism, and not even the concurrent scholastic turn was more laden with theological implication. Described in the familiar bipolar terms of strong Reformed theology, it represents an ambitious enlargement of the disciplinary pole, and at a time when no comparable adjustment of the solifidian element was achieved. This was more than a measurably greater ethical concern, more even than the "pietism grounded on moral legalism" that Basil Hall finds in turn-of-the-century Puritanism. Never consciously disputing belief that justification by faith alone is a polestar of the faith and deeply averse to the old church's monastic practice and theology, the Puritan godly pleaded all the same for a watched and restricted life that echoed monastic values. No wonder that Gisbertus Voetius (1589–1676), the famous Dutch scholastic and pietist of the mid-seventeenth century who regarded English pietist writers as the great masters of practical theology, published the Reformed magnum opus on the exercises in 1664 (879 pages) heavily dependent on English pietist authorities, and named it *Asketica*.[25]

The present chapter only begins to plumb the story of self-analysis. Overall, the trial of self had a twofold mission. It was to strengthen self-control but also to shore up flagging assurance, and these objectives were symbiotic. Both arose from a desire to transcend the average, to drive human beings to their limits of achievement, to achieve precision. As always in the strong Reformed tradition, a purer life and conscience were ends in themselves, shining with inherent value and beauty; but they possessed also a further excellency, the power to relieve worries about standing before God. That, however, brought hidden complications in tow. It associated the search for certitude with yet greater disciplinary expectations, and in particular it promised to ease uncer-

---

25. Catherine Bell, *Ritual: Perspectives and Dimensions* (New York, 1997), 188–189; *LBH*, 69 (the duty "dayly [to] arraigne, indite and judge our selves" was impressed upon Lady Joan Barrington by her Puritan family chaplain in 1629; see Arthur Searle, ed., *Barrington Family Letters, 1628–1632* [London, 1983], 74); Basil Hall, "The Early Rise and Gradual Decline of Lutheranism in England (1520–1600)," in Derek Baker, ed., *Reform and Reformation: England and the Continent, c. 1500–1750* (Oxford, 1979), 110; Gisbertus Voetius, *Ta asketika siue exercitia pietatis* (Gorichemi, Neth., 1664).

tain consciences by techniques of self-analysis and -management that would prove, to say the least, toilsome and ambiguous. To sketch the troubled Puritan engagement with the problem of religious assurance, and especially the disruptive impact of introspective drills upon religious certitude, is the aim below.

CHAPTER 7
CASES OF
CONSCIENCE

Medieval and Reformation Backgrounds

Martin Luther's preoccupation with the tormented conscience echoed anxieties widely shared on the eve of the Reformation. Since, for the medieval Christian, redemption could be assured "only in direct proportion to the degree to which the Christian is no longer sinful *in re*," anticipation of the Judgment seldom was free from fear and unrest. Yet a series of pre-Reformation developments closely related to the Catholic penitential system worked further to complicate the relation between morality and assurance. In the penitential manuals of the sixth through the tenth centuries, emphasis fell upon the gross and public transgression; there was less interest in the everyday sinfulness of individuals, and no demand for personal review and confession of a multitude of sins. During the following three centuries, however, attention shifted to the individual act and state of contrition and to the confession and amendment of offenses. The shift was both reflected and promoted by a decree of the Fourth Lateran Council (1215) that all adult Catholics henceforth must perform a complete penance, reviewing and confessing all their sins at least once a year.[1]

This enactment, understood to apply strictly only to mortal sins, gave rise to a large body of instruction in the "complete confession," a spiritual exercise that greatly enlarged the role of self-examination. In preparation for the Sacrament, penitents now were urged to conduct a diligent and prolonged search of their consciences to find out what sins had been committed. Since completeness—the identification and mortification of every single sin—now was a "ubiquitous criterion by which the work of the penitent is judged," scrutiny of

---

1. Steven E. Ozment, *"Homo Viator:* Luther and Late Medieval Theology," *Harvard Theological Review,* XLII (1969), 283, and see 275. For the decree and its reaffirmation by the Council of Trent in 1551, see *KG,* 364, 544. The decree was understood to require enumeration only of mortal sins. James McCue, *"Simul iustus et peccator* in Augustine, Aquinas, and Luther: Toward Putting the Debate in Context," *Journal of the American Academy of Religion,* XLVIII (1980), 88.

self must be conducted "methodically, deliberately, and extensively," perhaps using the Decalogue or the seven deadly sins as a systematic standard. Sins also must be appraised relative to circumstances of place, persons, knowledge, time, age, number, duration, motive, consent, and the like; and the inquiry should be deepened through a searching interrogation by the confessor. If performed with adequate rigor, an examen of conscience also might entail elusive niceties of distinction: Which of my sins were actually mortal and worthy of damnation unless fully confessed and absolved? Did my experience of temptation to a sin pass over into the more serious state of consent to its pleasure? Was my sorrow for sin the genuine contrition that some theologians required for a successful penance, or the imperfect sorrow called attrition? And if, as held especially within the via moderna in the later-medieval period, God grants mercy only "to those who do their very best," penitents also must determine whether in fact they had endeavored to the full.[2]

It is probable that the ideal of the complete confession was not easily conveyed to the great body of Catholic clergy and seldom was realized in practice, that confessors' manuals dwelt upon solace as much as the analysis of sins, and that in any event some of the laity could choose their confessors and avoid the unduly rigorous.[3] Nevertheless, those who took the rite seriously or could not avoid it could not easily have derived a firm trust in their ability to survive the Last Judgment. Late-medieval theologians and confessors agreed that the best that could be expected was "conjectural certainty." This was a reasonable but possibly mistaken inference as to one's current state of grace, and always it was subject to the fluctuations of human performance. Whether in fighting sin, accomplishing good works, or doing penance, the earnest Christian could become a homo viator, a "very anxious pilgrim, unsure, this side of eternity, whether he was worthy of divine love or divine wrath." Bal-

2. Thomas N. Tentler, *Sin and Confession on the Eve of the Reformation* (Princeton, N.J., 1977), 109–110 (first three quotes). Niceties of distinction: ibid., 148, 250–263; Heiko Augustinus Oberman, *The Harvest of Medieval Theology: Gabriel Biel and Late Medieval Nominalism* (Cambridge, Mass., 1963), 133. Circumstances: Angelus [Carletus] de Clavasio, *Summa angelica de casibus conscientiae* (Strasbourg, 1498), sig. xxxii; Antoninus of Florence, *Defecerunt: summula confessionalis utilissima* (Venice, 1538), 28–30. Searching interrogation: *Summa angelica*, clxvii–clxxvii, provided eighteen pages of detailed questions to guide the interrogation. See also Tentler, *Sin and Confession*, 88–93.

3. See Euan Cameron, *The European Reformation* (Oxford, 1991), 305–307; Anne T. Thayer, "Judge and Doctor: Images of the Confessor in Printed Model Sermon Collections, 1450–1520," in Katherine Jackson Lualdi and Anne T. Thayer, eds., *Penitence in the Age of Reformations* (Aldershot, 2000), 10–29.

anced thus unstably between righteousness and sin, guilt and pardon, he or she was vulnerable to despair. In response to this concern, some theologies of penance sought to anchor security primarily in the objective efficacy of the church and its sacraments and the power of priestly absolution, but others continued to explore and press the sinner's own ethical and psychological responsibilities. So it is no surprise that, from about 1300, "the scrupulous or sin-anguished conscience," which was never comfortable with its estate, and even "magnifie[d] or invent[ed] faults to its own torment" and doubted the efficacy of its own confession and contrition, became a prominent topic in penitential literature. To assist confessors in coping with such cases of conscience, penitential writers increased and gave more systematic attention to the consolation of troubled consciences. Numerous churchmen—Jean Gerson (1363–1429) and Johann Nider (1380–1438) were leading figures—became specialists in a new "science of comfort."[4]

Although it should not be exaggerated, the element of anxious uncertainty in late-medieval religion clarifies the early Protestant desire to deliver Christians from the burden of works-righteousness. Much of the Reformers' critique of the old church was leveled precisely against those features of the Catholic system that left people doubtful and anxious (as Steven Ozment notes). Luther and his colleagues indicted the mandatory annual review and confession of sins in particular as a source more of torment than of peace. To that rite and the fixation upon sins and sinning it represented, they now offered a clear-cut alternative: an understanding that faith only, looking entirely beyond the realm of behavior, mediates a clear, indeed "almost brash" certitude of redemption.[5]

A "certitude of salvation . . . unknown to . . . medieval man" was thus a major axiom of the early Reformation. Virtually every magisterial reformer on the Continent repudiated the "fable of the scholastics, that man must remain

4. David Curtis Steinmetz, *Misericordia Dei: The Theology of Johannes von Staupitz in Its Late Medieval Setting* (Leiden, 1968), 122; Steven E. Ozment, *"Homo Viator,"* Harvard *Theological Review,* LXII (1969), 275; Ozment, *The Reformation in the Cities: The Appeal of Protestantism to Sixteenth-Century Germany and Switzerland* (New Haven, Conn., 1975), 12; McCue, "Augustine, Aquinas, and Luther," *Jour. Am. Acad. Rel.,* XLVIII (1980), 90 (scrupulous conscience); Tentler, *Sin and Confession,* 76. For objective efficacy, see David C. Steinmetz, *Luther in Context* (Bloomington, Ind., 1986), 2–3.

5. Ozment, *Reformation in the Cities,* 70; and cf. the critique in Cameron, *European Reformation,* 307. See also the Augsburg Confession's statement on the "scrupulous enumeration of all sins," in Theodore G. Tappert, ed. and trans., *The Book of Concord: The Confessions of the Evangelical Lutheran Church* (Philadelphia, 1959), art. 25, 62.

uncertain, whether he is saved or not," and the English followed suit. Rejecting the doctrine and ritual of the Catholic confessional, they counted "faith that is not certain of salvation from God, . . . but doubts of it [as] either a weak faith, or else but a show of faith." A Christian who had learned not to rely upon the merit of his own imperfect deeds but to set his hope "upon a sewerer more certayne foundacion" in the objective work of Christ might live "withoute any dubitacion." The doctrine of predestination too, properly construed, dispelled the old church's merely conjectural certainty, for to anchor redemption in the Deity's unchangeable decree "comforteth most comfortably" the uncertain Christian.[6]

England's earliest Protestants wished likewise to transcend conjectural surety, but at no time did the consolation of anxious consciences become, as it had for Luther, the polestar of their Reformation; nor did many consistently embrace the Wittenberger's idea that "ethical activity was to flow from rather than toward religious security." To the extent that they wove legal and moral themes into their understanding of sola fides and, indeed, believed that redemption was mediated by a conditional pact, considerations of behavior remained ingredient to consolation. Most relied primarily upon the self-attesting character of faith and the inward witness of the Spirit but placed a strong secondary emphasis upon the evidential power of sanctification. Tyndale, in particular, given the conviction of his mature covenant theology that "none of us can be received to grace but upon a condition to keep the law," understood assurance as a dual product of trust in divine pardon and obedience to divine law. He and most of his Protestant colleagues attributed to good works the power "to make our vocation and election certain to ourselves." Saints with troubled consciences therefore were not to rest alone in the Atonement; they also must seek within themselves "a towardnes to be obedyente to do Goddes commaundement . . . to the uttermost of [your] . . . power." And so once again, now in the management of uncertainty, the familiar elliptical contour of strong Reformed divinity came into view.[7]

6. Ozment, *Reformation in the Cities*, 119; Emanuel Hirsch, *Hilfsbuch zum Studium der Dogmatik* (Berlin, 1951), 127; *WJB*, I, 308 ("comforteth most comfortably"), 325 ("faith . . . not certain"); George Joye, *A Present Consolacion* . . . ([Antwerp?], 1544), sig. E3 ("certaine foundacion"); Joye, *The Refutation of the Byshop of Winchesters Derke Declaration* . . . (n.p., 1546), xcii (without "dubitacion").

7. Ozment, *Reformation in the Cities*, 118; *WWT*, 185; Robert Eden, ed., *The Examinations and Writings of John Philpot* (Cambridge, 1842), 224; [Lancelot Ridley], *A Commentary in Englyshe upon Sayncte Paules Epystle to the Ephesyans* (London? 1540), sig. C. For Tyndale, see also *WWT*, 191; *LL*, 94–97, 102. Carl R. Trueman argues that Robert Barnes

The Problem of Assurance in Puritanism

When, after 1558, Puritan voices too found it necessary to address uncertain consciences, they had no quarrel with the standards laid down by their mid-Tudor forebears; indeed, they reinforced them. In conjunction with growing devotion to the divine honor and glory, a fuller Deuteronomic accent in contract theology, and a mounting interest in church discipline, more than ever it seemed clear that, in order to "come to heaven," men and women "muste addresse themselves to obedience." Consider the teaching of a militant presbyterian clergyman we have encountered before: George Gifford. At Maldon, Essex, in 1582 he spoke of "that wherein the stablenes of . . . faith doth stande, as upon a sure foundation, even the righteousnesse of God and of our Saviour Jesus Christe," but every one of his voluminous sermonic and polemical writings extending through two decades reveals that he understood "righteousness"—in full accord with the Reformed ellipse and his own disciplinary militance—as a synthesis of pardon and infused moral renewal. Accordingly, he did not reckon the Christian's standing before God in abstraction from his or her moral estate.[8]

Explicitly and repeatedly Gifford linked certitude to moral performance. How, he would ask, can we "attaine to this incomparable treasure, to bee out of doubt, and surely resolved in our selves . . . that we be chosen of God"? The answer was complex. In part the saints must look beyond themselves, trusting in the objective, immutable decree of election and its execution through Christ's atoning death. But in part too they should take care "to be richly decked with his [transforming] graces, or . . . vertues, for by these [too] wee shall undoubtedly know" that our faith and salvation are real. Thus Gifford's doctrine of certitude was bifocal. The crucial test, repeatedly applied, was, "Is [the inquirer] justified, is he sanctified"? On one side believers must look to the objectivity of election and Atonement; on the other they must engage in moral struggle. Those prone to "doubt and stagger" must ask themselves, "What is the cause, [and their] heart wil make answere, thou . . . art ful of foule sinnes, . . . thou art unfruitful . . . in good woorkes, [thus] thou canst not say, I am . . . sure I shal be saved." Wherefore they must "give al . . . diligence in good woorkes to come to the sure and undoubted knowledge, that we be chosen unto life." Since human obedience often faltered and the finest deeds

---

"does not make works a basis for assurance" (*LL*, 197). For other formulations, see *RMC*, 409; Charles Nevinson, ed., *Later Writings of Bishop [John] Hooper* (Cambridge, 1852), 60.

8. *CS*, sigs. C8, D; *SCV*, sig. A3.

remained imperfect and therefore damnable, continual recourse to the Redeemer's blood was necessary. Yet there was no suggestion that forgiveness could stand alone as the great warranty of salvation. The pardon of sin, and with it the saint's security, must be yoked to a painstakingly moral existence. In order, then, to attain to a rounded certitude, it was obligatory to *"fetch [a] warrant from within our selves."*[9]

This call for warrants found by self-inspection was the core of the famous "practical syllogism" of Reformed divinity, a proof of election by recourse to its biblically promised effects in the lives of believers. "Whosoeuer do truely beleeue in christ, they are elect . . . but I truely beleeue . . . therefore I am elected," is a typical example from the general literature. Gifford, however, like his fellow presbyterian Theodore Beza in Geneva, was party to a tendency in contemporary Reformed theology to accent the evidential significance of a reformed life as much as or more than the evidence of faith itself and the Spirit's witness.[10] If, again, one should wonder, "[How] may I come to . . . assurance: and which is the way?" Then, the Lord through the rule of the Word "pointeth him out the way" of disciplined life "wherein hee must painefully travel." And if God still "give[s] not this assurance, wee are to labour so much the more, and . . . call our selves to a more straite account, to set a watch over our affections too see with what mynde wee doe things, to foster no sin willingly in us, nor to bee slacke to any good worke." Here the point is drawn even more explicitly. Ethical activity was to flow toward, not away from, religious security. But that was not all, for Gifford's "labour so much the more" openly proportioned security to effort. As he put it even more pointedly, *"The more [one] wanteth [assurance], the more let him strive."* Clearly, in any case, for Gifford no less than for Thomas Cartwright, John Knewstub,

9. *SCV,* sig. E8 ("treasure," "richly decked," *"warrant,"* emphasis mine), F2 ("diligence"), F4 ("doubt and stagger," "foule sinnes"); *SSP,* 56 ("sanctified").

10. *A Briefe Discourse, Taken out of the Writinges of Her. Zanchius* (London, 1592), 50 (appended to [William Perkins], *A Case of Conscience: The Greatest That Ever Was* [London, 1592]); *FEW,* 127. For Puritan examples of the practical syllogism, see William Perkins, *A Commentarie, or Exposition upon the Fiue First Chapters of . . . Galatians* (London, 1617), 260–261; and Nehemiah Wallington, "A Record of Gods Mercies, or A Thankfull Remembrance," 197, MS 204, Guildhall Library, London, copy in the Genealogical Society of Utah, Salt Lake City. Beza's doctrine, "When Sathan putteth us in doubte of our election, we . . . must begin at the sanctification which we fele in our selves," also was available in English translation: Theodore de Beza, *A Briefe and Piththie Summe of the Christian Faith* (London, 1566?), 53 (error for 35). In *BWWP,* 172, Perkins appealed to Beza's teaching on the subject.

and many others, the quest for assurance—despite regular appeals to free pardon and the Spirit's inward witness—led squarely into the realm of behavior. Still attuned in a part of their minds to the age-old belief that personal worth and destiny were at least partly conditional upon moral activity, they made sheer pardon *plus* a monitored flow of regenerate behavior their provision against fear.[11]

From the complementary resources of pardon and moral renewal English Protestants through most of the sixteenth century appear to have extracted at least a tolerable minimum of security. Yet Gifford's several discussions of the problem of assurance suggested that a change was in the making in the later Elizabethan years, as did, for example, Cartwright's several "comfortable letters" to persons "tormented in their Consciences, and . . . not fully persuaded that their sins are forgiven them, by reason whereof, they are half in desperation." "Not fully persuaded," "half in desperation"—such phrases mark the entry into a new, long-lived, and troubled phase of religious complaint and consolation, and Gifford and Cartwright were but initial figures in that development. It was the aggressive spirituality in the tradition of Richard Greenham, William Perkins, and Richard Rogers, rechanneling hungers for purity into a multitude of arduous drills and ultimately into mazes of introspection, that drew moderate Puritanism into its age of anxiety.[12]

Buoyed by the devotional awakening and eager to effect a disciplinary reformation, pietistic Puritans strode forth to convert and order a nation. Less political but more self-analytical than their presbyterian forebears, they sought to make the English more "precise in the searching of . . . sins" and thus impel them to a higher life beyond the usual standards of English parochial religion. That was the theory, but a complication quickly arose; for this was the time, and affectionate Puritanism the primary carrier, of a "tremendous upsurge of interest in the question of a Christian's personal assurance of salvation." Never in mid-Tudor or early Elizabethan times had religious confidence been a dominant, widespread concern of evangelical theologians, but by the turn of the century Puritan utterance was shadowed by a sense of personal doubt and foreboding that, like the pietist turn itself, probably was of unique extent within the Protestant world. On this question as on many others, there were

11. *SCV*, sigs. F4–F5, G. See also *CS*, sig. M3.

12. Albert Peel and Leland H. Carlson, eds., *Cartwrightiana* (London, 1951), 97; the letters are reprinted at 75–108. Note also T[homas] W[ilcox], *Large Letters, Three in Number, Containing Much Necessarie Matter, for the Instruction and Comfort of Such, as Are Distressed in Conscience by Feeling of Sin, and Fear of Gods Wrath* (London, 1589).

substantial differences of emphasis. Among the divines, the foreboding ran stronger in Rogers and Henry Scudder, for instance, than in John Dod or Lewis Bayly. In Bayly's classic *Practice of Pietie*, to take one example, it was a relatively minor note. Among the laity, it emerged more forcibly in the notebooks of Nehemiah Wallingham than in the diary of Lady Margaret Hoby. Nevertheless, for a half-century and more, failing surety was a cardinal theme of pietist preaching and theological discussion.[13]

As framers of the first major "experimental" (experiential, "affectionate") divinity in the magisterial Protestant line, pietist Puritans dwelt frequently and at length upon the emotional states encountered in the saints' journey from preparation for conversion through all the cycles of spiritual warfare to the end of life. Their main concern was with a single axis of emotions from joy to sorrow, from the raptures occasionally experienced in prayer and meditation to dejecting experiences of contrition and "humiliation." Yet, within a worldview so absorbed in the struggle against sin, penitential states loomed larger than pleasurable ones, and this pattern was reproduced in discussions of assurance. Sometimes, at one extreme, the soul might be "sweetely crowned with a glorious, over-flowing confluence of all spiri[t]uall consolations." At such times, the soul "lies so peacefully in His armes of mercy, . . . that shee sweetly sings unto Her selfe, *my beloved [Christ] is mine, and I am His.*" Yet a majority of pietist spiritual directories, commentaries, sermons, and diaries testify that such moments were less frequent than those of loss and distress.[14]

Protestants of every stripe could agree that "the deare Children of God have interruptions . . . in their peace," but this was only a first step toward the conviction that was to rack the religious psychology of old and New England for half a century: interruption, with accompanying fear and distress, was as much the norm as the exception. By the early 1600s a legion of pietist voices had come to marvel and worry at how many of the converted, after some grasp of assurance, were driven from their hold; and, indeed, they had come to believe that the wavering and loss of peace and the arduous struggle to regain it (if only for a brief interval) were the regular fare of many of the saints. That belief helped to determine the content of affectionate divinity, for it slanted interest in religious affection toward the emotional trials of men and women

---

13. *WRG*, 131; Baird Tipson, "Invisible Saints: The 'Judgment of Charity' in the Early New England Churches," *CH*, XLIV (1975), 469; and see Dewey D. Wallace, Jr., *Puritans and Predestination: Grace in English Protestant Theology, 1525–1695* (Chapel Hill, N.C., 1982), 45–46; *WW*, 19, 196. The date of the first edition of Bayly's work is uncertain; the second edition appeared in 1612.

14. *CAC*, 485.

"caused to suspect their comfort to be a vain fancie, and so fall[en] into much feare and doubting." Breadth of coverage was necessary, since doubt was manifest in a medley of ways, ranging from minor worries to more serious and cyclical "spiritual desertions" and to such drastic "affliction of conscience" that the victims' "very *bones were broken* [and] their bodies possessed with strange tremblings." To alleviate these disorders, one had to know them; and, as they strove through the years to chart the "irkesome, and comfortlesse desolations" that befall saints with "no sense now of . . . assurance of His fauour," divines— joined by the few laity whose views are on record—created by far the largest inventory of religious affections within the Protestant world to that time. Dominated by despondent, wavering moods, that record suggests that the practical syllogism and other pietist antidotes to doubt were larger in promise than in delivery.[15]

Puritan Casuistry

To soothe troubled consciences, the "high and heavenly Art, of comforting afflicted consciences" now came to the fore. Just as sin-anguished Catholics could turn for assistance to confessor specialists trained in cases of conscience, so now on English and Protestant soil, for the first time within the international Reformed camp, the management of troubled consciences emerged again as a principal focus of pastoral activity. In this development, Greenham's role was large. His famous readiness to "succour the perplexed" attracted so many to Dry Drayton in the 1570s and 1580s, and his counseling work both in person and through the mails was so extensive, that he, not Perkins, as often claimed, was "the founder and original practitioner" of English Reformed casuistry.[16]

By the turn of the century, a devotion to resolving cases had become essential to the pietist fraternity's conception of the pastoral role, and a flair for the work did much to bring men to regional and even national prominence. When suitable nurture was not available at home, Puritan laity not only gadded to sermons across parish bounds, but they resorted in person and through corre-

15. *CDW*, 324; *CAC*, 88–90, 485. On spiritual desertions, a favorite topic of Puritan spiritual counsel, see *CDW*, 246; Paul Bayne[s], *Briefe Directions unto a Godly Life* . . . (London, 1637), 28–29; *WRS*, II, 100–115.

16. *CAC*, 130; Henry Holland, "The Preface to the Reader," in *WRG*, sig. A5; *PDRG*, 85, and see 95. Greenham's letters are in *WRG*, 232–247. See also *PDRG*, 68, for his epistolary counseling, 87–96 for his counseling theory and practice, and 134–252 for casuistical questions posed and resolved.

spondence to advisers of proven ability to comfort. To take a few examples, Perkins had such talent "at stating of a doubtfull conscience, so that the afflicted in spirit came far and near to him"; John Dod had "much employment in comforting such as were wounded in their spirits, being sent for, not only nigh at hand, but also into remote countries"; and Robert Bolton "had such art in . . . relieving afflicted consciences" that many from "farre and neare, [even] from beyond the sea . . . desired his resolution in divers cases of conscience." In some cases, laity too joined the counselors' ranks. Some turned to young John Winthrop "for advice in cases of conscience," and a godly artisan in early Stuart London served as "adviser to the spiritually troubled [and] . . . was sought out as a spiritual counselor." Devoted to a specialized ministry to the afflicted through personal counseling as well as letters, tracts, and treatises of spiritual guidance, these figures and many like them became the early modern equivalents of Jean Gerson or Johannes Nider in the later Middle Ages, supplying expert counsel for saints in doubt.[17]

A growing market for solace also contributed to the emergence of a more formal "casuistical divinity" in the later Elizabethan years. As with the theology of fast days or the Sabbath, Puritans held no monopoly upon this development, but much and probably most of the casuistical work on record is found in their sermons, commentaries, letters, and tracts of spiritual counsel. These reveal an absorption in cases so substantial as to constitute virtually a distinct branch of Protestant practical theology, and the most notable early manuals were works of the pietist brotherhood. Perkins's *Whole Treatise of the Cases of Conscience* was published posthumously in 1606, and William Ames's *Conscience with the Power and Cases Thereof* (1639) was written in the Protestant Netherlands by a Puritan in exile, an early congregational theorist. Presenting yet another example of re-Catholicization, the Protestant science of cases drew selectively upon the traditional consideration of cases of conscience in context of the sacrament of penance. Typical examples from medieval confessors' guides—"Whether simple fornication is a mortal sin?" and "Who should make restitution for injuries to the human body?"—mirror an underlying conception of casuistry as a science for resolving problems of moral judg-

17. Samuel Clark[e], *The Marrow of Ecclesiastical Historie* . . . (London, 1650), 415 (Perkins); Sa[muel] Clarke, *A Generall Martyrologie* . . . (London, 1651), 46 (Dod); E[dward] B[agshawe], "The Life and Death of Mr. Bolton," prefatory to [Robert Bolton], *Mr. Boltons Last and Learned Worke of the Foure Last Things* . . . (London, 1632), 11; *WP,* I, 156 (Winthrop); *WW,* 109 (artisan). For additional examples of lay consultation with clergy, see *WW,* 98, 105.

ment; and this conception remained dominant in the "anglican" casuistry of figures like Joseph Hall and Robert Sanderson.[18]

Puritan casuists too maintained the traditional interest in moral problems. Many of their concerns—fornication, oaths, usury, and the like—had been standard fare for centuries in the Catholic manuals. In a Protestant setting, however, detailed attention to such matters became a neatly co-optive means to rebut Catholic charges that justification by faith alone invited moral relativism and social chaos. It served as well to promote disciplinary reformation and to expedite adjustment to changing times. But the Puritan transaction with cases cannot be understood essentially as an aid to moral judgment. Echoing, again, trends within the contemporary Catholic evangelical and devotional revival, casuists of Puritan persuasion were engaged less with ethical than with existential problems. Like Greenham, they became specialists in the science of comfort, devising means to resolve "doubts, apprehensions, depressions, and temptations" as these eroded trust in one's state of grace. Works like John Downame's *Christian Warfare* (1604), Scudder's *Christians Daily Walke* (1627), or Bolton's *Instructions for a Right Comforting Afflicted Consciences* (1631) diagnosed and resolved hundreds of such cases. The "unique feature" of their approach, in fact, was a preoccupation with the problem of assurance.[19]

18. Thomas of Chobham, *Summa Confessorum* (ca. 1216), ed. F. Broomfield (Louvain, 1968), 341 ("Utrum simplex fornicatio sit pecccatum mortale"); Johannes Nider, *Manuale Confessorum* (Paris, 1479), sig. Iii ("quo[rum] restitutio fieri debeat circa lesiones corpis humani"). See also Josiah Pratt, ed., *The Works of . . . Joseph Hall* (London, 1808), VIII, 373–496; Robert Sanderson, *Eight Cases of Conscience . . .* (London, 1674). For contemporary recusant examples, see P. J. Holmes, ed., *Elizabethan Casuistry* (Thetford [Norfolk], 1981).

Ames's *Conscience* was a 1639 English translation made from the Latin original of 1632. "His library was well supplied with writings of Catholic casuists," and he grudgingly acknowledged dependence upon conventions of the Catholic *Summae de casibus conscientiae.* Keith L. Sprunger, *The Learned Doctor William Ames: Dutch Backgrounds of English and American Puritanism* (Urbana, Ill., 1972), 178; William Ames, *Conscience with the Power and Cases Thereof . . .* (n.p., 1639), sig. A5.

19. Norman Keith Clifford, "Casuistical Divinity in English Puritanism during the Seventeenth Century: Its Origins, Development, and Significance" (Ph.D. diss., University of London, 1957), 74; *WPEP,* xiv (and see Perkins's treatment of assurance in *WPEP,* 102–126). See also Keith Thomas, "Cases of Conscience in Seventeenth-Century England," in John Morrill, Paul Slack, and Daniel Woolf, eds., *Public Duty and Private Conscience in Seventeenth-Century England: Essays Presented to G. E. Aylmer* (Oxford, 1993), 34. For "felt and recognized differences" between Puritan and "anglican" approaches, see Ian Breward, "The Abolition of Puritanism," *Journal of Religious History,* VII (1972), 33. Margaret Sampson also sees the concern with assurance as the key to "a new

Just as, in the later Middle Ages, multiplying cases of conscience reflected heightened standards in the theology and ritual of penance, so did much of Puritan casuistry derive from the harder penitential routines that Greenham and others had introduced, and those routines were proposed, not to religious, but to lay men and women enmeshed in workaday life. When in the struggle with sin they were arrested by any difficulty, a moment of irresolution or weakness, a doubt about the nature of a sin and its aggravating or extenuating circumstances, a confusion about the degree or adequacy of a good work or an exercise of contrition or amendment, an inability to assess the evidences of a secure estate, or any of countless trials and afflictions (including extreme states of grief and despair)—there was prime material for a case of conscience. Perkins worried about the penitent who "findes himselfe hard hearted, and of a dead spirit, so as he cannot humble himselfe as he would"; and what, Bolton put the case, if "I . . . have cast my selfe . . . upon *Iesus Christ*; . . . and yet no comfort comes: What . . . should I thinke of my selfe, in this Case"? As, again, in the Catholic confessional, a major objective in the treatment of such matters was to relieve *"distresse of mind . . .* touching [one's] estate before God." And, in a most revealing development, often the question of assurance itself emerged as a, or *the,* capital case. Perkins identified the overall subject of his *Cases of Conscience* as the means "whereby the consciences of men distressed, may be quieted and relieved," and his poignant question there, "How [may] a man . . . be . . . assured of his owne salvation?" became, in a separate tract that spoke the mind of generations of pastoral counsellors and casuists, a case of conscience, "THE GREATEST THAT EVER WAS." By the time of Perkins's death in 1602, Puritan casuistry was becoming an art of consolation above all.[20]

Signs and Evidences of a Good Estate

The management of anxiety had climbed the agenda of Puritan concern, and now it both relied on and abetted the analysis and purification of behavior. The interest in psychological and behavioral "signs" of a genuine estate had by early Jacobean times become a pronounced feature of the new spirituality and a popular technique of case divinity. Convinced that faith was the great princi-

---

and distinctively Protestant casuistry in England," in "Laxity and Liberty in Seventeenth-Century English Political Thought," in Edmund Leites, ed., *Conscience and Casuistry in Early Modern Europe* (New York, 1988), 99.

20. *WPEP,* 104 ("dead spirit"), 118 *("distresse"),* 111 (overall subject, question); *CAC,* 432; [Perkins], *A Case of Conscience.*

ple of Christian identity and confidence, Luther had resisted the temptation to see good works as evidences of salvation. Yet by the 1620s Robert Burton was remarking upon the drive—a principal source of a mental disorder that he called religious melancholy—of "devout and precise" English spirits to "torture and crucify themselves" by seeking endlessly for "signs and tokens [to] . . . try themselves, whether they be God's true children." These were the "Supercilious Precisians," as another displeased observer said, who now had learned "to judge of any man's future state and salvation by more secret symptoms and . . . signs than the astronomers can find signs in Heaven."[21]

In the cultivation of signs, Greenham again seems to have set the pace. A cardinal aim of his pioneering effort to analyze "cases of conscience, [and] to succour the perplexed in them" was to help doubtful Christians document their estate. Although much of his literary corpus can be understood in these terms, of interest here are the lists of evidences that appear periodically, intended both for ministerial application through preaching and counseling and for private use by individuals. His four "Markes of a Righteous Man," fifteen "Sweete and sure Signes of Election," and seven "Notes of a true and upright Heart" are prototypical of yet another pietist exercise, self-scrutiny by a checklist of "evidences."[22]

Grounded in belief that it is possible to "iudge of the assurances and evidences of mens salvation: as the best Lawyer can iudge of [those] whereby men holde their lands and livings," the list of evidences became a standard device of spiritual direction and self-trial. From about 1600, pietist clergy routinely pressed their charges to "corroborate their title," to "get sound evidence of a good estate, and then likewise to keep [the] evidence clear." Countless sample lists were offered of varying length and content. Such were John

---

21. Robert Burton, *The Anatomy of Melancholy* (1621), ed. Floyd Dell (New York, 1927), 941–942; anonymous manuscript cited in Keith Thomas, *Religion and the Decline of Magic* (London, 1971), 376. In *Innovations Unjustly Charged upon the Present Church and State . . .* (London, 1637), 210, the Anglican writer Christopher Dow also noted and deplored the Puritan absorption in "innumerable signes and markes of Grace." Paul Seaver describes the analysis of "marks and signs" as "apparently the preoccupation of a generation of godly preachers and laymen" in early Stuart times (*WW*, 214 n. 26). For Luther's resistance, see Steven Ozment, *The Age of Reform, 1250–1550: An Intellectual and Religious History of Late Medieval and Reformation Europe* (New Haven, Conn., 1980), 377.

22. *WRG*, sig. A5. The cited lists are at 148–151, 152, 202. See also 52–57, 245; and cf. the account in John H. Primus, *Richard Greenham: Portrait of an Elizabethan Pastor* (Macon, Ga., 1998), 117–119.

Dod's four signs of election, John Downame's ten "signes and infallible notes of our election," Arthur Hildersam's four "notes, . . . whereby you may approve your hearts to be upright," Thomas Hooker's "Character of a Sound Christian, in Seventeen Markes," and countless other compilations.[23] And in some numbers the laity responded. Lady Margaret Hoby, an admirer of Greenham and Bownde and friend of Perkins, apparently made use of an early list of this type, an "examenation or triall of a christian" prepared by her Puritan chaplain in 1599; and by 1627 (in a prolonged exercise of prayer and fasting) Sir Simonds D'Ewes could matter-of-factly compile a volume of sixty-four "marks and signs . . . first in English and [with additions] afterward in Latin." Lady Anne D'Ewes shared fully in the project, beginning in the same year a record of "marks of her evidence to a better life" and completing it two years later. In one of the few extant expressions of nonelite Puritan spirituality, the London turner and shopkeeper Nehemiah Wallington made a book-length collection about 1632 of "The Marks that I am a Child of God" and advised others as well to "gather into some booke so much as in every signe [you] can clearly find . . . in [your] selfe."[24]

If Greenham pioneered the ritual of signs, Nicholas Byfield brought it to the acme of development. This decidedly Puritan minister of Chester (1600–1615) and Isleworth in Middlesex (1615–1622), whom we have met before as the

23. Arthur Dent, *The Plaine Mans Path-way to Heaven* . . . (London, 1603), 233 (the same comparison is made by *CWSR*, 45); *WRS*, I, 124 ("corroborate their title"); John Dod, *A Plaine and Familiar Exposition on the Lords Prayer*, 2d ed. (London, 1635), 33–34; *CW*, 235–247; Arthur Hildersam, *CVIII Lectures upon the Fourth of John*, 2d ed. (London, 1632), 59; T[homas] H[ooker], *The Paterne of Perfection* . . . (London, 1640), 376–392. See also Timothy Rogers, *The Righteous Mans Evidences for Heaven* . . . (London, 1619), 1–22.

24. Dorothy M. Meads, ed., *Diary of Lady Margaret Hoby, 1599–1605* (Boston, 1930), 63; *WWP*, I, 284–285; James Orchard Halliwell, ed., *The Autobiography and Correspondence of Sir Simonds D'Ewes* (London, 1845), I, 353–354, 375, 414; *WW*, 199; Wallington, "A Record of Gods Mercies," 300. Shorter lists of signs are in Wallington, "A Record of Gods Mercies," 131–137, 142, 287, 292–301. Richard Rhodes was private chaplain in the household of Thomas and Margaret Hoby. For his role as religious adviser to Lady Margaret, see *Diary of Lady Margaret Hoby*, 63, 65, 68, 69, 70, 71, 75, 243 n. 180. Ezekiel Rogers compiled a list of signs for a lay patron in 1630 (Ezekiel Rogers to Lady [Joan] Barrington, Feb. 2, 1629/30, fols. 142–143, Egerton MS 2645, British Library). Rogers's letter is printed in Arthur Searle, ed., *Barrington Family Letters, 1628–1632* (London, 1983), 130. For sample references to Greenham, Bownde, and Perkins, see *Diary of Lady Margaret Hoby*, 62, 71, 94. Margaret and Thomas Hoby apparently entertained Perkins at supper during a visit to London in 1600 (153).

foremost cataloger of biblical rules, published *The Signes* in 1614, then revised and expanded his material to produce *The Spirituall Touch-stone; or, The Signes of a Godly Man* in 1619. Promising his readers that they "may be infallibly assured of Gods favour" and should "use all diligence to get this full assurance," Byfield devoted *The Signes* to a detailed review of sixteen "infallible signes of a child of God," with multiple subdivisions under each. Then, in *The Spirituall Touch-stone*, he presented a far lengthier roster of major and subsidiary signs. It was designed to inspire and guide a private rite, a thorough examen of self to identify as many signs as possible, these to be "gather[ed] out into some litle paper-booke" for use in further rounds of self-examination. No one, Byfield warned, could possess the full range of signs, but he expected true saints to exhibit the "perhaps twentie, or thirtie, or fortie . . . distinct . . . markes" that would suffice for confident assurance.[25]

In what marks, precisely, did Byfield—or Sir Simonds and Lady D'Ewes—aspire to read human states and fates? Clearly the putative Protestant norm of *sola fides* was not the consistent and final rule of the ritual of evidences. What Greenham had proposed, and Byfield attested to the utmost, was that the gains made in the watch, the daily rule, and all the busy rituals of the pietist way counted with almost mechanical sureness as a ground of certitude. In most of the extant lists, trust in pardon and the inner witness of the Spirit were scattered entries amid more numerous marks of a regenerated, striving, sin-hating, and self-controlling nature. Characteristically, *"How stand you affected to sinne?"* and *"How stand you affected towards holines?"* stood in first and second position in Scudder's five queries: "If you can answer, yea, [even] to *any one* of these you may assure your selves that you are in Gods favour." "Do you resolve . . . [to] hang upon Christ" was fifth. In other lists, as in Greenham's "four speciall notes" by which to test one's estate (do I love God and hate sin? do I strive "to please and glorifie God"? do I "goe forward to leave sinne"? do I "love righteous men, and . . . things"?) the focus fell squarely upon the manifest fruits of faith in a highly regulated life. In this way, although neither Greenham nor Scudder might have desired to put the matter so, the rite of signs became itself a sign of piety's regimental aim. Doing more to valorize

---

25. Nicholas Byfield, *The Signes; or, An Essay concerning the Assurance of Gods Love, and Mans Salvation* . . . (London, 1614), 1–2, 7, 14, 20–23; N[icholas] B[y]field, *The Spirituall Touch-stone* . . . , in *MO*, 178–179, 181–182. Byfield's *Signes of the Wicked Man* . . . , a treatise separately published in 1619 and also included in *MO*, was a collection of negative signs, for example, a "lothnesse to examine themselves and trie their estates exactly" (*MO*, 201). Users were to gain assurance by noting the absence of such signs in themselves.

than to discount behavior, Puritan advice to anxious consciences subserved the overall design of a disciplinary reformation.[26]

Sources of Anxiety

At the same time, the heavy pietist traffic in signs was itself a sign that the issue of doubt and its management had become "the weightiest and chiefest poynt of all others in divinitie," and that was a development of some magnitude in Protestant history. Somehow the Puritan movement had worked back, as it were, toward the introspective, doubtful mood of the late Middle Ages—the very mood that original Protestantism was bent to dispel. Nor was this the exclusive result of trends within a religious tradition. The drift of an ardent fraction of the English nation into a phase of insecurity resulted from a snarled conjunction of forces both secular and religious. As suggested in Chapter 3, a changing demographic and economic pattern in the later sixteenth and early seventeenth centuries provoked anxieties. To generalized alarms about poverty and disorder were added more specific socioeconomic discomforts: the threat posed by emergent "economic appetite and entrepreneurial energy" to traditional social worlds like that of the London artisan Nehemiah Wallington or of Arthur Dent's rural commonwealth of South Shoebury, Essex; the "anxiety about status" generated by social polarization and mobility; the chronic risks and uncertainties of commerce; "ethical anxiety" arising from the tension "between the realities of an individualistic agrarian capitalism and the ethics of traditional social obligations"; and the difficulties of harmonizing worldly enterprise and prosperity with the strains of contemptus mundi that still ran strong in Protestant teaching. Given the climate of the age, it is a plausible surmise that such anxieties fed the pronouncedly Puritan experience of sin and "affliction" and thus fueled doubt about one's status before God. It is difficult to see how troubles of mind related to little-understood social dynamics could otherwise have been comprehended at the time.[27]

---

26. *CDW,* 256–258, and see Searle, ed., *Barrington Family Letters,* 130; *WRG,* 149–150. See also the inventory taken by John Rogers of Dedham of the "signes, by which examining our selves, we may certainly know whether we have a true faith or no" (*The Doctrine of Faith* . . . , 3d ed. [London, 1629], 348–383). Reliance "by faith on the promises" stands tenth in Thomas Hooker's seventeen signs of a sound Christian, and it was coupled to "abstaining from the use of any unlawfull . . . practices" (*Paterne of Perfection,* 384).

27. *ST,* 1; *WW,* 135 ("appetite"); *RRR,* 29 (status anxiety); *PM,* 125 ("ethical anxiety");

Yet the cases of troubled conscience that now crowded the schedules of counselors and casuists also fed upon sources rooted in the English Reformation and its radical Puritan manifestations. Certainly the wrenching changes of the earlier Reformation and again of 1553 and 1558 had left a legacy of insecurity. The elaborate Catholic system of mediations, consolations, wonder-working shrines, relics, images and masses, magical benedictions and exorcisms, and acts of communion between the living and the dead had been swept away, leaving some of the citizenry "bewildered, bereft." The traditional ministration of comfort through oral confession and priestly absolution was removed. Men and women now faced choices between the Catholic and Protestant ways to redemption and must make their way in hostile coexistence with their confessional opposites.[28]

Conforming Puritans, for their part, must occupy an often ambiguous middle ground defined by their commitment both to the state church and to their own semisectarian ways. Within their local communities, they must struggle to sustain subcultural values and identities sometimes stiffly contested by ungodly neighbors. They were likely as well to withdraw from the popular rites and recreations that defused tensions and bolstered "collective identity" in towns and parishes and were thus "of vital importance to the . . . emotional security of individuals and families." It is well to remember too that militant Protestantism made very slow headway among the general population before the Elizabethan period. Not until the mid-Elizabethan years did an actual reformation occur in large numbers of parishes, and this late-century expansion was largely the story of the rise of Puritanism, of its promulgation of a contractual, law-oriented, ethically stringent faith, and of its demand—as

---

ES, 60 (contradiction). For anxiety, see also C. G. A. Clay, *Economic Expansion and Social Change: England, 1500–1700* (Cambridge, 1984), II, 225; *RRR*, 9. In *CDW*, 48, Henry Scudder warned that the "desire of successe" can "make you ful of anxietie and feare." For a chronicle of the "endless worry and anxiety" that confronted a London Puritan artisan in the management of his business and household, see *WW*, 139, and Chapter 5. Hunt suggests that one result of commercial and ethical cares, "given the mental climate of the age, might be a morbid fear of damnation." *PM*, 125.

28. Susan Brigden, *London and the Reformation* (Oxford, 1989), 638; *ES*, 62; Jean Delumeau, "Prescription and Reality," trans. Ian Patterson, in Leites, ed., *Conscience and Casuistry*, 147. Ministration of comfort: the consolatory power of absolution was pointedly stressed in contemporary recusant literature, and the Laudian writer Immanuel Bourne in the 1620s urged "priestly absolution [as] . . . an alternative solution to . . . Calvinist despair" (Sampson, "Laxity and Liberty," in Leites, ed., *Conscience and Casuistry*, 105).

party to the contemporary and international reformation of manners—for "a severe moral and spiritual discipline of a sort which had never actually been demanded of . . . [Christian] forebears" outside the monastic state. Through the period, moreover, Protestants had reason to be alarmed by the belligerence and the many successes of the Counter Reformation, and scares of Catholic subversion at home abounded in the years of Elizabeth and the first Stuarts.[29]

Warm espousal of the doctrine of predestination was another mark of the Puritan breed, although its part in problematizing assurance is not fully clear. Presumably, the anchorage of election in unalterable divine decision was a boost to surety, but the accompanying harsh distinction between the chosen and the reprobate (accentuated by the removal of purgatory, which left the stark alternatives of heaven and hell) and the restriction of the elect to a small minority of humankind could become topics for anxious brooding and promote anxious resort to the ritual of signs. A related theme with similar potential was the pietist recapturing of the traditional affirmation that the Last Judgment is performed by Christ. Contrasting sharply with Luther's tendency to avoid portrayal of Christ as a condemning figure to be feared but in accord with Reformed characterizations of him as king and lawgiver, the expanded treatment of the Last Judgment and hell both in extent and graphic description exceeded all precedents in English Protestant thought. Reflection upon "what we shall answere that dreadfull Iudge" and upon the "incredible horror and exceeding great anguish" of the finally condemned was a frequent ingredient of pietist spiritual direction; and, together with the horrific depictions of Judgment and hell that appeared in Bayly's *Practice of Pietie*, Dent's *Plaine Mans Path-way*, Bolton's *Carnall Professor*, Shepard's *Sincere Convert*, and many other works of the genre, they reflected and no doubt fostered anxiety.[30]

29. Identity and security: for the vital psychosocial role played by neighborliness, goodfellowship, and the rites of popular culture in contemporary English communities, see *ES*, 51–57, 61–65; Marjorie Keniston McIntosh, *Controlling Misbehavior in England, 1370–1600* (Cambridge, 1998), 188–189.

30. *WRG*, 319, and see 322, 481–487; *BWWP*, 256. For extended treatments, see *POP*, 73–103; Dent, *Plaine Mans Path-way*, 352–357, 362–367; Robert Bolton, *The Carnall Professor* . . . (London, 1634), 122–161. Luther and Calvin tended toward a figurative understanding of hell and avoided dwelling upon physical details (Erhard Kunz, *Protestantische Eschatologie von der Reformation bis zur Aufklärung* [Freiburg, 1980], 15–17). For examples of Christ as judge, see *POP*, 91–94; Dent, *Plaine Mans Path-way*, 352–359, and *SF*, 373–400, 404–410. Concerning predestination: pietist writers emphasized the assuring function of predestinarian doctrine, but I am not persuaded that it was "*the* preeminently useful doctrine in the search for assurance." Wallace, *Puritans and Predestination*, 46, emphasis

Again the Ellipse: Exact Walking and "Certeintie"

At all events, in fidelity to principles laid down long before by advanced Protestants (illustrated above by the theology of George Gifford), pietist advisers met their growing load of cases with a two-pronged strategy: "resting upon [God's] promises" *and* "obeying his commandments. . . . [for] by th[ese] we . . . rest quietly about our Salvation." There were many variations in emphasis, to be sure. Downame sounded clearer solifidian notes than, say, Bolton. Yet all affirmed the freeness of pardon, the immutability of the saints' election and of God's covenant promises to them, and the inner testimony of the Spirit. Often they urged their charges to "renounce wholly all opinion . . . of that thine owne Righteousness and desert" and grasp Christ "aloane with the empty hand of faith," and some echoed the view of Calvin and other Reformed theorists that assurance was integral to the event of justification.[31]

Yet, in the last analysis, the clergy's response to multiplying cases of conscience remained twofold. Just as Abraham "was justified by his workes, that is, by such a faith as had workes joyned with it," no approach could succeed apart from the analysis and correction of behavior. Once again we see how the pietist turn was modifying the theological ellipse, accenting the disciplinary pole. Naturally enough, the practical syllogism, with the stronger performative spin already imparted to it by the turn of the century, came more decisively to shape strategies of consolation. Increasingly, assurance was proportioned to achievement, to the experience and exercise of transforming graces as much as or more than to passive justification. Dent, echoing and possibly quoting Gifford, underscored the duty to "fetch the warrant of our salvation from within our selves," specifically from how "a man feeleth in himselfe the increase of knowledge, obedience, and godlinesse." Here—as Scudder put it, "if you would have . . . profe" of your redemption, you must "feele for it in *the most certaine effect*, which is your Sanctification"—was a core element and often the crux of pietist counsel to afflicted consciences. In his *Christians Daily Walke*

---

mine; and cf. Charles Lloyd Cohen, *God's Caress: The Psychology of Puritan Religious Experience* (New York, 1986), 116.

31. Bayne[s], *Briefe Directions,* 182–183 (and see 51–53); Thomas Hooker, "The Rule of the New Creature" (undated), 71, Rawlinson E108, Bodleian Library, Oxford University. See also *CW,* 188 ("When we looke upon God and Christ, there is cause of firme assurance, but when we looke upon our selves, there is nothing but matter of doubting"); Ezek[i]el Culverwell, *A Treatise of Faith* . . . (London, 1623), 19, 26. On faith as assurance, see Wallace, *Puritans and Predestination,* 50, and the sources cited there. The best analysis of Puritan teaching on assurance is *FEW,* 119–137.

(1627), a best-seller of pietist spiritual direction, Scudder followed the trail of logic into outright contravention of sola fides. This militant pastor of Drayton, Oxfordshire, for whom *"to liue by faith . . .* is, to frame your life according to the will of God revealed in his word," now was ready to advise the doubting saint to explore, amend, and hold up his or her own "uprightnesse" to "answere the accusations of His accusing conscience."[32]

This was a relatively extreme statement, but it reveals the overall drift of pietist teaching, of its progressively intricate qualification of sola fides, its ever closer linkage of assurance and behavior, and its trademark demand for strictness and exactitude. Here, as in Richard Sibbes's dictum, "God's favour will not be kept without . . . a most narrow watch over our loose spirits, [and] . . . without exact walking, and serious self-denial," were definite echoes of the age-old Catholic belief that spiritual peace of mind is attained when the passions are watched and quieted and the virtues cultivated. Here too was a subtly backhanded reappropriation of the belief, underscored anew at the Council of Trent and basic to the Counter Reformation's devotional teaching, that a measure of uncertainty about one's status with God was a necessary source of moral energy. Always, pietist voices spurned the mere conjectural certainty allowed by the old church, yet implicitly they restored uncertainty to the economy of redemption, making the tension of doubt again a spur to moral effort. How, they asked, may we "have the angry face of our blessed God . . . turned into calmnesse and favour unto us"? How can we gain "the invalueable Iewel of peace"? To such queries an evident answer was to "embrace . . . strict and holy courses," for, by the plain logic of the practical syllogism: "The more sinne, the more guilt, and the lesse sin, the lesse guilt. Now the *lesse guilt* lyeth upon the *Conscience,* the *more peace of Conscience,* the *more guilt,* the *lesse peace.*" So the need for a merciful God, the same need that had moved Luther to assign morality a humbler place in Christian life and

32. John Preston, *The Breast-plate of Faith and Love . . .* , 5th ed. (London, 1634), 173; Dent, *Plaine Mans Path-way,* 240; *CDW,* 138 (emphasis mine), 4, 263. Bayly argued "Though good works are not necessary to *Iustification:* yet they are necessary to *salvation . . .* at the last day [Christ] will give the heavenly inheritance onely to them who haue done *good workes. . . .* At that day, [actual!] *Righteousnesse* shall weare the Crowne. . . . To be rich in good workes, [therefore] is the surest foundation of our *assurance"* (*POP,* 183–184, and see 212). Similarly, Bolton advised clergy: "Speake thus . . . to thy spirituall Patient[:] 'If [your] sorrowful soule . . . doth renounce . . . all manner of sinne [and] insatiably thirst *after righteousnesse; . . .* [then] notwithstanding all thy present terrour . . . of minde, thou are truly and euerlastingly happy.'" In this sense no spiritual adviser "can promise pardon, or apply the promises, but conditionally." *CAC,* 227, 278.

especially in the work of consolation, worked in this Puritan-Reformed tradition to enlarge its role and its prestige. In numerous parishes and through countless publications the message now resounded: "Thou must be a patrone, and in some good measure, a practiser of precise points, if ever thou wilt have true peace and assurance."[33]

And if "precise points" signified divine commands with their call for close and full observance, superior means of implementation now were at hand. After the pietist turn it was better understood that "the following of a well ordred course bringeth greatest peace" and that a course was best fixed and kept through a methodical plan of exercises. Thus, directly and immediately, the pietist rites were enlisted in the struggle against doubt. Sureness through exercises: this was a main article of practical divinity. Consider, for instance, its import in the two most notable pietist compendia of the early Stuart years. First published in 1603, Richard Rogers's *Seven Treatises* was the sorely needed aid that Greenham (according to Henry Holland) had failed to produce: the first English Protestant spiritual directory. Published between 1604 and 1618 in four parts encompassing nearly three thousand pages, Downame's *Christian Warfare* was the giant and peerless summa of English affectionate divinity. Each work had an expressly twofold design. The aim, in Rogers's words, was to explain "both how to come to the assurance of salvation and also how . . . to lead a godly and a Christian life"; and in his *Seven Treatises* the issue of assurance, rated the "chiefest poynt of all others in divinitie," became "the ground" of hundreds of pages of disciplinary instruction within a context of devotional drill organized in a daily rule. So too the design of *Christian Warfare* was "first . . . to comfort those . . . afflicted in conscience" by instruc-

---

33. *WRS*, IV, 143–144; *CAC*, 256–257; *CDW*, 284 (second pag.); *GD*, 58. Often the link between morality and consolation was expressed in the familiar "if . . . then" of federal theology. Greenham advised "poore [afflicted] soules" that "*if* they abhor sinne as sinne, *if* they examine them selues for it, *if* they . . . mislike them selues for it," then "the Lord will . . . giue them the sweetnes of his promises" (*WRG*, 133, emphasis mine). In explicitly contractual language, Thomas Hooker argued: "The Lord will manifeste himselfe to us . . . [i]f wee will love him and keepe his Commandements. But if we breake the condition . . . [he will] withdraw himselfe from us. . . . When Christians grow . . . carelesse in holy dutie, the Lord taketh away the light of his favour." T[homas] H[ooker], *The Soules Implantation into the Naturall Olive* (London, 1640), 148, 150.

Concerning moral energy, see Philip Schaff, ed., *The Creeds of Christendom*, rev. David S. Schaff (Grand Rapids, Mich., 1990), II, 98–99, 103–104. For contemporary examples in Catholic devotional writing, see L[uis] de Granada, *Of Prayer, and Meditation . . .* , trans. Richard Hopkins (Paris, 1582), sigs. avii–aviii; Granada, *The Sinners Guyde . . .* , trans. Francis Meres (London, 1598), 63–68.

tion in divine pardon and in the "signs and marks" of sainthood (itself an exercise), and "secondly, [to] labour to lead the Christian in an even course" through devotional rites. Thus did these and countless other texts assert the power of a regular course of rituals to contain sin *and* generate evidences of a safe estate. From the start the whole regimen of the tightly watched and ordered life was energized in part by a craving for more "certeintie."[34]

When, then, cases of conscience began to abound, pietist authorities did not highlight afresh the soothing power of sola fides; indeed, they found it increasingly difficult to affirm that faith alone reliably assured. Those who spoke of trust in God's acceptance despite the continued sinfulness of the heart were also veteran counselors struggling with cases of conscience that fell far short of the ideal. If the certainty of faith was relative in part to one's disciplinary drills and feats and if the solace drawn from spiritual combat could be faint or lost wholly for a time, then in practice certainty was divisible from faith. Since the objectively saving act of faith and the saints' perception of that act often did not coincide, by the early seventeenth century a distinction between faith that saves and faith that assures had become familiar.

Richard Sibbes (1577–1635) offers a prime example. For this famous Cambridge lecturer, educator, and president of the Puritan Feoffees for Impropriations from 1627 to 1629, pardon was the "main benefit" of the gracious covenant, and trust in "the blood of Christ!" the primary factor in assurance. "Nothing else can give rest to our souls." Yet in equally emphatic tones and with perfect consistency in his own mind, he divided the saints' faithful grasp of the Atonement from their assured knowledge of pardon. Faith in his reading is twofold. There are, "first, the direct act, whereby I cast myself upon Christ, and [second] a reflex act, whereby I know that I am in an estate of grace." The latter rests upon awareness of the regenerative "fruits of the Spirit" within and is "oftentimes divided from the first act." Here the familiar elliptical formula, its moral bias, and its bisecting impact upon the concept of faith

---

34. *ST,* 1 ("chiefest poynt," "ground"); 84 ("how to come"), 297 ("ordred course"), 498 ("certeintie"); *CW,* sigs. A4–A5. In the preface to *ST,* sig. A5, Rogers described the work as a "direction . . . for mens liues to gouerne and order them." The daily rule he offered as a means "to live according to the will of God, with sound peace." The alternative was to "live inordinately, and so voide of comfort" (*ST,* 314 [and see 411], 354). John Rogers of Dedham and Paul Baynes counted the daily rule as "the only way of true *peace.*" *MCA,* I, 424; and see Bayne[s], *Briefe Directions,* 310.

Concerning exercises: Ezekiel Culverwell argued that those who neglect family devotions, Sabbath practices, and other "holy exercises" lack "sound proofe" of their redemption. *Treatise of Faith,* 62.

are all starkly clear. Without question "it is by the first act that we are saved," yet at the same time "God gives the reflect act, which is *assured hope, as a reward of exact walking.*"[35]

In this respect, Puritan spiritual directors chose to treat troubled consciences in a manner adapted to ethical common sense and consistent both with the disciplinary accents in their tradition and their wish for a moral reformation. In so doing they proved again that their reading of the times was complex and their program versatile. Their summons to self-control through spiritual exercise and direction became more than a jealous response to the Catholic devotional awakening, more than a retort to Catholic attacks upon the dogma of faith alone, more than a means to reestablish order and identity in a changing society, and more than a way to serve the divine honor and to underscore federal and Deuteronomic concerns. It was also a remedy for anxious consciences, and one that met with some success. In the relentless pursuit of signs Robert Burton might see only a rite of self-torture, but eyes trained to the beauty of holiness could find there, in D'Ewes's phrase, comfort and reposedness of spirit. That, at least in theory, was the secret of the signs, and many could testify, with Sibbes, "We are never more in heaven, before we come thither, than when we can read our evidences." Making religious certainty ever more conditional upon self-analysis and purification was not the problem, as Luther held, but an indispensable part of the cure.[36]

Yet, if that is so, we are left with further questions. In many details the pietist synthesis was new, a challenge to select values of monastic and professional religiosity, and yet in other respects it was profoundly conservative.

35. *WRS,* II, 385, VII, 213, 263, emphasis mine. Although Sibbes emphasized the Spirit's inner witness to a good estate, he could speak of "no other way to gett assurance but by multiplieng in the worke of the Lord" ("The Christians Armor against the Feare of Death," 12, MS Add. 25037, manuscript division, British Library, London). Janice Knight clarifies Sibbes's covenant doctrine in *Orthodoxies in Massachusetts: Rereading American Puritanism* (Cambridge, Mass., 1994), 92–93. In early New England, the "Actus Reflexus" of assurance was a topic in Samuel Stone, "The whole body of Divinity in a Catecheticall way handled by Mr Samuel Stone, Teacher of the Church in Hartford, N.E.," 375–377, MS, MHS. For varying approaches to "justifying faith" and "the faith of assurance," see *FEW,* 66, 129–137; Cohen, *God's Caress,* 95 n. 72; John von Rohr, *The Covenant of Grace in Puritan Thought* (Atlanta, 1986), 65–66.

36. *WRS,* I, 124. John Davenport, the religious leader of the early New Haven colony, found the possession of a ready checklist of signs so precious that it was "as when an house is on fire, and all is in danger to be lost, the owner cries out, oh, let me have my . . . box of evidences, they are my treasure, the principal of my estate." *The Saints Anchor-Hold . . .* (London, 1661), 33–34.

Clearly, it appropriated ascetic and penitential modes of piety that had pre-vailed for centuries in the old church. Such modes might mesh well with a theology and a reform program in which moral regulation was complementary to pardon and pious affection, but was it disingenuous to seek warrants for assurance in a concept of spiritual combat redolent of the monastery and pursued through elaborate and ever-repeated rituals of introspection and self-management? And, if that concept was to play so large a role in the Protestant art of consolation, what then must be said of Luther's very different belief in the hopeless ambiguity of behavior? Since by the seventeenth century he was regarded in England as a great figure of the past but seldom as a living option in theology, it is unlikely that Greenham and his colleagues knew the extent of their difference with his teaching. Nevertheless, and to an even greater degree than in pre-Marian theology, their approach worked in the opposite direction from his. In the aftermath of a transforming conversion, deeper self-scrutiny and stricter constraint of thought and deed would do much to make election sure. Here was a gratifying thrust beyond the religion of the Prayer Book, but was it unduly hopeful to believe that severe analysis and control of the self would generate plain signs of a safe estate? Might the enlistment of strenuous devotion in the cause of peace serve in unplanned ways to *magnify* the problem of assurance? That is the question to engage us next.

CHAPTER 8

More Piety
and
More Doubt

At once the most prolific Elizabethan Puritan writer and the new piety's greatest literary popularizer, William Perkins shared the doctrinal and practical essentials described above (Chapters 4–7), including the belief that religious certainty flowed jointly from the Spirit's inward testimony and from signs of a regenerate life. His concern with the problem of assurance was especially evident in his doctrine of "a little or weak faith." A famous leitmotiv of his spiritual counsel, it was the subject of his 1597 tract *A Graine of Musterd-Seede*. Designed expressly for "troubled . . . consciences," it stated that even the smallest beginnings of faith and repentance, even a faint desire to believe and amend, indeed even a sense of grief for the lack thereof, all count before God as faith and repentance themselves. Here was a useful device of spiritual direction, one that acknowledged doubt as an ill of the time so urgent as to require a frank minimization of standards—and this within a religious movement that favored hard demands.[1]

Yet Perkins, like Greenham and Rogers, hoped grandly that more piety meant *less* doubt. Even those of weak faith, he seemed sure, could expect to ascend toward full and steady certainty, whereas persistent doubt was the lot of newborn saints unskilled in spiritual combat. In particular a strenuous practice of piety, in dialectic with sheer pardon, would purify lives and consciences and so reduce the incidence of doubting. By implication, the need for professional treatment of cases of conscience would recede, and with it the expanded flow of counsel, preaching, and writing about assurance.[2]

On the whole, however, pietist sermons, directories, and records of lay and clerical spirituality from the early Stuart era report a different outcome. Paul

1. *BWWP*, 401 (and see 230), 392. Perkins associated doubt particularly, yet not exclusively, with the early stage of conversion.

2. *BWWP*, 230; *WWP*, I, 126–127.

Baynes's *Briefe Directions unto a Godly Life* (1618), Mistress Anne Fenwick's *Saints Legacies* (1631), Robert Bolton's *Instructions for a Right Comforting Afflicted Consciences* (1631), the unpublished writings of the London artisan and shopkeeper Nehemiah Wallington (1598–1658), and other monuments of a maturing pietism do not evidence decreased anxiety. In truth, they reveal the opposite: an unrelenting absorption in "cases" and an increasingly refined analysis of affliction of conscience, its causes and cures. Thomas Goodwin, lecturer at Trinity Church, Cambridge, exhibited the pattern clearly enough in the late 1620s. Without apology he devoted an entire cycle of sermons (255 published pages) to the "maine proposition" that a Christian, sometimes for "many yeares," can slip into *"darknesse, . . .* filled with strong feares and jealousies, that God is not *His god."* Occupied with the sources and phenomenology of saintly doubt, and adding the usual fine distinctions between true and faked signs and a numbered array of ritual antidotes, Goodwin epitomized the scene near the time of the Great Migration to New England: more piety and *more* doubt. This was the very inference drawn by anti-Puritan clergy of the period like Robert Burton and Richard Napier. Both found an extraordinarily high incidence of religious insecurity among their Protestant contemporaries, and both found it concentrated precisely where one might least expect it: among the most "devout and precise" spirits given to fasting, meditation, and other penitential rites.[3]

It is well to remember that the hoped-for success in the treatment of doubt would have worked against important clerical interests. Members of the fraternity knew that the presbyterian attempt to magnify the ordinary clergy's authority had failed. Yet, from their many complaints of lay resistance and impudence and their emphatic self-promotion, we know of their strong desire for professional esteem and power. At the same time, their preference for painful preaching, for rites and sometimes conventicles not sanctioned by the official church, and in some cases for devious exercises in semiconformity weakened their office within the established church, making them vulnerable to official complaint by hostile laity and to episcopal interference or removal. To the careers of such men, the pietist turn was a boon. It multiplied their

3. Tho[mas] Goodwin, *A Childe of Light Walking in Darknes* . . . (London, 1636), 2–5, 174 (in an unpag. preface "To the Reader," Goodwin noted that he had preached the sermons about eight years earlier; he was appointed lecturer at Trinity in 1628); Robert Burton, *The Anatomy of Melancholy* (1621), ed. Floyd Dell (New York, 1927), 942, and see 939–942, 970; Michael MacDonald, *Mystical Bedlam: Madness, Anxiety, and Healing in Seventeenth-Century England* (Cambridge, 1981), 220–221. Burton also blamed "needless speculation" about predestination (941, 959).

necessary functions and hence their prestige. Saints, and many a hypocrite too, would honor the pastor who was not only liturgist but also orchestrator of a complex and emotionally engaging spirituality. And, since that spirituality was driven in part by a craving for certitude, the clergy became esteemed consultants in the heavenly science of comfort. So cross-purposes were at work. Pledged to dissolve anxiety, the brotherhood had a strong disincentive to discover a radically efficient means.[4]

Further, it is likely that the very directness and energy of their campaign against doubt proved counterproductive in several ways. Their efforts to impart and stabilize assurance met with many a success, but, when they insisted so habitually upon the need for certainty and dwelt at length upon states of doubt, when they treated the query, "Am I a child of God or no?" explicitly or implicitly as the grandest case of conscience, or when they connected their large repertoire of spiritual rites so directly to the struggle against doubt, they both advertised and complicated the very sickness they strove to heal. They rated security high among the gospel promises but taught as well that peace of conscience was, not a simple by-product of faith, but a fleeting state to be targeted and pursued. Now doubt too would serve moral reformation, but at a cost: acceptance that peace is an elusive quality that men and women perpetually must "labour to get" and "busie themselves about . . . for the obtaining and keeping of it." Unaware of the irony, Richard Rogers bade readers of *Seven Treatises* to "give no rest to your selves, till you can proove that you be in the estate of salvation"; and the proof, the array of signs and evidences, often was cloudy. The none-too-tacit message of pietist direction was that peace of mind was a toilsome and usually temporary achievement—and that pastoral consolation would remain in high demand.[5]

The Complete Confession in Protestant Dress

When cases of conscience failed to subside, men less gravely "precise" and, perhaps, less confident of their vocation might have paused to review their

---

4. Clerical self-promotion is discussed in *PM*, 113–114.

5. John Preston, *The Breast-plate of Faith and Love* . . . , 5th ed. (London, 1634), 110 ("labour"); *ST*, 30, 53. In a study of Elizabethan Calvinist piety that includes many of the figures treated here, Peter Iver Kaufman finds: "Anxiety was not something to be . . . gotten over once and for all. It was regularly to be renewed, interrogated or wrestled, and tamed each time pietists descended to their underworlds, encountered the sin within, and entertained grave doubts about their election." *Prayer, Despair, and Drama: Elizabethan Introspection* (Urbana, Ill., 1996), 57.

tactics in the cold light of history. In particular, they might have awakened to striking parallels between their present profusion of cases and the late-medieval phenomenon of the sin-anguished conscience. This, however, was not to be. Without doubt, they knew that the old church's frail grasp upon assurance was related to the confessional system and its demand for a regular survey and purgation of sins, but they did not detect its likeness to their own approach. Nor did they appreciate the obsessive strain in their own doctrines of sin and morality or imagine that their use of the practical syllogism was unsubtle. Nothing in their theology, they were sure, could compromise the consoling power of sola fides and make certitude again relative to morality. So there took form, beyond their power to recognize or hinder, a spiral of logic and counsel that fed the very anxieties they wished to resolve. At its center, unsettling the very confidence it aimed to increase, was the ritual of self-analysis.

"How may a man know," asked Perkins, "that he is justified before God? A[nswer]. He need . . . descend into his own heart to search whether he be sanctified or not."[6] Here in the trial of self was the chief means to implement the practical syllogism. For all their presumed expertise in the dynamics of the self and all their Protestant belief that the best of a Christian's thoughts and works are shadowed with sin, pietist directors still trusted that continual and tedious self-scanning would bolster certainty. From no other spiritual exercise, not even prayer, meditation, or fasting, did they expect so much. And now, even as they multiplied its occasions, the clergy also strove to enlarge the extent of its reach within and to upgrade its standard of thoroughness. Hear, for instance, the general directions given for the "triall of our estates" in John Downame's *Guide to Godlynesse* of 1622:

> The which [trial] is held . . . in the Court of Conscience, . . . wee sitting as Iudges upon our selues. . . . [We must] review and take a survey of all that wee haue done . . . , of all our parts and faculties of soule and body, examining how we haue imployed them to the glory of [God]; . . . [we must scan] all our thoughts . . . , words and actions, [and] all our course and carriage in our whole life and conversation, . . . More especially, wee may examine our selves, how wee haue . . . shaken off the seruice of sinne, . . . and deuoted our selues wholly to the seruice of God. How wee haue profited in mortification, and what corruptions wee haue subdued and weakened . . . ; how wee haue mastered and abated our pride, anger, ambition, couetousnesse, voluptuousnesse, impatiencie, euill concupiscence, and the rest

6. *BWWP*, 159. Perkins saw conscience as "a safe guide" to assurance "only so long as it was . . . constantly scrutinised for traces of sin." *BWWP*, 31.

of our corrupt affections. . . . How wee haue ruled that unruly member our tongues, . . . and how we haue renewed and increased our sorrow for sinne, . . . [and] haue performed the generall duties of Christianity, and the special duties of our callings; and how we have obserued or neglected the duties of our daily exercise [that is, daily rule]. . . . The chiefe things wherin we must most often and seriously examine our selues, are our sinnes, and the [Deuteronomic] punishments which attend upon them. . . . The rule of which examination . . . is the Law of God. . . . [We should move] from one Commandement [in the Decalogue] to another, examining our selues, how often and many wayes we haue offended against euery one of them, . . . reaching euen to our thoughts and first motions, which haue not the consent of will ioyned with them. . . . We shall heereby come to a cleere and liuely sense . . . of our sinnes in all the sorts and kinds of them; [and] we must then further examine our selues, how often and innumerable times we haue reiterated . . . the same sinnes, . . . And then wee shall plainely see, that our sinnes in number exceed the . . . starres of heauen. . . . we must [next] consider, how haynous they haue many of them beene, in respect of their quality and degree. Where we are carefully to take heed that we doe not . . . excuse, minse, and extenuate our sinnes; but that wee looke upon them in their naturall . . . outragiousnesse, and aggrauate them by all their circumstances of persons, manner, time, [and] place.

[The above considerations facilitate] the confession of our sinnes before God, [and] their remission, . . . For if Merchants . . . haue [their] bookes of accounts, which containe the maine matters of their estates, what they . . . owe, and what is owing to them; . . . [then] why should wee thinke such care too much, . . . for the . . . discharge and cleering of our debts unto God, which if they be found upon our account at the great Audit of Gods last Iudgement, shall neuer be forgiuen[?][7]

A small slice of the author's full instruction, this excerpt nevertheless supplies an extensive locus classicus of pietist instruction in self-scrutiny. Since Downame elsewhere acknowledged that, "when we looke upon our selues, there is nothing but matter of doubting" and was uncommonly careful to affirm faith and justification as the central assets of Christian faith and the primary sources of certitude, the passage is especially revealing. It suggests that in the Stuart years the examen of self had evolved into an aggressive, punctilious, and repeated survey of sins tied complexly to the question of assurance. Here, in the

7. *GG*, 605–611.

most militantly anti-Catholic sector of the English church, was an end result of devotional re-Catholicization. In striking fact, through his emphasis upon methodical procedure, his appeal to the Decalogue as a systematic standard for the exercise, his demand for completeness (the identification of every single sin) and for attention to "circumstances," his attention to elusive niceties of distinction (as in the need to determine "quality and degree" of sin), and his sense of the fearful Last Judgment overhanging all, Downame had achieved what one might have supposed unthinkable in a Reformation tradition: a near-approximation of the Catholic complete confession.[8]

The complete confession in Protestant dress! On the grounds that it incited anxious preoccupation with sin and even encouraged it, early Protestant theologians had derided the practice, and about 1571 Thomas Cartwright, the foremost English presbyterian, declared it an intolerable burden upon the Christian's conscience. But insistence that "as *Confession* must be *particular,* so also must it be *full*" was no peculiarity of Downame's in the early seventeenth century, but a commonplace of English pietist teaching. Making necessary allowances for solifidian principle, the brotherhood unfurled its program of self-analysis, often in striking symmetry to the old church's confessional teaching. Each of the elements cited above was ubiquitous in pietist direction, including belief that the earthly trial in the court of conscience removes sins from the roster at the Last Judgment and a pronounced interest in the "wayes, degrees, and circumstances, by which sins are made more notorious and hatefull"—both patent Catholic borrowings. The result, more than ever before in the Reformed tradition, was the construal of sin as a series of single and separately fateful acts, in turn reinforced by Protestant denial of the distinction between venial and mortal sins (as William Gouge put it, *"Every sinne is mortall"*) and by frequent warning of the Deuteronomic penalties due to breaches of the divine contract. As in Jane Ratcliffe's cry that "sinne like a leprosie hath . . . corrupted mee," the result could be a profound sense of personal impurity and danger.[9]

8. *CW,* 188. For the complete confession, see above, Chapter 7, n. 2, and text.

9. Daniel Dyke, *Two Treatises: The One, of Repentance; The Other, of Christs Temptations* (London, 1616), 73 (and see 59–73); *CAC,* 447–448; William Gouge, *A Guide to Goe to God . . .* (London, 1626), 136; John Ley, *A Patterne of Pietie; or, The Religious Life and Death of . . . Jane Ratcliffe* (London, 1640), 86. Gouge's point was echoed in T[homas] H[ooker], *The Soules Exaltation . . .* (London, 1638), 182; and *WRS,* V, 85–86. Ratcliffe owed her conversion to Nicholas Byfield. Ley, *Patterne of Pietie,* 23.

Concerning the complete confession, Thomas N. Tentler discusses early Protestant criticism of the Catholic rite in *Sin and Confession on the Eve of the Reformation* (Princeton,

Catalogs of Sins

Similar tendencies were evident in pietist annexation of yet another Catholic device, the "generall confession of thy wholle life." Traditionally required of novices entering religious orders and sometimes adapted for lay use in Counter Reformation handbooks of spirituality, this required a complete survey "beginning at the time thou first began to have use of reason, and so running over all thy yeeres."[10] Greenham, who deemed it fatal to "leaue the least sinne unespied," enjoined a full biographical review of sins: "Concerning sinnes past, we must call to minde the sinnes done of old, in our youth, in our middle age, in our old age." Possibly recalling a devotional technique of John Bradford's, Perkins suggested in 1593 that a self-inventory by the measure of the Decalogue should yield "large ... Catalogues of all our sins, even from the very cradle to any part of our age following"; and Bolton (d. 1631) in a posthumous work urged a thorough scan of "all [one's] sinnes past . . . , all that thou hast been guilty of ever since thou wast borne, *Originall, or Actuall, knowne, or unknowne, of thought, Word, and Deede.*" Like Bradford, Perkins and Bolton evidently meant that the sins disclosed should be gathered in a written record for use in subsequent penitential exercises, and this advice was repeated widely.[11]

N.J., 1977), 109–117. Cartwright, the foremost presbyterian, attacked it (Albert Peel and Leland H. Carlson, eds., *Cartwrightiana* [London, 1951], 104 [see 76 for probable date of composition]). For the hope, as Dod put it, that those who "iudge themselves . . . therefore shall not be iudged of the Lord," see J[ohn] Dod and R[obert] Cleaver, *Foure Godlie and Fruitful Sermons . . .* , 2d. ed. (London, 1611), 10; *WRG*, 94; *WWP,* I, 268. William Perkins allowed only two cases in which an incomplete confession was acceptable: when after thorough self-examination memory still fails to recover every sin, and in an emergency when time does not suffice. Perkins, *The Whole Treatise of the Cases of Conscience . . .* (London, 1606), in *WPEP,* 103–104.

Concerning circumstances, see also Perkins, *Cases of Conscience,* in *WPEP,* 96–98; *POP,* 253, 501, 627; *CDW,* 273. For circumstances in the Catholic confessional tradition, see Johannes Altenstaig and Joannes Tytz, *Lexicon theologicum . . .* (Cologne, 1619), s.v. "circumstantia," and above, Chapter 7, n. 2, and text.

10. [G]aspar Loarte, *The Exercise of a Christian Life* (n.p., [1597]), 2, 4. See also [Luis de Granada], *A Breefe Treatise Exhorting Sinners to Repentance, Commonly Called, The Conversion of a Sinner* (n.p., 1580?), 68.

11. *WRG,* 66, 130; *BWWP,* I, 459; Robert Bolton, *Helpes to Humiliation,* 4th ed. (London, 1637), 29; and see *CAC,* 283, 447. In *WWP,* I, 459–462, Perkins provided a model for self-examination by the Ten Commandments that identified nearly two hundred sins. He also advised compilation of a list of "the sins of [one's] whole life" in *A Commentarie, or Exposition upon the Five First Chapters of . . . Galatians* (London, 1617), 373, and of smaller-

Predictably, Nicholas Byfield's treatment was the fullest. Echoing the detailed inventories of sins used in contemporary Jesuit spirituality, he prepared a tract subtitled *A Catalogue of Sinnes* in 1619. There he described devising a list of sins as "the first rule" in preparation for conversion: "Take thee a Catalogue of all the sins thou . . . canst remember . . . , write them downe," and then classify them. The resulting digest would be the basis for additional rounds of self-examination that moved through one or two heads a day until finished. That procedure in turn should spur recollection of additional sins, these to be added to the catalog. Equipped now with a virtually complete and organized list of transgressions, the penitent next would hold a lengthy private confession in which all were confessed and rued before God and mercy was implored. Finally, after conversion, the catalog should be used (and presumably enlarged) repeatedly "after apostacie" and in preparation for the Eucharist.[12]

Byfield's zest for detail and technique probably was not matched elsewhere, but the catalog of sins was widely urged and used in pietist spirituality. Of course, there were many variations. Downame proposed a single inventory of sins, whether committed before or after conversion, supplemented by a "iournall or day-booke" with a running record of daily sins, whereas Bolton required "two Catalogues of thy sinnes, before conversion, and since." It is impossible to know how often such advice was taken, but about 1600 Samuel Ward decided "to record his sins in a volume," and later that decade young John Winthrop composed "a little catalogue of 'sinnes,' running through many days of many months, registered as in an account-current against himself." Lady Mary Gunter (d. 1633) "kept a *Catalogue* . . . of her daily slips" and "naughty thoughts" for use in a weekly rite of repentance; and, during a private fast about 1627, Simonds D'Ewes compiled and "wrote down a catalogue of all

---

scale "catalogues and bills of . . . sins" in *A Graine of Musterd-Seede* . . . (1597), in *WWP*, II, 406. Richard Sibbes enjoined penitents to "consider withal our former courses, rip up our lives from our childhood, consider the sins of our youth, together with our present sins" (*WRS*, 211). "Goe over all particular sinnes," John Preston advised, "and their multitude will amaze you. Remember the sinnes you have committed twenty years agoe. . . . And not that onely, but consider them with their circumstances" (*The Saints Qualification* . . . [London, 1633], 27–28). John Bradford reportedly had made written lists of his sins for private penitential exercises. *WJB*, I, 33, 35.

12. *MO*, 17–20, 35. The citations come from the first treatise in this collection, *The Beginning of the Doctrine of Christ; or, A Catalogue of Sinnes.* . . . It includes an inventory of every sin identified in the Bible. For Jesuit inventories, see John W. O'Malley, *The First Jesuits* (Cambridge, Mass., 1993), 143.

my known sins." In 1629 Nehemiah Wallington "begane to take another corsse with my selfe to over come my corrupt nature and that was to write down my sinnes in a booke." A "day Booke of my Sinns" (not extant) was among his many writings, and the list of sins was a standard device of his spirituality. In midcentury New England too, where Michael Wigglesworth "set [him]self seriously to meditate and call over the sins of my whole life by a Catalogue," the written roster of sins was in use.[13]

Pietist ardor for confessions and catalogs did not go unchallenged. "I grant," Arthur Hildersam told his parishioners at Ashby de la Zouch around 1630, that to dwell upon individual sins "is called precisenesse" by unconverted townspeople and unsympathetic church officials and that even among the godly complaints had arisen of the "endless worke" of "find[ing] out, and call[ing] to mind our sinnes." But, since in theological fact a single unrepented sin opened a man or woman to the full force of the wrath to come, censure and toil were costs gladly borne. With heavy Roman accent, clergy and laity worried that "every sin is written with a pen of Iron," that the "infinite, endless . . . evil of the least sin," if not repented with commensurate and anxious care, "bring[s] us out of fauour and credit with God." So the penitent's "particularizing of . . . sinnes" must be relentlessly inclusive. Always there was a lethal surplus of sin to detect and process. Every "old sinne," perhaps a forgotten lapse from "many yeeres agoe," or a transgression "hidden . . . in the darke corners of [the] . . . hearts," even a sin once repented of, but not soundly, would remain "hanging on the file" or "stand[ing] upon account" with potentially deadly effect both in this world and the next.[14]

---

13. *GG*, 610–611; Bolton, *Helpes to Humiliation*, 16; Margo Todd, "Puritan Self-Fashioning," in Francis J. Bremer, ed., *Puritanism: Transatlantic Perspectives on a Seventeenth-Century Anglo-American Faith* (Boston, 1993), 61; Robert C. Winthrop, *Life and Letters of John Winthrop*, 2d ed. (Boston, 1869), I, 66; Samuel Clark[e], *The Lives of Sundry Eminent Persons in This Later Age . . .* (London, 1683), 138; *SE*, I, 353; Nehemiah Wallington, "A Record of Gods Mercies, or A Thankfull Remembrance," 45, MS 204, Guildhall Library, London, copy in the Genealogical Society of Utah, Salt Lake City; Edmund S. Morgan, ed., *The Diary of Michael Wigglesworth, 1653–1657: The Conscience of a Puritan* (New York, 1965), 57. Preston too commended the use of "Catalogues" of sins, in *A Liveles Life; or, Mans Spirituall Death in Sinne . . .* (London, 1633), 65. For a sample of Wallington's lists, see "A Record of Gods Mercies," 15–28; "A Treatice Containing an Extract of Severall passages in my Life," 58, 155, 199, V.a. 436, Folger Shakespeare Library, Washington, D.C. (microfilm, University of Iowa Library).

14. Arthur Hildersam, *CVIII Lectures upon the Fourth of John*, 2d ed. (London, 1632),

And, indeed, the unsettling thought that "every sin . . . shall in the last day . . . accuse us" led some advisers, directly echoing Catholic penitential counsel, to require *repeated* acts of repentance for each sin. Bolton, in a characteristically extreme formulation, treated the peace of conscience attained by repentance as a mere stepping-stone to further, deeper rounds of "search into thy sins, or . . . more mourning."[15]

Such emphases, we must not forget, were balanced against other points of Reformed instruction, like the doctrines of justification and perseverance of the saints. At no time were those doctrines consciously weakened, but, when linked to the relentless disciplines of self-analysis and correction, their consolatory value inevitably declined. Say what they would about faith alone, precise

---

471; Hildersam, *The Doctrine of Fasting and Praier, and Humiliation for Sinne* . . . (London, 1633), 119, 121; Arthur Dent, *The Plaine Mans Path-way to Heaven* . . . (London, 1603), 342 ("pen of Iron"); *WTS*, II, 108 ("infinite . . . evil"); *WRG*, 6, 72 ("out of fauour," "dark corners"), 131 ("yeeres agoe"); Dyke, *Two Treatises*, 72 ("particularizing"); John Dod and Robert Cleaver, *A Plaine and Familiar Exposition of the Ten Commandments* (London, 1618), 12 ("old sinne"); *SHS*, 90; *WRS*, I, 158 ("hanging on the file," and see II, 316); *GG*, 613 ("upon account"); *CAC*, 289 ("mourning"). Hildersam's rejoinder to a complaint about "endless worke" conceded nothing: "I answer. . . . The more sinnes thou canst call to mind the better. . . . Take heed thou dost not in thy examination willingly forget or passe by any sinne." *Doctrine of Fasting*, 121–122.

Concerning individual sins, Greenham knew of "no sinne so little, but without repentance is damnable" and urged that each individual sin must be represented as "palpable, and plainely laid before our eyes" (*WRG*, 405, 493). "Every sin," concurred William Gouge, "maketh forfeiture of the covenant" and must be separately repented (*A Guide to Goe to God* . . . [London, 1626], 131, and see 135). For lay examples, see *SE*, I, 354; Wallington, "Severall passages in my Life," 232.

15. Dent, *Plaine Mans Path-way*, 343; *CAC*, 289 ("mourning").

Concerning repeated acts of repentance, Greenham had thought it "a good meditation often to unfold old sins" (*PDRG*, 245, and see 159–160). Declaring it "not enough that now the fresh horrour of ["old sinnes"] have wrought [remorse]," Bolton advised, "Thou must many and many a time hereafter, in . . . extraordinary exercises of renewed repentance, presse thy penitent spirit to bleede afresh within thee . . . for thy never sufficiently sorrowed-for abominations" (*CAC*, 280–281). In *GG*, 610–611, Downame urged that "though God hath forgiven" our sins, "wee must not forget them, but must retaine them in memory, and daily repent of them, using them as a chiefe motive to worke our hearts to hearty sorrow, both for them, and all our other sinnes." The manual in use at the recusant college at Douai in the late sixteenth century recommended the recall and repentance of individual sins "again and again." *Enchiridion sive manuale confessariorium et paenitentium*, in *Operum Martini ab Azpilcueta* . . . *tomus primus* (Rome, 1590), 43. For the Douai connection, see above, Chapter 4, n. 23.

divines had involved themselves and their tradition in a definite reprise of effects that had flowed from the papal legislation of 1215: a frankly quantitative fixation upon sins in the plural that swarmed in great numbers. Now every wayward thought and act endangered the saint. Each must be neutralized by a separate, focused, and sometimes reiterated task of identification, analysis, repentance, and reform.[16]

Puritan Depth Psychology

The elements surveyed above—the demand for completeness, the magnified import of individual sins, the interest in "circumstances," the general confession, and the written list of sins—are a small sample from the great palette of pietist techniques, but they reveal the central and virtuosic role now ascribed to the trial of self. Confident that stricter lives and quieter consciences would ensue, spiritual counselors urged themselves and their charges to push on in the spiritual war. When, as their own large roster of cases attested, the result often proved circular, inconclusive, and vexing, their will to discipline was too firm to recognize that a strategic error might have been made. They knew only to drive harder into the "world of worke within." With tasks unending to be done, persistence was a virtue, but in truth a deeper "prying with speciall curiositie and inquisitivenesse" into the self could lead to unanticipated and baffling results. Some might find relief for torture of conscience, but others would descend into complexities they could neither grasp nor resolve.[17]

The difficulty lay in assumptions about the self. One and all, the pietist clergy supposed that the human psyche, properly approached, was amenable to analysis. The regions of consciousness could be surveyed, the contents of memory retrieved, and a patrol established over the play of impulse. Fear of confronting the evil within, aversion to the strain and labor of inner analysis, and a lack of guidance or technique might delay or even arrest the process; but it was the business of spiritual direction, with divine aid, to overcome such obstacles. Thus the analysis, after all, could proceed on a relatively straight line into deeper levels of self-knowledge.

Well and good. But what if there were a point, incalculable by linear logic, at which one entered (in Bolton's telling phrase) a "maze of . . . windings and depths"? What if self-analysis relentless enough to find and mortify all sins

16. Note, for example, the ubiquitous emphasis upon the single "darling sin" that penitents withhold from confession. For examples, see *WRG*, 7–8; *CAC*, 174, 433.

17. *GD*, 128, 129.

should warp beyond normal awareness into realms of the subconscious and irrational? And what if, in that confusing region, one learned to be *less* confident about the knowledge and control of self? Pursuit of such questions will bring us to a little-known part of the Puritan story. For, as they probed and struggled to know the mind, spiritual directors finally pointed a way into blurry depths of the subconscious; as they sought to comprehend those regions, desirous to know more "about the heart, and the nature and properties of it," they wrote a prescient chapter in Western psychology.[18]

Actuated by belief that knowledge confers power, that a deeper grasp of the self must facilitate moral discipline and quiet of conscience, not all pietist clergy were willing to rest with a survey of manifest sins and their circumstances. Some found and began to blaze a deeper trail of analysis. In their hands, the ritual of self-scrutiny became, at least occasionally, an investigation of covert mental operations that here will be called Puritan depth psychology.

Protestant teaching always had emphasized the evasive and illusory qualities of self-knowledge in the unregenerate estate. It had a healthy respect too for the force and wiliness of Old Adam within the saints, and the doctrine of total depravity declared the intellect debilitated no less than the will or passions by the effects of original sin. Within the pietist awakening these concerns connected also to the increasingly systematized psychology developed in the Middle Ages to aid monastic contemplation as well as preparation for the confessional. The ascetic purposes of Catholic spirituality long had demanded an analysis of the ways by which sensual impulse gains entry and wins sway within the soul, and in some cases the inquiry had gone beyond normal consciousness to discern that the passage from temptation to sin was smoothed by a semi- or subconscious process of trickery and deceit. By the early sixteenth century, Bishop John Fisher could warn matter-of-factly against temptations that seem "so joyful to us that we [do not] . . . hear the privy guile hid under [the prospect of] bodily pleasure." Hidden guile—this concept so familiar to Fisher was axiomatic to the work of Robert Parsons, Luis de Granada, and other figures of the Catholic devotional awakening whose work was known in Elizabethan and early Stuart England. Now, in yet another demonstration of affectionate divinity's indebtedness to the past, it was to carry over into Puritan dissections of the "self-deceiving heart" and enjoy a vigorous separate evolution there.[19]

18. *GD*, 128; *ST*, 87.

19. John E. B. Mayor, ed., *The English Works of John Fisher, Bishop of Rochester* (London, 1876), 79. Ignatius of Loyola's warning that "it is characteristic of the evil one to . . .

Framers of the new piety acknowledged that "no man feeleth the heart of man so well as himselfe," but they were increasingly quick to add, "Yet himselfe, although hee haue liued with it euer since hee was borne, doth not know [fully] his owne heart." That was a root insight of the pietist way, but the decision to pursue it into the psychic underworld would have perplexing results. With the stakes of the spiritual combat now raised to the utmost, with moral mastery and peace of mind dependent more than ever upon an effective program of self-analysis, was this the moment to expose veiled, even inscrutable motions of deceit within the psyche? If the drive to amass knowledge "about the heart, and the nature and properties of it" had achieved a breakthrough in psychological science, if much had been learned of the devious means by which Old Adam works evils in the mind, the pattern of those operations seemed yet to defy the very idea of rational understanding and control.[20]

The pietist brotherhood, we recall, thought of the Old Adam within as a boiling libido from which illicit impulses continually stream. But they understood too that immoral urges do not always tread a direct path to conscious purpose and behavior; shying from frank exposure, they seek a means of disguise. It is a natural wonder, thought Arthur Dent, how men and women "writhe and wreath (like Snakes) to hide their sinnes." And, since Old Adam's sway within the intellect never finally is transcended in temporal life, the means of concealment is ready to hand. Reason itself, unless daily seasoned by meditations and kept precisely in check by the watch and the daily rule, strikes a working compact with sin that is fearfully efficient.[21]

Because ignorance of this "mutiny in [the human] understanding" could prove fatal in the combat against sin, affectionate divines became guides to the mind's unlighted, carnal side. Puritan voices long had portrayed reason, in its regenerate dimension, as an illuminated, illuminating power, showing straight paths of obedience and coaching the will in godly choices. This was doctrine to uphold against conservative critics who regarded pietist demands for conversion as a divisive force in the Church of England and as a dangerous flirting with spiritism, but in the context of spiritual direction a different emphasis

---

propos[e] fallacious reasonings, subtilties, and continual deceptions" is typical (Louis J. Puhl, trans., *The Spiritual Exercises of St. Ignatius* [Westminster, Md., 1959], 147). See also [Robert Parsons], *The First Booke of the Christian Exercise, Appertayning to Resolution . . .* ([Rouen], 1582), 185, 194; L[uis de] Granada, *The Sinners Guyde . . .* , trans. Francis Meres (London, 1598), 255–256, 269, 298–312, 314–334, 459.

20. *SHS*, 81; *ST*, 87.

21. Dent, *Plaine Mans Path-way*, 33.

was needed. There it was well to show that even in the best saints reason leads a second life, that it operates too on a lower, covert plane. Upon this terrain all is "intricately infolded together." No straight paths appear, but only "secret turnings and windings" and "perplexe labyrinths," for here "all . . . reasonings, and wisedome" subserve temptation and sin. Since it is a peculiar law of mind that more wit is required to obscure and dodge than to clarify and oblige the demands of the Lord's covenant and because carnal reason (in Richard Sibbes's words) is an outright "agent and factor for the flesh," exorbitant cleverness is its telltale mark. Not truth and clarity, but ruses, "shifts," "cunning trickes," and other arts "sophisticall" are its primary stock-in-trade. Like a "jugler, so full of cunning trickes and sleights," it has a host of devices for "extenuating, and mincing, and hiding . . . sin." This was a first, vexing result of Puritan depth psychology: the road from temptation to effected sin, that all-important avenue that the watch continually must patrol, was neither straight nor true.[22]

Convinced, nonetheless, that more careful analysis of the self would foster both a purer life and peace of mind, Sibbes and his pietist associates next sought out the specific techniques by which carnal reason cast its "mists upon the understanding." Their aim was strictly pragmatic. Survival at the Last Judgment—that was the objective, not systematic theoretical knowledge or a rounded theory of personality. To ensure this, a more detailed map of mental behavior was needed, a "verie anatomie and representation" of the psyche. If it was well to be alerted in general terms to unsanctified Adam's stealthy work within, elect men and women needed more detailed instruction to expose and defeat its daily and very particular sophistries. So pietist directors must probe for closer glimpses of carnal reason's agency. As they did so, gradually broadening their grasp of everyday psychopathology, they came to an extremely useful recognition: the sophistical arguments by which people "cast mists before their own eyes" fall into a few readily identifiable types. Consider, as a first example, the deceiving trick that a later age would call "projection."[23]

In classic Freudian psychology, projection is a subconscious ego defense that transforms an internal danger into an external one that is easier for the self

22. *WRS,* I, 153; *MSD,* 7 ("turnings," "labyrinths"), 12 ("infolded"); [Thomas Hooker], *The Soules Humiliation* (London, 1637), 147 ("reasonings"); *WRS,* I, 61 (and see II, 89–90); Preston, *A Liveles Life,* 68 ("shifts"); *MSD,* 357 ("tricks"); John Davenport, *The Saint's Anchor-hold . . .* (London, 1661), 58 ("sophisticall"); *EGJ,* 112 ("mincing"). The metaphor of "turnings and windings" in the psyche is a pietist commonplace.

23. *ST,* 122, and see 88; *WTS,* I, 71. See also the discussion of "sophistical fallacies" in *WRS,* I, 146.

to acknowledge and to handle. One gains relief from unacceptable thoughts, feelings, or behaviors by ascribing them to others. While no technical term emerged to describe it, the similar notion that "we are naturally addicted to blame others rather than our selves" was invoked by John Udall, John Knewstub, and other late Tudor figures who anticipated the pietist turn, and it became a familiar theme of pietist depth psychology after the turn of the century. In words later quoted without acknowledgment by John Dod, Greenham spoke bitingly of those who have "gored very bloodily into the consciences of others, who never once purged their owne unclean sinkes at home." Here, in the practice of those who "prie . . . into the wants of others, but . . . account the same wants no wants in them selues," was an example royal of the self-deceiving heart.[24]

Greenham's phrases identified projection in all but the name: an unconscious (or at best dimly conscious) maneuver to shift blame away from the self to an objective other. For Dod, Robert Cleaver, and (in earliest New England) John Warham, this was a nearly perfect crime by which sinners "put off the blame and shame of their sinnes upon others." In most such cases a lying ingenuity was at work to deceive family, neighbors, or other associates, as in Greenham's depiction of "the husband [who] knoweth what the wife should do; [while] the wife seeth the duties of her husband," or in Bolton's swipe at those who "impute . . . sinnes unto others, which are grosly predominant in themselves; that thereby they might purchase an opinion of supposed innocencie." But always, as in Thomas Hooker's image of the adulterer who "can easily confesse the danger and filthinesse of that sin in others, but hee thinks not his [own] sinne to be so vile," the projector too was befooled—and this was essential to the whole procedure. It was as "though a man can see to read abroad, yet hee cannot see to read in the house."[25]

Because projections are screened from normal awareness, pietist science knew of no more potent therapy than to draw them into the open. To shine the light of analysis upon the heart's secret displacements, and thus to pierce their indispensable cloak of secrecy, was greatly to sharpen the Christian's watch against temptation and sin. If this was true for projection, it was truer yet for lying reason's most common and versatile device: rationalization. In

24. *CL*, 169, and see *LJK*, 176; *WRG*, 66, and see *PDRG*, 179. Dod's quote varies slightly. Dod and Cleaver, *Fruitful Sermons*, 88–89.

25. J[ohn] Dod and R[obert] Cleaver, *Ten Sermons Tending Chiefly to the Fitting of Men for the Worthy Receiving of the Lords Supper* (London, 1610), 30–31; Douglas H. Shepard, ed., "The Wolcott Shorthand Notebook Transcribed" (Ph.D. diss., State University of Iowa, 1957), 48; *WRG*, 66 ("husband"); *GD*, 127; *SPC*, 23, 24.

modern terms, again, rationalization denotes the unconscious masking of dubious motives with a false, self-serving explanation of one's behavior. As enunciated here by no Freudian theorist, but by a member of the Puritan brotherhood best known in early Stuart times for a treatise on the Decalogue, the intuition, "Where lust hath dominion, it whets the wit to speake for it," did much to inform pietist discussion of the examen of self. Indeed, exposure and treatment of this reflex was depth psychology's core. In light of pietist commitments to self-examination and -control, to grasp that the understanding in its carnal mode "plays the lawyer" was a major gain. It was a large advance in knowledge and power to know that "the hidden, secret reason is one, the open is another," or that, since sin purposed or enacted "is afraid to appear in its own likeness," the intellect moves unseen to make "fair glosses for foul intentions."[26]

Therefore, pietist warnings rang out of "the hearts deceitfulnes in hiding that euill which she purposeth to doe" by inventing a "colourable pretence to shadow her malice." Believing as they did that the heart's pretenses could not survive exposure, spiritual directors were not content with general warnings alone. To make their charges to the fullest degree aware, suspicious, and watchful of themselves, they must particularize the skills of the watch; if fair-glossing was in some degree improvisational, in practice it often settled into specialized, readily identified routines. Usurers, for instance, may "read all [those] books, and go to all those ministers they suppose that hold it lawful" and "gather reasons" justifying their course; and a taste for "vaine and fond sports, and games" inspires many to seek—and wrest out of context—supporting passages from the Bible. To support "mixt dancing of men and women [some allege] that of *Solomon. There is a time to dance.*"[27]

With a flush of confidence in their ability to track such moves, the clergy labored to identify the more harmful species. In urgent need of exposure were the "shifts, evations, and all those tricks" of carnal reason that mask the threat of damnation for sin. Here a cardinal ploy to uncover was the designation of certain faults as "small sinnes. . . . It is too much precisenes to stand so strictly on every trifle." Another was the "strange reasoning" that God is a savior; it is his business to save sinners; he "has not made me to damn me." This line of thought, as Perkins knew, also undercut the Christian demand for personal

26. [Dod and Cleaver], *Ten Commandments*, 19; *WTS*, I, 88; *WRS*, I, 145. *SPC* and *CFS*, 85–156, are especially rich in their report of rationalizations.

27. *MSD*, 12–13 ("deceitfulness"), 220 (dancing); *WTS*, I, 88 (usurers); [Dod and Cleaver], *Ten Commandments*, 97–98 (sports).

reform. A seemingly gracious fix upon the Lord's "love, favor, and mercy," not to mention the more extreme pretense that salvation is universal, must also be exposed, since they secretly weaken commitment to be "strict and precise in hearing sermons, and reading and conferring about the word."[28]

It was equally imperative to lay bare the ways of those who, daunted by Puritan disciplinary demands, "plead the *corruption of nature*." "Wee cannot be Saints on earth and pure from all sinne," say these with a cozening twist, for "we are but flesh and blood." Or again, "Tush, the preacher is but a man as I am, I am sure he hath infirmities as others have; we are no Angels, our nature is corrupt, . . . I am sure you would not have us Gods." Likewise, the wish to evade Sabbath duties mothered a dazzling variety of ruses: "What can I heare there, which I may not heare or read at home? Have I not the Bible, and booke of common prayer at home?" What is the harm of "gathering a few sticks on the Sabbath"? "The family is great, children increase upon me, (and they are so busy and long a dressing on the Lord's day, that sermon is out before they come,) and we are not called to book it all day as ministers can, and worldly employments are so many."[29]

The above are a small sample of the "Armies of [furtive] Arguments" that the fraternity exposed. A full inventory of the "shifts lies excuses distinctions subtle evasions extenuations pretences [and] false condemnations of others" they identified would extend into regions of adultery, covetousness, commercial sharp dealing and price gouging, theft, sexual misbehavior, drunkenness, cursing, misliked ceremonies of the Prayer Book, and many others. These cannot be canvassed here, but the discussion is incomplete without mention of the greatest Puritan authority upon carnal shifts and tricks, Daniel Dyke (d. 1614). Not well known to students of Puritanism, Dyke was famous in his age as author of *The Mystery of Selfe-Deceiuing* (1614). The "book by Mr Dyke of the deceitfulness of the heart" went through at least fourteen editions in the seventeenth century and appeared in multiple Dutch, French, and German translations. Present as well in at least three early New England pastoral libraries and in the early holdings at Harvard College, "Dyke on the heart" offered the fullest instance of Puritan depth psychology on both the descriptive and theoretical levels. A virtual encyclopedia of "witty [clever] and col-

---

28. [Hooker], *Soules Humiliation*, 83; *CFS*, 115 (first ploy), and see 149; *SPC*, 52 (second ploy); Davenport, *Saints Anchor-hold*, 56 ("damn me"); *WWP*, III, 390.

29. *MSD*, 146; *WRG*, 134 ("Tush"); *DS*, 191 (first ruse); *MSD*, 186 (second ruse, and see 202–203); *WTS*, II, 248 (third ruse). Dyke reported the case of the "wearer of long haire," who explains, "I doe it not for pride, but onely to hide the deformitie of my eares, or to keepe my head warme." *MSD*, 176.

ourable excuses and extenuations," it offered also a full and partly original analysis of "the hearts deceitfulness in hiding . . . euill."[30]

The Mystery of Selfe-Deceiuing is a compend of colorable excuses crafted by that "olde foxe" the Old Adam within. Daily, Dyke knew, "sophisticall Iesuiticall equiuocation[s]" poured forth from the carnal heart. Their mere enumeration was enough to alarm and confound an already troubled conscience, and not even the most careful saint could analyze and counter them all individually. Yet, like his medieval predecessors and Puritan peers, Dyke believed that the multitude of sins reduced to a manageable number of types. To ease the work of spiritual counseling and self-analysis, the task now was to probe through the swarm of deceits to discern those types and their operating principles. To a large extent these were categories of equivocation familiar in spiritual direction. Dyke shared the judgment of Perkins, Downame, Lewis Bayly, Robert Cawdry, and others that carnal reason often adorns *"Vices* with the names of *Vertues."* Both to cloak sin and lessen embarrassment, it represents "niggardlinesse" as "parsimonie," or bloated pride of appearance as regard for cleanliness and neatness, or drunkenness as good fellowship, and the like.[31]

But Dyke's drive to classify and analyze also went a cautious step or two beyond his colleagues. In Puritan spiritual preaching and writing at large, the treatment of defense mechanisms was scattered and situational. No fixed roster of types or of descriptive terminology emerged, and this was the difficulty Dyke strove in part to redress. His effort was not systematic, but in some cases he attempted not only to isolate a class of ruses but also to fix it in his audience's memory with a technical name. For example, a sin so "grosse, as that it cannot be excused in it selfe," defines a discrete category of deceptions based upon a principle that Dyke called "extenuation." Sinners in the extenu-

---

30. *AR, 1–8,* 310; Shepard, ed., "Wolcott Shorthand Notebook," 48; R. C. Richardson, *Puritanism in North-West England: A Regional Study of the Diocese of Chester to 1642* (Manchester, 1972), 57; *MSD,* 145, 12. Libraries and holdings: Nathaniel B. Shurtleff, ed., *Records of the Governor and Company of the Massachusetts Bay in New England* (Boston, 1853–1854), I, sig. 37g; Charles F. Robinson and Robin Robinson, "Three Early Massachusetts Libraries," Colonial Society of Massachusetts, *Publications,* XXVIII, *Transactions* (1930–1933), 135, 141; Alfred C. Potter, "Catalogue of John Harvard's Library," Colonial Society of Massachusetts, *Publications,* XXI *Transactions* (1919), 207.

31. *MSD,* 4, 21, 181 ("niggardliness"); *POP,* 199–200. See also Perkins, *Galatians,* 343–344; Robert Cawdray *[sic], A Treasurie or Store-house of Similes* (London, 1600), 782; *CFS,* 114, and cf. 140. Calling "zeale in religion Puritanisme" and calling a "scruple of *Conscience,* precisenes" were two of Bayly's prime examples. *POP,* 200.

ating mode seek, not to excuse the fault entirely, but to lessen its gravity. They might, for instance, plead the unavoidable weakness of the flesh or recall the occasional lapses of persons of saintly renown. Drawing in part upon Seneca, Dyke also grouped an especially large set of rationalizations under the head of "*Translation.*" Its defining maneuver was to cast the entire blame for a fault upon an external cause. When men and women claim, for instance, that "we of our selves have good wills to doe otherwise, . . . but the *flesh* overmasters us," they perform a "translation upon the flesh." Or, in a translation upon secular calling, they may depict their secular business as so demanding "that they must needs neglect the kingdome of God in prayer, reading, meditation, sanctification of the Saboths; which if to doe be sinne, not *they* but their *callings* must be called into question."[32]

Much as Robert Cleaver and John Dod's *Godly Forme of Houshold Government* (1610) epitomizes Puritan approaches to family life and religion, Dyke's *Mystery of Self-Deceiuing* offers the fullest single conspectus of Puritan depth psychology in the years of its ascendancy. With a repertory of skills unknown in the days of Thomas Cranmer, William Tyndale, or Thomas Becon, and with a particular design to explode the Christian professor's normal innocence about him- or herself, it embodies the furthest methodological advance in the pietist project of self-analysis and control.

We have found no explicit conceptualization of a subconscious, and the material reviewed here qualifies a modern thesis that Puritan analysts found "the self and its contents . . . available for inspection" and thus were able to construct reliable cartographies of the soul. Pietist depth psychology marked a clear advance in understanding of the self, but it was of a sobering variety. It brought into view a surplus of mental activity and meaning well beyond the range of normal awareness, but it found it alarmingly inscrutable. By early Jacobean times, spiritual directors thus were approaching a difficult realization: "so *misticall* are these hearts of ours" as sharply to limit efforts to survey it. Not even intellects reborn by grace, illuminated by the Spirit, and experienced in depth psychology could master fully the soul's terrain.[33]

To realize that not all thought is scrutable was perturbing enough. Henceforth the saints, whose success in combat with sin hinged upon alert and skillful self-management, must reckon with forces at work beneath the level

32. *MSD*, 7, 144–145 (gross sin, "extenuation"), 138–139 (error for 150–151) ("*Translation*," "flesh"), 159. For other types, see *MSD*, 162, 153, 157.

33. James Hoopes, *Consciousness in New England: From Puritanism and Ideas to Psychoanalysis and Semiotic* (Baltimore, 1989), 11; *MSD*, 8.

of watchful control. It complicated matters further to view that force as a saboteur, a duping agency able to intervene in one's conscious judgments and choices without detection. Indeed, it seemed that reason was cleverest in its secret and contrary mode. Perhaps such insights framed the deeper science of the self to which Greenham had aspired, but their potential for good was unexpectedly mixed. They offered fresh advantages in spiritual combat, but they could breed troubling doubt about the ability of human beings to know and command themselves. If the mind's sharpest-witted feats are done in darkness, how can the saints fairly survey their sins? How can they take charge of their own personalities? Recognition that carnal reason can operate out of sight and yet enlist the self's best powers of ingenuity for evil ends evoked a sense, not of control, but of manipulation by an other. In one way, this was merely the familiar paradox of the Old and the New Adam. The regenerate self is two selves, each with its own logic and aim, yet in a manner that defies understanding the two are "mixed together in the whole man." A saint was not spiritual in one part and fleshly in another, but partly spiritual and partly of the flesh throughout, and so "the minde is carried against it selfe, the will against it selfe, and the affections against them selues." Old Adam in this equation was a regular, forceful shaper of the self's dispositions and choices.[34]

Who, then, was in charge? The answer must be cast in ambiguity. In some part the saints' evasions, as indeed all of the evils that professors commit, are an unwitting work elicited by Old Adam's arts "so subtill and secret[,] so deep and disguised." At the same time, the self envisioned by pietist direction is no puppet of carnal reason, but an active willer and maker of shifts and therefore a guilty party to them all. Nowhere was the mystery of self-deceiving deeper than here, in the pietist conviction that wholly or partly unconscious thought remains an action of the self, that the rationalizing professor "must . . . take *himselfe* for a lier." For that reason Sibbes portrayed rationalizing saints, not as inert victims, but as responsible agents who "play the sophisters with themselves," and Thomas Shepard spoke of the man savoring a sinful course who "covers it willingly from his own eyes." Here, then, was the perplexity. Errant Christians are "willingly deceived," else they could not be spoken guilty and

34. Perkins, *Galatians*, 367, 368. Preston makes the same point in *Saints Qualification*, 161. Cf. Hoopes's thesis that "Puritans little suspected the mysteries often connoted by the word 'self' today," including "the simultaneous existence of contradictory selves." *Consciousness in New England*, 11.

called to repentance; yet they remain susceptible to fraud beyond their ken or control.[35]

A sense of being manipulated was evident also in pietist belief that the soul's refractory motions are the personal work of Satan, that "great red dragon; . . . subtile, vigilant and malicious," a resident alien who schemes and bores steadily within. At once foreign and intimate, he has full "access to our spirits, to trouble them, . . . and the long experience he has of our corruption . . . from age to age gives him knowledge of our minds perfectly." Since centuries of experience have perfected, too, his delusional skills, his ways in the human psyche are "full of craft and very subtle." He exploits his knowledge of mental processes with a "subtiltie . . . so secretly wrought, that [humans] shall hardly perceive" it. To make the saints less "strict and precise," he prompts the heart's "strange reasonings for libertie in sinne." His "politicke strategems" wind into the arguments by which men and women "wonderfully diminish and extenuate those sins which [they] are about to commit." And all is done in secret. This is Satan's masterwork, to act as "a lying spirit in the mouth of a mans owne heart," to "join forces with us . . . *under our own colors,*" to make *"Reason* [his] secret friend [taking] part with him against our selues." Puritans conscious of these dynamics and aware of the devil's inordinate cleverness and power had good reason to doubt whether they fully understood and controlled their own personalities. No wonder they recoiled so sharply against the expanded estimate of human rational capability that surfaced in English Arminian theologies of the 1620s and beyond.[36]

Subtle Hypocrisy

Just how infernally difficult it might be to comprehend and steer one's self was evident in the extensive, sometimes tortuously fine analyses of the "hypocrite"

35. *CFS*, 87; *SHS*, 80–81, emphasis mine; *WRS*, I, 146 ("sophisters," "deceived"); *WTS*, I, 88.

36. *ST*, 42 ("access"), 415 ("dragon"); William Ames, *The Marrow of Theology*, ed. and trans. John D. Eusden (Boston, 1968), 115 ("craft"); *ST*, 420 ("subtlety"); *WWP*, III, 390 ("strict," "strange reasonings"); J[ohn] Downame, *The Second Part of the Christian Warfare* . . . (London, 1611), "To the Christian Reader," unpag. ("strategems"); *BWWP*, 241 ("diminish"); T[homas] H[ooker], *The Christians Two Chiefe Lessons* . . . (London, 1640), 207 ("lying spirit"); *WRS*, I, cix *("colors"),* emphasis mine; Robert Bolton, *The Carnall Professor* . . . (London, 1634), 214–215 *("Reason").* See also the section on "Satans *abilities to . . . invent false reasonings"* in Tho[mas] Goodwin, *A Childe of Light Walking in Darknes* . . . (London, 1636), 60–73.

that were another pietist commonplace. In its most general sense the term described the baptized but unregenerate member of the Church of England— a usage reflecting the mixture of the godly and profane in parish churches, the lack of apostolic discipline in the official church, and the often polarizing style of the godly. Yet, as attested by their many lists of criteria for distinguishing true from hypocritical Christians, by their numerous attempts to classify hypocrisy by degrees of resemblance to sainthood, and most tellingly by their recognition that the subtlest forms of hypocrisy are a divine work, pietist directors found it difficult and sometimes nearly impossible to distinguish true saints from false.[37]

Accordingly, the term *hypocrite* took on a second, more rarefied sense. A function of non-Separatist Puritan teaching that the validity of a half-reformed church hinges upon the presence of truly regenerated Christians within it, this usage pointed beyond the transparently phony to the jarringly close counterfeit of the real thing, to the refined type of "Artificiall [Chris]tian" that abounded *within the camp of the godly*. In all of this, Puritans remained committed Reformed predestinarians. They believed that "a stark abyss yawns between those who possess grace and those who remain . . . unredeemed by it," and expected the pietist way of conversion and spiritual warfare to build a sense of clear identity over against unregenerate others. Yet their slant on godly hypocrisy could also undercut that identity. For here, at least in the realm of human perception, there was no stark abyss, but only a faint margin between true faith and false.[38]

Greenham worked out four criteria involving some subtlety for distinguishing genuine and hypocritical saints, and the subtlety became profound when, drawing upon a familiar distinction in Reformed theology between saving and common grace, he drew upon the latter to define a type of gracious hypocrisy. In this category, hypocritical affections and deeds are gifts of God, unsaving but genuinely divine. Perkins pressed the argument further, consid-

---

37. For sample lists of criteria, see *WRG,* 56–57; *MO,* 218–222; *WTS,* II, 602–606. For classifications, see *MSD,* 58–68; T[homas] H[ooker], *The Soules Vocation; or, Effectual Calling to Christ* (London, 1638), 161, 269; *GD,* 44–51.

38. Thomas Shepard, "A Tryal of Regeneration" (n.d.), 380, MS Add. 45675, British Library, London; Larzer Ziff, *Puritanism in America: New Culture in a New World* (New York, 1973), 8. For non-Separatist belief that "only the presence of true Christians, . . . validated" English parish assemblies, see Patrick Collinson, "The Cohabitation of the Faithful with the Unfaithful," in Ole Peter Grell, Jonathan I. Israel, and Nicholas Tyacke, eds., *From Persecution to Toleration: The Glorious Revolution and Religion in England* (Oxford, 1991), 63.

ering "how farre a man may goe in the profession of the gospel, and yet be a . . . reprobate." How could some be saintly yet untrue, fooling the church and even themselves? Perkins's answer was one with Greenham's: such persons receive and exhibit genuine graces. With no power to redeem, the graces are but wisps of the real thing; yet they are graces still, able to produce strikingly realistic effects. A recipient may, for example, "be made partaker of the preaching of the Word, and be illuminated by the holy Ghost, and so may come to the knowledge of the revealed will of God in his Word. . . . He may acknowledge the truth of it, and confess it; [he may] be a defender of it . . . [and] have a feeling of his sins, and so acknowledge them" and "do outwardly all things which true Christians do." To make hypocrisy a divine work was well to explain its fine sleight of hand; but, by shrinking the observable distinctions between the reality and the imitation almost to a vanishing point, it also exposed unforeseen liabilities in pietist science itself.[39]

Those like young John Winthrop, who learned from "reading . . . Mr. Perkins and other books that a reprobate might . . . attaine to as much as I had done," might well begin "to grow very sad." Clerical warnings that hypocrites "may goe very farre in the probable resemblance" of a sound estate might serve as much to cloud as to ease the determination of their estate before God, and the same can be said of Byfield's discussion of the signs of "probable" hypocrites or of Richard Rogers's and Arthur Dent's attempts to devise a list of "infallible" signs of sainthood that cannot be simulated. Spelled out in detail in his best-selling *Plaine Mans Path-way to Heaven* (1601), Dent's approach illustrates the problem clearly. In this meandering dialogue he spoke most directly through the clergyman "Theologus." Presenting, first, "eight infallible notes . . . of a regenerate mind," Theologus later added nine additional signs by which a saintly estate might be "certainly discerned." In response to an objection that some of the nine are found in the nonelect, he acknowledged

39. *WRG*, 12–13, 55–57, and see John H. Primus, *Richard Greenham: Portrait of a Elizabethan Pastor* (Macon, Ga., 1998), 107–108; *WWP*, I, 356–361. For gracious hypocrisy, see also *ST*, 45–47; Paul Bayne[s], *Briefe Directions unto a Godly Life . . .* (London, 1637), 30–31. Preston allowed that hypocrites may converse about faith and repentance "better than many that haue the things indeed" and "many times exceed the godly" in virtues (*Saints Qualification*, 152–153). Thomas Wilson, *A Christian Dictionarie . . .* (London, 1612), 460, defined hypocrisy as "an inferior worke of the Spirit; generally, and slightly enlightening and reforming the reprobate." R. T. Kendall's assumption that the concept of hypocritical grace derives from Calvin and Theodore Beza to the exclusion of other Protestant and possibly Catholic sources is not proven. *Calvin and English Calvinism to 1649* (Oxford, 1979), 7, 22–23, 36.

that they are not so certain after all and devised a third and purportedly surer list of eight. Again the objection came that these too might be fraudulent, and again he had to agree. Challenged now to provide only such "demonstrative and infallible evidences, as no Lawyer can find fault with," he gathered a fourth and more refined set of seven "most sound and infallible" notes. Finally, to refute a claim that faith and not works is the essence of Christianity, he provided a fifth roster of nine signs. Readers of the *Path-way* (which went through twenty-five editions to 1640) thus must reckon with forty signs in five distinct sets. Clearly, many of the signs, like true love of God or "sinceritie of heart," could lead into confusing niceties of distinction, especially for users aware of carnal reason's double-dealing. But the more remarkable difficulty arose in Dent's elusive sense of what may be "certainly discerned." As constructed by this prominent spiritual director, the purportedly soothing rite of evidences was shadowed by an explicit and troubled warning: excepting the seven deemed most infallible, hypocrisy's divinely sharpened craft could reproduce and thus taint an indeterminate number of the signs.[40]

What Dent was forced to admit was granted as well by other colleagues in godly counsel. As spiritual advisers, they had experience of faked signs "shuffled in among true" and yet "able to speake the same thing true evidences doe." They knew that visible qualities of false and true saints can seem so nearly alike "that even the most iudicious, and discerning Christians, cannot perfectly distinguish betwixt them." Hypocrisy, as John Cotton warned his parishioners at Boston, Lincolnshire, about 1630, can be "spun with so fine a thread, and . . . so well dyed, . . . that you can hardly discern any difference." A little learning in depth psychology, it appeared, could be a dangerous thing for the project of self-analysis. Making the praxis of piety ever more laborious, it could vex the question of a safe estate. In some cases it could make it simply undecidable.[41]

40. *WP,* III, 340; *MSD,* 89, and see 128; *MO,* 222–226; *ST,* 63–64; Dent, *Plaine Mans Path-way,* 30 (first list), 231–232 (second list, "certainly discerned"), 233 (third list, "infallible"), 233–234 (fourth list, "sinceritie"), 250–251 (fifth list).

41. Goodwin, *Childe of Light,* 132; *MSD,* 67; *EGJ,* 249. For the probable date of composition of *EGJ,* see Everett H. Emerson, *John Cotton,* rev. ed. (Boston, 1990), 138.

CHAPTER 9

TAKING STOCK
PIETY'S GAINS
AND COSTS

B y early Stuart times the pietist way had created a legacy of grinding demand and, for some, a large potential for confusion and unfulfillment. Not without reason, Jean Delumeau makes it the supreme example of the unrelievedly morbid, ascetic, guilt- and fear-ridden spirituality that he finds pervasive in early modern Europe. Such a reading is understandable, yet overstated. It would have rung untrue to Puritan saints, most of whom deemed their penitential rigors not only endurable but fulfilling. Certainly the practice of piety, taken in the strictest sense, was impossibly hard. A composite of the godly life drawn from the works of, say, Richard Greenham, Richard Rogers, John Downame, Daniel Dyke, Nicholas Byfield, and Robert Bolton would have taxed the capacities of cloistered professionals. It must wed the legal, contractual, and Deuteronomic basics of Puritan theology to a battery of rites ordered by Byfield's rules of a holy life, fixed in a daily schedule and performed with an air of precision and rigor. Yet no record of practice I have found observes such a scheme in every punctilio and in steady regularity, although Nehemiah Wallington and probably a few others achieved a rough approximation. In reality, the clerical program appears to have functioned as a potent but unattainable ideal, softened in practice.[1]

How could it have been otherwise, since the pietist movement was necessarily a species of voluntary and amateur religion, since its claims upon time and energy and the degree of uncertainty that it generated were potentially infinite, and since spiritual directors differed among themselves on many

---

1. Jean Delumeau's analysis of sin-obsession and anxiety in Puritan spirituality is suggestive but sweeping and superficial, inattentive to countervailing themes, and marked by a personal revulsion against ascetic religion (*SF,* 544–554). For a critique of Delumeau that emphasizes the therapeutic value of contrition and despair in Elizabethan Calvinism, see Peter Iver Kaufman, *Prayer, Despair, and Drama: Elizabethan Introspection* (Urbana, Ill., 1996), 1, 8, 10–11, 25–26, 56–57, 160.

details? The diaries of Richard Rogers, Lady Margaret Hoby, and Thomas Shepard, the autobiography of Sir Simonds D'Ewes, the letters of Lady Brilliana Harley, the "Experiencia" of John Winthrop, and the "Dayly Directory" of Sir William Waller reveal lives impressively devout and ordered; but they record also selective applications of the theory and an overall gentling of the pace. None, for example, appears to have adopted Byfield's scheme of rules (Wallington again is an exception), and their ascetic practices varied notably in extent and rigor. The Hobys and Winthrops of the pietist awakening could persist in the rigorous work by moderating it in accord with their individual preferences and capacities.[2]

They could also find and savor its rewards. Greenham himself had disapproved of unrelieved "sorrowing," and, so far as we can judge, a majority of those swept up in the devotional awakening found it a wellspring of pleasure as well as of guilt and fear. This is an element easy to neglect. Like their European counterparts in ascetic religion, pietist Puritans spoke not only of struggle and incompletion but also of deep fulfillments. They were held to their labors in part by a cheering sense of achievement. The very choice and pursuit of an elite life was a source of content. As often in the history of religion, Puritan ascetic practice was a mode of human dignity and, indeed, of liberation. Breaking the tyranny of impulses, exercising endurance and virtuosity, and sharpening personal focus, it generated pleasures of self-mastery. It created types of "the fine self, the virtuous or excellent person" with an undeniable self-importance. Other satisfactions, too, offset the rigors of holy walking and the anguish of doubt. Critics like Robert Burton who found pietist praxis "unpleasant, mopish and melancholike" had misunderstood much. Heavy with verbal content, Puritan ritual continually invoked the all-

---

2. Thus Jane Ratcliffe was an ascetic virtuoso whose private fasts were so severe that she appeared weak and halting afterward. John Ley, one of her clerical advisers, worried that her ascetic "zeale would eate her up." Yet Lady Margaret Hoby's fasts were few and, so far as can be judged from her diary, relatively perfunctory. In 1638 Sir Simonds D'Ewes "began to feel the strain in his private exercises . . . and . . . found it necessary to reduce his ordinary fastings to one every quarter." See John Ley, *A Patterne of Pietie; or, The Religious Life and Death of . . . Jane Ratcliffe* (London, 1640), 79; Dorothy M. Meads, ed., *Diary of Lady Margaret Hoby, 1599–1605* (Boston, 1930), 206; *PG*, 35. D'Ewes was pledged to regular fasting "so long as my ability and health shall permit" and felt free to "vary the times and duration of my fasting" (*SE*, I, 353). In 1629 Nehemiah Wallington undertook to compile a catalog of his sins, but he later abandoned the project as "too daunting." *WW*, 35, 182.

sufficiency of grace and fullness of pardon, the Lord's unshakable election of his saints, the utter reliability of his covenant, and his wise purpose in all human afflictions. The harvest of signs and evidences yielded by introspection and the practical syllogism were at hand as well; they had power (however faltering in many cases) to reduce fear of the Last Judgment, to build a sense of security in the world and of vast fulfillments beyond. And undergirding all were the many social supports, from mutual consultation to public fasts to informal conventicles, of the godly community.[3]

Understandably, then, not all of the regenerate complained of a chronically troubled conscience, and spiritual counselors spoke of the strong as well as the weak. Perhaps the commonest figure among the weak was the newly regenerate "Babe in Christ," who normally (at least in clerical theory) would advance by degrees toward a more settled state. Indeed, Perkins's *Case of Conscience; The Greatest That Ever Was: How a Man May Knowe Whether He Be the Child of God or No* was addressed in particular to those who "begin to come on in Religion."[4]

Some of the godly, like Wallington or the landed gentleman and Canterbury politician Thomas Scott, were prone to "Mellincollie"; but others, like Lady Margaret Hoby and Lady Brilliana Harley, were upbeat much of the time. Like Sir Simonds and Lady Anne D'Ewes, they had found "that God's children in this life might attain to a certain knowledge of their own future salvation" and "much comfort and reposedness of spirit" in the ritual of signs. If some were overwhelmed by doubts at the approach of death, a majority of those of whose deaths we have some record met the end with comfort and hope. In preparation for her own death in 1620, "that [Puritan] Gentlewoman Mrs Rebekka Crisp" called godly friends together to share in a last review of

3. *PDRG,* 178; J. Giles Milhaven, "Asceticism and the Moral Good: A Tale of Two Pleasures," in Vincent L. Wimbush and Richard Valantasis, eds., *Asceticism* (New York), 1995), 376; *GG,* 836. Sirs Simonds D'Ewes and William Waller both attacked the view "that Religion is a dull flat melancholy thing" and emphasized the "mirth . . . which cometh from the Springs above" (Waller, *Divine Meditations upon Several Occasions: With a Dayly Directory* [London, 1680], 34; *PG,* 62). J. T. Cliffe finds Puritan gentry "often . . . convinced that their religion, far from inducing a sense of gloom, was a source of great happiness and joy" (*PG,* 62).

4. *WWP,* I, 125; [William Perkins], *A Case of Conscience: The Greatest That Ever Was . . .* (London, 1592), "To the Godlie Reader," A2. For the normal progression in faith, sanctification, and assurance, see *WWP,* I, 125–127; *ST,* 495–498; Paul Bayne[s], *Briefe Directions unto a Godly Life . . .* (London, 1637), 44–46.

"the grounds and notes of her assurance." Since her notes were many and cogent, Crisp was thereby prepared to work through the "conflicts" of her deathbed ordeal and attain to final peace of mind.[5]

It is true that the penitential course plotted in practical theology could not quell anxiety once and for all. It might generate a cyclical pattern sunk "in despaire / Five times a yeare, / And cur'd by reading Greenham." Yet its very repetition and cadence were consoling, and frequently it sparkled with "great ioyes" and moments of "most comfortable feeling." Clerical directors attested that spiritual duties, from Sabbath observance to the rebuke of a wrongdoing neighbor, conveyed "comfortable contentment, and secret sweetnesse." So too did diaries and other records of lay piety celebrate times of "joye and delight." "O it is a sweet thinge," exclaimed Lady Brilliana Harley, "to have privet conferance with our God"; and Sir William Waller found "delight of . . . soul" in his private rites. Clergy and laity, then, endured their spiritual drudgery by finding pleasures in the work; and they, by all reports, were of a transcendent order. Those pleasures did not rival the ecstasies acclaimed in Catholic mystical theology but were real and cheering enough. In Greenham's phrase, they "rauished" the pilgrim with "joy most unspeakable"; in Downame's, they lifted struggling saints into realms of "incomparable sweetnesse, above the

5. Nehemiah Wallington, "A Record of Gods Mercies, or A Thankfull Remembrance," 8, MS 204, Guildhall Library, London, copy in the Genealogical Society of Utah, Salt Lake City, and see 7; *SE,* I, 276 ("children"), 369 ("reposedness"); T[homas] G[ataker], *Pauls Desire of Dissolution . . . A Sermon Preached at the Funerall of That . . . Gentlewoman Mrs Rebekka Crisp . . .* (London, 1620), sigs. B3–B4. For Scott's "melancholic despair," see Peter Clark, "Thomas Scott and the Growth of Urban Opposition to the Early Stuart Regime," *Historical Journal,* XXI (1978), 4. Hoby's diary offers scant details, but she reported "good quiatt of Conscience" with some frequency. Meads, ed., *Diary of Lady Margaret Hoby,* 140, and see esp. 40, 62, 63, 107.

Concerning the rite of signs: Simonds D'Ewes also reported "inestimable comfort and satisfaction" in his "evidence of marks and signs" (*SE,* I, 353). When Lady D'Ewes died in 1641 in some anxiety about her estate, Sir Simonds, absent at the time of her death, sharply questioned his son, James, "Why did you not looke out comforte in Mr. Byfield's Marrow . . . for her[?]" (*SE,* II, 277–278). Byfield's *Marrow of the Oracles of God* was a collection of treatises including *The Spirituall Touch-stone; or, The Signes of a Godly Man* of 1619. For evidence that many Puritan gentry were able to take comfort in their signs, see *PG,* 20–22.

Concerning death: Lady Alice Lucy's "last words" were, "My God I come flying unto thee" (Samuel Clark[e], *The Lives of Sundry Eminent Persons in This Later Age . . .* [London, 1683], part 2, 143). For other examples, see *Lives,* 115; Ley, *Patterne of Pietie,* 160–161; and "Death of Thomasine Clopton Winthrop, 1616," *WP,* I, 182–190. Such accounts possibly minimized negatives in the interest of edification.

honey and honey combe"; and within their exercises Lady Harley and John Winthrop readily found and hailed "that joye which surpases the joy of the world."[6]

The Puritan scheme, then, was a delicate balance. Hard and depriving, it also conveyed rewards. Within the daily walk and watch there were sunlit moments, and they were frequent and generous enough to lift and maintain morale at least for a time. They emboldened the saints to bear their hardships and deprivations, sustain their faith in the system, and thus stop short of radical alternatives.

Yet the morbid view does not wholly miss the mark. However fine piety's delights might have been, they came at heavy cost. They had a quality of sheer enjoyment, giving moments of relief from the grind, but they were rooted in severity, in "strenuous, painstaking, almost punishing" modes of introspective piety. Wallington hailed "the goodnesse of my God in making me to hate sinne so much." For him and many others it was "Christs yoke" that was "easy" and "so sweet"; it was the path of privation and strain that became "cheereful and pleasant, sweet and delightful." With frequent salutes to "the sweet regement of our Lord Christ Jesus," Lady Harley made the connection clear: "How sweet did I finde . . . the endeavor, to walke in his ways." And for Harley, too, in accord both with spiritual direction and with Puritan ideals of physical recreation, the cheer and sweetness were a restorative, returning the soul refreshed to the via purgativa.[7]

Within so stringent a course, occasional refreshment was needed, for Puritan theorists granted frankly that the demand now laid upon the saint was extraordinary. Likening the way to heaven to a race where the saint must "sweat and strive," "put forth all his strength, and stretch every limb," Shepard instructed a congregation at Earls Colne in Essex around 1630 "that those that are saved are saved with much difficulty." For Joseph Bentham too (a close

6. J. A. W. Bennett and H. R. Trevor-Roper, eds., *The Poems of Richard Corbett* (Oxford, 1955), 58; *WRG*, 11 ("great ioyes"), 52 ("rauished"), 111 ("feeling"); *CAC*, 46 ("contentment"); *LBH*, 12 ("surpases," and see *WP*, I, 202–203, 210), 23 ("joye and delight"), 28 ("conference"); Waller, *Divine Meditations*, 25; *GG*, 837 ("honey"). For motifs of rapture, see Charles Lloyd Cohen, *God's Caress: The Psychology of Puritan Religious Experience* (New York, 1986), 126–130. For the "consoling cadence and repetition of the experiences of affliction and recovery," see Kaufman, *Prayer, Despair, and Drama*, 57.

7. Tom Webster, *Godly Clergy in Early Stuart England: The Caroline Puritan Movement, c. 1620–1643* (Cambridge, 1997), 128; Wallington, "A Record of Gods Mercies," 14; *WTS*, I, 64; *GG*, 837; *LBH*, 24, 34. The "delight and solace" found in discipline is a refrain, for instance, in *ST*, 62, 296, 325, 327, 331, 413, 430, 509, 577–579 (quote at 476).

associate of Bolton in Northamptonshire), the pietist trek was "a matter of great difficulty, . . . of much hardship and no easie labour . . . [of] solicitous cares, painefull labours . . . [and] excessive diligence." In the early seventeenth century, the straitness of the way, its "hardnesse and difficultie," and the "violent, eager, strong, endeavours" and "restless pursuits" that it required became routine parts of the propaganda; and they reveal much.[8]

The emergence of laborious effort itself as a topic of analysis and exhortation was of some importance in Puritan history. Restating the precisianist ideal, it recorded the cumulative impact of the pietist rites that assumed, echoed, and supplemented one another with heavily involuted effect. Wallington, again, was a case in point of rising levels of discomfort among some of the saints. "My goeing to heaven," he acknowledged, was "like unto Pharoths Charets when the wheles ware strocke off they went heavily." "O what Striving and Strugelling have I had this day to keepe my heart up in duty" is a typical passage from his spiritual diary, and he complained in particular that "the work of [self-]Examination is very hard." Yet, as plainly for him as for Shepard and Bentham, to depict the holy walk as a draining ordeal was a means, not to reduce, but to sustain and even heighten the pressure, to name strenuousness a cardinal virtue. No wonder that the pietist turn evoked charges of "bringing in . . . Monkery againe" and of making demands "beyond the ability of mortalls to performe." More and more, it prescribed a care of the self so strenuous and subtle that it requires some effort to recall that it applied not to professional contemplatives but to lay men and women laden with worldly responsibilities.[9]

Again, even as they acclaimed the many available remedies for doubt and fear, spiritual directors constantly, worriedly returned to the trials of wavering consciences, with some agreement that even "the highest degree" of faith was a varying quantity; it was "better setled in some then in other . . . and this hath assurance accompanying it [only] for the most part usually." In these phrases from Richard Rogers and Baynes, the instinctive retraction, the double quali-

---

8. *WTS*, I, 64; Joseph Bentham, *The Christian Conflict* . . . (London, 1635), 14–15; [Thomas Hooker], *The Soules Humiliation* (London, 1637), 63; *WRS*, VI, 307; *WTS*, II, 247. Bolton and Bentham shared in a combination lecture in Northamptonshire in the early 1630s. Webster, *Godly Clergy*, 49.

9. Nehemiah Wallington, "A Record of Gods Mercies," 45; Wallington, "A Treatice Containing an Extract of Severall passages in my Life," 20, 188, 302, V.a. 436, Folger Shakespeare Library, Washington, D.C. (microfilm, University of Iowa Library) (and see 496, 513, 516, 523, 526); *ST*, 575 ("monkery"); Christopher Dow, *A Discourse of the Sabbath and the Lords Day* . . . , 2d ed. (London, 1636), 73.

fication, are revealing. Considered with all the evidence thus far, they suggest the deeply ambiguous nature of Puritan transactions with doubt. As in many other historic settings, ritual in this context served both to allay and to create anxiety. "Rest comfort and quietnesse I could find none" was the complaint of a zealot wholly immersed in pietist rites. Given the many points of symbiosis between the penitential warfare and the struggle to be sure, the means chosen to bolster and stabilize security functioned as well to delay and frustrate it. Rites so intertwined with the quest for certainty needed continual inputs of doubt to continue flourishing. In this sense, troubles of conscience were a necessary asset as well as a painful liability.[10]

Shaped also by the cautious realism of non-Separating dissent, the pietist way affirmed no ready end to the struggle. Fitly named a walk, journey, course, or race, it worked always "forwards, on and on." Offering no decisive moment, act, or resolution in history and thus no sense of arrival and finality, it verified the suggestion that religious ritual "never yields a definitive answer" to human concerns, but addresses them through a technique of "orchestrated deferral." In just this way, the exercises functioned to postpone closure and flow on to the next circuit of performance. Often, perhaps typically, the hopes bred by self-inquiry and confession were short-lived, soon displaced by weakness, sin, fear, repentance, and hope again, and so recursively forth from round to round. At worst, the penitent could drift into a vortex of psychologizing, in which few stable handholds appeared and no exit was clearly marked. Those drawn within it spiraled toward the finicky exercises of the complete confession. There, as they constantly scrutinized their consciences for traces of sin and strove to assess their quality, degree, and circumstances in light of carnal reason's finespun tricks, they might find it difficult enough to fulfill the conditions of their gracious covenant; but it was harder yet to find and hold proofs of their election and transcend hypocrisy, especially amid a welter of behavioral signs often of an elusive sort.[11]

10. *ST,* 71; Bayne[s], *Briefe Directions,* 45–46 (here, as often, Baynes's text is an adaptation of Rogers's); Wallington, "A Record of Gods Mercies," 47.

11. A[dam] H[arsnett], *A Touch-Stone of Grace* (London, 1630), 261; Catherine Bell, *Ritual Theory, Ritual Practice* (New York, 1992), 106. The cyclical pattern is captured nicely by Kaufman, *Prayer, Despair, and Drama,* 25, 47, 56–57, although he relates doubt primarily to predestinarian belief and downplays its force and role in the overall pattern of piety; and by Janice Knight, *Orthodoxies in Massachusetts: Rereading American Puritanism* (Cambridge, Mass., 1994), 81, 99. In his study of an early Stuart lay member of the Puritan gentry, Clark suggests that the very "technique for spiritual self-analysis—fasting and rigorous prayer—in most cases only heightened the subject's psychological distress and

Held upon their treadmill of ever-returning sins, knowing no subject "so subtill and secret so deepe and disguised" as the human heart, and perhaps unable to distinguish real from hypocritical faith, the godly well might waver and stumble and continue to generate new cases of conscience. By the clergy's own report, they could fall to an "overmuch *viewing of their own daily infirmities,*" become *"wicked overmuch"* in their own estimation, and so lose their hold upon assurance. In the worst case they might fall for a time into hapless despair. Persons in this condition, despite their "manifest signes of faith, and the new birth," yet "are perswaded that they are utter reprobates, and have no remedie. . . . They feele (they say) . . . anguish of conscience most intolerable: and can finde no release. . . . And if any Scripture be recited to them; oh, it belongeth not to them, they say: they are past hope: . . . they are never satisfied; but raise new obiections against themselues." The hypersensitive and inconsolable state of mind here on display was a frequent case of conscience in its own right, a species of spiritual pathology in which "one little sin" could occasion a "plunge . . . into the depth of extremest horrour, and a very Hell upon Earth." Often associated with suicidal tendencies (and occasional suicides), it was familiar and worrisome to Puritan spiritual directors. As illustrated by the famous case of Joanna Drake in Esher, Surrey, around 1620, extreme and "needlesse scrupulosity" was its defining feature. This was manifest primarily in an invincible conviction that one's sins are so profound as to disqualify for mercy, and secondarily in a tendency to torment oneself with magnified or invented faults.[12]

---

thereby served to create a vicious circle of self-doubt." "Thomas Scott," *Hist. Jour.,* XXI (1978), 4.

12. *CFS,* 87; *MO,* 205–206 ("overmuch," *"wicked"*); *ST,* 40 ("signes"), 42 ("past hope"); *CAC,* 89 ("little sin," "Hell"); John Rogers of Dedham, *The Doctrine of Faith . . . ,* 3d ed. (London, 1629), 369 ("scrupulosity"). John Downame directed his *Christian Warfare* to those "so affrighted, astonished, and continually tormented with doubtings, feares, . . . that they goe mourning all the day long" (*CW,* sig. 3). Many scruples are cataloged in *CDW,* 12–14, 19, 22, 31, 39, 97–99 (new numbering after 372). See also Bolton's discussion in *CAC,* 81, of the scrupulous saint "fill[ing] His darke and dreadfull Fancy with a world of fained horrours . . . and imaginary Hells," and John Ball's strategies for counseling such persons in *A Treatise of Faith . . .* (London, 1632), 283–291, and *The Power of Godlines . . .* (London, 1657), 155–157. In *The Anatomy of Melancholy,* 941–943, Robert Burton identified the hyperscrupulous conscience as a logical outcome of Puritan teaching. *The Anatomy of Melancholy* (1621), ed. Floyd Dell (New York, 1927), 941–943.

Concerning suicidal tendencies, see *WRG,* 126; Wallington, "A Record of Gods Mercies," 2–9; and Michael MacDonald, *Mystical Bedlam: Madness, Anxiety, and Healing in*

And what other result could be imagined when ordinary men and women troubled in conscience were given counsel fraught with ideals of monastic spirituality? When they were urged *positively to value* a spiritual struggle "full of dreadfull feares, solicitous cares, [and] painefull labours"? When, not always gifted with acuity and patience, they were advised to pinpoint, dissect, and order countless and often subtle details of their own behavior that increasingly included states of mind? When they were advised knowingly to *cultivate* a prickly "conscience . . . sensible of the least offence, and apprehensive of Gods wrath attending the same"? When, in particular, the self-searching self became a mystery and problem to itself? For all his or her weaponry, skill, and brave aspect, the spiritual warrior featured in pietist sermons and books understandably was prey to a doubting, sin-obsessed conscience that stood recognizably descended from the scrupulous conscience of the fourteenth and fifteenth centuries. Indeed, a medievalist reading of a "tormented soul, constantly examining his every thought and action, now convinced that hell awaits him, now lunging after the straw of hope that he is saved, and then once more falling into despair. . . . always on the cycle of alternating moods," reasonably might identify it as a creature from the pages of Johann Nider's *Consolatorium timoratae conscientiae* of the early fifteenth century. Yet this is Robert Middlekauff's depiction of "the most familiar figure among Puritans."[13]

Persons so tortured as this might have been rarer than so alleged, but the self-preoccupied, wavering, often anxious *homo viator* undoubtedly lived again in the Puritan setting. It was no monastic confessor, but the godly preacher Henry Smith who considered the Christian "set upon the side of a hill, alwayes declining and slipping" toward Satan's allures, and then "ris[ing] again" through repentance, dialectically hopeful of redemption and bowed down by the threat of "Hell's mouth, under [his] feet . . . ready to swallow [him] up." It was the harshly anti-Catholic John Downame who worried over

---

Seventeenth-Century England (Cambridge, 1981), 133–134. For actual suicides, see *WRG*, 126; *GV*, 27–28; *WW*, 31, 60.

Concerning the Drake case, see [John Hart?], *The Firebrand Taken out of the Fire* (London, 1654). (Hart's authorship is disputed by George Huntston Williams, "Called by Thy Name, Leave Us Not: The Case of Mrs. Joan Drake . . . ," *Harvard Library Bulletin*, XVI [1968], 111–128, 278–300.) For similar cases, see *SE*, I, 284–287; *WW*, 109–110; and "PH," 110–113.

13. Bentham, *Christian Conflict*, 15; Robert Bolton, *The Carnall Professor . . .* (London, 1634), 201; Robert Middlekauff, "Piety and Intellect in Puritanism," *WMQ*, 3d Ser., XXII (1965), 459. For scrupulosity in the Middle Ages, see *SF*, 314–321.

those who "hang as it were[,] wavering in the ayre, sometime lifted up with hope, sometime deiected and cast downe with feare." And it was the godly shopkeeper Wallington who, in a dream, found himself "dead and the day of iudgment was come, and I was raised, and stoode betwixt heaven and hell, but wheither[?] I should goe I knew not."[14]

Since the clergy themselves were deeply immersed in the spiritual awakening and considered their own lives exemplary, their portrayal of "an interchangeable course of sorrow and comfort, of faith and feare" contained elements of their own experience. "I haue my self languished long," Richard Rogers acknowledged, "(though not without Christ . . . and . . . flitting comfort) sometimes to see such unsettlednesse in my life," and it was precisely this "wofull experience [that] droue" him to devise the daily rule outlined in *Seven Treatises*. John Cotton, Thomas Shepard, Samuel Whiting, and others also reported severe troubles of conscience. God, Cotton wrote, had often roiled him with "Fears . . . about mine own spiritual estate," and Shepard's spiritual journal, indeed, records "the full range . . . of the spiritual anxieties to which Puritan saints were subject."[15]

Similar patterns appear in the few records of lay experience. Thus the case of Joanna Drake again, or of Lady Joan Barrington, who complained to Hildersam and Ezekiel Rogers of "doubtings and feares" and that neither "could give her firm assurance that she was saved." Or of Sir Thomas Bouchier, who suffered from "such infinite sadness springing from fears of my union with Christ that I have scarce been able to subsist." Or of the glassmaker and weaver Obadiah Holmes, who "had no rest in the soul, though I was in the manner strict as any." Or of the wife of Robert Harris, a member of the brotherhood, who was "so buffeted . . . by Satan, that she was under the greatest horror of mind imaginable." Or of Mrs. Katherine Clark, whom "it pleased God . . . for many years, to keep . . . (for the most part) in a sad . . . Estate, . . . not cleerly Evidencing the certain Assurance of his love to my Soul: So that many times I questioned whether I was a child of God or no." In their times of affliction, these members of the godly subculture indeed were viatores: pilgrims uncertain of their destiny.[16]

14. *SHS*, 496, 500; *CW*, 185; Wallington, "A Record of Gods Mercies," 47.

15. *WRG*, 243; *ST*, 571–572; Cotton to Samuel Stone, Mar. 27, 1638, Ms. Am., 1506, pt. 2, no. 12, Boston Public Library (now published in *CJC*, 273–274); *FEW*, 148. Whiting described his "deserted condition" at length in a letter to Cotton, imploring him, "Helpe me out of this maze." Whiting to Cotton, undated, in *CJC*, 510.

16. Ezekiel Rogers to Lady [Joan] Barrington, Feb. 2, 1629/30, fols. 142–143, Egerton

At least for men and women such as these, the pietist turn had struck a balance of gains and costs weighted toward the latter. It had so leavened the gospel of pardon with disciplinary interests that it could not well function—certainly not in the manner Luther had early envisioned—as the reasonably steady center of Christian consciousness freeing men and women from anxious concern about themselves and their religious destinies. As in the well-recorded case of Wallington, "driven by religious scruples and wracked . . . by religious anxieties," strain and fear often were more the stuff of their daily experience than consolation and peace of mind. This was a cost, hidden but excruciating, of decisions long since taken to embed devotion and self-analysis within a master plan of disciplinary reformation.[17]

Nevertheless, as the case of Wallington also makes clear, if piety's rewards were recessive much of the time, they remained ingredient to the faith. He could sense, even if he could not easily grasp, their comforting potential. Finding that years of struggle had failed to purge the "sty of filthiness" within and dispel his fear of Judgment Day, he could realize, "I looked too much to myself and not upon Christ." Is Christ "very merciful?" he could ask. "Then he will . . . take pity on me." Pursuing thoughts such as these, Wallington enjoyed intervals of relative security in his early fifties, and in some fine moments he heard the Spirit "whisper[ing] in my soule saying 'Sonn, thy sins are forgiven thee.' "[18]

Though he did not recognize it as such, this was the germ of a different vision, of an openly contrapietist strain of piety that had emerged in the 1610s and risen to prominence during his lifetime, which scholarship today names "antinomian." It tempered or cast off the morality of rule and law, abhorred

---

MS 2645, British Library (also published in Arthur Searle, ed., *Barrington Family Letters, 1628–1632* [London, 1983], 129); *PM,* 221 (Barrington), 222 (Bouchier); Edwin S. Gaustad, ed., *Baptist Piety: The Last Will and Testimony of Obadiah Holmes* (Grand Rapids, Mich., 1978), 75; Erasmus Middleton, *Biographia Evangelica* (London, 1774–1817), III, 383–384 (Harris); Clark[e], *Lives of Sundry Eminent Persons,* 158 (and see 156). Ezekiel Rogers recalled his "watchings" with Sir Thomas Barrington "in the time of yor melancholy, and risings at midnight to . . . comfort yo." Ezekiel Rogers to Sir Thomas Barrington, Nov. 2, 1636, Egerton MS 2646, British Library.

17. *WW,* 110. Paul S. Seaver finds Wallington "given to endless and searching introspection, to constant worry not only about the moral rightness of his actions but also about the correctness of his motives and feelings" and tormented (in his own words) by the "hags and terrors and continual chiding and brawling" of his conscience. *WW,* 145, 195.

18. Wallington, "Severall passages in my Life," 357 (and see 535); and see *WW,* 43–44. For Judgment Day, see *WW,* 7.

strictness and exactitude, and adhered exclusively to the suprahuman sources of redemption that Reformed doctrine also supplied. Wallington himself rejected it. Like most parties to the pietist way, he could not envision a life not harshly scanned, policed, and tensely fearful much of the time. Unable and indeed unwilling to claim assurance as a secure possession, he kept faith with the exercises until the end, remained troubled by sins, and found his old doubts returning in his last years.[19] Yet, if Wallington disdained the antinomian move, the desire to fix less on the self and its faults and duties and more on the Deity's sheer largesse was its very essence. Antinomian theorists might draw upon sources outside the Protestant mainline, but their prime objective was to unbind the solifidian gospel that the godly had lashed to a disciplinary program. Speaking to those, like Wallington, vexed by sins and disappointments, they spoke of a vast potential of relief that lay choked and coiled back within the Puritan ellipse. Into ears tuned to "free grace," the Spirit would whisper relief. He would convey gifts without conditions of duty or feverish introspection. In deliberate reversal of the pietist way, he would offer a life in which fulfillments, not denials and delays, were foremost—and were securely possessed.

19. *WW*, 195–196. Wallington rebuked current antinomian and other radical trends in "Severall passages in my Life," 178, 188, 536.

ANTINOMIAN
BACKLASH

CHAPTER 10
JOHN EATON
AND THE
ANTINOMIAN
FIRST WAVE

Our modern understanding of early New England's antinomian conflict has been enriched by a growing appreciation of its English roots. It is now clear that the controversial ideas of Anne Hutchinson, John Wheelwright, and their followers must be understood in the context of a theological insurgency that predated the founding of the Bay colony. Almost certainly the American antinomians drew upon English antecedents. Before their emigration, Thomas Hooker, John Cotton, John Davenport, and possibly other Massachusetts clergy had jousted with antinomian doctrines. Thomas Shepard briefly had been drawn to the Grindletonian variant (discussed below) early in his religious pilgrimage. Martha Collins, a prospective member of Shepard's New England congregation in 1640, appears to have acknowledged contact with the infamous Peter Shaw; and William Dyer, one of the most radical members of First Church in 1636–1638, had been apprenticed in the London parish of Saint Michaels, Crooked Lane, while Shaw preached from its pulpit.[1]

The importance of the transatlantic background was recognized by New Englanders who found traces in the antinomian outbreak of the already in-

---

1. For jousts with antinomians, see T[homas] H[ooker], *The Soules Vocation; or, Effectual Calling to Christ* (London, 1635), 65; H[ooker], *The Soules Implantation into the Naturall Olive* (London, 1640), 232–233; *GP,* 42–43; *WTS,* III, 276; George Selement and Bruce C. Woolley, eds., *Thomas Shepard's Confessions,* Colonial Society of Massachusetts, *Publications,* LVIII, *Collections* (1981), 131. For Cotton's engagement with antinomian ideas, see below, Chapter 11, n. 29, and text. Probably in 1633 or 1634, John Davenport rebutted a critic who rejected the ritual of signs and evidences in favor of a direct gift of divine assurance ("PH," 76). Collins attended sermons of "Mr. Shaw" before her emigration. The identification of this figure with Peter Shaw is plausible but uncertain ("PS," 685). For Dyer and Shaw, see Michael P. Winship, *Making Heretics: Militant Protestantism and Free Grace in Massachusetts, 1636–1641* (Princeton, N.J., 2002), 52.

famous ideas of Robert Towne, Roger Brierley, and probably others and passed an alien act in May 1637 designed to bar members of "Mr Brierly his church" from joining forces with the insurgents. Given both the surprising extent of antinomian dissent in the quarter-century before the English Civil War and the strongly interactive ways of the English godly, we can assume that those who made the Great Migration were familiar with a variety of antinomian prophets and their opinions. The migrants would have known too of the several court cases that antinomian heterodoxies already had provoked, together with conflicts and debates among the godly themselves. Indeed, the first years of the Great Migration coincided with a well-publicized cycle of struggles in London that has been termed "the first antinomian crisis." A sketch of the English backgrounds to about 1635 will clarify later New England developments.[2]

Beginning in the century's second decade, some men and women of Puritan persuasion defected from the practice of piety. Non-Separatists of a sort, they did not aim to secede from the larger godly community, but to reform it from within; yet they proved agents of strain and division. They found the community's program for the good life in reality burdensome and disquieting and saw little value in individual adjustments in, say, private fasting or the use of a daily schedule that left the overall scheme intact. In their cry for relief there appeared what we have come to call the antinomian (that is, "antilegal") movement. Its critique of contemporary religion was broad in scope, hostile to Catholic and Arminian values, to the nominal, unregenerate religion of the Prayer Book, and to legalistic tendencies in any form; but regimental Puritanism was its major target. The critics saw a fateful contradiction in godly religion, in its declaring grace free and then chaining the saints to conditions and duties. To end the bondage, a forceful countermovement was needed. Free grace was its stinging party slogan, and "sainthood without obligation or anxiety" its grand ideal.[3]

Of its lay constituency relatively little is known. With some regularity hostile contemporaries portrayed it as largely plebeian and female, but the

2. "PS," 705. For Towne and Brierley, see *AC*, 32. The ordinance is in Nathaniel B. Shurtleff, ed., *Records of the Governor and Company of the Massachusetts Bay in New England* (Boston, 1853–1854) I, 196 (and see *JJW*, 219). Winthrop might not have known that in 1631 Brierley had moved from Yorkshire to a clerical living in Burnley, Lancashire, where he apparently entered a mellower phase. *BDR*, I, s.v. "Brierley, Roger."

3. The phrase is from Stephen Foster, "New England and the Challenge of Heresy, 1630 to 1660: The Puritan Crisis in Transatlantic Perspective," *WMQ*, 3d Ser., XXXVIII (1981), 638.

fullest modern study finds that it drew from every social stratum and mirrored the composition of the larger godly community. "Artizans and illiterate men" and women certainly took part, yet antinomian views won an audience "not alone [among] the lesser sort, but [also] the more exquisite"; and in the New England outbreak of the mid-1630s merchants and their families and other citizens of rank were prominent. As to the pastoral leadership, most of the figures whose views are on record were well-spoken men with university training or substantial self-education. Presumably they and their audiences shared the need of the time for personal and social reorientation amid rapid changes, but in their quest to master new forces and recast identity they had found—or had been persuaded by antinomian criticism to find—the pietist awakening self-defeating.[4]

Antinomians sought no return to the religion of unregenerate parishioners attached to older and laxer ways, but many of their grievances reiterated long-familiar complaints. From early Elizabethan times Puritan clergy had kept a running catalog of gripes they encountered against the godly, their strict and judgmental deity, and the "precise nicenesse and needlesse scrupulositie" that they paraded and sought to intrude upon the church and nation. "Wee cannot brooke this exactnesse" was the standard complaint. "Shall we alwayes be poring on our corruptions? [It was asked,] . . . shall a man set his soule on a continuall racke?" "To be pent up all the day long in doing God's work, watching, praying, fighting against every sin, this is a burden, this is too strict." Presuming a less demanding God, such grumblers sought to keep "the way to [heaven] wide and broad," and always they "complain[ed] of preachers that they straiten the way." Their religion, to change the metaphor, marked out "a shorter cut to heaven," a way to safety and fulfillment without undue exertion or cost.[5]

Protests and proposals such as these had hounded Puritan efforts since early Elizabethan times, but from the mid-1610s they were to be voiced anew by disillusioned men and women who had attempted to live by precisianist ideals but found them despotic and unfulfilling. Uncommonly sensitive, impatient, or simply weaker travelers in the pietist way, their immediate aim was to carve a path out of the punctilious, troubled religion that Puritanism since

4. *RV,* 129; *HP,* 10. The role of women was emphasized in *RV,* sig. A7, 64; *LG,* sig. B4, and see *RC,* 320. For plebeian associations, see *WRS,* II, 316; *HP,* 6. The modern study is "PH," 44–45, 361.

5. *MSD,* 225; [Thomas Hooker], *The Soules Humiliation* (London, 1640), 149 ("exactnesse"); *SPC,* 55 ("shorter cut"), 88 ("racke"); *WTS,* I, 84 ("pent up"); *WRS,* VII, 12 ("wide and broad," "preachers").

Richard Greenham had become. Leaving behind all that was demanding or fearful, particularly the sense of Christian identity as a volatile work-in-progress, they reimagined sainthood as stable, confident, and relaxed. The result was a very rare thing in the Puritan century: a highly committed approach to Christian redemption that was not fundamentally shaped by disciplinary ideals.

There was a surprisingly large cast of antinomian characters and activities in early-seventeenth-century England. In different places and under apparently unrelated circumstances, at least five distinct varieties of antilegal opinion had emerged before 1630. Peter Lake and David Como have identified eight to ten antinomian clergy in London alone by that date, together with an indeterminate number of committed laity; and their increasingly aggressive activities sparked a series of conflicts, debates both within and outside the godly community, flurries of literary controversy and of investigations and high-profile cases before the Court of High Commission (the highest ecclesiastical court) in the years around 1630, which constituted a substantial "Antinomian Controversy" a half-decade before the American struggle. Only a few such figures left a substantial record of their teaching, but at least six in England made a mark in the record of pre–Civil War antinomian doctrine: John Eaton (1575–1630?), John Traske (1585–1636), Roger Brierley (1586–1637), Robert Towne (1593–1663), Tobias Crisp (1600–1643), and John Everard (1575?–1650?). To these we may add Peter Shaw (d. 1660?), the tenor of whose teaching is evident in a dossier of materials gathered for his trial before the High Commission in 1629; the author of a brief tract published in 1622 as *Antinomus Anonymus;* and the authors—Como dubs them the "Cambridge Antinomian" and "Oxford Antinomian"—of two surviving antilegal manuscripts held by Cambridge University Library and the Bodleian Library of the University of Oxford. Collectively their ideas constituted a substantial first wave of antinomian opinion, and at least Eaton, Traske, Brierley, Towne, Shaw, and Everard had gained notoriety by the time of the New England controversies of the mid-1630s, where Brierley and Towne were mentioned by name.[6]

Brierley's iconoclastic career began at Grindleton Chapel, Milton in Cra-

---

6. "PH," 38 (Como has in mind the patterns associated with Eaton, John Etherington, John Traske, Roger Brierley, and John Everard), 312, 337; "PS," 699; Peter Lake and David Como, "'Orthodoxy' and Its Discontents: Dispute Settlement and the Production of 'Consensus' in the London (Puritan) 'Underground,'" *Jour. Brit. Stud.*, XXXIX (2000), 61. "London's Antinomian Controversy" is reconstructed in "PH," 52–66. The contents of the Shaw dossier are printed in "PS," 706–715.

ven, Yorkshire, where his preaching sparked a long-lived Grindletonian movement. In 1617 he was tried before the Court of High Commission for Nonconformity and doctrinal errors of antinomian tendency. Eaton emerged even
earlier, sparking conflict at Wickham Market, Suffolk, in the mid-1610s.
Among the first clergymen to be punished by the High Commission for
spreading antinomian views, he was deprived of his clerical living in 1619. He
completed his masterwork, *The Honey-Combe of Free Justification by Christ
Alone*, about 1630, sometime before his death, although it was not published
until 1642.[7]

Traske exhibited shifting antinomian tendencies from the mid-1610s into
the 1620s, then fell in with Eatonist views during the later 1620s or 1630s and
aired them in *The True Gospel Vindicated* (1636). Little is known of Towne's
activities before the 1640s, but he was suspended by the High Commission in
June of 1629 and was known to John Cotton at least by 1636 as a spiritist "Ring
Leader" in Nottinghamshire. His earliest and fundamental statement, *The
Assertion of Grace* (1644), was composed about 1632 and leaned heavily upon
Eaton's ideas. Crisp's antinomian conversion probably occurred about 1630
when he held a pastorate at Brinksworth, Wiltshire, but was making connections with London antinomian circles. A first collection of his sermons, *Christ
Alone Exalted*, appeared in 1643, but their date of composition is unclear. Shaw,
a controversialist from the North drawn to London in the later 1620s, was
found guilty of antinomian error and suspended by the High Commission

7. *AC*, 32 ("ring leader"). Brierley: *DNB*, s.v. "Brierley, Roger"; Ronald A. Marchant,
The Puritans and the Church Courts in the Diocese of York, 1560–1642 (London, 1960), 40,
233–234; Christopher Hill, *The World Turned Upside Down: Radical Ideas during the English Revolution* (Harmondsworth, 1975), 81–83; *BDR*, I, s.v. "Brierley, Roger"; David B.
Foss, "Grindletonianism," *Yorkshire Archaeological Journal*, LXVII (1995), 146–153. The
"secte called Grindletonians" was known to the York High Commission from at least 1617.
Brierley moved to Kildwick about 1622 and in 1627 was haled again before the High
Commission for holding conventicles. Marchant, *Puritans and the Church Courts*, 281, 233,
and see 40, 45–48. A first collection of Brierley's sermons appeared in 1670 as *A Bundle of
Soul-Convincing, Directing, and Comforting Truths;* to the 1677 edition a series of poems
was appended.

Eaton probably died about 1631 (Foster, "Challenge of Heresy," *WMQ*, 3d Ser.,
XXXVIII [1981], 633). Eaton's principal idea—that God neither sees nor punishes sin in
the justified—was in place by 1615. Gunter reported that in previous years neighboring
clergy and other "friends" had organized a number of private conferences in an effort to
persuade him of his "dangerous and blasphemous" course (*HP*, sig. B). Sometime after his
degradation from the ministry, Eaton was readmitted to a curacy, but he soon was removed
and punished for "broach[ing] all his opinions (formerlie denyed) againe." *RC*, 320.

early in 1629—only to resume his career in the North. Standing in a class by himself as representative of a perfectionist strain of antinomian opinion, Everard by about 1625 had evolved an eccentric and heavily allegorical view of the Christian redemption that nevertheless shared standard antinomian complaints and concerns. The main source of his ideas is a series of sermons preached at Kensington between 1625 and 1636 and published posthumously as *Some Gospel-Treasures Opened* (1653). In 1636 he was suspended and fined by the High Commission on charges of Familist and antinomian as well as Anabaptist heresy.[8]

John Eaton, "the first antinomian among us"

Among the expositions of free grace these varied spirits produced, Eaton's was the most thoughtful and influential. From about 1620 he broadcast his views through conversation, preaching, and "scatered [probably unpublished] pamphlets"; and his *Honey-Combe,* completed by the decade's end, was hands down the fullest and most systematic statement of early English antinomian opinion. Born in 1575, he was the senior member among the first antinomian publicists. Ardent and forceful in manner, he seems to have exerted the greatest influence in the early agitations. He might not have been the first prophet of antilegal religion, but he was unquestionably its most notable early exponent and "standard-bearer." In his *Heresiography* of 1645, Ephraim Pagitt reported that "the first *antinomian* among us (that I can hear of) was one Mr. Iohn *Eaton,*" and Thomas Gataker later grudgingly attested the power of Eaton's ideas in an attack upon "those, who from one of the first authours

8. On Traske, see *BDR,* III, s.v. "Traske, John," and "PH," 116–161, 295–312. On Towne, see A. G. Mathews, *Calamy Revised . . .* (Oxford, 1934), 489–490; Marchant, *Puritans and the Church Courts,* 313; *CJC,* 232. For his suspension, see "PH," 58. *The Assertion of Grace* was a rebuttal of Thomas Taylor's *Regula Vitae* of 1631. The title page indicates that Towne had sent the work in manuscript "to the said Doctor [Taylor] a little before his death" in 1633 *(AG).*

Crisp: *DNB; BDR,* I, s.v. "Crisp, Tobias"; Christopher Hill, "Dr Tobias Crisp, 1600–43," in *The Collected Essays of Christopher Hill* (Brighton, 1986), II, 141–161. Crisp seems to have attracted little attention before 1642, but a surviving set of notes from a sermon he preached on a visit to London in 1634/5 records "identifiably antinomian sentiments" ("PH," 68–69).

Shaw: "PS," 684–686. Everard: *DNB; BDR,* I, s.v. "Everard, John." "PH," 215–266, surveys Everard's theology and its antinomian proclivities.

thereof are commonly called *Eatonists,* [and] from their opposition to the *mandatory . . . power* of the *law morall* [are called] *Antinomians.*"[9]

By about 1630, a circle of Eatonists that included Traske and Towne had become the most visible antinomian presence in the mother country, and by 1632 the archbishop of Canterbury had come to see Eaton as the "Patriarch" of at least four outspoken men who by then had stood accused before the High Commission for disseminating antinomian views, explicitly Eatonist for the most part. Three of the earliest anti-antinomian tracts, Peter Gunter's *Sermon Preached for the Discoverie and Confutation of Hereticall Positions Held by a Certaine Factious Preacher of Wickam Market* (1615), Henry Burton's *Law and the Gospell Reconciled* (1631), and Thomas Taylor's *Regula Vitae: The Rule of the Law under the Gospel* (1631), all took particular aim at Eaton and those influenced by him, and all perceived a "large dispersion" of his message, which "as an infectious leprosie . . . spreads it selfe farre and neere." In his lectureship at Chelmsford, Essex, in the later 1620s, Thomas Hooker expressly censured "Eatonists," and about this time Richard Sibbes too was complaining of the Eatonist error recently "crept in . . . [that] God sees no sin when he had once pardoned men in justification."[10]

Certainly Eaton and his followers were not the only antinomian witnesses of the period, but arguably they were "the English antinomians who most directly and palpably challenged Puritan orthodoxy" at the time of the Great Migration, and it was their ideas that New Englanders of the mid-1630s were most likely to have known, whether directly or by hearsay, in the growing literature of refutation or in reports of the High Commission cases. We begin, therefore, with a sketch of Eaton's teaching.[11]

Eaton's theology of free grace (and with it the entire antinomian upheaval from about 1615 to 1660) took form in wrathful opposition to the Puritan and precisianist ideals we have tracked through a century and more into the pietist

9. *LG,* 16; Stephen Geree, *The Doctrine of the Antinomians . . . Confuted, in Answer to . . . Sermons of Dr. Crisp* (London, 1644), 5; E[phraim] Pagitt, *Heresiography; or, A Description of the Hereticks and Sectaries of These Latter Times* (London, 1645), 89 (Thomas Bakewell also saw Eaton as the first notable antinomian publicist in *The Antinomians Christ Confounded . . .* [London, 1644], 28); Tho[mas] Gataker, *Gods Eye on His Israel . . .* (London, 1645), 2.

10. *RC,* 320 ("patriarch"; the four were Towne, Traske, Samuel Pretty, and John Eachard, a vicar in a town near Wickham Market); *HP,* 8 ("dispersion," "leprosie"), and see *LG,* sig. B2;, *RV,* sig. A8; H[ooker], *Soules Vocation,* 65; *WRS,* II, 316–317. For Eaton's ardent manner, see *HP,* 6, *LG,* 22; but cf. *RC,* 320.

11. Foster, "Challenge of Heresy," *WMQ,* 3d Ser., XXXVIII (1981), 632, and see 634.

program of introspection and spiritual exercises. Born in 1575, he had lived through the pietist turn, and his passion was to reverse it. Although little is known of his pre-antinomian career, he studied theology under a member of the spiritual brotherhood, and his almost obsessive critique of pietist Puritanism suggests personal, bitter experience of its ways and effects. In the last years of his life, as he distilled the lessons of years of reflection and controversy into a literary magnum opus, he aimed his harshest criticism at the brotherhood and their lay charges. An overweening tribe of clergy—unmistakably the brotherhood, or some of them—had arisen to "boast themselves . . . the most sincere preachers of the Gospel." Devoted chiefly to "the holy walking of sanctification," they had bred a strain of Christians who claimed elite status. "Both in their owne opinion, and in the judgment of others [the godly are in] their legall, zealous, holy, and godly living, the most religious, and most holy men in the world. . . . In outward appearance, they seeme to excell all others in good workes, in holinesse and straightnesse of life, and thinke themselves to lie in the very lap of god, and to be his true Saints by mortification." Regularly enough they "glance at *Free Iustification,*" but their religion now was a swirl of covenants, conditions, works, threats, and penalties, all reinforced by mortifications, fasts, and other "legall devotions." The result was a "hotchpotch," a rhetorically Protestant theology ruled really by zest for "works, works, works, and a preposterous holy walking." "Hotchpotch," of course, was Eaton's perception of the strong Reformed ellipse. Precisely its "double-minded" logic worked the harm.[12]

To see the deviance of that logic one need only consult the original Protestant standard. Yet Eaton, in implicit recognition that the pietist turn arose from distinctive Reformed principles, found that standard best expressed—not in Calvin, Beza, or the Thirty-nine Articles—but in Luther. In *Honey-Combe* Luther is cited or quoted more than one hundred times, a quotation from John Foxe's edition of his commentary on Galatians appears on the title page, and many of the more striking ideas and turns of phrase clearly are borrowed from the Wittenberger. So to find the truest transcript of the apostolic gospel, and therewith the strongest antidote to the dogma of godly walking, one must move wholly outside the Reformed, and English, world.[13]

But, even as Eaton used Luther, he changed him. Of the Luther who saw the Decalogue as an indispensable guide to Christian conduct, who required

12. *HC*, 84 ("hotchpotch"), 86 (boasting), 114 ("glance"), 145 ("sanctification"), 172–173 ("holy men"), 193 ("devotions"), 218 ("works, works"), 382 ("double-minded").

13. *RV*, 53 (and see 191); Geree, *Antinomians Confuted,* sig. b4.

severe self-discipline, denounced libertine misconstructions of sola fides, and warned congregations of misbehaving Christians that they must obey the law or go to hell, he knew, grasped, or regarded little. Eaton's Luther was defined exclusively by his advocacy of free justification, or pardon. Directly echoing and often quoting him, Eaton hailed the supremacy of justification. Within the temporal order, it was redemption itself. It alone focused Christian teaching. It did not *co*define the faith, but was itself "the mother and abundant grace, of graces," "the touchstone of all truth and doctrine, as the only principall originall of our salvation."[14]

Mother, rock, touchstone—these were no mere hyperbole, once one had grasped the real meaning of justification, or free pardon. One prominent metaphor of pietist religion fixed the saints always under the gaze of a "Royall eye," there to be wholly transparent and exactly surveyed. Bound to move and act with "that precisenesse, which is commended" in the Bible, they were held accountable for every misstep and liable to both temporal and eternal punishment. With this construction in mind, Eaton reframed the question of how the Deity sees human beings. God is of too pure eyes to gaze upon sinful humanity, yet sin belongs to the human condition. Even the best of Christian deeds, the most adequate signs and evidences in the Puritan sense, are rankly corrupt by the divine standard. How, then, can we stand before God worthy of his gaze? How can we "endure the triall of his justice"? Solely by justification. Its work, full and final, is to cloak human imperfections with "the wedding-garment of Christs righteousnesse." Made thus "perfectly holy . . . in the sight of God freely all day long," the justified escapes the Deity's harsh surveillance and all attendant threats.[15]

Thinking, again, in a Lutheran mode, Eaton cast the mother doctrine in an alien, otherworldly light. The core of the New Testament message, the hiding of sin and its ugliness before God by a mantle of purity, repeals every standard of deduction and common sense. Imputed innocence, canceling appearances and blinding the Deity, cannot be reckoned by any human mind or conscience. Since it stands opposite to ordinary morality, the faith that seizes it is a daily

14. *HC*, 5, 95. For obeying the law or going to hell, see James F. McCue, "Luther and the Problem of Popular Preaching," *Sixteenth Century Journal*, XVI (1985), 33–43. In *"Sola Fide, Sola Gratia:* The Battle for Luther in Seventeenth-Century England," *Sixteenth Century Journal*, XVI (1985), 115–133, J. Wayne Baker underestimates Eaton's many substantial departures from Luther's teaching.

15. *GD*, 32, 58; *HC*, 2, 160, 279. Further details are in T. D. Bozeman, "The Glory of the 'Third Time': John Eaton as Contra-Puritan," *Journal of Ecclesiastical History*, XLVII (1996), 645.

exertion of trust in the impossible. And to repose that trust, a faithful man or woman "turnes quite from, and forgetteth the order of nature . . . and [believes] things that doe to reason, sense, sight, and feeling, shew a contrariety and impossibility." So the gospel's call to belief that God is kind and that believers' imperfections "are mystically, that is, above their reason, sense, and feeling, utterly abolished out of [his] sight," became alike a leitmotiv of Eaton's argument and a stark elucidation of the Puritan apostasy. How cozily reasonable pietist religion really was, with its calculable system of contracts, controls, and temporal punishments! How apparent it was too that the whole routine of constraint and fear had taken hold because it "seemes both in preachers and people a good and plausible course to flesh and blood, because it is the teaching of reason, and the *light of nature*".[16]

Surpassing logic and sense to grasp their unaccountable purity before God, the justified achieve as well a new vision of the Deity. As Eaton's critics noted, the god beheld in his scheme is not the complex being of mercy *and* justice described in Reformed divinity. Although outspokenly hostile to Arminianism, Eaton shared a central Arminian emotion: revulsion against the despotic and cruel deity of orthodox theology. When addressing the faithful, he was at pains to avoid current designations of God as ruler, legislator, judge, and avenger; nor did he share the Reformed enthusiasm for divine glory manifest in ethical demand and the punishment of sin. In his pages the Deity is defined almost exclusively by acts of affection and especially by forgiving, forgetting, casting away, burying, or not seeing sin; and it is through those acts alone that the divine glory is shown. To approach this God is, not to cringe before an exacting "Majestie," but only to "perceive the love, goodnesse and sweetnesse of God how great it is." The deity known by Christians, in brief, is a being of no anger who sees and punishes no sin, who "embraces us . . . with a true fatherlike, and well-pleased affection of love" and intends always to "make merry with us." He is kindhearted through and through.[17]

A god of all good favor, an immaculate reconception of the human self—so great a honeycomb of benefits must change dramatically the affective charge of English religion. Since the fraternity claimed not only minds but hearts for their philosophy of mortification, Eaton became a critic of prevailing moods as well as of doctrine; he urged people to feel as well as to think differently. When with the eye of faith believers and churches see only an angerless lord,

16. *HC*, 78 ("abolished," and see 50, 59), 114 (plausibility), 178 (things contrary). On making God blind and weak, see *HC*, 52.

17. *HC*, 62–63, 420. For the divine glory, see *HC*, 52.

they will experience an emotional sea change. Then they will grasp another great truth of the gospel: that the god who sees no sin "loveth not heavinesse . . . of spirit" and "hateth . . . heavie and sorrowfull cogitations," and then the somber atmosphere of affectionate divinity must disperse. Even in the lives of the justified, contrition and mortification of sin will play an occasional role, since "wee fall sometimes into sinnes, which by nature bring . . . sorrow with them"; yet that role is minor and transient. In the overall view, "Joy . . . ought alwayes to have the first place with us." Rituals of self-abasement must give way to "sweet cogitations of Christ, wholesome exhortations, pleasant Songs and Psalmes, praises and thanksgiving." Under the friendly gaze of a pacified father, a happier, more upbeat, even tuneful human temperament can take form.[18]

Yet if penitential moods are swept away and if the principal glory of the faith lies in the hiding and not the curing of sin, how are people induced to do good? How can personal and social discipline be secured? Again echoing but going further than Luther, Eaton proposed that the experience of justification imparts an ethical sense and will that is simply irrepressible and almost wholly reliable. Here was an estimate of what pardon does to a person that could be found in no Reformed or Lutheran confession. There was no denying that impulses to sin remain, but these were mere remnants of the Old Man. Gone was the notion that sweepingly powerful impulses vie for control of the redeemed self and that violence must be done to them if a sanctified life is to emerge. Disciplinary schemes were superfluous, for justified persons are ruled by "good and holy desires"; their new and cheerful mood embraces a grateful goodwill that must simply "abound" in good acts. Here, despite all the emphasis on a righteousness beyond the self and its capacities, was a larger trust in the power of conversion to remodel personality than a Greenham or Robert Bolton—or even Luther—could allow.[19]

Here was a fuller capacity as well to resolve doubt and fear. Onerous though it was, Puritan faith might be credited if it built in the end a stable footing before God, but Eaton knew too well that, despite all upright walking and warfaring, "doubts of the assurance of . . . Justification" continued to abound and indeed to multiply; and the source of those doubts was readily apparent. As ever, the binary impulse was at work: the intransigent need to complement

18. *HC,* 449–450. On repentance, see also *HC,* 95.

19. *HC,* 27, 142. For Crisp, Christ "doth take as strict an order, to restraine and keep in the spirits of a man, as to save that man" (*CA,* 37); and see John Eaton, *The Discovery of the Most Dangerous Dead Faith* (London, 1642), 77–79. For gratitude, see *HC,* 144, 169, 211, 457.

(and hence in effect to supplant) the gospel with a regimen of precise walking. Inevitably the delusion that God continues to see and hate sin in the Christian fostered belief that the event of justification was a deficient source of hope. It revived the Catholic conviction that the saints' sins disrupt and poison their relationship to God, and bred a "secret hope . . . of procuring . . . Gods favour [by] mortifying sinne out of the sight of God." There began the doomed search for bases of certainty in the murk of behavior, a search that could but make status before God probationary and unstable. This was the final reduction of the religion of trust and cheer to a careworn ordeal.[20]

Again we see that Eaton's deepest quarrel was with the set of tendencies that we have called "strong Reformed." Against a deep-seated need to combine, link, and correlate pardon and morality, his instinct was to sunder and distance them. None of the familiar pairings—gospel and law, the New and the Old Testaments, or the Deuteronomic calculus tying divine favor to temporal rewards and punishments—had been spared; and now the crowning duality, the practical syllogism joining certainty of pardon to ethical states and works, also must be unlinked. Acting at once to lever apart the two poles and restore the supremacy of justification, Eaton tabooed behavior as a factor in assurance: "When thou desirest to bee holy and righteous before God, *leane not to thy life.*"[21]

Simply to take and enjoy the costless gift of purity before God—there was a downright leisurely way to dispel doubt and fear. But suppose, as Eaton assuredly did, that the source of doubt lay deep and engrained. Suppose, specifically, that it arose from the obsession with sin and repentance that two generations of pietist counselors had nursed with such success. In that case, to take and trust the Lord's free favor must work a hard reversal of trust in human behavior. That was the essential insight that eluded Puritan spiritual direction and its twinned cure for the anxious conscience. Plotting a track to peace, not through, but around and beyond morality, Eaton thus required troubled saints to move contrary to their normal instincts, to count their "owne holy walking of Sanctification as *nothing* and *dung,*" and then to dare (by pietist lights) the unthinkable: to abandon the holy walk. Not the redoubling, but the suspension of effort would silence doubt. Indeed, the deeper the doubt, "so much the more [should persons] goe by faith wholly out of themselves." The more the

---

20. *HC,* 12, 170. For the godly's "secret inbred delight" in works, see also Eaton, *Dead Faith,* sig. A12.

21. *HC,* 184, emphasis mine. Eaton allowed good works a role in declaring to others the excellence of the justified estate. *HC,* 66, 164, 379.

wise saint is distressed by his behavior, "the more he flies . . . to the absolute perfection of his justification," blanking the mottled realm of works from his consciousness as much as possible. Peace, in sum, flows from a passively trustful, not from a tensed and striving, state of mind and body. Since by this alone could one "sleep one night . . . in any security," Eaton had discovered how to "lie downe safely, and sleep sweetly." From the mother doctrine Eaton drew boon after boon, but perhaps this one, untroubled sleep, captures the nub of the matter most poignantly.[22]

To seal his exit from the Puritan and pietist frame of mind, Eaton also drew expressly antinomian conclusions. Since the "willing, cheerfull and ready practising of all duties" was a dependable trait of the justified life, legal codes were obsolete. Designed for the childlike citizens of biblical Israel, law remained needful in later times to convict the unregenerate (a category that included the Puritan godly!) and prepare them for conversion. Sounding now like an Enlightenment philosophe, Eaton construed justification as the portal to moral adulthood. Leaving all tutelage behind, those who experience it come fully of age and can be trusted to steer themselves. Sometimes their obedience might slacken, and then "a little help of direction, and exhortation" might be useful. So there is a continuing role for pastors and preaching as well as for biblical study, but now the saints simply "cannot chuse but" to order themselves and to perform good works. In a way unimagined in Puritan quarters, *the less they worried and strained, the more their power for good would increase,* and works would flow of their own accord. In this vision of effortless discipline, of duties "voluntarily flowing" from relief and joy, we find at once the core of Eaton's (and of much antinomian) ethics and the revolutionary corollary of his theory of redemption: Christian morality is virtually automatic. Ethical behavior flows so readily, indeed so "unfallibly" from the saints—and with all its imperfection removed from God's gaze and concern—as to exempt them outright from law.[23]

22. *HC,* 87 ("goe by faith"), 154 ("perfection"), 168 ("dung," and see sigs. b2–b3), sig. b3 ("sleep," "lie down").

23. *HC,* 75 ("chuse"), 78 "infallibly"), 457 ("cheerfull"), 466 ("help"), 474 ("flowing"). For the saints as *haeredes adulti et emancipati* (come-of-age and freed from "schoolmaster-like government"), see *HC,* 110–111, 117. For preaching the law to the unconverted as the "hammer of death, [and] the thundring of Hell," see *HC,* 464. Exclusively in this context, Eaton urged a review of self by the touchstone of the Decalogue (*HC,* 10–17). He also adopted the strong preparationist teaching that the soul is a contaminated space ("a foule hog-stie"), which requires detoxification before the divine entry, but he reversed its intent by making justification the exclusive cleansing agent. *HC,* 424.

In context of his time, Eaton's story was thus arresting. Antinomian in the literal, antilegal sense, his theology was much more. Its positive element was the advocacy of free grace and its cornucopia of benefits, and the benefits were linked unashamedly to pleasures. Affectionate divinity too, Eaton knew, spoke of free grace. It endorsed gifts and gratifications, but it involved them so closely with disciplinary aims as to cloud the divine largesse. So it was time to reverse field. Focusing now as much on earthly as heavenly gifts, Eaton made of the Christian redemption a lavish giveaway. No longer the port of entry to a difficult life, the event of justification now was a kind of divine potlatch, a sheer repletion and feast of unearned favors. No longer pummeled with exactions and penalties, those who experienced it were showered with gifts. They were, not plunged into contrition, but encouraged to make merry. Here, we suggest, in a dizzyingly sharp tilt from costs to gains and enjoyments, is the most telling overall trend not only in Eaton's thought but throughout the antinomian insurgency on the eve of the Great Migration.

The Other Antinomians: A Collective Profile of First-Wave Theology

A greathearted deity pouring out free grace, saints standing pure and confident before him, relaxed obedience without the law, and gay and carefree moods—were these Eaton's idiosyncrasies, or broader distinctions of the antinomian first wave? The answer is mixed but clear. Eaton was the most influential proponent as of about 1630, but he shared the stage with other creative and controversial spirits. Their theologies formed no uniform project, but an array of varied and often contrasting points of view, and none centered on the metaphor of the Deity's piercing or blinkered gaze. Although after the publication of Honey-Combe the term "Eatonist" was to become a familiar label for those who declared Christians free from the law—and indeed by the 1630s an Eaton circle that included Towne and Traske had formed in London to keep the gracious message before the Protestant public—none of the other early theorists shared the full range of Eaton's concerns. Nor, excepting Traske, Towne, and probably Crisp, do they appear to have been dependent upon or clearly familiar with his distinctive polemical strategies. Tobias Crisp was damned as an apostle of "his Master Eaton, from whom he hath borrowed most of his new Divinity"; but, if Crisp framed part of his argument in terms of the divine sight of sin, that metaphor did not become central to his work. Moreover, he differed at many points from Eaton, taking more radical positions on preparation for conversion and the compatibility of justification with sin in the believer. Shaw shared many positions with Eaton but joined them to

eccentric opinions that Eaton could not have endorsed. Brierley valued contrite, self-abnegating moods that contrasted with Eaton's favored accent upon
cheer, and clung to the notion of Deuteronomic punishments. Neither Crisp,
Traske, nor Brierley shared Eaton's vision of a golden era in the early Reformation years, and each held ideas incompatible with his. Traske, Antinomus
Anonymus, and the Oxford Antinomian, for example, (in contrast also to
Towne) denied to the law its familiar role in the conversion of a sinner,
preferring to believe that "Repentance and faith bee wrought onely by the
Gospel," whereas Brierley maintained a positive conception of the Hebraic
Scriptures and drew a majority of his sermon texts from the older Testament;
and neither Crisp nor Brierley fully accepted Eaton's outright removal of law
from the Christian dispensation.[24]

Should these differences outweigh the similarities, our inquiry would take a
greatly complicating turn. Then the free grace witness in New England must
be plotted relative to a medley of interests pulling in varied directions. Yet it
was not so. With respect to the issues we are pursuing, Eaton's theology was a
true epitome. Just as John Downame's works of spiritual direction typified
practical theology despite his numerous special concerns and accents, so too
did Eaton's *Honey-Combe* represent the major interests of the early wave of
free grace radicalism. All of the figures above shared more with than they
differed from Eaton and one another. They held a common vision of Protestantism in crisis, and their diagnosis and remedy were the same in most
essentials. Several, with Eaton, drew heavily upon Luther. The pattern is not
apparent in New England, but in the parent country the early antinomian
agitation constituted (aside from the minor activity associated with John Foxe

---

24. Gataker, *Gods Eye*, 2 ("Eatonist"); Geree, *Antinomians Confuted*, 5 ("Master
Eaton"); *GV*, 52 ("Gospel"), and see *Antinomus Anonymus . . .* , in William Hinde, *The
Office and Use of the Morall Law of God . . .* (London, 1622), sig. B3; "PH," 337–340. The
Eaton circle is discussed in Foster, "Challenge of Heresy," *WMQ*, 3d Ser., XXXVIII (1981),
632–633, 633 n. 20, 639. For Crisp on the divine sight of sin, see *CA*, I, 8–11. A variant
metaphor is more prominent in his work: God does see and punish the sin of the justified
but diverts the punishment wholly to Christ (*CA*, I, 12–14, 28–29, II, 69–111, 316–344).
Going beyond Eaton, Crisp held that God requires no "qualifications or spiritual disposition before or upon the communicating of . . . Christ" (*CA*, I, 60–73, 195–196, 411–423,
quote at I, 184). For his view that "God will never call you to an account for the sins you
commit," see *CA*, I, 34, 243–244, 311–312, 397, II, 272 (quote at I, 399). At this and other
points, Crisp's doctrine is not well described as a return "to pristine Calvinist theology"
(Hill, "Crisp," in *Essays of Hill*, II, 144). On Shaw's eccentric opinions, see "PS," 700–704.
Brierley on self-negating moods: *CT*, 4, 36, 45, 73, 89, 167, 182–183, 225–226, 238. On
Deuteronomic punishments: *CT*, 153–155, 169, 202.

in the 1580s) the first *Lutherrenaissance* in an English-speaking land. For several of the publicists covered here, Luther was the favored Protestant authority. The judgment of Thomas Taylor and other critics that it was *"Mr. Luther,* whom [antinomians] challendge as their friend, and favourer" and who is their "Hercules of Gods glory in the point of free Justification" is borne out fully in their work. More single-mindedly than other Reformers, they believed, Luther had named justification apart from works the heart and sum of Christian faith, but to review his teaching was to realize how little it counted in the present day. A new message vaunting "obedience [as] the way to heaven" had shouldered it aside, and for this usurpation it was easy to fix the blame. Within the theological parties of the day there was fault enough to go around, but the principal revisionists were the Puritan clergy, their devotional awakening, their flood of published propaganda, and their aggressive followers. Under their ministrations the doctrine of justification had died the death of a thousand qualifications.[25]

Not only Eaton but also Brierley, Traske, Shaw, Crisp, the Cambridge Antinomian, and probably others were disillusioned veterans of godly religion. Unlike most of their Arminian contemporaries, they were deviant insiders, mavericks of the godly movement itself. Like Eaton's theology, their mature theologies recoiled point for point from the pietist way. Its agents, who styled themselves "the greatest Protestants" in the land and had established a practical hegemony in the English pulpit and in spiritual direction, in reality had revived a faith of Catholic or Judaic type. Accolades to free grace fell from their lips, but over the Bible's delighting disclosure of mercy they had inscribed bolder messages of law and punitive rule. Blotting out Christianity's core belief—*"The Lord Jesus Christ hath already done all that is to bee done"*—they had so expanded their regimen of efforts, evidences, and exercises that the human self and its own "qualifications and dispositions" came to the fore. Not Christ and his extrinsic purity, but the saints' "blamelesse walking according to the law" was their operative dogma, construed in the strictest imaginable

---

25. *RV,* 53 (and see 191); Geree, *Antinomians Confuted,* sig. b4; *CA,* I, 88. Crisp and Traske cited only biblical authorities. Others drew on Luther's work as a fundamental alternative to Puritan soteriology. In *AG,* Towne cited Luther at least twenty-eight times, and one quote extends to three pages. "Is now Luther yours or ours?" Towne asked his Puritan antagonist, Thomas Taylor. "If you condemn us, why not him . . . ?" (*AG,* 58–60, 74; and see 10, 16, 21, 42, 44, 124). See also *Antinomus Anonymus,* in Hinde, *Morall Law,* 1–3, 5, 7; and *CT,* 143, 223. Blasts against Puritan clergy: *CA,* I, 386–387; *GV,* 27–38; *CT,* 46, 77, 164, 225; *AG,* 14–15, 25, 42, 119–120 (and note Towne's strictures upon "holy walking" at 25, 60, 168).

terms. To find men and women dedicated to "beating down of the body by exactest fastings" and other suppressive techniques, one need not visit a monastery but only behold the nearest clique of the godly. Their practical ideal, nurtured in "the dead groves of . . . devotions," was "a strict, austere, and severe life: a precisenesse and exactnesse without giving to a man[']s self any liberty whatsoever." And when their tiresome course of "humiliations, sorrows, [and] mournings" fails to calm doubt, "whither do they run [for assurance]?" Not to the already completed work of justification, but to their volatile signs and evidences, "to their humiliations, . . . reformations, universall obedience, and the like."[26]

Whether or not they came to the judgment by separate paths, on this point antinomian spokesmen were at one with Eaton: pietist Puritans were the foremost agents of ruin in English religion. Of Christianity they had made a religion of command that always demanded more and was never satisfied with what the believer gave. By this means they had driven a whole generation of well-meaning Protestants to loathe, lacerate, and regiment themselves. They so merged identity with performance that the saints virtually *became* the blur of busy, unstable forces at play in their daily drills. Since little sense remained of selfhood forged outside of themselves in Christ, let alone of its passive, restful, and stable qualities, the gospel was robbed of power to save and console.

Because the fault lay in the very constitution of pietist thought, a top-to-bottom overhaul was needed, and its principal objectives were Eaton's: to bring home the full extent of human impotence before God, to re-vision the Bible as a book of favors and freedoms, to reimagine the Deity as a being of

---

26. John Traske, *The Rule of Faith*, appended to *GV*, sig. G3 (core belief); *CA*, I, 87 ("fastings"), 109 ("precisenesse"), 203 ("sorrows"), 213 ("reformations"), 268 ("blamelesse walking," and see *CT*, 1–3, 53, 77), 322 ("qualifications," and see also *CT*, 3, 38, 46), II, 178 ("greatest Protestants"); *CT*, 179 ("devotions").

Disillusioned veterans: for Brierley's Puritanism, see "Of True Christian Liberty," poem appended to *CT*, 1–2; Marchant, *Puritans and the Church Courts*, 233. Como discusses the Puritan backgrounds of Shaw, Traske, and Crisp in "PH," 17 n. 9, and of the "Cambridge Antinomian" at 323–324. Antipathy to Puritanism: "PH," 241–244, 297–298, 314–315, 325. Catholic or Judaic type: *CA*, 88, and see 290–292; *CT*, 69, 77, 164. Critique of devotional mourning: *AG*, 13, 114, 120; Edw[ard] Nor[r]i[s], *The New Gospel, Not the True Gospel; or, A Discovery of the Life, and Death, Doctrin, and Doings of Mr. Iohn Traske . . .* (London, 1638), 6, 17. Critique of evidences: *GV*, 17–20, 30, 48; "PS," 702. Como notes the particular opposition to signs by John Pordage and the Cambridge Antinomian ("PH," 76, 315).

"ravishing and overcoming love" who does not judge or punish the elect but showers them with mercy, to fix pardon sheer and free as the focal Christian value, and to lift disciplinary burdens. Realization of these values would lift the pietist cloud of self-hatred and suppression, restore the saints' ability to affirm and trust themselves, and—abjuring all proportionality between the capacities and graces of the converted and their religious certainty—exorcise the famous syllogism of practical divinity.[27]

A theology redrawn along such lines would offer no scheme of holy labor and strain, but, as with Eaton, a revolutionary *devaluation of human endeavor*. To the Puritan brood in particular, and to all religious athletes tensed to do their utmost, it would bring jolting news: your exertions can neither pacify God nor produce evidence of a gracious state. The "exactest, strictest, precisest person" has no more credit before the Lord, and no more assurance, than the worst of sinners. Defying all reason and common sense, God calls you to run no race, win no battle, labor for no reward, fulfill no conditions, toil over no preparations, avert no punishment, and grub for no evidences. To the contrary, he instills and prizes passive virtues, virtues often deemed feminine in contemporary culture.[28]

"The whole Doctrine of the Gospel, is not what we should do to [serve] God, but what we should receive from him." The words are Brierley's, but he shared the message with Eaton and all the figures treated here. To stop the godly's performative compulsions, they advanced a contrary ethic. "We at the best work but passively" was its core. In part it merely expanded Reformed teaching that all saintly powers and effects flow from God, but it may reflect too the theme of *Gelassenheit* ("abandonment," "resignation") in the medieval mystical classic *Theologia germanica* (Everard and probably Brierley made English translations) and within the Radical Reformation; and there is a striking resemblance to the later "quietist" teaching of Miguel Molinos (about 1628–1696), which was condemned by the Catholic Church in 1687. Though less radically than Molinos, antinomians minimized human capability. To the godly with their touching belief in "mans power, by diligence," Brierley posed this question: where "is that power . . . to order man[']s heart, to rule his passions. . . ? Is it in man[']s good husbandrie[?] [N]o . . . It is in man[']s lying

27. *AG*, 6, and see 104, 107–109. For divine benevolence, see also *CA*, I, 194, 219, 400–401. Crisp explicitly rejected the practical "syllogisme" in *CA*, II, 431.

28. *CA*, I, 235. "Even the most blamelesse walking according to Gods law," Crisp added elsewhere, "is truly but losse and dung" (*CA*, II, 6). For contrariness to sense and reason, see *CT*, 5, 218, 221–222; *CA*, I, 398. Traske reportedly called his critics "silly naturalists that understand not the mysterie of the Gospell" (quoted in Nor[r]i[s], *New Gospel*, 2).

dead in himself, [and] waiting for help" from beyond. No charter for the going scheme of controls and exercises, Christian faith aimed, not to empower, but to deactivate. It declared godly striving the Lord's alone and left "passive receiving" for the human part. Although male antinomian theorists probably did not have considerations of gender in mind, this approach would give the saints a more feminine turn, to make them more patients than agents. Graciously *dis*empowered, not self-moved, but impelled by Christ within, they achieve without doing. Simply to yield to his persuasions, and to let God "do *all*, speak *all*, work *all*, think *all*"—that was the quietist credo, and it applied through all the drama of redemption. Before, during, and after conversion, to "sit" and "wait," "rest" and "submit" is the primary art that saves. Even the act of faith itself owes nothing to human agency, and it is wildly misconceived as a covenantal condition to be met by a human partner. Not a reach to grasp Christ, but an attestation of Christ's arrival in the soul to do his saving work, faith is the welcoming echo of an already completed event.[29]

"We find experience of the Grace of Christ, *especially when we stir up ourselves to endeavour*." "This . . . you are able to do," for God "makes you instruments: . . . not . . . dead instruments, but . . . living [ones] to move of your selves." Richard Sibbes and John Preston spoke here with the true voice of Puritan practical and federal divinity. It valued states of passivity too but balanced them against active endeavors. Brusquely, antinomian theology broke the balance. Belief that grace "animates, and acts" a supine believer discredited the striving spirit. Henceforth, just as Eaton held, all "labouring

29. *AG*, 91 ("work . . . passively"); *CT*, 67 ("mans power"), 63 ("that power"), 73 ("whole Doctrine"); *CA*, I, 195 ("receiving"); John Everard, *The Gospel-Treasury Opened* . . . (London, 1657), 36 ("*all*," and see 77, 132–133). The four verbs ("sit" etc.) are from *CT*, 112, 171, 178, 225. Human "power": see also *CA*, I, 167–169, 204, 215–216; *GV*, 55; *AG*, 12; and "PS," 707. For Everard and the Cambridge Antinomian, "the pinnacle of religiosity was to escape the self completely"; Christ moved believers "like a great mind or soul energizing a lifeless body" ("PH," 321, 328). *Theologia germanica*: the author urged the Christian to "be concerned with his own self as little . . . as though he did not exist" (Bengt Hoffman, trans., *The Theologia Germanica of Martin Luther* [New York, 1980], 76; and see *Lexikon für Theologie und Kirche* [Freiburg, 1995–], IV, s.v. "Gelassenheit"). For Everard's and Brierley's translations, see Nigel Smith, *Perfection Proclaimed: Language and Literature in English Radical Religion, 1640–1660* (Oxford, 1989), 112, 117, 120. Welcoming echo: *CT*, 164; *CA*, I, 167–169, 204; *GV*, 55; and "PS," 707; this was the thrust of the much-mooted antinomian thesis that justification *precedes* faith. Molinos: *The Oxford Dictionary of the Christian Church*, 3d ed. (Oxford, 1997), s.vv. "Molinos, Miguel" and "Quietism." "Velle operari active, est Deum offendere, qui vult esse ipse solus agens" was one of the condemned theses attributed to Molinos (*KG*, 1687).

and tugging" in religion was but wasted effort, and the godly's compulsion to "sweat and toile and moile all the day long" through their daily march and war now seemed especially incomprehensible and repugnant. If the Lord justifies persons without regard to their deserts, if, in short, "justification is past over to a person whilst he is ungodly," then the premise that likes attract (and opposites repel) is inverted, and the great pietist struggle to break, cleanse, and otherwise prepare the heart for pardon is exposed as an empty project.[30]

And when extended to the everyday practice of Christianity, the quietist principle cut a huge, scythelike swath through the reigning praxis of piety. "Be careful to do exersis[es]" was precious advice from Lady Brilliana Harley to her son Edward in 1639, but by antinomian lights it was gross misguidance. If all human acts are flawed, and if in biblical truth the "the creature['s] concurrence" was reduced to null, why should the saints absorb themselves in churchly ordinances or the strenuous private liturgy that had come in with the pietist turn? Hence, much as Molinos would encourage nuns under his direction to discard their rosaries and holy pictures, to abandon their daily offices and the practice of confession and even all active resistance to temptations, so Eaton, Towne, Brierley, Crisp, and Shaw urged their hearers to strike free from the tyranny of rites. With fitting scorn they sheared away (or witheringly ignored) the fasts and Sabbath duties, the daily schedule, the regulated prayers and introspections, the catalog of sins, the self-canvass for signs and evidences, and the numerous other means used by the fraternity to spur saints to their limits of achievement. Since the practice of piety might have been pursued disproportionally by upper-class women whose circumstances often allowed ample time to perform daily exercises, such dismissal of rites, joined to the elevation of passivity, possibly had special appeal for them. By the going rules

---

30. *WRS*, II, 105, emphasis mine; John Preston, *The Breast-plate of Faith and Love . . .*, 5th ed. (London, 1634), 239; *CA*, I, 65 ("animates"), 214 ("labouring," "sweat"), 166 ("justification"). Looking askance at human "actions," "endeavor," and "doeing," Shaw expressly disconnected salvation from goal-directed activity ("PS," 708, 711). Preparation: Crisp's critique was the fullest: "Whatever thou art . . . , suppose a drunkard, a whore-master, suppose a swearer, . . . [you need] but come to Jesus Christ" (*CA*, I, 411, and see 180, 184, 203, 411). Emphasizing God's "readinesse to receive all that come," Traske scorned in particular the strong preparationist requirement of a "change of life, [in the mistaken belief that Christ] will not . . . take up his habitation in such as are sinners" (*GV*, 30–31, 35–36). Brierley and Towne continued to insist upon a powerful conviction of sin as a prelude to conversion but strongly disapproved protracted rituals of preparation with their emphasis on "this and that qualitie or diligence" (*CT*, 15, 22, 38, 45 [quote on 33]; *AG*, 13–16, 19–20, 111–112, 147).

of gender, they might have found it a relatively natural act to reduce active engagement, to lay down the drills and wait on the Deity to pardon and enact.[31]

In full accord with Eaton, again, this dismissive estimate of human agency and action rested upon a paradoxical surmise: that justification, despite its deliberate focus away from morality, transfigures the moral life. Roving and dangerous as a wild animal before conversion, the natural self is "so tamed [by justification], that he may be set as loose as he was before; yet he will not runne unrulily. . . . Hee will never break loose [or] run away, though the gate stand open on every side." Only on such supposition—that the justified self was so altered as to "walk [uprightly] without his Keeper" of legal, coercive religion— was it plausible and safe to redirect concern away from behavior and possible also to rebut charges that the doctrine of free grace "opens a wide gap to . . . licentiousnesse." Therein did early antinomian ethics affirm a far fuller gent-ling of Old Adam and a stabler desire to do good than even the precisest notion of holy walking.[32]

No more than Eaton did the theorists treated here argue that repose in supernatural agency brings freedom from any rule of law. With their implica-tion of lawless release, the labels "libertine" and "antinomian" were as odious to them as to their critics. When Traske, Towne, and Antinomus Anonymus declared "the morall Law . . . utterly abrogated . . . by the comming in of the Gospell," they spoke, not of the principles of biblical morality, but of their temporary and imperfect outward expression in scriptural statutes and their attendant ethos of demand and threat. Law in that sense is annulled for believers, but only to make possible their fuller realization of its underlying intent. For that intent, summarized in the biblical command to love God and neighbor, now is divinely written in the soul and flows naturally into behavior. Further, since in antinomian doctrine the saints' acts are worked by Christ and the Spirit within, they directly manifest the divine will and hence are lawful

31. *LBH,* 522; *RMC,* II, 189. See the derisive treatment of spiritual exercises in "PS," 711, 712, and *CA,* 271, 300–301, 373. For upper-class women, see Felicity Heal and Clive Holmes, *The Gentry in England and Wales, 1500–1700* (Stanford, Calif., 1994), 364, and the sources cited there.

32. *CA,* I, 37, 39 (and see Towne's example of the tamed mule, *AG,* 137), II, 157 ("gap"); *AG,* 5 ("keeper," and see 172). See also *GV,* 14–16, 60, and John Traske, *Rule of Life,* appended to *GV,* sig. G7. One possible source of the perfectionist strain is the Familist teaching that "the perfected believer . . . 'cannot geeve-fourth els-what from him, but all . . . Vertues and Righteousnesses.'" Christopher W. Marsh, *The Family of Love in English Society, 1550–1630* (Cambridge, 1994), 22.

through and through. Law understood this way, not as an exacting code, but as gentle invitations and admonitions that harmonize with the saints' abounding desire for good, remains wholly in effect. Antinomian theory silently presumed that biblical morality is the only morality, and Christian Scripture its normative statement. It gave no charter to defy the Bible's proscriptions of adultery or greed or its call to truthfulness and charity. To the obvious accusation that their doctrine licensed lawless behavior, early antinomian theorists therefore could retort—often and with high indignation—that the opposite was true. They offered the means to a more virtuous "course of living agreeable to the Law" than was possible in slavery to codes and rules.[33]

In what sense, then, are theologians of the first wave termed "antinomian"? Few if any made law per se the master issue, and all rejected implications of lawless release. Further, "antinomian" points more to their negative stance than to their exultant affirmation of pardon. Yet the affirmation itself arose within opposition, as a thrill of release from the religion of command. To free justification as a great positive ideal, law was a vital foil and antipode. Thus when Eaton or Crisp deployed the word "legal" as an epithet, or when Burton or Taylor labeled the dissidents antinomian and rallied to defend *"the rule of the law* under the gospel," their choice of terms was apt. Both sides knew that law in this context was more than a body of statutes. Critics of legal walking made it symbolic of the practice of piety in all its regimental array and its bruising demands and penalties. For Eaton and his colleagues in dissent, that was the complaint packed into the terms, "law" and "legal." And the larger target, ancient and persistent, was the very conception of religion as a regulatory system. (Construed this way, in productive dialectic with "free grace" or an equivalent, the antinomian label remains useful, and is so used in the present study.)[34]

On the question of law, Crisp and Brierley offered a variant reading. They

33. Nor[r]i[s], *New Gospel*, 4, and see *GV*, 49–51; *AG*, 172. Traske also disavowed those who "slip Collar by Familisme or Antinomisme, or flat Libertinisme" (*GV*, 32, misnumbered 16). For Towne the law remained "an eternal and inviolable Rule of Righteousness" by which "a believer is to walk and live." The Spirit moving in the justified "freely and chearfully . . . encline[s them] to the way of the Law." *AG*, 6, 32, 170 (and see 43, 105, 127), and see *CA*, II, 161.

34. The cited phrase is the subtitle of *RV*, emphasis mine. The proposal that "free grace" encapsulates the issues of the Antinomian Controversy of 1636–1638 offers a needed corrective to glib usages of the "antinomian" label, but it overlooks the symbolic impact of law in that context (and in the broader English context) and implies that "free grace" was a nonpartisan term. Winship, *Making Heretics*, 1.

avoided the language of abrogation and thus were not antinomian in the strict sense (although some of their disciples probably took the extra step). Yet the difference should not be exaggerated. If they did not reject outright law's claim to rule the saints, they did largely ignore it. Perhaps they merely wished to skirt a dangerous subject, but they scarcely concealed their aversion to the reigning religion of command and the contractual and Deuteronomic theory that underwrote it, and they could but shudder at the fantastic scheme of rules enjoined in Nicholas Byfield's *Rules of a Holy Life*. So they too described moral acts as the uncoerced expression of divine power and love within. Yet at the same time, in apparent response to libertine misunderstandings, they defined love as a law-based force that "doth cause [the justified] to walke in [God's] statutes." Early champions of free grace espoused an easier style of virtue, based upon inner suasion and not hard submission to rules; but they hastened to add, with Eaton, that self-control and loving service were its reliable fruits.[35]

Nevertheless, the vision of spontaneous virtue stood poignantly opposite to the ethic of "hardnesse and difficultie" cried up by the pietist tribe. The work of dogmatic sectarians, antinomian plans of salvation were single, uniform, and exclusive; but, at least in theory, they were easy. They sketched a style of life within the capacities of ordinary people. It made the path to heaven "of all the wayes in the world the *most easie* to be hit; there is no hardnesse to find it out, no difficulty to [make] . . . progresse in it": and it yielded ready peace and cheer.[36] Freedom from the pietist treadmill was relief and pleasure enough,

35. *CA*, I, 89 (and see 37–39, 229). Brierley denounced "Drunkennesse, . . . Chambring and wantonnesse, . . . swilling and drinking . . . carding, and dicing [and] whoring" (*CT*, 30–31, and see 9, 24–25, 82, 173). He seems to have assumed a continuing, modest, non-threatening role for the law among Christians (*CT*, 133, and "Of True Christian Liberty," appended to *CT*, 47). Crisp expressed a similar view in *CA*, I, 242. Presumably representing a conservative reaction to the turmoil and mounting religious radicalism of the early 1640s, a set of Crisp's late sermons that his son added to the 1690 edition of *Christ Alone Exalted* laid more emphasis upon the law, moral effort, and discipline: Tobias Crisp, *Christ Alone Exalted: Being the Compleat Works of Tobias Crisp, D.D.* (London, 1690), IV, 25, and see 46, 89–90. Disclaimers of antinomian radicalism also appear in the poem "Of True Christian Liberty" appended to *CT*, 5–7, 10, 14, 19, 45, 53, 59.

36. [Hooker], *The Soules Humiliation*, 63; *CA*, I, 106–107. See also Norris's attack on Traske's "easier way to heaven" and Traske's complaint that pietist clergy make "easily gotten" faith "very hard to attaine unto" (Nor[r]i[s], *New Gospel*, 34; *GV*, 28). The "easier way" metaphor also appears in *RV*, 117, and John Sedgwick, *Antinomianisme Anatomized . . .* (London, 1643), 32. "The way" to heaven, countered a chorus of Puritan critics,

but, when this was joined to realization that God in principle is never "of-fended and angry" with the justified no matter how great their sins, when in antinomian preaching they heard him say, "I will never call you to an account for the sins you commit," the result was exhilarating. In a single moment, without exertion on their part, the saints, as Towne put it in obvious depen-dence on Eaton, were veiled for all time from the Deity's "overlooking eye." Now they could taste freedom not only from doubt and the anxious pietist traffic in evidences but also from the most thoroughly templated and self-repressive course of devotional asceticism known in the Protestant world to that time and from its attendant scheme of Deuteronomic threats and penalties.[37]

Buoyed by the freeness of pardon and flinging off those yokes and all the "joylesse-sorrow" that marked the pietist spirit, they could affirm and trust themselves again and so rise into states of delight: "For it is not written, Weepe evermore, but Rejoyce evermore." When Samuel Pretty, a follower of Eaton tried before the High Commission in 1631, told the court that believers dis-tressed by doubt or fear should, not mourn, but simply "singe all care away," or when John Traske told Edward Norris later in the decade that "carelesse Christians are the choisest beleevers," they put in question the whole Refor-mation heritage of contrition for sins. But they were specially adverse to the "sadnesse and heavinesse of spirit" that was pietism's dominant affect. Whether, with Crisp, they affirmed that "there is matter of nothing but joy" in Christian teaching, or, with Brierley's auditors, found themselves "danc[ing] for joy," or gave themselves with Traske and his followers to "such triumphing

---

"is strict and austere, and requires precisenesse and exactnesse." Geree, *Antinomians Con-futed*, 62; and see *RV*, 137–138.

37. *AG*, 23 ("angry"), 105 ("eye"); *CA*, I, 399 ("account"). Shaw and Crisp most radically disconnected divine favor from the saints' actual moral estate, even in "the highth of iniquity" (*CA*, II, 272, and see 243–244). The issue arose repeatedly in the rash of antino-mian cases—including Shaw's—before the High Commission about 1630 and amid the "errors" of the Massachusetts antinomians. "PS," 708; *RC*, 182, 270; *AC*, 202, 224.

Deuteronomic punishments: for Crisp, Towne, Shaw, and the "Cambridge Antino-mian," as for Eaton, "God doth not punish any believer." Christians remain subject to providential afflictions, but these are "the gentle *purges* of a tender Father" designed to "make his love appear," and no longer *"rods of Gods anger"* (*CA*, I, 31, 54, and see 34; see also *AG*, 111–113; "PS," 708–709; "PH," 317). Brierley laid more stress upon afflictions but saw them more as trials and purges than as punishments (*CT*, 154–155, 202). Yet he held that God dealt more severely with the English people collectively, punishing their sins with plagues and other disasters and threatening a Catholic invasion. *CT*, 153–155, 169.

and glorying, laughter and glee" as to "make mirth and joy, the substance of their religion," they expressed a spectacular sense of relief from penitential religion. "Rivers of pleasures" little tainted by struggle and fear were their portion now.[38]

And exactly that, once more, was the contra-Puritan crux of free grace. It must be emphasized again that the first wave of antinomian theorists remained children of the Puritan movement in several respects. Most shared selectively in its bibliocentric, evangelical, conversionist, and predestinarian emphases, its hostility to Arminianism, its search for a higher life beyond the tepid norms and forms of the official church, and its preoccupation with the problem of assurance. Without doubt, the liberties and pleasures of free grace bore little resemblance to those defined by Robert Burton, the anti-Puritan cleric whose *Anatomy of Melancholy* (1621) defended "feasts, mirth, musick, hawking, hunting, singing, dancing, etc." against the "too stern, too rigid, too precise" negations of the brotherhood and their disciples. Nor could freely gracious pleasures include the "bacchanalian" enjoyments of Nicholas Assheton, an untitled and very un-Puritan gentleman whose *Journal* of the late 1620s virtually enacts Burton's ideal. Not sensual, but spiritual (and in some cases spiritist) pursuits were the stuff of antinomian merrymaking.[39]

Yet, if antinomian mirth was not sensual, it was worldly, to be enjoyed here and now in some fullness, and in this respect too it was calculatedly alien to the pietist project. The godly also were driven by a sense of unrealized possibility and a wish to exceed normal limits. During the turbulent 1640s that wish would lead many to dream of an earthly transfiguration in which the normal restraints of finitude would be removed and felicity achieved, but few Puritans in the earlier period were devoted to millennial speculations, and their impulse to transcend the ordinary was sharply qualified. As social conservatives they were natural foes of extremism in any form, and their theology breathed a profound sense of the trials and limits of life in finitude. That theology nur-

---

38. *GV*, 24, 27; *RC*, 182 ("singe"); Nor[r]i[s], *New Gospel*, 3 ("glee"), 6 ("substance"), 31 ("carelesse"); *CA*, I, 101 ("sadnesse," "matter"); J. C., "An Epistle to the Reader," in *CT*, sig. A3 ("danc[ing]"); *CA*, I, 105 ("rivers"). Traske, who blamed the "desperate mourning" of pietist religion for a high rate of contemporary suicides, wondered: "Why may not carelessnesse be used in an holy sense? seeing, All our care is to be cast upon the Lord" (*GV*, 27–28, 39, and see *RC*, 183, *LG*, 35). Brierley, who highlighted contrite, passive "lowness" as an antidote to activist religion, did not highlight joy. For lowness, see *CT*, 4, 162, 225–226.

39. Robert Burton, *Anatomy of Melancholy* (1621), ed. Floyd Dell (New York, 1927), 921; F. R. Raines, ed., *The Journal of Nicholas Assheton . . .* , in Chetham Society, *Remains Historical and Literary*, XIV (London, 1848), 50, and see 22–23, 26, 31.

tured a keen sense of human imperfection and a healthy respect for Old
Adam's continuing power within the regenerate elect and depicted coercion
and fear, instability and uncertainty as integral to human experience within
history.

For these reasons the kind of spiritual direction espoused by Perkins or
Downame was a sober realist's art. They could not project the Christian course
and combat as a path to utopia this side of heaven. To them it was important not
to exaggerate the saints' ability to know, do, and enjoy the good during their
temporal passage. At once driven forward and held within tight limits, the elect
faced a life of hard endeavor for limited objectives. Theirs was an uphill struggle
for gains that, while inestimably valuable in themselves, were always proximate
and unstable, always pointing past themselves to fulfillments beyond. As laity
like Nehemiah Wallington also knew, "there is no perfection heare in this Life"
where all holiness and assurance "ebbs and flows and flows and ebbs." Transient
foretastes of heaven are granted here, but the real and abiding pleasures come
with a rush after the Last Judgment. Heavy demand and deferred enjoyment, a
sense of limits befitting persons who "have a great journey [still] to goe"—in
affectionate divinity as in the larger history of ascetic Christianity, this seemed a
rightly modest estimate of the life in earthly imperfection.[40]

When the witness to free grace is set against this backdrop, we see more
clearly both the high degree of consensus within the first antinomian wave and
the sharp reversals of attitude that it expressed. Teachers of free grace might
have been weary of pietist duress, but they voiced a firm and total demand of
their own: they required fewer costs and more gains, less labor and ambiguity,
and—beyond the blurry forms of hypocrisy—a clear, unwavering sense of
identity. Surfeited with burdens and delays, they judged a failure the whole
historic effort to make deprivation a redemptive strategy, and so they moved to
lift the accepted limits upon fulfillment, exacting little but promising instant
ease and delight. They esteemed, not effort, but passivity; not control, but release; not deferral, but prompt gratification. Measured within the Reformed-
Puritan tradition with its many Catholic retentions, and indeed from within
any sector of mainstream Protestantism and even the Anabaptist fringe, the
effect was revolutionary. Breaking with age-old ascetic convictions, antino-

40. Nehemiah Wallington, "A Record of Gods Mercies, or A Thankfull Remem-
brance," 156, MS 204, Guildhall Library, London, copy in the Genealogical Society of
Utah, Salt Lake City; Wallington, "A Treatice Containing an Extract of Severall passages
in my Life," 530, V.a. 436, Folger Shakespeare Library, Washington, D.C. (microfilm,
University of Iowa Library) (and see 109); A[dam] H[arsnett], *A Touch-Stone of Grace*
(London, 1630), 261.

mian spirits sought to *replace deprivation with fulfillment as the dominant value of Christian thought and practice* within history.

Blandly familiar today, in Eaton's time this emphasis was provocative. It implied a greatly expanded sense of historical possibility. If God is, not judge, but loving Father, and if grace refines the worst evils out of human nature and with it the need for massive, steady coercion, what need for laws and duties? Then justified Christians are swept up onto higher planes of fulfillment, there to be showered with gifts. There too the endless cycle of hope and doubt in the individual pilgrimage will give way to a confidence both stable and progressive, "gro[wing] stronger and stronger, to a plerophory and full assurance unto joy unspeakable." Furthermore, although publicists of free grace spoke primarily of and to the church, their rebuke of a theology based upon law and force implied a wish to transcend hierarchical social relations and their underlying basis of coercion. Leaving behind the great contemporary dread of disorder, they promised that, if people struggled less and trusted more, seldom would they cease to pour forth virtue; and their spontaneous love and goodness would at at once remedy sin and harmonize human relations. Part of the larger history of pent-up utopian yearnings, these were promises of a life without sacrifices and postponements, and they would surge up anew in New England during the 1630s.[41]

Now a theology that judged the historic struggle for moral purity as misbegotten from the start well might be said to have "flowed from the [Puritan] movement's heart as its characteristic and defining heresy." It was no accident that all of the early and strident literary opponents of free grace—Peter Gunter, William Hinde, Henry Burton, Joseph Bentham, Thomas Taylor, and Edward Norris—were known Puritans. Further, the antinomian first wave did not disconnect cleanly from the godly subculture. Often enough men and women pledged to free grace kept important ties to the Puritan community, and their theologies (including the core value, self-abnegation and dependence on the Deity) expanded upon Reformed and Puritan teaching and spirituality. In this sense it belonged to a single continuum that extended far leftward of the pietist mainstream. But, again, it arose from a hard disillusionment that went beyond this or that component to the paradigm of piety itself. The devil was surely in the details, in, say, fast days or the assembly of signs and evidences. But the evil was also general, engrained in the full scheme. So the overall aim was, not to make limited adjustments, but to remake the faith as defined in the tradition of Greenham. In the reading preferred here, antino-

41. *HC,* 155.

mians were *contra*pietist spirits who judged bankrupt and aspired to quash the entire program of discipline through piety and its train of problematic psychological effects. Radical Puritans they might have been, but the terminology can mislead. It was a curious Puritanism indeed that had ceased to view the Bible as a legal book, not only lacked but decried passion for exactitude and purity, and devalued behavior and called the saints to slacken their pace.[42]

Probably no theorist of free grace knew legal faith's deeper history. None realized how far back its roots extended, how it built logically and psychologically upon elements long favored in English Protestantism, or how much collateral strength it drew both from ancient and continuing traditions of Catholic spirituality and from Reformed sources and trends abroad. Nevertheless, antinomians did have a strong and, despite their differences, a remarkably uniform sense of the enemy's endowments. Eaton and his colleagues defined the religion of purification as the principal threat (after the Roman Antichrist) to human happiness in their day. It could be neither ignored nor circumvented but must be met head-on with a radical critique and alternative. Indeed, without the pietist turn or some equally strenuous equivalent, it is difficult to understand why the freeness of grace was proclaimed with such feeling from about 1615 or why it was received with that infectious "greedinesse" that made a movement and, in both Englands, bred spiritual combat of a different sort.[43]

---

42. Michael McGiffert, "The Perkinsian Moment of Federal Theology," *Calvin Theological Journal*, XXIX (1994), 131. Como's critique of my earlier description of first-wave antinomians as "post- and contra-puritan" persuades me that the language is too unqualified, and I revise the emphasis here (Bozeman, "John Eaton," *Jour. Eccl. Hist.*, XLVII [1996], 641, 654; "PH," 163, 395–396). For the Puritan credentials of the figures cited, excepting Gunter and Bentham, see *DNB. HP,* Gunter's tract against Eaton, expresses standard pietist ideals (see, e.g., 44, 50, 53–58). Joseph Bentham's *Societie of the Saints . . .* (London, 1630?) is a prime statement of covenantal, Sabbatarian, and pietist ideals that identifies explicitly with "Puritans" (29).

43. *HP,* 10.

CHAPTER II

JOHN COTTON
ANTINOMIAN
ADUMBRATIONS

Since by and large the religiosity of early congregational New England was shaped by the pietist way, it is easy to understand why the largest insurgency of free grace before the midcentury period of turmoil in England happened there. In that eruption, however, an eminent pietist divine was to play a cardinal role. John Cotton in midcareer made two seemingly contradictory moves. First, he joined the emergent congregational wing of the fraternity. But, even as he affirmed the strong disciplinary commitments of the congregational way, he began to develop contrary tendencies. Unwilling to break with the tradition of Richard Greenham and William Perkins, he yet came to favor a set of initially modest changes in the practice of piety that became more pronounced either late in his English career or later in New England. Attacked as an antinomian fellow traveler but unprepared to follow Anne Hutchinson and her radical associates as they veered to extremes, he brought to the controversy an intriguingly eclectic and ambivalent state of mind.

Cotton's contributions to New England discussion should be understood in light of his previous experience, embracing a virtual quarter-century from his conversion in 1609 to his emigration in 1633, as theologian, pastor, and spiritual director in the English Puritan context. Nearly half of his voluminous literary output dates from his tenure (1612–1632) as vicar at Saint Botolph's church in Boston, Lincolnshire. For our purposes, one feature of his English career is of paramount importance: at least until his last years in old Boston, he remained true both to the ethos and doctrine of the pietist renaissance, and indeed through exceptionally articulate emphases upon purity and likeness to God he advanced the regimental aim further than most of his peers.

Five works dating from Cotton's tenure in old Boston are of particular importance here: *A Brief Exposition of the Whole Book of Canticles, Gods Mercie Mixed with His Justice, Christ the Fountaine of Life, A Practical Commentary upon the First Epistle Generall of John*, and *The Way of Life*. To begin with, they document Cotton's interest in a reformation of Boston manners, including the suppression of popular games and feast days, and the resulting division of local community; but, more to the point, they illustrate virtually the entire range of strong Reformed and pietist concerns that we have surveyed. Justification took its place in a series of benefits, and everywhere the familiar theological ellipse governed the discussion—as in christological formulas focused dually on pardon and reformatory power, or in an interpretation of the saints' cloak of righteousness as a symbol both of imputed and inherent purity, or in a striking doctrine of "double Justification" that, to "justification . . . from sin in the sight of God," joined justification "from Hypocrisie in the sight both of God and Man . . . by good Works."[1]

Never failing to acclaim the Lord's lavish care and pardon for sinners, Cotton in this period drew a milder portrait of deity than, say, Thomas Hooker, but he remained a little-troubled proponent of divine sovereignty, law, the Israelite paradigm and pact, and Deuteronomic punishment. God could appear as kindly father of his people and, especially in *Canticles*, the amorous wooer of souls, but rulership was his primary role and the Bible his book of regulations and threats. Since Christ's purpose too was "not onely [to] save us, but [to] rule us," redemption, as usual in Reformed perspective, became a special administration of the Deity's overarching government. Within the covenant the part of the elect was to believe and trust, but it was as well, and with more frequent emphasis, to "run . . . the way of [biblical] commandements." The reborn, to be sure, were freed from "slavish," anxious obedience to law, but never were they freed from the law itself, for Christian freedom also meant release from evil desires in order to perform the commands. In this sense the saints were "free to every duty," to show indeed with their lives that *"the law hath dominion over a man as long as he lives."* Nor did this entail a merely general deference to the laws. Like many other members of the brotherhood, the Lincolnshire pastor-theologian pushed the claim of law to a typically precisianist extreme: so tightly does Scripture regulate human behavior that "a man is not to dare to allow himselfe in so much as a thought, unlesse it be in a way of obedience to the will and Word of God."[2]

---

1. Justification: *EGJ*, 5, 9, 31 ("justification," "double Justification"). Dual christology: *WL*, 232–233, 256–257. Cloak of righteousness: Cotton, *GM*, 40–42.

Dates of composition of the five cited works are estimated in Everett Emerson, *John Cotton*, rev. ed. (Boston, 1990), 138–139. For sample echoes of local moral reform and the resulting division of community, see *EGJ*, 69, 118, 232, and *MCA*, I, 260.

2. *EGJ*, 278 ("commandments"), 392 ("slavish"); *CF*, 12 ("will and Word"), 74 ("rule us");

Purity and Likeness

Sufficient in their own right to tax human energy and patience, these teachings drew both extra force and complication from the pietist awakening. No less than Greenham and Perkins (whom Cotton named together with Paul Baynes as chief influences upon his thought) or Richard Sibbes (who had converted Cotton), Cotton in his Lincolnshire pastorate was absorbed in the inward saga of the soul, and in the main he made pietist priorities his own. In light of his later modification of the brotherhood's doctrine of preparation, it is especially noteworthy that his English works affirmed that doctrine in its strong form: the unregenerate soul is a toxic space to be cleansed before conversion. On the premise that "when we abandon all our lusts, then Christ shall suddenly come into his holy Temple [that is, the cleansed soul]," he sought to help unregenerate parishioners ready themselves both for justification and the accompanying "new birth" that in good Reformed fashion he equated essentially with personal transformation—and then to train and drill them in routines of holy walking. So in old Boston too, the *"daylie warre"* against sin (including a periodic return to rue "old sins"), vigilant analysis of the self-deceiving heart, meditation, and other historically Catholic exercises became the stuff of advanced Protestant teaching, together with Sabbatarian and other Protestant additions, and all were steeped in profound contrition.[3]

Like Perkins, John Dod, or Robert Bolton, Cotton advised the saints regularly to question and review their status before God. Like them, too, he specialized in cases of conscience. "What is the reason that many Chris-

---

WL, 231, 238 (citing Rom. 7:13). Federal and Deuteronomic doctrine: *EGJ*, 386–387; and *CF*, 31–39. Cf. the claim that Cotton in England "preached not a reciprocal covenant based on human obligation but an unconditional testament" (Janice Knight, *Orthodoxies in Massachusetts: Rereading American Puritanism* [Cambridge, Mass., 1994], 86). In *WL*, 283–286, 351–353, 359–361, 392–397, Cotton emphasized the act of faith as an appropriation of ethical power and purity, of biblical law and Deuteronomic paradigm. In *WL*, 359, he summarized biblical content as "[Deuteronomic] threatnings, Commandements, and promises." For variations of this formula, see *WL*, 274, 392.

3. *EGJ*, 4 ("old sins"), 384 ("lusts"); *CF*, 96 ("birth"); *WL*, 205 ("warre"). Preparation: see also *EGJ*, 384–388; *WL*, 129–130, 326. Conversion as transformation: *EGJ*, 207, 246; *CF*, 92–99. Indebtedness to Greenham and Perkins: Tom Webster, *Godly Clergy in Early Stuart England: The Caroline Puritan Movement, c. 1620–1643* (Cambridge, 1997), 298. Exercises: Cotton accepted the conventions of Puritan depth psychology (*EGJ*, 112; *WL*, 203–204, 211). To intensify mourning for sin, he cultivated one spiritual exercise in particular: visualization of one's sins as "darting against [and wounding] Christ." *WL*, 36–41, 56.

tians . . . fall into doubt concerning their estate?" "How comes it to pass . . . , that so many Christians are so troubled?" Through a decade or more before his emigration, such recurrent questioning defined, as it had for Perkins and Richard Rogers, the supreme case of conscience, and it did much to focus his preaching and biblical exegesis. It was expressly the central concern of his *Practical Commentary upon the First Epistle Generall of John,* and *Christ the Fountaine of Life* laid out at length the "grounds of triall" of a safe estate. In light, again, of his later challenge to Puritan wisdom on the subject of assurance, we note that Cotton the Lincolnshire counselor not only took most of his cues from affectionate divinity but devised an unusual strategy to strengthen the links between discipline and certitude.[4]

For, to an unusual degree among affectionate divines, Cotton in old Boston was a theologian of likeness and purity. As in the traditional call for an imitatio Christi, the desire to resemble God's immaculacy (and its underlying premise that likes attract and opposites repel) was a prime value of historic Catholic faith that had proved selectively congenial to Puritan designs since the 1570s. Indeed, preparationist belief in the "impossib[ility] that two Contraries [that is, sin and the divine presence] should be in the same [human] subject at the same time" may be its bluntest Protestant expression in the seventeenth century. In Cotton's thought, the assumption that "if we would have Christ, our lusts must be parted with" led to an emphasis on moral cleansing as an essential element of preparation for conversion, but it also informed other fundamental doctrines. Thus purification and resemblance became keynotes of a notable variation upon Puritan faith that, far from tending toward a semi-antinomian position that putatively was to attract Anne Hutchinson, moved a measurable degree or two in the opposite direction.[5]

When he lauded "the name of *Puritans*" as "the name of purity in . . . Christians," the vicar of Boston invoked an already heavily credentialed ideal. The purity there esteemed was primitive and moral as well as imputed, and thus the rhetoric suited well a pietist orator and counselor's purpose to lift his audience to a stricter standard of life. But, in pursuit of that purpose, he gave special play to themes of likeness to God. Purity in this sense involved the whole Trinity of divine persons. It could mean the saints' participation in the Father's ethical attributes, although most often it referred to their sharing of

---

4. *EGJ,* 45, 199; *CF,* 5. For Cotton's management of cases, see *CJC,* 19–21.

5. *AR, 1–8,* 373; *EGJ,* 384. Cotton emphasized that "the Spirit will not lodge in an uncleane heart." *WL,* 326, and see *EGJ,* 28, 307, 319.

traits with Christ the Redeemer; and, as usual in Reformed divinity, the mediation was provided by the Holy Spirit.[6]

In the brotherhood's teaching the Spirit performed a medley of functions. He illuminated and confirmed biblical truths, worked remorse of conscience, and imparted assurance, to mention only a few. Yet the moral bias of Reformed and Puritan theology determined the dominant role, for in this context he appeared most prominently as a moral force, as the sanctifier or agent of regeneration. This was exactly Cotton's emphasis: God "gives us . . . his Spirit to be our Sanctifier" to work "inherent righteousnesse in us"; the Spirit poured out at the first Pentecost wrought *"griefe for sin,* and *care for the reformation of it."* Often enough, and in yet another marked continuity with traditional Catholic thought, that transforming work was described with an idiom of resemblance and imitation. Cast in these terms, the Christian redemption became a progressive achievement of likeness to God. The Spirit "communicat[es] to us" qualities of the Father's nature, so that "we become gracious as he is gracious, holy, wise, and patient as he is," and the like.[7]

Puritan Trinitarian teaching, however, tended to a focus upon the Second Person, and Cotton retained this focus too. For in his theology Christlikeness is the norm of the Spirit's remodeling work. Working usually through the ordinances of preaching and the sacraments, he "conforms us to the image of Christ," as when he "makes [us] meek and lowly, as [Christ] was."[8] In all the vast body of literature produced by Reformed theologians of the period, there may be no more marked instance of this theme than a sermon in Cotton's *Christ the Fountaine of Life* devoted to the "secret fellowship between Christ and the Spirit." The Spirit, Cotton told his East Anglian parishioners,

> make[s] us one with the Lord Jesus, it unites us into one fellowship of nature, a likenesse in affection and disposition, and a likenesse in all the graces of God, . . . [The Spirit] makes. . . . a conformity between Christ and

6. *EGJ,* 232.

7. *EGJ,* 194; *GM,* 40 ("righteousnesse"); *WL,* 4 ("communicat[es]"), 127 ("griefe"); and see *EGJ,* 24–25, 304, and esp. 247: "To be *born again,* is when the Word and Spirit hath framed a man to the image of God"). Spirit as sanctifier: Tho[mas] Wilson, *A Christian Dictionarie* . . . (London, 1612), 460, matter-of-factly defining "the worke of the Spirit; to wit, the new quality of holinesse, created by the Spirit in the . . . elect." Sanctification was the predominant role of the Spirit in Puritan theology, not the illuminist function emphasized in Geoffrey F. Nuttall, *The Holy Spirit in Puritan Faith and Experience* (Chicago, 1992), and see below, Chapter 14, n. 26.

8. *EGJ,* 364.

us; one and the same Image stamped upon us both, . . . a like in grace, a like in affection, and in continuance of affection, a like in every thing. . . . The same spirit . . . doth worke a threefold . . . likenesse betweene Christ and us. First, A likenesse in Nature. . . . There is a likenesse and a participation of the divine nature, . . . and that *grace for grace:* Look what grace . . . you see in Christ, the resemblance of it is stamped upon every child of God, by the spirit of Christ. . . . [Hence the saints are like Christ in] innocency, and gravity, and purity. . . . [Secondly] there is also . . . a conformity to Christ in his Offices, . . . As he was *both King, Priest and Prophet to God his Father,* so are we. . . . Kings, to rule over all our lusts. . . . And *Priests* also we are, . . . able to offer up sacrifices of prayer and thanksgiving . . . And so are we also *Prophets,* . . . [able to] understand many secrets of Gods counsell. . . . Thirdly, there is a conformity in their *Estates,* [that is, the "estates"] of *humiliation,* and *exaltation.* . . . [In all the above we remark the saints'] proportion . . . to Christ in holinesse and righteousnesse.[9]

Unidentified and out of context, this passage well might be taken as a *Catholic* exhortation to likeness. Expunged by Luther, who "ruled out almost every trace of Christ's exemplarism," the motif of likeness was eminently useful to a Protestant fixed on moral transformation. Regularly, as he stressed the Redeemer's sacrificial death, the placation of the Father, and the undeserved imputing of pardon, Cotton worked the solifidian side of the ellipse. But his ardor for likeness pushed strongly in the other direction. How better to acclaim regeneration and to affirm its coordinate status within the Christian redemption than to represent it as a "fellowship of nature" with deity? So Cotton's Christ resumed his time-honored place as exemplar. As Protestant belief required, all of his benefits were gifts seized by faith alone; yet faith became exactly what Luther could not condone: a mode of participation, conformity, proportion, and likeness.[10]

And though the sense of filiation to a divine person must be grandly satisfying in itself, Cotton in England valued it most as a spur to moral

9. *CF,* 58–72. See also *CA,* 137, and *EGJ,* 390–391. Like many a medieval theologian, Cotton aimed "to advance the mimetic transformation of the soul according to the image of Christ" (Karl F. Morrison, *The Mimetic Tradition of Reform in the West* [Princeton, N.J., 1982], 132). Christlikeness was a special interest of Richard Sibbes's, who had converted Cotton and remained a friend and supporter; and Cotton might have followed his lead on this point. *WRS,* IV, 132–135, V, 435, VI, 376.

10. Morrison, *Mimetic Tradition,* 231. The threefold offices of Christ are a familiar distinctive of Calvin's theology, but Calvin explicitly described those offices as "inimitable" and did not in this context stress "the assimilation of like to like" (236).

reformation, as a way of making persons "tractable to the yoke of Christ, and [to] any course of obedience he shall shew us." For, wholly unlike imputation, resemblance comes about by a transfer of actual virtues, as the Spirit stamps the self with Christlike qualities, which included a penchant for devotional exercise. These, it should be added, were not quietist graces inviting Christians to relax and yield, but dynamic forces spurring them to "walk as Christ hath walked . . . in [active] imitation of Christ"; and among them purity engaged Cotton the most. Repeatedly he urged his hearers to "strive to [Christ's] exactnesse of purity, *to purifie our selves as he is pure.*" Bound and empowered by the heavenly contract to "purge" and "cleanse" away impurities, the saint who stood forth in his sermons was therefore the rare man or woman who lived this virtue, who *"purifieth himself,"* who "labors to purge himself [and] . . . to purifie himself," and "to keep himself pure . . . as Christ is pure," and the like.[11]

As he pondered the selfsame purity of Christ and his saints in light of his preparationist convictions, Cotton thus came to a still deeper insight: purity does not live by resemblance and imitation alone but also by repulsion. The notion here affirmed, that unlikeness repels, became another Cottonian emphasis. In effect it made the premise of preparationist teaching—that "the Sun-shine of Gods favour will not shine upon a dunghill soule"—into a general axiom of the moral life. "Suppose [Christ] be come [into the soul]," Cotton asked his parishioners and students to consider, "there is . . . much . . . required . . . to keep him there, we must look there be no unholy thing remaining there. . . . *Christ loves to lye cleane.*"[12]

For a partisan of disciplinary religion, this was a highly exploitable realization: *after* conversion as before, sins create a toxic effect repellent to deity and adverse to salvation. Simple, lucid, yet incisive if rightly applied, the principle that opposites repel opened rhetorical opportunities that Cotton was quick to see and seize. Warnings that "the Lamb of God will not lye in a den of Lyons" or that "Christ will not dwell in a house of drunkennesse, and prophanenesse" helped define his distinctive voice within the brotherhood, but, he hoped, they also resonated with his hearers, inciting desires to repel and expel the impure. To lend the lesson even greater force, on several occasions he expanded the

---

11. *EGJ,* 20, 74 ("walk," and see *WL,* 258–259), 224–225 *("purifieth himself")*, 232 ("strive"). Linking purity conditionally to redemption, he added that if the saint "do but endeavour . . . to purge himself as Christ is pure, he shall . . . come to a blessed . . . estate in the heavens." *EGJ,* 225.

12. *WL,* 426; *CF,* 44.

metaphor of repulsion into a kind of Aristotelian mechanics: the divine "life" infused by the Spirit in the soul

> hath an expulsive power to expell . . . out of the body that which is . . . hurtfull to it, . . . Nature cannot endure to be clogged with superfluity, out it must one way or other[.] Nature will ease it selfe, . . . so if grace be but living in the soule, there is an expulsive power . . . that will purge away that which is contrary to it.

Unlikeness, then, joined and bolstered likeness as a theme of Cottonian divinity, adding yet another charge to its disciplinary pole. Yet, in the train of thought we have traced from purity and resemblance, Cotton also found means to comfort the soul who, whatever his or her mimetic state, remained subject to doubt.[13]

Behavior's Evidential Power

Consistently in his old Boston sermons and commentaries, Cotton followed pietist pathways all the way to their critical juncture with assurance. His approach to doubt and surety hewed to all the familiar protocols, meshing "the peace of that soul whose sins are pardoned" with "the peace of that soul whose sins are mortified," and then tending to emphasize the latter. When assurance was in question, few members of the brotherhood made franker use of the conditional "if . . . then" of Reformed contractual thought. To put the issue another way, again in this setting we find the preparationist assumption—"If wee would have God to pardon sinne, it is for us to leave sinne"—applied as fully after conversion as before. Accordingly, and while Luther's shade tossed in the grave, Cotton gave this advice:

> If a man would have comfort, he must consider whether he live in any sin voluntarily . . . ; if there be no sin, but he is willing to avoyd it; no duty, but he desires to perform it, and amend all, it is a sign he walks in light; [so] if you see what is amiss and labour to mend it, then . . . assure your selves the bloud of Christ [therefore] will cleanse you from all your sins.

Or again:

> *If you be willing and obedient, you shall eat the good things of the land.* . . . [So] though my sins were as scarlet, they shall be white as wooll; How shall I

---

13. *CF,* 44 (the image of repulsion recurs in *EGJ,* 388), 141 ("expulsive power"); *WL,* 273 (error for 303; "house").

know that? because God hath given me an heart willing to obey. . . . If I can make the Command my counsell, I may claime the promise.[14]

Never did Cotton forget to hail the power of faith alone as the ground of assurance, but his frequent and unblushing linkage of certitude to duty, striving, amendment, and law shows that he was no readier than George Gifford or Greenham to estimate the Christian's standing before God in abstraction from moral activity. His principal works of the Lincolnshire years brimmed with confidence in behavior's evidential power. Repeatedly they dwelt upon "divers marks and signes," by which Christians "so knowing their estate, . . . might have . . . joy." And there as in pietist literature at large, self-forgetful trust in the Savior's death was a single element in a broader program of consolation whose predominating focus was moral reformation. Standing before Boston audiences that included future emigrants who would choose different sides in the American Antinomian Controversy, Cotton argued this point unequivocally: sanctification, properly understood, necessarily and reliably evidences justification. Almost certainly in the presence of future dissidents like William Coddington, Thomas Leverett, and possibly Anne Hutchinson, he urged the use of behavioral signs. Are we troubled and insecure? he asked. Let us seek then "an evident signe of tryall of our own estates," and much of the time the sign was sought and found in the pietist holy walk. To examine, for example, whether "thy faith . . . [has] brought thee into subjection to God's will," or whether you join in "Closet [private devotional] duties": these were sound "tryall[s], whereby we may take an estimate of our faith" and, perhaps, find peace.[15]

Amid the many behavioral signs of trial Cotton proposed (at least forty appear in *The First Epistle Generall of John*), all in principle anathema to his antinomian contemporaries, obedience to law and self-purification loomed large. Thus in one roster of "certaine signes, by . . . which you may know, whether you have the Lord Jesus Christ or not," Cotton declared: "If God give us a conscionable care to keep his Commandements, we know that we know him. And [there are] other signes, as . . . if God give us hearts to *purge and cleanse our selves from . . . sins*." Turning up with some regularity in discussions of assurance in most of the Lincolnshire works, legal observance and purity

14. *EGJ*, 35 ("If a man"), 307 ("peace of that soul"); *GM*, 69 ("leave sinne"); *WL*, 324 (*"If you be willing,"* and see *EGJ*, 278: "If a Christian shall grow up in obedience to Christ, then Christ . . . will comfort us with the consolations of his Holy Spirit").

15. *EGJ*, 345 ("subjection," "estimate"), 348 ("marks"); *WL*, 24 ("signe of tryall"), 95 ("Closet duties").

were featured most fully in *The First Epistle Generall of John*, a work of Cotton's last decade in England. "Keeping his commandements" and "Purifying our selves from sin" appeared there as items two and three in a review of five marks of "an estate of eternal life," and a multitude of other references left readers (and the original auditors) in no doubt of their role in Cotton's strategy of consolation. When, in a context of pervasive anxiety, a prominent spiritual guide could announce unchallenged that only the conscience cleansed by obedience and purity of life might enjoy assurance, the late Middle Ages were not far away.[16]

What, he asked repeatedly, is "the Evidence whereby we come to know that we know Christ"? "How do I know that I know him?" The answer seemed self-evident: "Why[,] if I keep his Commandements." So great was Cotton's trust in the legal sign of trial that he elevated it to a formal "Doct[rine]" of Boston theology: *"Sincere obedience, or keeping the Commandements of Christ, is a scientifical argument, and sign of . . . fellowship with Christ."* Keeping the laws also was a mode of cleansing, of course, and it was only logical that one who saw in Christian faith a moral detoxification aimed at likeness to God would find an equally scientific role for purity. "The more peace, the more care of purity": this was a cardinal premise too of Cotton's healing art. As with observance of law, self-purification was a consolatory as well as a disciplinary move, generating certified evidence of divine acceptance.[17]

Moral achievement and status before God, poles asunder in antinomian (and Luther's) treatment of doubting consciences, were wedded firmly in Cotton's ritual of signs. Solifidian themes were prominent too, defining moral achievements as menstruous rags and debarring Catholic claims for merit and synergy, and often enough the purity won solely by forgiveness came to the fore. Yet Cotton showed not the slightest inclination toward John Eaton's univocal concept of purity as the shining raiment of pardon or as the divine blindness to sin. Hewing tightly to the Reformed ellipse, he made the *"white robes. . . . pure and cleane"* of apostolic teaching a compendious symbol of pardon imputed *and* of the inherent virtues that the Spirit implants; and often, as in many texts cited in this chapter, the focus fell on purity won by effort and exercises.[18]

The truth is that, as in Puritan teaching generally, for Cotton in his pre-

16. *CF,* 189 (roster, and see *WL,* 216: "Let but the heart be kept clean, that in his heart he doth not close with any wickednesse; then shall [he be] acceptable in the sight of God"); *EGJ,* 413 (five marks).

17. *EGJ,* 31 ("How do I know," "Commandements"), 60 ("Evidence," *"scientifical argument,"* and see 68, 70), 365 ("care of purity").

18. *GM,* 40. In *EGJ,* 359, purification of conscience is construed as a double work of pardon and purgation of "uncleannesse" by implanted virtues.

migration years the Protestant concern for justification and faith alone served to magnify as well as to restrict the importance of behavior. Like Greenham or Bolton, he knew that obedience derives alone from election, repentance, trust, the blood of the Lamb, and the work of the Spirit; but like them he also esteemed the obedient life drawn from those wells as a miraculous complement of justification bearing power to silence doubt. Like them, accordingly, he saw in cases of wavering certainty (which for Luther as for Eaton mandated a counterintuitive turn away from law and duty) another disciplinary opportunity. Certainly, victims of doubt should trust in the Lord's death, but they also must heed biblical commands and keep the holy walk and watch. What was it to declare that "purity of heart" understood as aversion to sin keeps "a conscience voyd of offence before God and man," or that *"such as keep Gods commandements, they keep a good conscience, and Gods favour together,"* if not to impart moral instruction in another form? And so did counsel to the anxious become, albeit never wholly, another agency of moral reformation.[19]

A Magnet for Anne Hutchinson?

The works cited in this chapter cannot be dated precisely, so we do not know whether Cotton's latest views in the parent country are on record. If, as he seems to have claimed in mid-1636, he had developed the doctrines that stirred conflict in Massachusetts before the effective end of his ministry at old Boston in mid-1632, then without exception the extant writings appear to predate that development, for they register the views of a pietist clergyman who stood square and unchallenged (save on questions of ceremonial conformity and ecclesiastical polity) in the tradition of Greenham. With the limited exceptions to be noted below, they offer a study in miniature of affectionate divinity, of its silent Catholic borrowings and affinities and its construal of religion as a system of discipline as well as of mercy and pardon. So far as the literary record indicates, if Cotton tended in any direction in his English years, he was angling *away from* free grace positions. Not the semi-antinomian who is said to have attracted Anne Hutchinson, he was an uncommonly bold theologian of moral faith.[20]

That, however, presents us with a puzzle. How could Cotton the disciple of

19. *WL*, 411; *EGJ*, 271.

20. In June 1636, Cotton claimed in a letter to Thomas Shepard that he had taught the same way of "holding out of christ . . . many yeares both in old Boston, and in New" (*AC*, 33). Yet the precise meaning of this text is unclear, since his recorded old England and New England views differ substantially.

law and purity become a magnet for Anne Hutchinson, probably drawing her to visit his sermons on some occasions during his final years there and then to follow him across the Atlantic? Before we can attempt an answer, there is another factor to consider. Cotton's lengthiest English works, the *The Epistle Generall of John* and *The Way of Life*, reveal that he was familiar with an array of antinomian ideas and had condemned them unreservedly.

Cotton might have had a radicalized antinomian teaching partly in mind when he rebuked those "who say, after they have once received the spirit of regeneration, ... they need not the Scriptures," but in at least seven other cases the reference is plain. In a passage prepared about 1630 that suggests familiarity with antinomian controversies since the rise of Eaton and Roger Brierley in the mid-1610s, he ranked advocates of "free grace" alongside Catholics, Arminians, Separatists, and those content with a church-type, unregenerate Christianity as the most harmful "false Prophets" of the time. Naming no names and using only the flexible "Familist" tag already widely applied to radical views, he portrayed a coherent heresy centered upon belief that grace and its effects are unqualifiedly free. From that center emanated three particularly noxious errors: that "godly and regenerate men are in nowise subject to the Law," that they are exempt from all legal and Deuteronomic *"threatnings* of condemnation,"" and that right obedience flows "freely, and not [in response] to commandements." Possibly taking cues from Stephen Denison's critique of the Grindletonians in *The White Wolfe* (1627), he also traced a direct line from these to abandonment of "prayer, preaching, and any [other prescribed] Christian duty." Beyond this point he acknowledged variations, identifying in particular the belief (promoted well before 1630 by John Traske, Antinomus Anonymus, the Oxford Antinomian, and probably others) that law plays no legitimate role in conversion as the peculiarity of a minority of Familist prophets. There is no clear sign of acquaintance with the distinctive ideas of Brierley, Robert Towne, or Tobias Crisp, but hostility to the Eatonist dogma that God sees no sin in the regenerate may underlie Cotton's strong insistence that "God hath a speciall eye to [the Christian's] whole course." Therefore (quoting Isa. 40:27), *"Why sayest thou, my way is hid from the Lord?"*[21]

Well before his emigration, then, and possibly before his first contact with

---

21. *EGJ*, 19 ("who say"), 191 ("Familist," "Law," and see *WL*, 236–238), 278 ("freely"), 285 ("free grace," "false prophets," "prayers, preaching"; cf. Stephen Denison, *The White Wolfe* . . . [London, 1627], 39); *WL*, 245 ("speciall eye," and quoting Isa. 40:27), 398 ("threatnings"). The seven cases are in *EGJ*, 234–235, 278, 285, and *WL*, 134, 236–238, 398–401, 405. For law and conversion, see *WL*, 134, 405. For another attempt to identify subvarieties of antinomian belief, see *WL*, 236–237.

Hutchinson, Cotton had given thought to a variety of antinomian beliefs, real or reported. In doing so, we should note, he made no reference to religious assurance, despite his own deep concern with that issue. "Free grace" with its corollaries struck him as, first, a solvent of self-control. It imperiled the whole venture, already fraught with difficulty, to set the saints in their ordered course and constrain them to paths of likeness and purity. Another possibility might have occurred to him. Did the Familists have a point? Was the rising interest in freedom a sign that the clamor for command and control had begun to obscure other messages of the Word? If, alone with his thoughts, he entertained such a question, no certain trace of it appears in many hundreds of pages of expression. There, he weighed the prophets of freedom in the balances of law and duty and judged them enemies of the continuing Reformation.

If contemporary criticism of legal religion drew no sympathy from Cotton and might indeed have hardened his commitments to the pietist way, then his initial appeal to Anne Hutchinson becomes more puzzling. Since his published sermons were not the work of a semi-antinomian, the basis of that appeal may be more complex than often supposed. If we may assume that Hutchinson's views by about 1630 were unsettled in some degree and that she had commenced or at least was predisposed to shift away from her father's rigorously pietistic Puritanism toward the positions she professed in Massachusetts, then how might Cotton's teaching have facilitated that shift?[22]

Three basics of his doctrine offer likely points of connection: a portrayal of the saints' direct dependence upon Christ both for ethical purification and assurance, an emphasis upon the Holy Spirit as the agent of assurance, and an unusually strong formulation of the Protestant principle of private judgment. These were stock items of Protestant belief, and Cotton's treatment of them does not appear to have been controversial. Yet there is reason to suppose that this trio of elements, amplified and creatively misunderstood, contributed to Hutchinson's, and perhaps others', move toward free grace.

Reformed Protestants knew no more basic truth than this: that the gifts of redemption flow to believers through an intimate bond to the Redeemer.

---

22. Anne's father was Francis Marbury (d. ca. 1611), a Puritan cleric, critic of non-preaching ministry, and author of a commendatory preface to Richard Rogers's pietist classic *Seven Treatises*, with its stark division of the godly from the ungodly (*ST,* sig. A5). Marbury urged the saint "to examine himselfe every night in his bed" and "speedilie repent" even of "the least" indulgence. Untitled, undated notes of three sermons by Marbury, Egerton MS 28776, fols. 62–64, British Library. His *Notes of the Doctrine of Repentance* (London, 1602) repeated familiar motifs of godly and painful spirituality blended with depth-psychogical motifs.

Forged by the Spirit, the tie to him establishes an exhilarating relationship, but it is also the conduit through which pass all the goods of redemption. As Cotton put it, there is "no benefit, but its conveyed through him; Christ first, and then the benefit."[23]

Benefits, in this usage, embraced (a) private graces like justification or the virtue of sobriety, and (b) public and private ordinances or means like preaching or meditation. For reasons not entirely clear, Cotton came to believe that in his parishioners', and perhaps his own, experience, a troubling imbalance had emerged in the relation between Christ and the benefits. True, so rich were the goods rained on the godly that one scarcely could praise or enjoy them too much. Yet precisely there, in a perhaps understandable tendency to fix on the gifts as much as or more than on the giver, lay a serious error; and to help his audiences avoid it Cotton offered strong enjoinders: "Live not upon the flock of your own graces," and beware of too-fond attachment to the ordinances. All your new being is derivative, contingent on the Source. Savor, for instance, your passion for "zealous reformation," your ability to "pray powerfully" or to draw benefit from sermons and sacraments, "but while you enjoy them, trust not in them." Do not "looke for life in the Word, or Sacraments, [but] . . . looke for it all in Christ." And, as you strive to walk and stay your self-denying course, perceive your works as fruits, not of your own exertions, but of transcendental power acting within.[24]

Together with tributes to free grace, such directions were common coin of pietist counsel, but Cotton took them to unusual lengths. He could so press the need to "relye upon Christ, to lean on him, to rowl towards him" as, momentarily, to shrink the human element almost to null. Declaring that *a living Christian lives not himselfe, but Christ in him*," or that "*the life of a Christian is not his owne life, but the life of Christ Jesus,*" he made the bond to deity so close that the normal sense of human presence and agency (a sense well manifest elsewhere in his work) began to blur, or at least could be so understood. The tendency was carried further in portraits of the Christian in action, who seeks "that Christ and his life in him might worke all his workes in him and for him" and who, "as a Mill moved by the breath of the wind," has "no further motion . . . but as Christ moves him." Nor was this an unintended

23. *CF*, 51.

24. *EGJ*, 380, and see 388–390; *CF*, 21 ("looke"), 22 ("pray," "trust not"), 27 ("reformation"). The terms "grace," "ordinance," and "means," as defined here, are ubiquitous in Puritan discourse.

by-product of devotion to Christ, but a deliberate self-abasement in light of a conviction that grace is and does all.[25]

Why had the need arisen so insistently to deny innate value to the benefits, which included biblically certified ordinances and the saints' new sense of power to do good and perform religious exercises? Possibly Cotton's pietist discipleship was attended by an ambivalent sense of its excesses and dangers. His comment that "zeale and humility, and gifts of grace. . . . [are] but a dead businesse" apart from Christ, accompanied by advice to "put away all confidence in saving graces," may define observed tendencies in the godly to over-occupy themselves with their own states and efforts and to make the exercises a mechanical routine, as may his denial of legitimate motion to the self. Likewise, and despite his own as yet unaltered commitment to the practical syllogism, his frequent warning, "Unlesse you finde Christ more than his gifts, you shall finde little peace," may reflect awareness that his own and others' quest for behavioral tokens of certitude had proved more difficult than pietist theory foresaw. His many and graphic descriptions of the "horrors and terrors" of a stricken conscience lend force to this suggestion.[26]

Here, at all events, in a theme of union with Christ that came with special accent from Cotton's pulpit and pen, we see at once an affinity to free grace theory and (as will become clearer below) a first plausible basis in his doctrine for Hutchinson's reported views in the mid-1630s. A second emerges in his vision of the Holy Spirit's assuring role. In Massachusetts, Hutchinson was to define Christian assurance as an immediate work of the Spirit above the realm of signs and evidences, and that doctrine expanded upon ideas Cotton had begun to express before 1632. In company with other affectionate divines, Cotton in old Boston assigned the stilling of doubt and fear to the Third Person, a "witness" who imparts "such peace of Conscience . . . as passeth understanding." Possibly taking cues from Paul Baynes, John Preston, and Richard Sibbes, he also portrayed this inward comfort with the metaphor of a

25. *EGJ,* 267 ("Mill," and see *WL,* 277), 375 ("relye"); *WL,* 268 (*"living Christian," "life of a Christian,"* and see 275–276); *CF,* 50 ("life in him"), 137 ("motion"). For divine power "working all [the saints'] works for them," see also *EGJ,* 278, and *WL,* 275–277. For "rolling" upon Christ, see also *WL,* 311.

26. *CF,* 29–30, 56 ("Unlesse," and see the entire sermon at 46–57, and *EGJ,* 380); *EGJ,* 266 ("horrours," and see 324–325: "The estate of a soul troubled with fear, . . . is [in] *a state of torment.* . . . [a] melting of spirit, . . . as if the heart were like waxe, and Gods wrath like burning fire. . . . This fear sometimes brings men into trembling of body. . . . Sometimes it causeth terrible dreams," and the like).

seal: "The Spirit . . . doth seale it . . . that my sin is pardoned." On another occasion he described the sealing work as "an immediate work of the Spirit, [which] . . . makes us that we never doubt more." In this last passage, students of the New England controversy will recognize not only an early version of the seal motif but also two hotly argued topics of 1636–1638: the immediacy and finality of the sealing work.[27]

The familiar Protestant principle of private judgment, which requires a faith grounded in personal inquiry and intellectual conviction (in contrast to the Catholic "implicit faith," which believes what the church believes), offers a third likely point of influence. In line with his ventures in Puritan dissent, Cotton cast this principle.in exceptionally bold form. When at a conference at Emmanuel College about 1611 he advanced the controversial thesis that observance of the Sabbath should begin Saturday evening rather than Sunday morning, he defended the presumption of his "private motion discrepante from the common consente of the body of Christ" by appealing to private judgment: "We are commanded to try all things [by Scripture] and as we beleive so to speake."[28]

Then, sometime in his first decade as vicar of Saint Botolph's, Cotton grew anxious for the future of religious reform as militantly anti-Puritan forces came to the fore in the English church. Many "bad Ministers" were abroad; and, when "they see good Christians make a conscience of keeping the Sabbath, of performing family duties, and abstaining from sin, [they] will doe as much as they can to pervert their faith." To turn away the challenge, Cotton devised a more forceful statement of private judgment and extended it without qualification to the laity. Now he authorized all men and women of godly bent

27. *EGJ*, 198–199 (and see 200), and see *CF*, 231; *WL*, 325–326. The seal motif is from Eph. 1:13. "Seal of the spirit," denoting a sense of assurance conveyed by the Spirit, is a routine entry in Wilson's *Christian Dictionarie*, 429. Baynes, Preston, and Sibbes emphasized the seal, but Cotton's New England elaborations upon the doctrine went far beyond theirs. See below, Chapter 13, n. 21.

28. Winton U. Solberg, ed., "John Cotton's Treatise on the Duration of the Lord's Day," in *Sibley's Heir*, Colonial Society of Massachusetts, *Publications*, LIX (1982), 509. I cite the date assigned by Solberg, which is disputed in Webster, *Godly Clergy*, 20 n. 16. In 1624, as Cotton moved toward greater ceremonial nonconformity, he wrestled again with the issue of "private Conceyte" at odds with *"the* rest of *the* members of *the* body of Christ" (Cotton to the bishop of Lincoln, Jan. 31, 1624/5, in *CJC*, 101). In a context of Reformed divinity, Cotton's boldly semi-Arminian critique of prelapsarian predestination was also an exercise of private judgment; see William Twisse, *A Treatise of Mr. Cottons, Clearing Certaine Doubts concerning Predestination* . . . (London, 1646). The treatise probably was written in 1625 (*CJC*, 110).

to "search the Scriptures daily, . . . [to] be the better able to try the spirits of their Ministers." Leave trustful attitudes aside, he advised, and consider that "a Preacher speaks not the expresse words of the Scripture, but comments and explications of the Scriptures." "Do not," therefore, "take every thing as true from your Minister, . . . [but] try his spirit, try every word." Hear his words in respect, but afterward "goe home and consider whether the things that have been taught were true or no: whether agreeable to the holy Scriptures or no." Saints, indeed, may absent themselves from unsaintly preaching and "ride to such places, where the Word of God is . . . taught."[29]

To expand the prerogatives of individual lay judgment and conscience, to encourage discrimination between the Word and the worldly mix of "comments" in the preaching of duly ordained men, and to validate active opposition to doctrine deemed unscriptural: here already was the "radical potential for lay activism and self-help" that Peter Lake finds in godly preaching of the era. But more, so strong and incautious was Cotton's Dissenting mood by his last Lincolnshire years that he conceded to private judgment—to *godly* private judgment—a further and ultimate sanction: the Deity's fail-safe guidance. At one level this simply reiterated the familiar. That the Spirit illumines intellects applied prayerfully to the Word was an axiom of Protestant teaching, and at Cambridge in 1611 Cotton had rebutted the charge of irresponsible "private motion" partly by appeal to "the voyce of the Holy Ghost" heard in the sacred text. Now he reinvoked his Cambridge doctrine, but in a more radical frame of mind and in the face of express warnings of its dangerous potential. Twice in *The Epistle Generall of John* he recorded the "objection," perhaps from voices in his own congregation, that glib or untutored resort to the Spirit might *"pin the Scripture upon our own private spirit."* "May not a mans spirit bee a delusion?" Yet he made short shrift of such fears, together with their underlying concerns about spiritist tendencies. Confident that no "private sp[i]rit" showed saints the error of bad ministers beyond "the same spirit that breaths in the Scripture," he ventured an even bolder formulation: "The Spirit breaths where it lists. . . . Then let us . . . not . . . rest in what Ministers . . . teach, but what the Spirit teacheth." "One dayes Instruction of the Spirit, will lead you into more knowledge than a hundred Sermons." This evidence may shed light on a report dating from the early 1640s that long before his migration to America Cotton was suspected of Montanism, an early Christian spiritist heresy that

29. *EGJ,* 282 ("search the Scriptures"), 284 ("your Minister"), 291 ("bad ministers," "good Christians," "ride"; and see the approval of "gadding to Sermons" in *WL,* 156); *CF,* 200 ("Preacher," "goe home").

affirmed "the personal inhabitation of the Spirit" imparting "immediate revelations" to the godly.[30]

In early Caroline England, in a context of conservative, non-Separating Puritanism hostile to religiously radical and certainly spiritist tendencies, these utterances from *The Epistle Generall of John* were extraordinary. That they were no momentary excess but were Cotton's considered conviction is clear from a fuller passage in *Christ the Fountaine*—so rhapsodic, and so pertinent to the question of influence upon Hutchinson:

> [God] poures out his spirit in a rich and plentifull measure; he poures out his spirit *upon all flesh;* whence it comes to passe, that the servants of God understand many secrets of Gods counsell, . . . that many a godly man by the same spirit discernes many secret hidden mysteries, and meanings of the Holy Ghost in Scripture more then ever he could by any reading or instruction; and many times discernes some speciall work of the spirit of God, which inables them to fore-see some speciall blessings, . . . and so leads them on to many good things which they did little thinke of, and so makes them of *Propheticall spirits,* and bowes them to teach others also, to lead on others of their neighbours in the wayes of God.[31]

In such texts, hindsight permits us to see a virtual charter for Hutchinson's future career in religious deviance, controversy, and withdrawal. Direct evidence is lacking, but she probably went on several occasions to old Boston to be where God's word was taught. There, she would have found glimpses of a partially relaxed spirituality in which the inner enjoyment of Christ stood above the active graces featured in the pietist regimen, and learned to cherish the Spirit's assuring seal. Seated in the visitor's place at Saint Botolph's, she would find sanction to try every word of authority, to claim a right independent of established authority to consider and perhaps to revise and resist such

30. Peter Lake, *The Boxmaker's Revenge: "Orthodoxy," "Heterodoxy," and the Politics of the Parish in Early Stuart London* (Stanford, Calif., 2001), 58 (referring to a similar emphasis in the preaching of Stephen Denison); Solberg, ed., "Cotton's Treatise," in *Sibley's Heir,* 509; *EGJ,* 197, 363. For Cotton's teaching on private, spirit-aided judgment and its possible influence on Hutchinson, see Michael G. Ditmore, "A Prophetess in Her Own Country: An Exegesis of Anne Hutchinson's 'Immediate Revelation,'" *WMQ,* 3d Ser., LVII (2000), 361–368. Cotton was accused of Montanism in Robert Ba[illie], *A Dissuasive from the Errours of the Time . . .* (London, 1645), 57, 61. He answered the charge in *WCC,* 218–222, and Baillie responded in *The Disswasive from the Errors of the Time, Vindicated . . .* (London, 1654), 23.

31. *CF,* 62, and see Chapter 13, n. 69.

words; and it was a right reinforced by Cotton's brief for prophetical spirits, with its promise of transport beyond the mediate realm of reading and instruction to direct, unearthly discernment. Place Christ above his benefits, rely on the Spirit's seal more than on created graces, and learn the deepest truths, not from sermons, lectures, or sacred writ themselves, but from the Spirit's voice within: each privileging a direct relation to the Deity, these three Cottonian counsels correlate with her reported later views.[32]

While Cotton probably intended no special application to women, on one occasion and possibly with Hutchinson in the audience he cited a biblical forecast of the Spirit poured out upon all flesh, including *"Maids."* So might a daughter learn more from the Spirit than from sermons, discern hidden mysteries, be endowed with special foresight, and take up the role of teacher to her neighbors. These were the very presumptions that, somehow speaking true to her condition, encouraged her in a course of religious deviance that led into the stirring events of 1636–1638.[33]

Always, however, we should recall the ruling Puritan cast of Cotton's Lincolnshire sermons and commentaries. Perhaps he had select misgivings about the pietist way, its heavy moral and devotional demands and the sense of insecurity it seemed to spawn; but he developed no open critique, upheld the usual exercises, including preparation in its strongest form, and flatly denounced free grace and antilegal beliefs. His reminders that graces and ordinances apart from Christ are but dead forms were balanced by a devotion both to the standard graces and to apostolic ordinances, including the congregational polity, that was itself almost ecstatic; and he nurtured a lively eucharistic piety that viewed the communion service as well as the other liturgical and devotional "meanes" as necessary vehicles of Christ and mediators of assurance to the troubled. If he affirmed a state of recessive agency in which the self acts only by the Deity's impulse, yet, in sharp contrast to free grace theory, his larger religious program mandated diligent effort and hard self-control in

32. The date of Hutchinson's first contact with Cotton is not known, but in late 1637 she recalled that "when our teacher came to New-England it was a great trouble unto me" and contributed to her decision to emigrate. The reference to "our teacher" almost certainly means Cotton and suggests a close bond to him. Emery Battis suggests that she was already attached to his preaching by about 1630, but direct evidence is wanting. Cotton acknowledged that, in England, Hutchinson and her family were "well beloved" by him. *AC,* 337, and see 272; Emery Battis, *Saints and Sectaries: Anne Hutchinson and the Antinomian Controversy in the Massachusetts Bay Colony* (Chapel Hill, N.C., 1962), 49; *WCC,* 238.

33. *WL,* 100; and see *CF,* 62, and Acts 2:17, which quotes Joel 2:28. These were to become the great proof texts in America of women's right to preach.

the brotherhood's customary fashion. And there is no evidence that Cotton at any time, even in New England, espoused unconventional views of the role of women.[34]

Certainly it is possible that, in the months of crisis preceding Cotton's decision to leave his pulpit and later to emigrate, he took further steps in an antinomian direction and that his revised views influenced Hutchinson, perhaps even sparking her decision to follow him abroad. But even *The Epistle Generall of John,* which internal evidence indicates could not have been composed before about 1628, and *Christ the Fountaine,* which most insistently subordinates benefits to Christ, offer no evidence of such a change. The most that can be said, in light of the literary record and with the aid of hindsight, is that a limited set of tendencies appears in Cotton's latest English works that worked toward but stopped short of his later semi-antinomian position.

At this time a great gulf still separated Cotton from Eaton, Brierley, and other true teachers of free grace. He could not have foreseen his own eventual departure from key preparationist premises, his break with the practical syllogism, or his collusion with a free grace party at serious odds with Puritan affectionate divinity. As to Hutchinson's initial relation to him, there are at least two broad possibilities. First, she might have grasped his doctrine fairly in context before her departure to the New World and later, in continued contact with her mentor, moved on to a more advanced position. There is evidence that before her emigration she shared her favorite lecturer's preoccupation with religious certitude and had begun to claim prophetic foresight. Second, Cotton's trio of special elements, possibly joined to ideas from the radical Protestant fringe, might have begun already to fuse in her mind into a custom-made antinomianism untrue in some respects to his actual intent. In either case, his frequent blasts against free grace would have sufficed to acquaint her with contemporary antinomian ideas and possibly led her to explore them further. What we know allows us to discount neither of the above possibilities or to determine how much her thought as of 1637 or 1638 owed to distinctively New England developments.[35]

---

34. *WL,* 330. For eucharistic piety, see 365–366, 374; *CF,* 134–138. In *CF,* 137, being "conformable to . . . Christ by the Ordinances" itself becomes "an evident sign" of a safe relation to Christ. Congregational themes are most prominent in Cotton, *A Brief Exposition . . . upon the Whole Book of Canticles* (ca. 1641) (London, 1655).

35. For certitude and foresight, see *AC,* 322, 338–339.

CHAPTER 12

John Cotton
in America
Hypocrisy and
Crisis

n light of the Puritan pietist awakening and the antinomian backlash
it evoked, it is time to approach the famed controversy that wracked
Massachusetts in 1636–1638. The key ingredients were in place by
mid-1636, and John Cotton, teacher at Boston's First Church, his
disciple Anne Hutchinson, and possibly Henry Vane (invited lodger
in Cotton's house and member of First Church, elected governor in May)
were catalysts. Completing a doctrinal shift begun in Lincolnshire, Cotton by
that date had begun to air opinions akin to those of John Eaton and other
exponents of free grace in the parent country. The women's meetings that
Anne Hutchinson had organized the previous year for admiring discussion of
his sermons had expanded to include men—including numerous successful
merchants and craftsmen, other notables and officeholders, and probably
Governor Vane—and to feature Hutchinson's progressively sharp criticism of
those in the colony, including the great majority of the clergy, who emphasized law and the holy walk. Another major actor, the Reverend John Wheelwright, recently had arrived in Boston and associated himself with Hutchinson's views, as had a great majority of the members of the First Church by late
in the year. By the year's end the polarization of opinion had grown so severe
and "antinomian" behavior so disruptive as to threaten authority both in
church and state.

In an atmosphere of crisis (to be heightened by the Pequot War beginning
in April 1637) and with the government in tumult, a clerical and political
counterattack now began. Attempts by the First Church to call Wheelwright
as a second teacher (October 1636) and to censure its pastor, John Wilson, for
his public critique of the new opinions (December 1636) were defeated with
difficulty. When Wheelwright used the occasion of a Fast Day (January 19,
1637) for a belligerent attack upon opponents of grace, the General Court—

with John Winthrop now governor and an agricultural majority—disfran-
chised and banished him. Hutchinson and other unrepentant antinomians,
including signers of a "remonstrance" protesting the treatment of Wheelwright, received the same treatment.

Beginning late in 1636, members of the clergy had held intensive debates
with Cotton, Hutchinson, and Wheelwright; and in August 1637 a synod of
clergy and laymen confronted the issues in dispute. The members inventoried,
refuted, and condemned a medley of presumed antinomian opinions and
urged an end to private religious meetings such as those Hutchinson had held.
By the year's end the controversy was largely over, although it remained for the
First Church to try, convict, and excommunicate Hutchinson in March 1638,
before her departure for Rhode Island. Harried by criticism and alarmed by
the increasingly heterodox ideas voiced by Hutchinson and others in the
aftermath of the banishments and the synod's condemnations, Cotton dissoci-
ated himself from the radicals, moderated his views to a degree, and sustained
his position at First Church.

Why did this traumatic collision occur? There is no simple answer. By the
mid-1630s radical theories of free grace were abroad in England, and, although the early Great Migration was subject to screening, it was informal
and porous enough to admit a few settlers of antinomian tendency or suscep-
tibility; and the private exercises for discussion and devotion that flourished in
the first years of settlement provided an opportunity to share and develop their
special interests. The emergence of heterodox ideas in Hutchinson's discussion group recapitulated the "transition from repetition [of sermons] to original exposition" already evident in some English Dissenting conventicles. Possibly the consolatory element of free grace theology had special appeal to
colonists uprooted from their parent society and struggling to build a new one
in a difficult, sometimes dangerous, environment, and the spiritual egalitari-
anism might have offered psychological compensation to adherents of modest
socioeconomic status. Perhaps it positively transvalued the feminine experience of humility, and perhaps Anne Hutchinson's assumption of the right to
give dogmatic religious instruction and her insistent spiritism suggested to
women—and perhaps to military men with their zeal for personal honor—
larger possibilities of worth and power. Both the wish for freedom from
controls and the curtailment of time-consuming religious duties might have
addressed the special concerns of merchants, artisans, and farmers developing
their businesses within an expanding commercial economy. Perhaps, too, the
devaluation of behavior and achievement spoke to those grown weary under

"ordinances to the full, sermons too long, and lectures too many, and private meetings too frequent" in the first energetic decade.[1]

New England and the Practice of Piety

In New and in old England, however, the main precipitant of antinomian rebellion was the same: the grueling, costly regime of precise and pietist faith. At some remove from the religion of the earliest Elizabethan Puritans of the 1560s, American Puritanism was grounded in the distinct cycles of religious evolution discussed earlier. As seen in their devotional disciplines, the great majority both of the early New England clergy and the religiously active laity in the seventeenth century were committed heirs of the pietist renaissance. Most of the clergy had been members of godly clerical networks in the parent country and maintained ties thereafter by correspondence and, in a few cases, by visitation. Thomas Hooker, for example, was closely associated before his emigration with Richard Sibbes, John Rogers of Dedham, William Gouge, John Dod, Arthur Hildersam, John Preston, and others. Hugh Peter, who had studied at Thomas Gataker's household seminary, joined Sibbes, John Preston, and others during the 1620s in a regular London gathering for religious exercises. After a conversion inspired by Richard Rogers's *Seven Treatises,* John Wilson joined a godly devotional group at Cambridge University that

1. *RP,* 267; *WTS,* II, 375. Business and agricultural concerns: William Coddington, William Hutchinson, Edmund Quincy, and Atherton Hough, for example, were engaged in farming and developing large tracts of land they recently had acquired at Mount Wollaston (Emery Battis, *Saints and Sectaries: Anne Hutchinson and the Antinomian Controversy in the Massachusetts Bay Colony* [Chapel Hill, N.C., 1962], 123). Male membership in Massachusetts churches, moreover, was at its seventeenth-century peak during the lifetime of the founders (Gerald F. Moran and Maris A. Vinovskis, *Religion, Family, and the Life Course: Explorations in the Social History of Early America* [Ann Arbor, Mich., 1992], 89). Thomas Shepard directly linked absorption in economic affairs and the antinomian attitude to sanctification as an evidence of justification (*WTS,* II, 443, and for clarification see 66–67, 152, 164, 376–378). Darren Staloff, *The Making of an American Thinking Class: Intellectuals and Intelligentsia in Puritan Massachusetts* (New York, 1998), and Louise A. Breen, *Transgressing the Bounds: Subversive Enterprises among the Puritan Elite in Massachussetts, 1630–1692* (Oxford, 2001), make cases for "urban bourgeois" concerns behind the antinomian insurgency. Breen also affiliates antinomianism with the military ideals represented in the Artillery Company of Boston. On psychological compensation, see Philip F. Gura, *A Glimpse of Sion's Glory: Puritan Radicalism in New England, 1620–1660* (Middletown, Conn., 1984), 52, 79.

included Preston, Sibbes, Gouge, Thomas Taylor, and Cotton. He also made several visits to Wethersfield to hear Rogers preach and accepted a living at Sudbury to be near him. Prominent lay leaders like John Winthrop and Thomas Dudley also had close associations with pietist clergy. Winthrop, who read Perkins, Richard Rogers, and Robert Bolton and cited them in his Suffolk spiritual diary, was a friend of John Rogers of Dedham and maintained correspondence with him until the latter's death in 1636. Winthrop "first found the ministry of the word to come to [his] heart with power" under the ministry of Ezekiel Culverwell, a pietist minister who once had joined in a pact with Richard Rogers "to watch over each other and help each other lead godly lives" and who in 1587 made a pilgrimage in Rogers's company to Greenham's household seminary at Dry Drayton.[2]

Among English holdings in the early New England clerical libraries of which we have record, in the few records of lay literary taste, and in John Harvard's founding bequest of books to the college in Cambridge, one set of authors predominated: Richard Greenham, William Perkins, John Downame, Daniel Dyke, Nicholas Byfield, Robert Bolton, and other members of the pietist intelligentsia. In one telling example, Daniel Dyke's depth-psychological classic, *The Mystery of Selfe-Deceiuing*, appeared in at least three clerical libraries of the founding era and in the Harvard library—and Richard Mather featured its concept of "translation" in a lecture at Dorchester in the 1640s. Indeed, the abundant literary record of New England's early years reveals a religious faith by and large continuous with the specialized pietism in the tradition of Greenham sampled earlier—the very pattern that had roused antinomian opposition at least a decade and a half before the Great Migration began.[3]

2. *WP*, I, 155 ("first found," and see 156, 199, 211, and Rogers's letters to Winthrop in *WP*, II, 316–317, III, 8–9); Francis J. Bremer, *Congregational Communion: Clerical Friendship in the Anglo-American Puritan Community, 1610–1692* (Boston, 1994), 57 (Culverwell and Rogers's pact), 53 ("pilgrimage"). For Hooker, see Bremer, *Congregational Communion*, 29, 47, 51, 58, 61, 99. For Peter, see Bremer, *Congregational Communion*, 37, 50. For Wilson, see also Tom Webster, *Godly Clergy in Early Stuart England: The Caroline Puritan Movement, c. 1620–1643* (Cambridge, 1997), 20–22, 37, 296. The social network of Puritan clergy is detailed in Bremer, *Congregational Communion*, and see Janice Knight, *Orthodoxies in Massachusetts: Rereading American Puritanism* (Cambridge, Mass., 1994), 34–71, although her analysis of "Amesian" and "Sibbesian" networks is problematic. On devotional disciplines, see *PPPDD*.

3. Charles F. Robinson and Robin Robinson, "Three Early Massachusetts Libraries," Colonial Society of Massachusetts, *Publications*, XXVIII, *Transactions* (1930–1933), 107–

Thomas Shepard's *Parable of the Ten Virgins*, Peter Bulkeley's *Gospel-Covenant*, and Richard Mather's unpublished "Summe of Seventie Lectures upon the First Chapter of the Second Epistle of Peter," to take but three texts from the founding generation, belong to the pietist genre of sternly edifying literature. Despite topical differences, their largest religious objective was one. On the premise, "Sin is the great evil; hence the end of Christ's coming is to take it away," they strove to orchestrate the soul's complex struggle to achieve conversion, to coordinate pardon by faith only with the scheme of exercises and the war against sin, and by the same means to expel doubts of "standing in a happy estate." Although these and similar works bore marks of American experience, they continued to define that struggle in line with the norms of strenuous endeavor, sheer difficulty, and mournful mood espoused by the reigning masters of Puritan spiritual direction—and with all their fervor for introspection and their compulsive fix upon law and self-rule. Neither in the settlers' new-won freedom from resistance and persecution nor in the antinomian rebellion in the founding decade did New World clergy find occasion to lighten the pietist load or slacken its strain. On the contrary, they continued to extol difficulty and pain as validating marks of the regenerate life and demanded from their charges a virtually sectarian absorption in their own religious states and duties. Hooker, for instance, recapitulated the elaborate preparationist rituals worked out in his Chelmsford years, including for good measure a fresh statement of the art of meditation and the medieval ideal of the complete confession.[4]

156; Alfred C. Potter, "Catalogue of John Harvard's Library," Colonial Society of Massachusetts, *Publications*, XXI, *Transactions* (1919), 190–230; "Mr. Skeltons Note of Bookes," in Nathaniel B. Shurtleff, ed., *Records of the Governor and Company of the Massachusetts Bay in New England* (Boston, 1853–1854), I, 37g–37h; Richard Mather, "The Summe of Seventie Lectures upon the First Chapter of the Second Epistle of Peter," 117, Mather Family Papers, box 1, folder 8, American Antiquarian Society, Worcester, Mass. Candidates for membership in the church at Cambridge around 1640 cited books or sermons by Richard Rogers, John Rogers of Dedham, William Perkins, Arthur Dent, Thomas Goodwin, John Dod, Thomas Hooker, John Preston, and Daniel Dyke (George Selement and Bruce C. Woolley, eds., *Thomas Shepard's Confessions*, Colonial Society of Massachusetts, *Publications*, LVIII, *Collections* [1981], references indexed). For Byfield, see also Virginia DeJohn Anderson, *New England's Generation: The Great Migration and the Formation of Society and Culture in the Seventeenth Century* (Cambridge, 1991), 174. Writing to Winthrop in 1639, Ezekiel Rogers reminded him of the "peece of Godlinesse, called the Dayly Direction" without which "a Christian shalbe maimed at the best." *WP*, IV, 150.

4. *WTS*, II, 118, 134 ("great evil"), 190. For difficulty, see also Richard Mather, "Seventie

In a rare eyewitness account of an early American congregational church founding, we may glimpse a pietist Puritan community immersed in strenuous ritual work. As they gathered their church in 1637–1638, the townspeople of Dedham were engaged by the primitivist dimension in Puritan thinking, the recovery and emulation of biblical precept, and normative example. Yet they also matter-of-factly assumed that the ancient congregationalism there regained was of a piece with the pietist way. Professing dual commitment to "faith and holynes" and attentive to "the inward workings and dealings of the lord with . . . soules," they planned and executed a lengthy, laborious set of rites. Enacted step by step in weekly meetings and perhaps more frequently upon occasion, they extended through six months of doctrinal debate and another six of selection and mutual testing and retesting of prospective "pillars," or initial members. Rounds of biblical study and debate, cycles of "solemne fasting and prayer," and examination of "cases of conscience" were involved, and the core of the work among the pillars was a detailed and repeated "scrutiny or triall of ourselues." Only then, and after a final fast, was the covenant drawn and subscribed and the church brought into being. As those who poured time and energy into these activities were, not focused religious professionals, but busy pioneers, the entire experience must have strained the limits of possibility.[5]

In the spiritual diary of Thomas Shepard, pastor of the church at Cambridge from 1636, Governor John Winthrop's recollection of his "Christian Experience" written during the Antinomian Controversy, and other records of individual spirituality from the first decade of settlement, indications of rigorous performance are accompanied by the usual pietist signs of discouragement and doubt. Shepard offered a running account both of Sabbaths, fasts, meditations, and introspections and of intertwined obsessions with obedience, sins in the plural, and assurance. "Uncertainties concerning [one's] own Eternal estate" were evident too in the American careers of John Cotton and Richard Mather, and Winthrop told of "many falls" suffered in his spiritual combat. Roger Clap, a founding member of the church gathered at Dorchester in 1630, recalled an interval early in that decade of his "saddest Troubles for want of a

---

Lectures," 256; *AR*, *9–10*, 343. For meditation and confession, see *AR*, *9–10*, 208–283, 630–641.

5. Don Gleason Hill, ed., *The Record of Baptisms, Marriages and Deaths, and Admissions to the Church and Dismissals Therefrom . . . in the Town of Dedham, Massachusetts, 1638–1845 . . .* (Dedham, Mass., 1888), 4 (see also 12), 5, 8, 5 *(sic)*. For primitivist themes in Dedham, see Theodore Dwight Bozeman, *To Live Ancient Lives: The Primitivist Dimension in Puritanism* (Chapel Hill, N.C., 1988), 131–135.

clear Evidence of my good Estate," and the famous attempt to gather a new church at Dorchester in 1636 failed because "most . . . had builded their Comfort of salvation upon unsonde gro[u]ndes." In autumn 1637 a female member of Boston's First Church, possibly unsettled by the antinomian dispute then raging, fell, like Joanna Drake and many others before her, into such "trouble of mind about her sp[i]ritual estate" that she "grew into utter desperation, and could not endure to hear of any comfort."[6]

Of the fifty-one lay applicants for membership in the church at Newtown (Cambridge) whose professions of faith Shepard recorded about 1640, at least five expressed a fear of being hypocrites, eighteen described an interval of spiritual discouragement shortly after arrival, and two explicitly denied that they had found settled assurance. Shepard himself identified "deep and frequent [spiritual] desertions" as "the great . . . temptation of this place." In North Andover, Massachusetts, recovering from an illness of uncertain date, Anne Bradstreet too reported of the recurrent demoralization that dogged the pietist way:

> Beclouded was my Soul with fear
> of thy Displeasure sore,
> Nor could I read my Evidence
> Which oft I read before.[7]

6. *WP,* I, 154 (and the entire text at 154–169), 160 ("falls"); Increase Mather, *The Life and Death of . . . Richard Mather . . .* (Cambridge, Mass., 1670), 25 ("uncertainties"); Roger Clap, *Memoirs of Captain Roger Clap* (Boston, 1766), 11; *JJW,* 173 (Dorchester, and see Gura's interpretation of the incident in *A Glimpse of Sion's Glory,* 61), 229–230 ("desperation"). For Cotton's "falls," see below, Chapter 13, n. 19, and text. Shepard's diary, in *GP,* 81–238, records regular oscillations between assurance and despair, with confidence rising and falling in proportion to his achievements in spiritual combat. After intensive self-analysis "upon my Bed in the Night," Clap received "full Assurance that Christ was mine," predicated upon a sense of his ability to resist temptations. He also echoed the pietist doctrine that each sin counts against the sinner and must be separately recalled and repented. Clap, *Memoirs,* 11–12, 31–32.

7. *WTS,* II, 170–171 ("desertions"); John Harvard Ellis, ed., *The Works of Anne Bradstreet, in Prose and Verse* (New York, 1932), 12, and see Bradstreet's brief record of her "religious experiences," 3–10. Among the Newtown applicants, fears of hypocrisy are recorded in Selement and Woolley, eds., *Shepard's Confessions,* 51, 74, 80, 112–113, 154; spiritual discouragements at 41, 48, 51, 66–67, 87, 90, 103–104, 121, 123, 127, 131, 136–137, 140, 143, 145, 151, 179, 191; and denials of assurance at 64, 69. "Doubts about his spiritual state" fill three pages of John Brock's spiritual diary for 1639–1640 and are prominent in Obadiah Holmes's account of his "trial of things in several [New England] churches" in the same period. Clifford K. Shipton,

But if such utterances record familiar concerns of the English devotional awakening, they do more than mirror the parent movement. Forces were at work in the period 1630–1640 that, at least temporarily, must have enhanced the imported piety's effect. The difficulty, cost, and risk of the uprooting from England and the voyage over tended to restrict migration to committed believers, many already radicalized beyond the Puritan average by policies of the Caroline regime, and early efforts to winnow out the idle and vicious and limit participation to the orthodox and well-behaved were reasonably efficient. Both during the journey and in the earliest period of settlement, levels of commitment were lifted by a spirit of common adventure, by the experience of Puritan leadership and evangelism, all in relative freedom from interference by English authorities. So there arose in New England a "very special population," which would give the emergent religious establishment wider support than the contested, short-lived regimes that godly minorities had been able to establish in a few English towns since mid-Elizabethan times.[8]

No complete blueprint of that establishment existed at the start. The founders did not arrive with a fully rounded plan for managing their religious affairs. But, although the arrangements that shortly took form did reflect trial and error, debate and compromise in light of present circumstances, they also achieved historic objectives that had been realized only in part, if at all, within the Church of England. Consider the exercises of fasting and prayer, of Bible study and discussion, and the other informal gatherings that, although officially condemned as "conventicles," had grown from scattered beginnings under Elizabeth to become a Puritan mainstay by the early seventeenth century. In the now officially Puritan colony of Massachusetts, such private and prayerful exercises could be indulged without stigma or censure so long as they appeared orthodox; and, as in the Dedham church-gathering, they were fortified now by strong collective endorsements.[9]

---

ed., "The Autobiographical Memoranda of John Brock, 1636–1659," American Antiquarian Society, *Proceedings*, N.S., LIII (1943), 98; Edwin S. Gaustad, ed., *Baptist Piety: The Last Will and Testimony of Obadiah Holmes* (Grand Rapids, Mich., 1978), 76.

8. David Hackett Fischer, *Albion's Seed: Four British Folkways in America* (New York, 1989), 25. For effects of evangelism, see David Cressy, *Coming Over: Migration and Communication between England and New England in the Seventeenth Century* (Cambridge, 1987), 102, 158.

9. Stephen Foster, "New England and the Challenge of Heresy, 1630–1660: The Puritan Crisis in Transatlantic Perspective," *WMQ*, 3d Ser., XXXVIII (1981), 626–628. Hambrick-Stowe surveys spiritual exercises in early Congregational New England in *PPPDD*, 137–241.

Sabbaths and fast days likewise were freer to unfold in the New World, and they too enjoyed fuller communal support. Never embraced by the official church, Puritan Sabbatarianism had existed as much in theory as in practice in the parent country since the 1570s. Days of humiliation and fasting were more widely accepted in Elizabethan and early Stuart culture and were proclaimed routinely by the government at times of crop failure, military crisis, and other occasions of special worry or peril. Few authorities in state and church, however, favored either the strict Deuteronomic canons of Puritan fast day theory or its tendency to define "speaking evill of . . . the life and power of godlinesse," its persecution of committed ministers, and the like among the causes of divine punishment to be confessed and removed by the ritual. Nor did they approve private, unauthorized fasts. Yet in America, in virtually total freedom from episcopal control, Sabbaths and public Fast Days (the latter now proclaimed, and frequently, on occasions deemed suitable by solidly Puritan authorities) became official, inescapable observances.[10]

So there is reason to suppose that pietist ideals and rites, powered now by corporate purpose and backed both by central and local government, became yet more stringent in their claims upon the saints. But there remains the most exacting development of all. By 1636, the American Puritan authorities both in church and state had substantially realized the disciplinary reorganization of the church for which advanced English Protestants for nearly a century had hoped and worked. Pre-Marian proponents of discipline as a structural mark of the church, and even Thomas Cartwright and his fellow presbyterian theorists of the 1570s and 1580s, well might have quarreled with some features of the Massachusetts system, although William Ames, Robert Parker, Paul Baynes, and other early-seventeenth-century theorists of nonseparating congregational polity would have found less to fault. But all would have recognized the system as a fruit of their own promotion of strong institutional supplements to the inward fervor for obedience that the Reformed tradition so heavily prized. We can understand Thomas Shepard's regard for Cartwright as a "burning and shining light of our times" when we recognize that in most essentials the Bay colony adopted the presbyterian program of moral supervision and correction, including its appointment of lay elders as disciplinary specialists and its potent array of censures.[11]

10. Arth[ur] Hildersam, *The Doctrine of Fasting and Praier, and Humiliation for Sinne* . . . (London, 1633), 20.

11. *WTS*, II, 68. See also Cotton's comment on Cartwright in *WCC*, 207–208. For the earlier advocates of discipline, see above, Chapter 1, n. 15.

The elements of that familiar program need not be reviewed here, but in its effort to copy apostolic discipline we encounter again the strong Reformed concept of the Bible as a compend of rules and archetypes. We note also a clear institutional expression of two long-standing staples of Puritan teaching: the careful "watch" for sins and the personal rebuke of sinners. Further, in at least two significant ways, the emergent church order in the Bay intensified the already rigorous presbyterian standards. First, and in direct dependence upon the congregational theory of Ames, Baynes, and Parker, the New Englanders moved to strengthen the moral as well as spiritual caliber of their congregations with stiffer criteria for membership. From 1636, prospective members were required to make a public testimony of faith; it in turn was expected to exhibit the spiritual combat and "mourning for sin" that marked the pietist way. Second, formal disciplinary actions were made the business of the lay male membership as well as of the elders. Thus, as seldom before in English history and as nowhere else in colonial America, an exceptionally strong regimen of discipline had emerged, reinforced by institutional procedures involving the entire membership of religious congregations.[12]

When to this was added a relatively severe monitoring of the colonists' behavior by government officials, most if not all of whom were committed to the congregational enterprise, it is clear that an impressively rigorous and thorough set of controls was in place. It was no accident that, in their English careers, leading American clergy like Cotton, Hooker, Thomas Weld, and probably others had nursed local cliques of the godly with their characteristic hostility to alehouses and popular merriments, and one contingent of immigrants stemmed directly from the Puritan reformation at Dorchester, Dorsetshire, in the 1610s and 1620s. Absent the unregenerate majorities, the culture of good-fellowship, and other elements of resistance in traditional English parishes, and with ministry and magistracy "walk[ing] hand in hand, discountenancing and punishing sin," at least some of the early Bay towns had effected a more thorough and durable reformation of manners than had been possible in the parent country.[13]

12. In *A Defence of the Answer Made unto . . . Nine Questions* (London, 1648), 193, John Allin and Thomas Shepard described the New England testimonies as reports of "such a faith as is joined with evident repentance, and sorrow, and mourning for sin." This emphasis is confirmed in Shepard's summaries of testimonies delivered at Cambridge about 1640. Selement and Woolley, eds., *Shepard's Confessions*, 36, 61, 127–129.

13. Everett Emerson, ed., *Letters from New England: The Massachusetts Bay Colony, 1629–1638* (Amherst, Mass., 1976), 232, and see Cressy, *Coming Over*, 102. For Cotton,

As they revised Protestant culture along apostolic, pietist, and disciplinary lines, congregational Americans by the mid-1630s became a late party of the international second, or later, Reformation. Many expressed satisfaction and pride in the accomplishment, but not all were equally gratified. By 1636 if not earlier, a substantial minority, most of them church members in good standing, were discovering serious liabilities in their religious tradition. They were the ones who, feeling the lures of free grace, went "eager after them, and were streight infected."[14]

A Mind in Motion

In making free grace attractive, John Cotton had the pivotal role. Without him, without his special emendations of pietist divinity, the famed Antinomian Controversy of 1636–1638 is difficult to imagine. For all his credentials as a Puritan dissenter and spiritual director, he became the New World theologian around whom the greatest controversy swirled in 1636–1638. At the same time, in a fateful complication for Anne Hutchinson and other more radical spirits who claimed discipleship in his ideas, he was much more restrained than English leaders like John Traske or Peter Shaw or than his American colleague John Wheelwright. Constitutionally hesitant and averse to conflict, he did not indulge, say, in the "particularitie in cariage, [the] shew of zeale, [the] vehement deliverie, [and] vociferations" with which John Eaton sang the glories of the third time, or share his doctrinal boldness. Because Cotton's antinomian tendency was peculiarly ambivalent, limited in range and contained by larger loyalties both social and theological, Cotton offers a far more elusive and intriguing problem in interpretation.[15]

Ambivalent as he was, Cotton's challenge to Puritan business as usual was both potent and disturbing. Had his American teaching merely reiterated his recorded English views, it might have bred conflict. Shortly after his arrival a wave of spiritual enthusiasm arose in the Boston church, resulting in a flurry of conversions and applications for church membership there and probably affecting other Bay towns as well. Evidence of this event is scant; but, if amid that emotional excitement Cotton had reiterated his later Lincolnshire emphases upon divine agency, the assuring seal, and private judgment, he

---

Weld, and Hooker, see below, Chapter 11, n. 1, and text; *PP,* 73–74, 137, 158–160; *SPC,* 20, 41, 90, 179. For the migration from Dorchester, see David Underdown, *Fire From Heaven: Life in an English Town in the Seventeenth Century* (New Haven, Conn., 1992), 131–140.

14. *AC,* 202.

15. *HP,* 6, and see *LG,* 22.

might have found a crucial seedtime for the church's antinomian spree in the mid-1630s.[16]

In any case, Cotton's was a mind in motion, and his teaching unquestionably had taken a sharper turn by 1636 at the latest. Just as we cannot be sure that *Way of Life, Christ the Fountaine,* and other collections from old Boston record the full progress of his thought to the time of his emigration, so the literary record does not permit us to follow in any detail possible changes in outlook between his arrival in Massachusetts in September 1633 and his first recorded expression of controversial ideas in spring 1636. At all events, his writings during the New England struggle reveal that by further reflection upon the role of Christ and the Spirit in the pietist saga of the soul he had created a provocative revision of Puritan divinity. In broadest terms, the point at issue was the bifocal thrust of Puritan theology. A willing spokesman for the congregational program of church discipline, he hardly could disclaim the strong Reformed ellipse outright; yet by 1636 he valued less its moral pole, including the special interest in purification and likeness to God that had flavored his teaching at least into the later 1620s. His counsel to New Englanders striving to enter and walk comfortably in the Christian way now tended toward a single focus. With limited but clear harmony of purpose with English theorists of free grace, he pointed beyond human agency to the power and solace found in deity alone.[17]

Throughout this period, even as he cast his semi-antinomian net in waters troubled by the practice of piety, Cotton remained in many ways a typically energetic pietist. He led himself and his family through a rigorous schedule of daily devotions, with redoubled activities on the Sabbath. When personal or civic trials arose, he "would set days apart to seek the face of God in secret; . . .

16. For the Boston's church's "burst of fervor akin to latter-day revivals," see David D. Hall, *The Faithful Shepherd: A History of the New England Ministry in the Seventeenth Century* (Chapel Hill, N.C., 1972), 157; *AC,* 13–16. Hall's account of this event as prelude to the antinomian conflict is suggestive, but many of its details are speculative, as is my suggestion here. In his preface to the *Short Story,* Weld claimed that antinomian doctrine appealed especially to recent converts. *AC,* 205.

17. The extant record of Cotton's views in 1636–1638 includes individual exchanges with Thomas Shepard and Peter Bulkeley (in *AC,* 24–42); *SPS,* 39–68; [John] Cotton, *The New Covenant* . . . (London, 1654), included with separate title page in John Cotton, *The Covenant of Grace* . . . (London, 1655); *Sixteene Questions of Serious and Necessary Consequence* . . . (London, 1644); "Mr. Cottons Rejoynder," in *AC,* 78–151; and *A Conference Mr. Cotton Held at Boston with the Elders of New-England* (London, 1646). All of these items except the *SPS* and *New Covenant* are available in *AC.*

He was in fastings often." A generous level of pietist and disciplinary content persisted too in his theological message. He continued to see Christian conversion as a remolding of personality that suppressed the passions and spurred the faithful to good works. The theme of likeness to God remained important, for Cotton continued to feature the Spirit as the regenerating agent and to envision his work as a stamping, or *"ingraving the likeness,"* of Christ and his moral virtues upon the soul. The idiom of purification was still in evidence, as in the Spirit's "work of cleansing in the hearts and wayes" of believers. As always, Christian liberty meant freedom from the harsh demand and curse of the legal covenant of works, not from obedience to divine commandments, and a sound hammering with the law remained an essential prelude to conversion. Possibly in response to ideas abroad in Boston's First Church, in late 1636 or 1637 he censured those who, "under pretence of the Covenant of Grace, have thought it . . . bootless to bind Christians unto the Law of God." As firmly as ever, he insisted that Christians "lie under the authority of [the law], and dare not pluck their necks from under that yoke" and that God sees and is angered by sins. He required regular use of outward ordinances and exercises, including the practice of mourning for "evils . . . wrought in God's sight" together with its underlying premise of *"fatherly displeasure"* and Deuteronomic punishment for sin. Perhaps most notably, his writings on church order present in unsoftened form the familiar Presbyterian and Congregational vision of the church as a domain of Christ's "Kingly Government" regulated by his "Lawes and ordinances" and enforced by punishments on a scale of ascending severity.[18]

From daily devotions to Deuteronomic penalties, all of these elements were present as of 1636, yet now their place and value within the larger horizon of thought had become problematic. Startling when viewed alone, this develop-

---

18. *TCG,* 76; John Norton, *Abel Being Dead yet Speaketh; or, The Life and Death of . . . Mr John Cotton* (London, 1658), 28 (and see 26–27, and *MCA,* I, 277–279); *TCG,* 64 ("cleansing"), 76 ("Covenant of Grace," *"fatherly displeasure,"* "lie under," and see the fuller discussion of law at 69–79), 188 *("ingraving"); SPS,* 50 ("evils wrought," and see *TCG,* 24); John Cotton, *The True Constitution of a Particular Visible Church . . .* (London, 1642), 8 ("Government," "lawes"), and see 2–3, 8–12. The *True Constitution* probably dates from 1635 (Everett Emerson, *John Cotton,* rev. ed. [Boston, 1990], 139).

　　Spirit as sanctifier: see also *TCG,* 158–165. Likeness: see also *TCG,* 67, 206, and *AC,* 41–42, 81. Christian liberty: *TCG,* 137–138, 152. Legal hammering as a factor in conversion: *TCG,* 69, 114. God's sight of sin: *SPS,* 50, and *TCG,* 88. Divine anger at sin: *SPS,* 52, and *TCG,* 76, 88. Use of ordinances and exercises: *TCG,* 7–9, 108, 123, 148, 213. Deuteronomic punishment: see also *TCG,* 87–88, and *SPS,* 51–52.

ment in fact accorded with the long-range pattern of Cotton's intellectual life. He shared the dominant belief of the time that Christianity is a fixed and final body of truth, a conviction deeply inbred in Reformed Protestantism and accented by trends since the later sixteenth century toward a scholastic organization of doctrine. Yet to this belief he joined a second: that humanity's comprehension of that truth was not yet perfect and that to earnest seekers the Deity imparts corrective epiphanies of "further light." Accordingly, fresh insights and changes of mind punctuated his English career. Thus was his determination, while a student at Cambridge about 1611, that observance of the Sabbath should begin Saturday evening, and a decade or so later he formulated a daringly softened version of the Reformed doctrine of reprobation. For several years before his emigration, Cotton gradually was changing his mind about other issues as well, not only about the believer's relation to Christ and the Spirit but also about the Church of England and its resistance to apostolic ways in worship and polity. As early as 1615 he decided that he could no longer be a party to the sign of the cross in baptism and other required elements of the official liturgy, and organized like-minded parishioners into a covenanted society that avoided use of them. Concerning liturgical conformity, a hardening of doctrine and tone can be traced from a letter Cotton wrote to the bishop of Lincolnshire in 1624, to his sermon of farewell to the departing Winthrop fleet in 1630, to his letter of resignation from the Boston post in 1633. Well before he arrived in Boston Harbor, then, and to an unusual degree within nonseparating Puritan circles, Cotton had shown a persistent readiness to adjust his theological sights and take provocative stands.[19]

As we may see, for instance, in his repentant approval in mid-1636 of the conception of an exclusive church covenant that he had rejected in a letter to New England in late 1630, Cotton expected new light to shine as well in the New World as in the Old. Yet here we are concerned with a far more fateful change, with a severe but silent shift in his theological center that ran counter

19. Bozeman, *Ancient Lives*, 104 ("ceremonies"), 126 ("further light," and see 72–75, 124–127). Sabbath: Winton U. Solberg, ed., "John Cotton's Treatise on the Duration of the Lord's Day," in *Sibley's Heir*, Colonial Society of Massachusetts, *Publications*, LIX (1982), 505–522. Reprobation: William Twisse, *A Treatise of Mr. Cottons, Clearing Certaine Doubts concerning Predestination* (London, 1646) (the work probably dates from 1618–1625). Cotton's hardening: Cotton to the bishop of Lincoln, Jan. 31, 1624/5, in *CJC*, 98–103, May 7, 1633, 179–189; Cotton, *Gods Promise to His Plantations*, Old South Leaflets (Boston, n.d.), no. 53 (sep. pag.). The town of Boston accepted Cotton's resignation on July 22, 1633. MHS, *Collections*, 3d Ser., VIII (1843), 343.

both to the major trend of his English doctrine and to central Reformed tenets.[20]

Consider his portrait, drawn repeatedly during 1636–1638, of the misled soul who "confesseth . . . sin unto God, and forsaketh it, and therefore . . . looketh for mercy," or of those who "find themselves discouraged from sin, and so reform their lives, and give up themselves to obey the Word, and find comfort therein," or interpret "their Duties as so many tokens of the love of God unto their souls." What was the offense of such behaviors? That, in effect, was the question posed to Cotton by the majority of his clerical colleagues. They knew that obedience did not earn redemption and that to hold otherwise was Pelagian and papist, but Cotton appeared to target rites of the pilgrim struggling toward conversion or, after conversion, pursuing the spiritual walk and warfare and taking comfort in signs and evidences—the same praiseworthy figure he had acclaimed, albeit with occasional qualification, in his English works. In the small and well-connected world of the Puritan clerical brotherhood, men like Thomas Shepard and Peter Bulkeley must have known of Cotton's rise through the 1620s as a star in the pietist firmament. Perhaps they knew too that in the parent country he had condemned antinomian ideas unreservedly. Their dismay and chagrin as of 1636 were natural reactions to a valued colleague's shockingly altered attitude toward the historic pietist program.[21]

Although it is not clear whether Cotton's decisive turn to a new position occurred in old or New England, now he related it directly to American experience. The venture into the New World had begotten religious troubles that existing doctrine could not resolve and in fact seemed to compound. Cotton in old Boston had warned against works-righteousness, to be sure, and proclaimed free pardon, but these were joined to a larger and resisted disciplinary program that included a civic reformation of manners. Thus the greater emphasis in the English sermons fell upon law and duty, likeness and purity. Yet his *Treatise of the Covenant of Grace,* a collection of lectures delivered during the Antinomian Controversy, reflects a different reading of the audience and its primary religious need. His American parishioners, Cotton now believed, had learned too well their tradition's moral instructions. Relying too heavily upon them, they had slipped into confusion and anxiety.[22]

20. David D. Hall discusses Cotton's change of mind about the church covenant in "John Cotton's Letter to Samuel Skelton," *WMQ*, 3d Ser., XXII (1965), 480.

21. *TCG*, 39, 72, 86.

22. More than half of the material included in the *Treatise* had been first published in

The religious excitement of the earliest years, in short, was a shadowed blessing. Cotton never put the issue directly, but his analysis implied that circumstances in "this Countrey," the very site where Puritan faith was freest to unfold, encouraged defection to the covenant of works. Beyond the reach of Laudian bishops, in the unimpeded pursuit of their prayers, conferences, family devotions, fasts, self-examinations, and apostolic ordinances, some of the Puritan settlers had become too absorbed in their exercises and performances, shunting the Deity to the margin. "Being full of . . . *gifts*," they had come to focus upon *"themselves*, and not . . . *Christ*,*"* and so fell into spiritual depression. As he continued his pastoral counseling on a new continent, Cotton also heard his charges grumble that "they cannot pray fervently, nor hear the word with profit, nor receive the seals with comfort: they wonder what is become of their old . . . lively spirits in holy duties." Amid the broader freedoms and hopeful prospects of founding times, he also found complaints of failing assurance, of saints pressed by "sad doubts of their own estates." As of 1636, the colonial adventure had produced, not a finer spirituality, but disappointment and fear.[23]

Some evidence from the period supports Cotton's perception of flagging morale, such as the "spiritual depression of 1635–1636." Since the colonists were free as never before to fulfill their tradition of piety, this was an unexpected, even baffling occurrence. It may reflect natural disappointment as the enthusiasms of 1633 ebbed away and perhaps the settlers' growing prosperity and absorption in secular affairs as they began to move beyond cruder pioneer times. Yet, to understand Cotton's diagnosis, we must also view it in light of the history of strong Reformed and pious religion traced earlier. By the time of

---

1654 as *The New Covenant*. It was reedited with additions and published as *A Treatise of the Covenant of Grace* in 1659 and again in 1671. In this study I cite the 1671 edition *(TCG)*. All editions probably were compiled from auditors' notes, although Cotton reportedly had read and corrected the text before his death in 1652 (Emerson, *John Cotton*, 63). *TCG* addresses a "controversie . . . stirring in the Country" about "grace," describes the evidencing of justification from sanctification as "yield[ing] as much agitation as any other Doctrine that is taught among us," and defends against charges of *"Antinomianism"* (*TCG*, 38, 87, 130). Larzer Ziff and Emerson date the sermons on which it is based in 1636 (Ziff, *The Career of John Cotton: Puritanism and the American Experience* [Princeton, N.J., 1962], 265; Emerson, *John Cotton*, 63–64, 139). Although I detect no shifts of emphasis in the added matter (120–223) in *TCG*, I have checked all citations against the 1654 edition and marked noteworthy variations in the notes below. For the reformation of manners in Boston, see above, Chapter 11, n. 1.

23. *TCG*, 90, 200; *AC*, 130.

the Great Migration the project of disciplinary devotion had increased the saints' burden of duties and complicated the quest for certitude but promised a rich harvest of returns. Self-control and good works were a badge of sainthood and a way of escape from disorder and doom. Aggressive analysis of the soul's obscurities and deceits could perplex the search for signs of a good estate, but saintly patience and skill finally could discern those signs, setting them in reasonably clear relief against the grey horizon of hypocrisy.[24]

A Crisis of Hypocrisy

By 1636 at the latest, Cotton could sustain such trust no longer; he sensed that affectionate divinity was flawed. Despite its promise of better things, in practice it had proved a step backward within the continuing Reformation. This was the unwanted lesson that New World conditions taught. Consider, for instance, the strangely booming state of hypocrisy in the Bay. Yes, in theory the colonial churches had achieved a higher level of purity, but their members' freer pursuit of gifts and graces actually bred fakery. In his Thursday lectures of the mid-1630s, Cotton not only resumed the study of hypocrisy already familiar to pietist immigrants; he offered a more worried analysis of it than ever before. Within their sainted community, he argued, ungenuine members abounded. Among the elect and reborn many had lapsed into faulty ways, but, he seemed to suppose, the most numerous and dangerous offenders were the nonelect in camouflage. "Blessed souls they [take] themselves to be," and so complete is their deception and so great their strength in numbers that they demoralize the people of God.[25]

They could demoralize God's people because their vigor was matched by skill. All the godly knew that hypocrites flourish through artful deceit, and Cotton in Lincolnshire had found hypocrisy "so well dyed, . . . that you can hardly discern any difference." But in the early Bay colony, where sainthood was privileged and a much larger fraction of the population claimed the name, the difficulty was compounded. There, the most finely drawn counterfeits

24. *AC*, 15. For evidence of "grim, gray disappointment" in the lay testimonies recorded by Thomas Shepard probably between 1638 and 1645, see Patricia Caldwell, *The Puritan Conversion Narrative: The Beginnings of American Expression* (Cambridge, 1983), 31, and see 32, 120–122. See also above, n. 6, and text.

25. *TCG*, 46. In a discussion of "evangelical hypocrites," the "secret and subtle enemies, yet seeming friends" who are a distinctive plague of the "purest [gathered, congregational] churches," Shepard declared it "the chief work for Christ here, there being no profane ones among us, to overthrow the kingdom of hypocrisy." *WTS*, II, preface, 184, 189, 191–192.

came to the fore. Cotton dubbed them "Goats," but he meant bluffers of the subtlest, most self-deceiving kind who blended all but perfectly among the sheep. Many no doubt appeared among those who had not yet achieved church membership, but often enough Cotton's language indicted ranking visible saints of the congregational churches.[26]

How could so bald a case of mistaken identity have arisen? How could forged credentials have misled so many? Cotton's answer leaned heavily upon an insight that Greenham and Perkins had elaborated: the defter forms of hypocrisy are too finespun to be a human work. God himself augments their effects, making the mimicry masterful. During the mid-1630s, this was a leitmotiv of Cotton's preaching. To a Salem audience in June of 1636 he flung a provoking thought: some of you visible saints are pious frauds, and the deceit is refined supernaturally. You

> believe; and . . . receive sundry spiritual gifts, and that with joy.

> [You are in a fashion] married to Christ. . . . You . . . resolve to walk in all ordinances, and undertake to reform both church and commonwealth; [and Christ may] take you by the hand and become a husband to you. . . . And what will a husband do, he will rejoice with you, and you will find comfort in duties; your heart hath been refreshed that you may see you have Jesus Christ in your bosom. He will also reveal secrets unto you, He will cast in seeds of sundry good things among you, so that you shall prophecy in his name. . . . [Yet all these things] thou mayest have and yet run upon a covenant of works.

While Cotton at Salem did not offer a full solution, he yet supplied a disturbing analysis of the problem of New World hypocrisy. Gracious gifts do not animate the saints alone. They also rouse and buoy the doomed, producing a saintly realism as persuasive as it is hollow.[27]

Cotton's message to Salem—that the enemy, finely masked, now prospers within the camp of presumedly visible saints—was a staple of his teaching in the years of controversy. Before the local parishioners and visitors who thronged his lectures, he held up an unflattering mirror. To look into its deep reflections was to see the falsity beneath the surface, falsity that was no mere counterfeit but so adorned by gifts from above as to be virtually undetectable. To suppose that "there is no reality in hypocritical sanctification" is a serious

---

26. *EGJ*, 249; *TCG*, 46, and see 31. Cf. the analysis of "secret and subtle enemies, yet seeming friends," whose outward "operations are chiefly evangelical," in *WTS*, II, 191–192.
27. *SPS*, 54, 58. For Greenham and Perkins, see above, Chapter 8, n. 39, and text.

mistake, for "certainly it is a real work, the gifts be real, . . . and not imaginary," though nonsaving. As with Saul or Judas of biblical story, the Spirit may touch hypocrites today, "acting them mightily" to perform religious duties. They may "come willingly [and] . . . delight to come" to Fast Days and play out the whole ritual with conviction. They may possess "gifts of Tongues, and utterance, and wisdom, and discerning of Spirits." They may even join the anxious wait for the Bridegroom of the Second Coming and with true conviction *"stay themselves upon the God of Israel."* In disagreeable fact, what congregational America had labored to bring forth was hypocrisy of a higher order.[28]

And it got worse. Average Christians, through daily contact with replicas of sainthood real enough to "dazle the eyes," understandably found their self-image growing faint. Consider the "poor Christian," a recurrent figure in the Thursday lectures that surely mirrored Cotton's pastoral observations in new Boston. This is a portrait of a saint unnerved by hypocrisy's fine pretense. Comparing his or her deeds with what hypocrites forge, "a poor Christian [is] put to much exercise, to find a difference." When, for instance, "a poor Christian cometh, and seeth how much [a hypocrite] doth magnifie God both in doing and suffering, and yet falleth away; it maketh him conclude, Surely I also shall at length turn away from the Lord." Some Christians, again, are simply unable to stand the pace that the best fakers set. Consider adolescents, barely able to contain their sexual drives, who then must compare themselves with "such hypocrites as run along with more freedome of spirit then themselves." No matter, it would seem, what grace or work poor Christians might find in themselves, "they will find it in Hypocrites also" and perhaps learn that "hypocrites have gone beyond it."[29]

Here was a dilemma that also cut to the quick of Puritan identity, for, since the years of Cartwright, that identity had derived in part from a sense of sharp contrast with the impure. In English parishes, techniques of rigid self-management (and concomitant moods) had been the saints' shining insignia, separating them from the unregenerate and their permissive lifeways. But now, just as the dream of widespread citizen involvement in precise and pious religion was close to realization, with tightened measures in place to exclude as many hypocrites as possible from the religious community, the accustomed

28. *TCG*, 30 ("Tongues"), 41 ("acting"), 42 *("stay")*, 46 ("come willingly"), 48 ("real work," "no reality"), and see *AC*, 122. A hypocrite may "carry all [these] things in so fair a way, that you shall hardly discover him to his very death." *TCG*, 48.

29. *TCG*, 42–43 ("Hypocrites also"), 47 ("much exercise"), 48 ("dazle," "falleth away"), 49 ("freedome"), 133 ("gone beyond").

contrast faded. Because few of the migrants and fewer still of the church members were visibly impure and some hypocrites outshone the saints, godly life seemed more a source of confusion than a badge of honor. Where the real and the illusory had drawn so damnably "close together" that the difference "is very hard to be discerned" and where "Eagle-eyed Christians" and indeed even "Angels in Heaven have much ado" to distinguish reality from bluff in others' behavior or their own, how could God's people hold their oppositional self-image? Who could see themselves now as an elite, as exemplars of a pointedly higher style of life? How, in the end, could the settlers keep faith with the ideal of visible sainthood that was congregationalism's prized distinction? And who, now, could be confident that one's best colleagues and confidants in the congregational inner circle were of genuine coin? So, Cotton ruefully had to conclude, in the Bay colony many a "poor Christian is discouraged."[30]

Not a beaming City on a Hill, but a scene of discouragement: that was what Cotton made of Puritan America's religious project. The Bay's congregational reformation might press on from strength to strength, but the spirit within was unsound. The free practice of piety had brought, not the expected fullness, but, at least for the moment, checkmate. Absorption in benefits, forgetfulness of Christ, spiritual depression, faltering consolation and surety, rampant hypocrisy, blurred identity—taken together, these were, not scattered aberrations, but connected symptoms of a movement in crisis. In a setting where saintly effects were feigned widely and well, simulation had so overtaken reality that both the prestige and the evidential power of behavior were ebbing away; and deductions of a safe estate from sanctified behavior seemed as fleeting as "songs in the Night" or "Castles in the air." Hence abounded cases of conscience that, in Cotton's opinion, the dominant casuistry did not know how to resolve. Clearly, within a scheme of things in which so much had gone wrong, in which the costs weighed heavier than the gains and the delicate Reformed balance tilted out of control, it was time to audit and overhaul.[31]

This, let us note, was a partly implicit message. No citizen of New England, certainly no one charged with the cure of souls, could have announced it baldly and survived. Cotton weathered the antinomian storm in part because he excelled in elliptical speech, and this too cohered with his long-range career

---

30. *TCG,* 39 ("Angels"), 40 ("close together"), 42 ("discerned"), 43 ("Eagle-eyed"), 49 ("discouraged"). See also *FEW,* 48–49.

31. *AC,* 32; *TCG,* 192. For skillful hypocrisy's erosive effect upon "consolation [built] upon conditions of obedience," see especially *TCG,* 133.

pattern. As with many other nonseparating clergy, his pastorate in England had rested on uneasy and shifting compromises between a generally conservative outlook averse to disorder and the sometimes disruptive demands of private conscience. In correspondence with the bishop of Lincolnshire he maintained a Dissenting posture in a pronouncedly hedging style. In a letter of 1624/5 he veiled the devious means he had devised at Saint Botolph's to avoid nonapostolic ceremonies with generous equivocation and deference to authority. Reflecting upon the whole experience at old Boston in his letter of resignation in 1633, he described the search for a balance between "true-hearted loyaltie and christian liberty" as the overall "bent of my course" and the great struggle of his career to that date. Although at the end he made a bold decision to "live by mine own fayth" and not that of others, he still found it worrisome to flout the weight and wisdom of tradition and its many distinguished representatives ("in comparison of whom, what am I[,] poore sparke?"). At old Boston, Cotton earned an unquestioned place in the roll call of Puritan radicals, but his radicalism was qualified, sometimes twistily evasive, and betrayed a genuine ambivalence.[32]

Cotton might have hoped that his decision to flee England and to join an apostolic reformation would resolve the ambivalence, but New World circumstances served to sustain it. Apparent in his vision of congregationalism as a delicate "walk[ing] with an even foote betweene [the] two extreames" of Separatism and conformity to the Laudian church, it was clearer still in his approach to Roger Williams, whose one-sidedness and freedom from self-doubt chafed him as much as his doctrinal irregularities. As Cotton, writing sometime in 1636, scored both Williams's haste to find "failings (yea intolerable errours) in all the Churches and brethren, rather then in your selfe" and his proud dismissal of the "testimony, and judgement of so many Elders and Brethren" in America, he cast in favorable relief his own more guarded manner; and certainly in the difficult years ahead he seldom was to know the luxury of single-mindedness. When he assailed the warped religion of duties and performances, he spoke as a disciplinary congregationalist emotionally committed to Puritan tradition, to the nonseparating clerical network, and now to the Bay project. As averse as ever to disorder, he did not aspire to dismantle and replace, but to modify and save, to remove impediments and set the stalled venture in motion again. Possibly he could not admit to himself the full

32. Cotton to the bishop of Lincoln, May 7, 1633, in *CJC*, 179. In the earlier letter Cotton also avoided reference to his covenanted subgroup that circumvented objectionable ceremonies. Cotton to the bishop of Lincoln, Jan. 31 1624/5, in *CJC*, 98–103.

magnitude of the crisis he diagnosed and did not wholly appreciate how the pietist awakening itself supplied the fuel of hypocrisy. Possibly, too, he could not acknowledge the degree of his own departure from Puritan canons, let alone the sizable overlap between his newer teaching and that of Eaton and other known apostles of free grace. So was the ambiguity compounded; accordingly, unlike Williams's or Eaton's frontal attacks upon the parent tradition, his own critique could be so elusively shaded as to seem "darkly and doubtfully delivered" both to contemporaries and modern historians.[33]

Yet it was not always so, and of course it was the part of ambivalent speech to be at once guarded and probing. Through all his caution Cotton's followers and critics could read a plainly disruptive message: American conditions had exposed a pathology inherent in their religious movement. They had made more apparent the tendency of an activist religion to give human qualities, exertions, and rituals a life of their own. Here was the same fault Cotton had identified in his old Boston congregation, the same fatal tilt away from the Savior, but now it stood at the center of his message. Now the analysis came back, almost obsessively, to the relation to deity, to the settlers' "faith in *themselves*, and not . . . *Christ*." Reliance on "such changes or graces, or Deutyes or ordinances (as church-fellowship etc.) as may leave them short of saveing fellow-ship with Jesus christ"—by Cotton's observation, this false move had so upset morale in Boston, and perhaps in other Puritan towns, as to become the besetting malady of "this Countrey of universall Profession" and a rousing challenge to an able and experienced spiritual director. "The desire of my heart," Cotton told Shepard in an opening salvo of the conflict, was to meet that challenge; and his attempt to do so defined his role in the antinomian troubles.[34]

Downgrading Covenant Conditions

To cure so deep a disorder, harsh medicine was required, which many said would kill the patient. But how else to resolve pandemic hypocrisy, to recuperate saintly reality, and to make the Lord again the sovereign focus of faith than to downgrade, and decisively, the place of "benefits"? In Lincolnshire Cotton already had gestured in this direction, but now he was ready to press further and to try to carry the other settlers (many came from outlying settlements to

33. Cotton to Roger Williams, early 1636, in *CJC*, 213, 214, 220 (and see Emerson, ed., *Letters from New England*, 196–199); *AC*, 62. On Cotton's verbal obscurity, see *CJC*, 10.
34. *TCG*, 90, 200; *AC*, 32.

his Thursday lectures in Boston) with him. This was a wrenching move, for the category of benefits included all the forms of regenerate behavior, all new powers and emotions, all the saintly round of devotional and self-managing performances, and all transactions with apostolic means and ordinances. It included, in short, a large share of that which made the colonists' religion Puritan.

As veteran assayers of the Old Man and his wiles, Puritan directors from Richard Rogers to Daniel Dyke to Cotton himself in Lincolnshire and most of the founding clergy in the Bay had learned to live with a measure of ambivalence in their estimate of behavior; yet by and large it remained an undertone, worrying but controlled. By 1636, however, and climaxing a trend already begun in old Boston, disciplinary *"reformation"* held an uneasy station in Cotton's thought. It was not simply that he valued it less, or that his disciplinary exhortations now grew as much from a need to counter charges of laxity or, in some cases, from a sense that irresponsible tendencies actually had arisen among the Hutchinsonians, as from doctrinal or psychological need, but that the radiant worth of duties now gained his attention less than their "frequent abuse." To treasure them now as an index of gain in the fight against sin and troubles of conscience was to traffic with "promises made unto [be-havioral] conditions in us" and not to trust in the Savior.[35]

As Cotton's own Lincolnshire utterances attest, the denial of redemptive value to "conditions" was a routine gesture of Reformed thought, one of whose purposes was to square covenant theory with solifidian principle. In a single cycle of sermons, and with no sense of incongruity, he could affirm both the unconditional and the contractual aspect of the gracious pact. He offered "the Covenant of Grace . . . [as] absolute without condition" and added that, when God "do[es] require a condition, yet it is such as he himself will perform." He then spoke with equal conviction of "the free covenant of grace, by which [God] hath promised everlasting fellowship to those that keep his com-mandements." So the two elements, the free promise and the positing of conditions, came comfortably together in a unified contract theology; once he had acknowledged the former, Cotton then felt free to adapt the latter to his equally urgent legal and disciplinary interests. Relying heavily upon formula-tions of the Israelite covenant in Genesis, Exodus, and Deuteronomy, he exhorted his old Boston parishioners to "enter into a Covenant with [God], to

35. *TCG*, 132 (*"reformation,"* and see 126), 133 ("promises," and see 200, *AC*, 122); *AC*, 121 ("abuse").

keep his Commandements for ever; [for] . . . this is the way of having him for our God."[36]

Yet Cotton's teachings of 1636–1638, most pertinently his lecture cycle devoted to the covenant of grace, record a definite change of mind. Here his cautious nature was at work, stopping well short of positions taken by Eaton or Traske. He continued to employ the covenantal paradigm and recognized that "conditional Promises . . . (that is to say, Promises to such and such Qualifications)" are a common scriptural formula and serve a variety of edifying purposes. They identify, for instance, the many gifts that Christ confers, and they stir up the elect to prayerful appeal to him for such gifts. Accordingly, Cotton would allow himself and others to "speak of Conditions" from time to time in a positive sense, but the allowance was hesitant and qualified. Now the once occasional caveat, "Trust not . . . unto . . . conditional Promises," dominated. As Thomas Dudley, William Coddington, and other former members of Saint Botolph's church must have noted, a concern increasingly prominent but still secondary in old Boston (at least in the extant sermons) now was central to their teacher's message. It could appear, for instance, as an argument that faith "is not built upon any conditional promise" or as an indictment of those who claim a "right unto any *conditional promise*, by . . . performance of the condition." For in these and a medley of similar statements in which the concept of a conditional promise functions as a virtual oxymoron, Cotton signaled his belief that the going theory of the gracious covenant had blundered into connivance with the covenant of works. With its call for human partnership and active input into the pact, not to mention its linkage with the practical syllogism, it was partly responsible for the obsession with performances that was ruining the American project. Accordingly, he must act to mute the conditional note.[37]

Not content to problematize conditions, Cotton also deployed terms that antinomian theorists had established as disparaging tags for the godly's sanctified states and feats: "qualification" (sometimes "quality") and "disposition." Eaton, Traske, Towne, and Antinomus Anonymus made no special use of

36. *EGJ*, 152 (first two quotes), 280; *CF*, 31, and see 32–39, and the baldly conditional statement in *EGJ*, 386.

37. *TCG*, 13 ("Conditions"), 19 ("not built"), 56 ("conditional Promises"), 66 ("trust not"), 86 ("right unto"). The qualifiers that Cotton now attached to conditional promises, that "if the Promise be conditional, it is a condition subsequent to Faith, not antecedent," and that the Deity himself "performeth all those conditions that are required on our parts," were commonplaces of covenant teaching, but Cotton pressed them so often and hard as to shrink the genuinely reciprocal element beyond recognition. *TCG*, 20, 25.

them, but, almost certainly by the mid-1630s, they were common coin both to Brierley and Crisp, highlighting the defective status of the saints' graces and works. "How far are we . . . from Christs Religion," declared Brierley in a typical phrase, "when all our Religion is. . . . in some singular conceit of quality and disposition which we conceive in our selves"; and Crisp found in pietist divinity "an hundred times more poring on . . . Qualifications, than on Christ, and his Free Grace." We cannot know how familiar Cotton was with such rhetoric, but by 1636 he had become one of the first (and few) credentialed Puritan clergy to use "qualification" and "disposition" with some frequency and in a sense critical of pietist tradition. Both terms rang through his popular lectures and his debates with other clergy during 1636–1638.[38]

At no time did he cease to affirm a "good Qualification" as a "good work . . . in the heart of a Christian" or to celebrate "gracious dispositions"; yet such expressions now belonged to a larger unit of argument focused on the divine source and not the human effect. It was "the Lord . . . working . . . qualifications" in his chosen that occupied stage center. Moreover, like Brierley and Crisp, typically Cotton used the terms in a negative sense. Now openly critical of the conditional element in covenant doctrine, he warned repeatedly that biblical "Promises to such and such qualifications" were not intended to build confidence in human moral capability or worth. "Good conditions or qualifications," likewise, offer a sandy ground for religious assurance. To depict the faithful Christian as one scrupulously "fearful to build . . . upon *qualifications*"—that was now a deliberate means to lower the rank and role of benefits.[39]

38. *CT*, 3, and see 33, 35, 40, 44; Tobias Crisp, *Christ Alone Exalted: Being the Compleat Works of Tobias Crisp, D.D.* (London, 1690), IV, 100. Reflecting scholastic Latin usages, "qualification" and "quality" in this context signified any divinely worked attribute in the self's nature and behavior, and "disposition" was an approximate synonym for "habit," or an infused virtuous inclination. Brierley preferred "qualities"; Crisp preferred "qualifications" and "dispositions," but the three terms pointed to pietist gifts and graces, to "prayers, . . . teares, . . . humiliations, . . . sorrows, . . . reformations, universall obedience and the like" (*CA*, I, 213 [and see *CA*, 322, 443]). The date of the materials in *CT* is uncertain, but Brierley died in 1637. Samuel Crisp, Tobias's son and editor of the 1690 edition of *Christ Alone Exalted*, ascribes most of the sermons in vol. IV to his father's Brinksworth pastorate (1627–1642). The text cited in this note probably dates from Crisp's brief term in London in 1642–1643, but the usage is consistent with the earlier sermons.

39. *TCG*, 20 (see also 63), 66 ("such and such," and see 65), 67 (the Lord "working"), 133 ("fearful"); *AC*, 97 ("good conditions"), 135 ("gracious dispositions"). In their public testimonies of faith, at least two applicants for membership in the church at Cambridge

Demote the benefits! Mistrust qualifications! Uttered by a blue-chip member of the pietist and congregational intelligentsia, these were inciting suggestions indeed. Yet, as he struggled to meet a religious crisis, Cotton saw that merely cosmetic changes would not suffice. The time had come to redraft sainthood, leaving the present absorption in personal acts and states out of the design. Professors now, he hoped, would be known by a reluctant frame of mind in which regard for graces was tempered with caution, even suspicion, and thus in the mid-1630s Cotton labored to infect the colonists with ambivalence about behavior. Always would holy walking flow from the bond with Christ, but it would fall into relative twilight while the spotlight shifted elsewhere.

—————

appealed to their "qualification[s]" and "dispositions" as a ground of religious assurance. Selement and Woolley, eds., *Shepard's Confessions*, 61, 83.

CHAPTER 13

John Cotton
in America
Transcendent Gifts
and Operations

I n America, Cotton retrenched the holy walk, but he did so by accenting the vintage Puritan urge to make religion less human and more
divine. The objects of his critique were akin to the liturgical and
ecclesiological "human inventions" that Puritans long had assailed.
To the practice of piety in the 1630s he applied the same rule he was to
apply to New England lawmaking in the 1640s—that the more a statute
"smells of man, the more unprofitable." Yet, to remove the human savor, a
critique of duties, conditions, and qualifications was but an initial step. A
positive strategy also was required.[1]

Accordingly, Cotton complemented his lowered estimate of human behavior with a greatly magnified interest in the divine being and agency. This
too built upon tendencies apparent already in his later Lincolnshire doctrine,
but now it was carried with force and consistency to the forefront of discussion, and again it unfolded in partial yet evident accord with English radical
theories of free grace since the 1610s. Throughout, Cotton's concept of God
remained dynamically Trinitarian, but with special emphasis upon Christ and
the Spirit as his frequent operative agent. If, in the 1620s, "Christ first, and
then the benefit" had become a favored motif of Cotton's pastorate, in Massachusetts it became a fundamental rule of thumb. Christ always had been
first, of course, in Cotton's overall outlook, but the primacy now was construed
in a different way. The Christ (and by extension the Spirit) of Cotton's semi-
antinomian years was less directly tied to the pietist system of moral and ritual
mediation. He was less the sanctifier, lawgiver, ruler of souls, or model of

1. John Cotton, "How Far Moses' Judicials Bind Mass[achusetts]," MHS, *Proceedings*,
2d Ser., XVI (1902), 284 ("smells of man"). For human inventions, see Theodore Dwight
Bozeman, *To Live Ancient Lives: The Primitivist Dimension in Puritanism* (Chapel Hill,
N.C., 1988), 51–78, 136–138.

purity, and more a mirror of the "the absolute freeness of the Grace of God." That was what Cotton had in mind when he told of the Lord's "absolute free Promise" or when he acclaimed the "marvellous freedome" with which God dispensed with contractual conditions in a human sense and, simply, gave gifts.[2]

All of Cotton's revisionist tacks, however, were constrained by a strongly residual loyalty to Reformed principles. How, he asked, do free promises square with the reciprocal demands that federal theory laid upon the human partner? In search of an answer, he faced a characteristic ambiguity. He did not wish either to eject the covenant idea or to question its disciplinary require- ments, yet his overriding aim was to curb the exaggeration of human agency and accomplishment that, in his view, it had helped to foster. How, then, could he present the Lord's redeeming acts as both free and conditional? How could he preserve his gracious covenant's bilateral structure and yet overshadow the human part with the divine?

The Divine Work in the Saints

In fact, a potent means already was at hand. To secure the gracious character of the pact, Puritan federal theologians since Elizabethan times, including Cot- ton in Lincolnshire, typically had added a proviso: the triune God himself fulfills the conditions he requires. He does this by imbuing otherwise helpless humanity with the vision and desire to keep the covenant. This was no after- thought, but a featured element of the theory, yet it was qualified by a larger passion to maximize human performance. Now Cotton invoked the proviso: God "will work . . . what He doth require; so that doth He require, that they should walk holily before Him, He himself doth also work this." But now the equation was altered. Here again the traditionalist spoke, appealing to federal routine; but the revisionist spoke too, using a free grace accent. A parallel case is found in contemporary Brinksworth, Wiltshire, where Tobias Crisp (on virtually identical grounds) was advancing a quietist version of covenant di- vinity. For both men, the larger passion now was to restrain the human role, making God more the potter and mankind more the clay.[3]

"Come to any holy duty," Cotton told his Thursday audiences sometime in 1636, "and it is the *Holy Ghost* [Christ's operative agent] that leadeth you

2. *CF,* 51 ("Christ first"; for New England expressions, see *TCG,* 10, 21, 107); *TCG,* 11 ("marvellous"), 19 ("Promise"), 20 ("freeness").

3. *SPS,* 51, and see *TCG,* 11–12, 25, 66 (Reformed teaching on this point is summarized in *FEW,* 9). For Crisp's version, see *CA,* I, 146–183, and cf. *GV,* 55.

along, and *Acteth* in you." Again, any member of the fraternity could have made this statement, and then, as both covenantal logic and the Reformed ellipse dictated, he must add the usual heavy complement of appeal to human agency. But, since the purpose now was to restrain such appeal, the federal ideal must yield to one more singular and divine. As Cotton hailed "the precedency of Jesus Christ" or pledged to put "not obedience first, nor . . . any thing else first, but [Christ] Himself [as] *Donum primum, et primarium,*" he also assigned to him (and the Spirit) much more than a merely forensic part. Moving "to *act* [graces] in us," to "work all our works for us" and so also to perform the covenant conditions, the Savior whom Cotton now revered was no mere vicarious actor on the elect's behalf. He was also the direct "Author and Finisher" of Christian humanity's deeds. More than Reformed theories of Providence normally allowed, and more than Bay colonists seemed to know, he was the dynamic worker of saintly effects; and active verbs abounded in the portrayal.[4]

Exploiting one of the many traditional Catholic ideas that by the early 1600s had resurfaced in Reformed scholastic thought, Cotton also magnified the divine work in the saints by representing it as an instance of the *concursus divinus:* a concurrent, continuous exertion of divine power that enables and upholds all earthly effects. By 1636 the divine concursus (or concurrence), adapted to his special purposes, had become an explicit premise of Cotton's attempt to expand the operative power of God at the expense of humanity's. It echoed through his lectures and polemical writings of the period. It was heard, for example, in his insistence that graces "are nothing, without the working of [divine] Grace" and in his argument that Christian duties are enacted in men and women and not in the first instance by them.[5]

The divine concurrence came most explicitly to expression, not in Cotton's Thursday lectures, but in his strenuous debate with the clerical majority in late 1636 and early 1637. There, a full complex of argument turned upon differing

4. *TCG,* 10 ("precedency," *"Donum"*), 11 ("Author"), 13 ("all our works," and see 24), 94 *("act"),* 95 ("holy duty"). John Everard put a similar emphasis on Christ's "precedency." See Everard, *The Gospel-Treasury Opened* . . . (London, 1657), 21–22, 35, 77. The passages cited appear to date from the 1620s or early 1630s.

5. *TCG,* 12. For the concursus, see Richard Muller, *Dictionary of Greek and Latin Theological Terms Drawn Principally from Protestant Scholastic Theology* (Grand Rapids, Mich., 1985), 76. For a typical Protestant statement, see *WWP,* III, 98. The concursus permitted an emphasis on either divine or human action. Cotton in America stressed the former. Dagobert D. Runes, ed., *Dictionary of Philosophy* (Totowa, N.J., 1966), s.v. "concursus dei."

estimates of the operative power of graces or, to put a scholastic point upon it, of the "habits" or virtuous dispositions implanted by the Spirit in the saints. With the Antinomian Controversy in rapid crescendo, the worried ministers sought to learn how Cotton was interpreting regenerate behavior to his parishioners, many of whom stood in the antinomian forefront. Did he, in silent accord with existing antinomian theory, deny that the "graces of Christ in his members are . . . active in their proper nature"? Or, to vary the question, did he deny that "habits infused" are a motor of saintly works? That is, do they carry an operative capacity of their own? To Thomas Hooker, Thomas Shepard, and their fellow inquirers, the correct answer was a qualified but definite yes. They granted the weakness and instability of graces as well as their dependence on "dayly [concurrent] assistance" from the Source and, indeed, defined the Spirit as the "procreant and conservant Cause" of all the phenomena of sanctification. Yet that cause must not be construed as to deny saintly graces an actuating power of their own. For what is a grace or habit but a name for the new traits and capabilities of the godly? "What are habits for," John Preston had asked, "but for action?" And what are the godly if not active and responsible agents? Were Cotton to deny all inherent capacity to graces, he would arrest the striving spirit that pietist awakeners had labored for half a century to instil. To the ministers, nothing less than that was at stake.[6]

To a man now fixed upon transhuman initiatives, however, the ministers' stance was pietist business as usual, more fuel for the reigning obsession with human dynamics. The concursus, it was true, described no simply unilateral process. In literal Latin, the term suggested a running-together of forces, and this was roughly the clergy's conception of divine and human (habitual) exertions joining to produce a saintly life. Of course, they cast the doctrine in a Protestant idiom of divine supremacy and prevenience, but to Cotton's eyes their version seemed nonetheless to trivialize the Deity's share. His acts became merely external (embedding graces and habits that then operate of themselves) and supplementary ("conservant" of their action). Cotton's retort to the inquiry, delivered with scarcely concealed irritation, therefore had to be

6. *AC,* 51 ("habits infused"), 67 ("procreant"), 76 ("members," "assistance"); John Preston, *The Breast-plate of Faith and Love* . . . , 5th ed. (London, 1634), 240. For orthodox positions on infused habits, see *FEW,* 44–46, 68–69. Emphasizing that without an "Operation of the creature, there is no [concurrent] Cooperation of God," Samuel Stone restated the doctrine in New England. "The whole body of Divinity in a Catecheticall way handled by Mr Samuel Stone, Teacher of the Church in Hartford, N.E.," 103, MS, MHS, and see 102–105, 358. Baird Tipson is preparing the text for publication.

blunt: "The Holy Ghost doth not work in us gifts and habits . . . [which then] work by their own strength." To argue the contrary was to establish that "we our selves produce the acts . . . by vertue of those habits received by us," and it was to dash this inference that Cotton now invoked the concursus.[7]

Even as he did so, he remained the vigorous advocate of transformation and obedience. Ever ardent for the congregational disciplinary reformation and for private and family spiritual exercises, he found the concursus doubly useful, since, with due qualifications, it affirmed human agency. Because the divine work is, not sole, but concurrent, he need not deny outright the "voluntary concourse" of human with divine agency that was so vital a link in Puritan divinity. The actuated self is not inactive; it is firmly "going forth" in the tasks of the daily walk.[8]

That activity, nevertheless, is tied immediately to the power that undergirds it in every instant of time. Duly to know this power was to see that absorption in human tasks was the ministers'—and by implication mainstream Puritanism's—fateful error. Through their program of duties and their reliance on graces and habits they had so far forgotten that God is God as to "deny [Christ and the Spirit] to have any . . . concourse in our Sanctification." In point of fact, Cotton was saying, the Lord may infuse and conserve, but he also must do more. Graces are wholly contingent, able only to lie inert or even to "vapour out into smoak" unless the Deity acts in and through them. From fasting to prayer to relief of the poor, therefore, every godly deed requires an extra, separate activation. This is the divine "concurr[ence] . . . in [the saints'] every act," and it is both immediate and determinative. Indeed, in the language of scholastic philosophy it also may be named the formal cause of sanctification, as what imparts the form or principle that makes a thing to be what it is. Construed this way, the congregational reformation derived its energetic goodness—first and moment by moment—from the Lord's "formal . . . concourse." When Cotton spoke, then, of the Spirit "working and acting in us" not only our habits but our very "actions," or affirmed his "in-

7. *AC*, 102–103 (and see 144). Cotton emphasized that "God . . . worketh in us, not only the habits but the acts." *AC*, 143.

8. *TCG*, 26. In *TCG*, 92, Cotton affirmed the saints' "holy . . . pursuit" after "duties." The Lord calls them "to follow [purity of life], and pursue it." Although the language does not recur, his teaching in the antinomian years was consistent with his affirmation about 1634 of "the voluntary concourse of every Child of God, with the Holy Ghost in every Spiritual Work." John Cotton, *A Treatise: I, Of Faith* . . . ([Boston], 1713), 17.

dwelling Power . . . to act and keep Holinesse in us all," he made the Deity more directly and fully than ever the actuating force in sanctification.[9]

We Are Not Actors

Whether cast in scholastic or popular idiom, Cotton's message was therefore one: we are, not actors, but reactors. Even those who admired that proposal must have marveled at its revisionist edge. For if deity is said to act and form all, and if, simultaneously, the array of human duties, conditions, qualifications, and dispositions are downgraded, then what truly human role remains? If action is shorn of self-assertion, what must become of the dynamic psychology that long had underlain the drive for further reformation of church and society, or of the kinetic, projective qualities of personality needed in the Puritan walk and warfare? Within a religious tradition that urged the self into states of effort and tension as much as or more than into states of compliance and surrender, these were urgent questions, but Cotton was undeterred. Busy qualities must diminish. New England's crisis would end when the realization, "We cannot be active of our selves," rings in the colonists' consciousness day in and day out. Awakened to their impotence and knowing themselves, not as powerful, but as powered, they would ease into a state of mind and conduct that "quietly resteth upon the Lord." Within the larger community with its many unconverted and hypocrites, their distinguishing mark would be, not the self-mobilizing style of the traditional godly, but an actionless action, a peculiar readiness to "yeeld" or "to be led."[10]

Yield and be led—among Reformed Protestants in Europe, Great Britain, and New England this was common advice. It expressed a common belief in the all-sufficiency of grace and a will to preserve it against Catholic and Arminian criticism. Yet, so Cotton thought, in recent times the wheel had turned. Since he and those for whom he spoke were now the embattled champions of grace, it was a scandal to find such counsel in the mouths of his opponents; and on one occasion in the Thursday lectures, treading dangerous ground, he hinted that their views were akin to *"Arminianism."* Alternating with calls for self-absorption and hyperactivity, the standard praises of sub-

9. *AC*, 51 ("working and acting," and see 143, *TCG*, 24), 102 ("concurr[ence]," and see 144), 103 ("deny," "formal concourse"); *TCG*, 156 ("smoak").

10. *TCG*, 19, 31, 63, 222. See also *FEW*, 10–11, 45–46.

mission before God served only to veil a drift toward human autonomy in pietist direction and practice.[11]

In Cotton's sermons and debates of 1636–1638, the call to "yeeld" therefore took on a new meaning. It stood in striking accord with free grace radicalism, as with Roger Brierley's characteristic design to "bring all things down in man . . . and to lay him low" and Peter Shaw's reported view that "the humane nature of a Christian is not a person, but that his personalitie is in Christ, in whom he subsists." Devising as well a potent counter-Arminian strategy, Cotton now replotted saintly action in strikingly quietist terms. How, for instance, are covenantal conditions to be met? Human instinct, and too much of practical divinity, suggests an active approach: "Here is the [condition], and here the blessing promised to it, and therefore I will take it to my self"—and so the fruitless round of striving and hypocrisy begins again. The condition, however, truly is met, and the blessing gained, by an opposite means. Echoing, again, Brierley's principle that "a quiet sense of . . . Weaknesse" is the ethically potent state, Cotton argued that, "the more empty we are of our own strength," the more the Spirit moves us to do good. A helpless and waiting suspense, a "lowly, sheep-like frame," is what opens the valves of power. When one thinks, not to act and grasp, but to yield and depend—then alone may the Deity intervene, and then the reactive work may begin, when "the Lord doth secretly transform [the saint] . . . working [the conditions] in him." A purely reactive obedience—to advocate this was to blur the bipolar, contractual focus of affectionate divinity. But how better to remind a forgetful audience that the power that moved them was divine and total, and so to make a sounder basis for the American venture?[12]

Nowhere was the reactive ideal more evident than in Cotton's American treatment of the doctrine of preparation. There again we find a tellingly ambiguous mixture of disciplinary and quietist themes. As in Lincolnshire, the necessity of an extensive, traumatic ritual of preparation is taken for granted; moreover, the strong preparationist demand for moral cleansing prior to union with Christ is explicitly restated. If these elements echo Cotton's earlier teaching, they also record a shift in viewpoint. In old Boston he had

11. *TCG*, 32–33. For other reflections on Arminianism, see 48–49, 217, and John Cotton to Hugh Goodyear, Apr. 12, 1630, in *CJC*, 140.

12. *CT*, 4, 243 ("Weaknesse"); "PS," 707; *TCG*, 31 ("sheep-like"), 66 ("Here is"), 67 ("secretly transform"), 109 ("empty"). For Brierley's devotion to "low," receptive states, see also *CT*, 36, 215, 225–226, 239.

spoken unperturbed of active human input to "prepare a way" for Christ. As a Reformed theologian, he knew that human beings depend utterly upon divine power to perform such deeds; but, since he felt too the Puritan craving to lift Christian practice to higher planes, he made generous appeals to human volition and effort. Christ, he told his English congregation, enters the soul when we act, when we "discover our sins openly," or when we set "to turn from all our evill wayes."[13]

By 1636, however, the emphasis had changed: "The Lord prepareth." Christ enters the soul when, passively disposed, we *undergo* preparation. Divine, not human, agency discovers, turns, and subjects. By a work of "Bondage," it is "the Lord [who] setteth home unto the Consciences of men . . . the sense of his wrath" and "draweth them from all their sinful lusts, and passions." What is more, he enforces his unilateral privilege in a still more drastic work of *"burning."* There expressly the human spirit of "undertaking" is targeted; the presumption to act "of thy own accord" is consumed, as are *"fastings, and humiliations,* and *alms-deeds,* and *prayers"* infected with any presumption of *"self-sufficiency."* In these two ways, "God . . . prepareth us," and the result of his work, the soul prepared for divine entry, is one from which every conviction of "power in himself" has been cauterized and that lies wholly pliant to the Deity's operations.[14]

How, then, can a soul laid supine produce the act of faith that makes the saving link to Christ? "Faith" in Reformed and Puritan thought was active and passive at once. Since the natural self had neither inclination nor power to believe the gospel, faith was a gift passively received, and the gift gave power for a "positive act of the will" to grasp Christ. In the summary of John White, a leading English clerical supporter of the Massachusetts project, the will "is meerly passive, till grace have renewed it, and no more but the subject wherein God worketh"; but "then being renewed it wils the conversion, and becometh a voluntarie instrument of God . . . to apprehend his grace." This was the

<hr />

13. *EGJ,* 384, 388, and see above, Chapter 11, n. 3, and text. For moral cleansing, see *TCG,* 14, 114–115. The frequent claim that Cotton in America rejected preparation is corrected in *FEW,* 194–195, and Charles Lloyd Cohen, *God's Caress: The Psychology of Puritan Religious Experience* (New York, 1986), 84. Janice Knight, *Orthodoxies in Massachusetts: Rereading American Puritanism* (Cambridge, Mass., 1994), 111, 115–117, understates differences between Cotton's English and American teaching on preparation.

14. *TCG,* 14 ("Lord prepareth," "Bondage," "setteth," "draweth"), 17 ("God prepareth"), 117–118 (*"burning,"* "undertaking," "own accord," *"fastings,"* "self-sufficiency"), 119 ("power"). See also *TCG,* 131: God "will make thee to lie flat at his feet, and to say, If he will kill me, here I am."

doctrine of the New England ministers—their theological outlook tried and sanctioned by the adult male members of the congregations who elected them to pastoral office—locked in debate with Cotton in 1636 and 1637. For them the event of faith was both gift and embrace, a "mutuall giving and taking," and, if stripped of the latter, it ceased to be a meaningfully human act. Be it ever so much a gift, the faith known both from biblical study and experience is at the same time a potently "instrumentall cause," reaching forth to seize Christ. By comparison, Cotton's categorically passive faith, "Empty" and "without . . . power," ran "opposite unto the streame" of traditional interpretation. Thus, by mid-1636 if not earlier, the issue of faith's operative role had become another focus of controversy and debate.[15]

In Lincolnshire, Cotton himself had affirmed faith's active "power *to establish and fixe* the heart upon Christ." Yet, as if in silent retraction of those words and with some dependence upon the radical predestinarian teaching of William Twisse, William Pemble, and Richard Rothwell, he now laid virtually exclusive emphasis upon "Passive Reception." As a child actively sucks milk from its mother's breasts, the soul after union with Christ exerts a force of "active Receyving," but even such modest agency must be excluded from the moment of union itself. In union, unequivocally, the soul is "not active, but passive." And what, in this context, did passivity mean? Was it a readiness to comply or accommodate? Certainly, the soul prepared wishes to meet God's every demand. If called to believe, one "would run through fire and water" to perform it. But, and this was the core of the matter, he "findeth himself unable." Utter impotence enfolds him, so that "to believe is as impossible . . . as to build a world." And if advised to wait in hope that strength will come, one can only scoff. "Wait?, saith he; I . . . cannot wait"; for such advice construes waiting itself as an active strategy, a tactical postponement. It therefore commends an act that persons on the brink of conversion are wholly unable to perform.[16]

---

15. Gisbertus Voetius, *De praxi fidei* (1638), in *Selectarum disputationum theologicarum* (Utrecht, 1655), II, 510; John White, *The Way to the True Church* . . . (London, 1616), 283; *AC*, 36 ("giving and taking," "instrumentall cause"), 195 ("streame"). For the Reformed doctrine of human agency, see *FEW*, 41, 63–65, 104–106. Voetius was the chief theologian of the precisianist movement in the Protestant Netherlands.

16. *WL*, 311; *AC*, 37 ("actyve Receyving," "not active"); *TCG*, 120 (remaining quotes). In *WL*, 312, note also the strongly transitive sense of faith, which "put[s] forth that act, by which we are justified." In New England lectures, however, Cotton distinctly affirmed that union with Christ, together with justification, precedes faith. Faith merely registers the union already achieved (*TCG*, 35, 218). For Twisse and Pemble, see *WCC*, 236–237; Dewey

How, then, can one link to Christ? To clarify the means, Cotton enlisted an age-old metaphor of Christian spirituality: emptiness. Like passivity, it too was a familiar preparationist motif, but one that stood in counterpoint to human volition. Yet so deep was Cotton's mistrust of volition now that emptiness, like passivity, stood, not as its dialectical, but as its negating opposite. Relative to human agency, faith's first motion arises in a void. Indeed, faith itself is "an emptying grace"; it has "an Emptying Nature, emptying the soule . . . , constituting the soule as an empty vessell." With no motion of its own, lacking even the ability to embrace, it is like a bowl that merely "receyveth oyle poured into it, when it self is passive." In the crucial, formative time, faith's sole office—and that only so far as it is enabled—is to lie open and receive.[17]

In one sense this concept is continuous with Cotton's preparationist teaching in old Boston. There, we recall, he viewed the unregenerate soul as a toxic space to be purified for Christ's entry. Yet, in America, human undertaking itself, any bent to be "stirring and busie in [one's] own strength," became the ultimate impurity; and this was a complicating shift. The purgation of desire was an easily comprehensible concern, but Cotton now called for surrender of something deeper, of the instinctual human sense of agency itself. Now it was a man or woman's natural conviction of a "root, or power [of action] in [my] self" that must be expelled, and hence the Spirit, in the preparatory works of bondage and burning, "cometh to act contrary things to nature." He induces in the self "a state quite contrary to nature." As if taking a cue from John Eaton, Cotton thus lifted the issue to a plane beyond sense and reason; for now the defining moment of preparation arrives when the soul, "convinced that neither

<hr>

D. Wallace, Jr., *Puritans and Predestination: Grace in English Protestant Theology, 1525–1695* (Chapel Hill, N.C., 1982), 119. For Richard Rothwell, a clerical colleague whose manuscript papers Cotton gathered and sought to publish in the late 1620s, see "PH," 196–199. Cotton's distinction between faith before and after union with Christ was a commonplace of contemporary Reformed dogmatics, with the emphasis upon passivity before union directed normally against Catholic and Arminian errors. See Muller, *Greek and Latin Theological Terms*, 82–83.

17. *AC*, 37–38, 40, 196, and see 197–198. To Cotton's written debate with the ministers in mid-1637, "The good Lord empty us more," was thus a fitting close (*AC*, 198). Here also, in reference to the soul's motionless state in the first (not the second and active) moment of faith, is the context of Cotton's oft-quoted statement, "For our first union, there are no steps unto that *Altar*" (*TCG*, 36). In Knight, *Orthodoxies*, 113, Cotton's construal of emptiness and passivity in 1636–1638 becomes an unexceptional expression of a "Sibbesian" orientation that Cotton long had shared with Richard Sibbes, John Preston, and others.

his working, nor believing, nor waiting, nor seeking . . . will do him any good," is stunned into inaction. Now the initial linkage to Christ, the most dynamic effect available to humankind, occurs (and can only occur) in a total vacuum of effort. The supposition here, that "emptiness of . . . abilities" is the religiously powering state, frames the whole doctrine in paradox—again in striking accord with existing antinomian theory.[18]

The Seal of the Spirit

A vision of God as plenary actor was the core too of Cotton's American revision of the doctrine of assurance. As we have seen, complaints of failing certainty loomed large in his portrayal of the religious crisis. That New Englanders in the flush of social, political, and religious reformation had found no release from "sad houres" when "faith [is] suspected" became a prime exhibit of his antipietist case. Yet he also reported troubles of his own. In a letter written during the Antinomian Controversy he acknowledged that an acute personal need underlay his controversial ideas. God, he wrote, "hath so often exercised me with renewed Feares and Agonyes about mine owne spirituall estate, . . . that I could not rest" upon the usual signs and evidences. So the eminent casuist confronted his own painful case of conscience and was forced to reconsider conventional antidotes to doubt.[19]

Uncertainty of one's standing before God, the familiar anguish that pietist Puritans had named the ultimate casuistical challenge in their day, thus remained a pressing issue on American soil; and we know enough of Cotton's outlook as of 1636 and its overlap with free grace radicalism to foresee the basic results. The cause of the difficulty was clear. Doubt thrives among those tempted by pietist counsel to "lay the feeling of their Sanctification as the corner stone of their peace." Accordingly, the solution was equally clear: "When my Spirit is in a swoon, the Aqua vitae bottle hangeth not at my girdle but standeth at the right hand of the grace of Christ." In the trial of doubt, in

18. *TCG*, 118 ("emptiness"), 119 ("root," "busie," "cometh"), 120 (contrary state), 129 ("convinced").

19. *AC*, 109 (see also 113, and *TCG*, 134); Cotton to Samuel Stone, Mar. 27, 1638, Ms. Am., 1506, pt. 2, no. 12, Boston Public Library (published in *CJC*, 273–274), and see William K. B. Stoever's comment on the letter in *FEW*, 169. A report by Cotton Mather that "no less than 3 years disconsolate apprehensions" had preceded Cotton's conversion may evidence an unusual proneness to spiritual troubles. Mather also reported that Cotton as a young minister suffered from a "want of internal *peace*" until he first received assurance in 1613. *MCA*, I, 255, 257–258.

other words: resort to Christ's mercy and pardon alone, and away with re-course to works in any form.[20]

Yet when scanned more closely, the matter was not so simple. Like the presbyterian Thomas Wilcox, who in the later 1580s was offering similar advice to those demoralized by doubt, Cotton drew the basics of consolation from the solifidian side of Reformed theology. Unlike Wilcox, he spoke as one increasingly at odds with a fully formed and vigorous tradition of Protestant spiritual direction that specialized in distresses of conscience. Through long complicity with it, he knew of its frequently infirm hold upon assurance, but he also appreciated its power and cogency as a system of casuistry; and he was well aware that, with few exceptions, the religious leaders of the New England reformation were its committed agents. To restore the American settlers to certainty, therefore, a sharpened appeal to free grace was only a point of departure. To gladden their sad hours, and more truly to break the ties that so long and securely had bound religious certainty to behavior, a major doctrinal supplement was needed. It was one that, whether Cotton knew it or not, went a noteworthy step beyond English antinomian teaching as of the mid-1630s. Building upon standard Protestant teaching of the inward-assuring testimony of the Spirit, and probably taking additional cues from Paul Baynes (a pupil of Richard Rogers, and Perkins's successor as lecturer at Great Saint Andrews Church, Cambridge) and from Richard Sibbes but going far beyond them, he found it in the apostle Paul's references to the Spirit's sealing work.[21]

20. *AC*, 113, 130.

21. For Cotton and sealing, see *SPS*, 65; *TCG*, 183–184. Thomas Wilson, *A Christian Dictionarie* . . . (London, 1612), 429, and John Ball, *A Treatise of Faith* . . . (London, 1632), 85, 115, provide standard teaching on the inward testimony as a spiritual seal. In possible dependence upon Paul Baynes, John Preston and Sibbes gave exceptional emphasis to the seal, styling it a distinctive but repeated gift after justification in times of doubt; but in their construction it was linked firmly to pietist disciplinary standards and did not register a shift toward free grace in Cotton's later sense. See *WRS*, IV, 132–135, 138–139, V, 432–435, VI, 376–377, 483–484; and Mark Dever, *Richard Sibbes: Puritanism and Calvinism in Late Elizabethan and Early Stuart England* (Macon, Ga., 2000), 175–185. See also Paul Bayne[s], *A Commentarie upon the First Chapter of the Epistle . . . to the Ephesians* (London, 1618), 280, 289–293, with a preface by Sibbes; and John Preston, *The New Covenant; or, The Saints Portion* . . . (London, 1634), 399–403. Preston, Sibbes, and Cotton were close associates in the 1620s; see Francis J. Bremer, *Congregational Communion: Clerical Friend-ship in the Anglo-American Puritan Community, 1610–1692* (Boston, 1994), 42, 50–51, 62. For additional discussion of the seal, see also Michael P. Winship, *Making Heretics: Militant Protestantism and Free Grace in Massachusetts, 1636–1641* (Princeton, N.J., 2002), 21–23.

By 1636–1637 Cotton had revised previous Reformed and Puritan estimates of the believer's initial act of faith and of the redemptive role of the Trinity. The convergent effect was to find the event of justification an imperfect ground of security. For Eaton, Crisp, and other antinomian theorists, the act of faith that joins to Christ was the medium of certainty; properly understood, one's trust in Christ and his pardon supplies unfailing knowledge that one is elect and redeemed. But Cotton now took an opposite tack. Expanding a theme he had begun to develop in England, he offered a humbler estimate of what the initial act of faith accomplishes. Faith makes the link to Christ and so remains a watershed event in the Christian life, but, if only temporarily, it lacks power clearly to attest that union to the believer and thus is not itself the definitive ground of assurance. This emphasis reappeared in context of a distinction between the Father's, Son's, and Spirit's distinctive roles in re-demption, which was a mainstay of Cotton's argument at the time of the controversy. The Father prepares and justifies the soul, the Son performs the atonement and frees the soul from the bondage and curse of the law, but their work is incomplete. The conjoined work of the Father and Son and the believer's faith confer but a partial certitude, still laced with doubt and fear. When and whence, then, is the deficiency overcome? Firm assurance arrives with a separate and subsequent grace, a "most clear, most certain and most powerfull" attestation expressly targeting and curing anxiety of conscience. Cotton sometimes called it the seal of the Spirit. Although the evidence is uncertain, he might have experienced the seal, or a foretaste of it, on the day of his wedding in 1613. Eventually to become the showpiece of his theology of assurance, it was heavy with implications.[22]

To begin with, widening the already familiar divide between justification and the calming of conscience, the seal accented their temporal separation and qualitative difference. By the same token, it distinguished the sealed elite from the lower and deficient subclass of those as yet unsealed. It also met New England's crying need for a *"difference . . . discernable"* that would distinguish believers from hypocrites, restore confidence to the colonial venture, and at last make it possible, in words that echo Eaton, to "sleep in quietness, and

22. *AC*, 141. I thank Michael Winship for assistance with the works of the Trinity. For the Father-Son-Spirit schema, see *AC*, 80, 83, 115; *TCG*, 124–194. It also appeared among the eighty-two errors identified by the synod of 1637 (*AC*, 230). The experience of 1613 is reported in Cotton Mather, *MCA*, I, 258. Cotton declared early in 1637 that he preferred the term "Witnesse of the Spirit," but the terminology of the seal was more common in the Antinomian Controversy and is used here (*AC*, 48). The first five of the sixteen ques-tions that the other ministers posed to Cotton in late 1636 focused on the seal. *AC*, 46–47.

ha[ve] full contentment." Crowning the entire cycle of conversion, this was no doctrinal footnote or corollary, but a pillar of the faith in its own right, a distinct rubric within the *ordo salutis*. As such, it bears comparison with John Wesley's eighteenth-century invention of a "second blessing" of Christian perfection that occurs after the event of faith itself or with the later Pentecostalist addition of a glossalalic baptism of the Holy Spirit.[23]

Like all of Cotton's doctrines canvassed in this chapter, the concept of the seal was informed by a Platonic and scholastic distinction between creaturely and "increated" operations. Sealing was above all a transcendent event, a source of confidence wholly untouched by human imperfection and mutability. Like the earlier union with Christ, it takes effect when the self, like wax ready for a seal, stands in yielding suspense; and it comes from without and above. Arriving abruptly "from on high," it is "instamped and ingraven" in the soul. Thus the impress is wholly supernatural, the direct act and insignia of the Spirit "expressing his own proper and peculiar [witness and] work."[24]

That witness and work, moreover, is an exertion of "imediate power above the . . . work of any creature." As Eaton might have said, it leads unimaginably far "beyond what any created understanding can search into the depth of." Hence, as in his treatment of preparation and justification, but now climactically, Cotton sought to preclude human input by magnifying its fallible creatureliness. Most of all in New England of the mid-1630s, where astonishingly artful hypocrisy embarrassed true saints and bred in them doubt and fear, there was need to recall that "works of Sanctification [are] . . . created things." If the seal is bestowed at such a time, it comes to those alone persuaded that their "best works are but creatures."[25]

By construing assurance as an exclusive bounty from on high, Cotton sought virtually to refound the art of consolation, and nowhere was his recoil

23. *TCG*, 51; *SPS*, 65. For unsealed believers, see *AC*, 48: "Every Beleever is not sealed with the Seale of the Spirit." In *A Treatise: I, Of Faith*, 64, Cotton described the interval before sealing as a state of "weak hope." For his English teaching on the seal, see above, Chapter 11, n. 27, and text.

In Reformed divinity, the *ordo salutis* (order of salvation) is the chain of events, from justification to heavenly glorification, through which God effected the salvation of the elect.

24. *AC*, 82–84. The scholastic distinction appears in Cotton, *A Treatise: I, Of Faith*, 15. For examples of medieval usage, see Roy J. DeFerrari and M. Inviolata Barry, eds., *A Lexicon of St. Thomas Aquinas* . . . (Washington, D.C., 1948), 535. The importance of the distinction in the Antinomian Controversy was first shown in *FEW*, 14, 170–174.

25. *AC*, 80, 134, 141; *TCG*, 167.

from pietist ideals more evident. Although qualified, his construction of the seal as a moment of direct contact with the increated was in tension with Reformed teaching that divine communication necessarily is refracted through finite media (sacred Scripture, human faculties) and conditioned accordingly. More, what was it to tell men and women of troubled conscience that "the power of the creature cannot help you" but to say that the Spirit stamps his seal with sublime disregard for the ritual of signs and evidences? Few pietist counselors had commended that ritual more often and more trustfully than Cotton in his Lincolnshire years, but in this respect too his debates with the American ministers and his lecture cycle on the covenant of grace delivered during the Antinomian Controversy offer a startling contrast. Not only has the apparatus of "marks" vanished, but the underlying rationale of the practical syllogism— by now an internationally estimable device of Reformed Protestantism—had come largely undone.[26]

Ambivalent to a fault, Cotton did not flatly dismiss the demonstrative value of behavior, but he now viewed estimates of "that close walking with god, upon which . . . the Assurance of a Christian mans good estate [commonly is made] to depend" as absurdly inflated. He conceded sanctification a part in the work of consolation but soft-pedaled it now as a mere "inferiour helpe." So reduced was its part in the management of troubled consciences as to require major corrections in Puritan casuistry. Current casuistical advice did not distinguish properly between troubles of conscience preceding and troubles following the event of sealing. Nor did it fully appreciate the creaturely weakness of the signs themselves.[27]

Within Cotton's scheme as of 1636, the difficult cases of conscience arise in the limited, twilight segment of the *ordo salutis* between justification and sealing. And in this interval there can be no thought of signs and evidences. It is the pure occasion to silence works and await the Lord's act. What, then, the other ministers asked, are we to make of the legion of biblical passages that plainly endorse sanctification as evidence? What, for one, of the apostle Peter's exhortation to link faith to virtue, knowledge, temperance, patience, godliness, brotherly kindness, and charity, "thereby to make our calling and Elec-

26. *TCG*, 187. An example of Reformed teaching on finite media is Franciscus Junius's emphasis upon the mediated and conditioned character of revelation. *De vera theologiae D. Francisci Junii opuscula theologica selecta*, in Abraham Kuyper, ed., *Bibliotheca Reformata* (Amsterdam, 1882–1896), I, 53–55, 61–63.

27. *AC*, 90, 184. By late 1636 or early 1637 Cotton had advanced to the position that it is "not by the chain of . . . graces, nor by the march of . . . duties, but even by faith looking up to Christ . . . , [that] the walls of Assurance are built up, out of . . . free grace." *AC*, 124–125.

tion sure"? Cotton's reply was provocative but consistent: such texts exclusively address cases that arise *after* sealing. They "were not given at all to [those lacking] the first Assurance of their good estates: but to such only as are formerly assured . . . by the seal of the Spirit." Within that context, sanctified acts may play an important—if decidedly secondary—part. To those already bonded to Christ and consoled by the Spirit, they may provide supplementary verification.[28]

Sealed saints, moreover, are a buoyant lot. They suffer anxiety neither "so frequently nor so desperately as before." "Ordinarily" their security is much "more *constant*, and leaveth faith even . . . [in anxious moments] more *constant* and *firm*" than before the seal was applied. So great was Cotton's trust in the steady surety of the sealed that in his debate with the other ministers in late 1636 and 1637 he sounded a controversial theme that Philip Nye, a longtime associate in the Puritan clerical fraternity, had espoused at the time of the London Antinomian Controversy about 1630 and that had yet more notorious associations with Peter Shaw and Tobias Crisp: Since assurance is rooted in a source wholly extrinsic to behavior, not even serious sins like adultery and murder normally can disturb it. This was a dangerous admission, shrinking the importance of likeness to God and weakening incentive to self-control, and the elders argued hard against it. But Cotton stood his ground. Provoking the doctrine might be, but it was a plain corollary of the seal. To show that even "gross sin . . . is no just ground why [one] should weaken [one's] assurance" was further to illustrate the seal's consoling power, and it offered a needed challenge to pietist belief that assurance stands in at least partly calculable proportion to the mix of good and evil in the self.[29]

If, however, the saints' security is so firm, why do they require further assurance? The answer was that the seal, for all its decisive impact, does not lift the godly into pure certitude beyond all sins and troubles. Their assurance "is not so constant or permanent (at least not in all Beleevers) but that a man after he hath received [the seal], may come in time of Temptation . . . [to] question his Estate"; and at times the Lord deliberately "eclipse[s]" assurance in order

---

28. *AC*, 72 (citing 2 Pet. 1:5–11, and see 68), 106 ("not given," and see 87). In the phase between justification and sealing, one's security may be "wholly prostrate" (*TCG*, 38). This phrase does not appear in the original edition. Cotton, *The New Covenant* . . . (London, 1654), 57.

29. *AC*, 49, 89 ("gross sin," and see 50); *TCG*, 183 *("constant")*. For Cotton's debate with the elders on assurance and gross sin, see *AC*, 27, 31, 50, 65–66, 88–90. English antinomian associations: above, Chapter 10, n. 37, and text. Nye's doctrine: "PS," 714–715, and, for his links to Cotton, see Bremer, *Congregational Communion*, 4, 58, 60

to test and firm faith. At those moments, signs of sanctification may play an auxiliary part.[30]

Yet here too casuistical divinity had erred. "Master *Nicholas Byfield*" and other specialists in the "Doctrine of Marks and Signes" had assigned behavioral evidences a major role in the art of comfort. Their strategy, however, was misconceived. It both underrated the "trembling and wavering" of all human effects and exaggerated the saints' powers of self-analysis. Cotton shared the Reformed belief that men and women of faith possess a gift of intellectual illumination, but by 1636 his greater experience of hypocrisy and its untraceable subtleties had persuaded him that human fate is but dimly echoed in behavior. Even the saintliest signs, even heartfelt hope or thirst for Christ or acts of repentance or love, often darken, and hypocrites can fake and even surpass them all; but, more to the point, their very construction as signs remains earthly and fallible, for the gift of illumination itself is a creature. Neither divine itself nor an immediate act of God, it is "a created gift" made by the Deity and infused in the soul. Enlightening it may be, but it shines with "created light." It enhances but must continue to employ frail human modes of "reasoning and discoursing." And therein lay the fallacy of the practical syllogism as commonly understood.[31]

Take, for instance, this version of the syllogism:

He that Repenteth and beleeveth the Gospel shall be saved[;]
But I repent and beleeve the Gospel[.]
Therefore I shall be saved.[32]

Here, etched clear, was a charter for "an enlightned Conscience reasoning and concluding" to dissolve doubt, but Cotton now tartly undermined it. For in all such formulas, even when illumination is present, "the Conclusion followeth but from the strength of reasonings," and so are heavenly purposes computed with earthly arithmetic. To probe the divine mystery of election, this form of the syllogism applies a creaturely analysis ("Therefore . . .") to the creaturely

30. *AC,* 49; *TCG,* 183. It is in this sense that "afterwards from the Effects we may argue to the Cause, and from our . . . Sanctification argue to the Lords Justification of us." *AC,* 142.

31. *AC,* 140–141 ("reasoning"), 146 ("light"), 183 ("gift"), 190–191 (Byfield); *TCG,* 21 ("trembling"). Since "our best works are but creatures, and our renewed knowledg by which we see them is but a creature," understandably "true Christian Sanctification . . . is *many times dark to a sincere Christian." AC,* 134 (and see 85, 146–147, 149); *TCG,* 49.

32. *AC,* 148. For explicit discussion of the practical syllogism, see *AC,* 146–150, 182–183, and the analysis in *FEW,* 49–51.

web of works ("I repent and beleeve the Gospel"). When put into practice, so faulty a procedure naturally proves inept. It proves only that faith's light is too faint, and behavior too frail an index, to permit even the most "Eagle-eyed Christians" to read human fates. In yet another risky departure from ruling Puritan ways, Cotton therefore asked to be counted among those who "think it an unsafe way to conclude a safe estate by way of such a practical Syllogisme."[33]

These were provoking words, but their design was, not to ban appeal to works, but to conform it to the overall thesis that graces "are nothing, without the [immediate] working of his Grace"; and this could be accomplished by a simple but fundamental amendment of the syllogism. Take again the above example. Of its three elements, the difficulty lay in the second and third, the minor and the conclusion, both of which Cotton represented as acts of the creaturely "I." But he now knew—and here is the critical point—that the conclusion contains more than a rational process can provide, that "more [is] required to clear spirituall sight" than the act of a regenerate intellect. To divine a person's good estate from a cloudy mixture of works is nothing less than a miracle, a vision through murk of Christ's embrace of a soul, and from where can it come but above? Since here again creaturely power falls short, the transcendent must intervene in person. In a kind of secondary sealing, repeated whenever the Lord sees fit to console a sealed but momentarily anxious conscience, he "set[s] in [to] clear up the truth" in sanctified works by "imediate light from himself," that is, by "a concourse of the Spirit."[34]

Cotton himself attempted no such reformulation, but he had in mind, effectively, a remodeled syllogism that pivots on the Deity's inputs. Expressed, again, in terms of our working example, it might run like this:

He that Repenteth and beleeveth the Gospel shall be saved[;]
But [by "imediate light" from the Spirit I see that]
 I repent and beleeve the Gospel[.]

33. *AC*, 85, 149, 182; *TCG*, 43. Saints are not by "reasonings, . . . able to gather clear evidences of their estates" (*AC*, 141). Henry Bull was excommunicated from the Dorchester church in 1638 in part for his doctrine "that a Ch[ris]tian must never take any assurances at all, of Faith by way of Reasoning." Thomas Weld and John Eliot, "The Causes of Hen. Bull[']s Excommunication . . . ," in "Transcriptions by Edward Holden of documents in the Prince Library, Boston Public Library," 85, in Cotton Family Papers, MHS.

34. *TCG*, 12; *AC*, 140–141. Cotton emphasized that the concursus is "an immediate light . . . above the created light of the Conscience" (*AC*, 146). See also *AC*, 150: "The Spirit of god doth often concur to bear witness to our Spirits that the works of our Spirits are of God and accepted of him." For the secondary, repeatable "word of comfort" given to the sealed, see also *AC*, 86–87; *TCG*, 62–63, 77–78.

Therefore, [enabled by divine concurrence, I grasp that]
   I shall be saved.

Redrafted in this or a similar way, the syllogism would embody a far safer notion of how "the walls of Assurance are built up." It would preserve reference to saintly works and capacities yet severely restrict it. Strictly accessory to the Deity's immediate agency, signs would function best as they negated themselves, pointing away from the creaturely context. Indeed, "Weaknesse and Emptinesse" mark the best signs, and Cotton accordingly favored those like the hope of heaven or desire for Christ that represent persons "go[ing] out of themselves" and looking to God beyond. In all cases, to seek comfort, not in works, but in the direct acts of deity that both work the works and reveal their meaning—for the relatively few and usually minor troubles of conscience that occur after the seal, that was the fitting cure.[35]

Above, and beyond the Letter

Weakness and emptiness: on that vintage Brierleyan note, the chapter might well end, but the conclusion would be hasty. Making God dispose and do all, Cotton's newer creed abridged the ordinary Puritan sense of strong selfhood, capability, and partnership within the Christian redemption, but it also harbored powerfully contrary implications. His intent was to curb absorption in personal acts and states, but the recent history of the Radical Reformation had demonstrated that doctrines of direct divine endowment and actuation could breed tendencies to an individualist, highly subjective, and ultimately overweening spiritism. Ever a foe of "familist" excesses, Cotton nevertheless in the 1630s revised and restated his Lincolnshire belief in Spirit-aided private judgment. That belief (discussed in Chapter 11) emerged in response, not to perceived problems in Puritan spirituality, but to the Laudian anti-Puritan campaign around 1630. In America, however, Cotton strewed his message with spiritist leaven. He accentuated his earlier doctrine of the seal, expanded his appeal to the Spirit's individual counsel to the saints into a virtual sanction of private revelation, and wove both into his multifaceted plan to subordinate graces to grace.

As ever, his cautious and hedging style was still in evidence. He continued to value his place as a congregational reformer and elite member of the brotherhood. His fervid primitivist regard for apostolic and indubitably objective ordinances placed some restraint upon his spiritist inclinations. He neither

35. *AC,* 59, 124–125, 148.

joined nor countenanced the attack upon godly clergy that had been a defining antinomian gesture since the rise of Eaton and Brierley in the 1610s, and he resisted attempts of the more forward members of his congregation to pit him against his brother ministers as agents of the covenant of works. Immediately before Wheelwright delivered his disruptive Fast Day sermon (January 19, 1637), Cotton advised the Boston congregation to avoid further "strife and debate." Mindful that the other clergy held him partly responsible for the current troubles, and perhaps uneasily aware that they had arisen from exercise of the very right of individual judgment he had promoted in old Boston, Cotton (at least in his surviving works) no longer openly urged the laity to scrutinize clerical sermons for conformity to the Word. He must have known, too, that early in 1637 some of the more militant antinomians had begun to forsake their own parish services and flock to his sermons and that some from First Church formed truth squads to visit services in other towns and openly criticize the doctrine there delivered. And so he no longer spoke directly of ungodly ministers or urged the dissatisfied to seek a purer gospel beyond their own parish. Further, he continued to insist that the Spirit speaks to men and women in and through the sacred text and the objective ordinances of preaching and sacraments, and there is no evidence that at any time he devalued or suspended either his (and his family's) private exercises or the communal ordinances and Fast Days that were a New England fixture.[36]

In context, however, of his expanded interest in transcendent gifts and operations, his doctrine of prophetic inspiration took on a less equivocal hue. The trend of his thinking was apparent initially in an exchange of letters with Shepard probably in early 1636. There Shepard agreed with Cotton's claim in a recent Thursday lecture that possession of a personal grace or "qualification" cited in Scripture should be validated as a sign of divine acceptance by a "farther revelation" of the Spirit, but Cotton's forceful statement of the point also led Shepard to sense danger to Reformed theology's carefully balanced dialectic of Word and Spirit. He wondered "whether this revelation of the spirit, is a thing . . . above the woord; and whether tis safe so to say." Yet, if the Cambridge pastor's natural interest was to *restrain* the motions of the Spirit, Cotton inclined to *magnify* his transcendent freedom: "Though I consent to you, that the spirit is not separated from the word, but in it, and ever according to it: yet above, and beyond the letter of the word it reacheth forth comfort, and Power to the soule."[37]

36. *AC*, 291.
37. *AC*, 25–26, 30.

Above, and beyond the letter—there was the telltale accent of 1636–1638, and it appeared most often in discussion of the Spirit's sealing work. From old Boston days Cotton had stressed the supernatural and immediate character of that work and its very loose relationship to humankind's performances and "signs," but further musing upon the seal in light of circumstances in the Bay led him to realize more fully that "the word of God it self hath no power in itself . . . to encrease faith or the assurance of faith." This was a way to soften the concept of the sacred text as omnicompetent rule upon which rested not only nonseparating Puritanism's vigorous antispiritism but also much of its fixation on duty and performance. In the development of this point, Cotton remained cautious to a degree. He retained the mainline Protestant dread of religious enthusiasm. He knew that incautious reliance on the Spirit could foment dangerous delusions, and professed a healthy abhorrence for the English Familists (among whom he named Robert Towne) and their pretense to freedom from the biblical letter. Thus far he agreed with Shepard and the other clergy that "the Lord couples his *word,* and his *Spirit* together," but such statements now were preliminaries to a larger interest. For, if it were true that "the *word* of God . . . is the *medium*" of spiritual comfort, it was fully as true— and much more germane to the present crisis—that the *"word* . . . [cannot] clear up the grace of God unto the soul: it is the *Spirit* of God that must do it."[38]

To press the issue further, and to highlight a dangerously suggestive notion in ways that must have made Shepard and the other ministers wince, Cotton also argued that the Spirit's gift of certitude is immediate. Granted, the seal comes through the medium of the Word. Yet it does not come to all who read and hear Scripture, but is stamped only in that rare moment when the Spirit makes the medium come alive. Further, sealing is a transcendent work, the act of a free deity who must exceed the biblical medium even as he uses it. Only thus could the seal have sweeping power against doubt. Sealing works where all other pietist antidotes fail precisely because it embodies the Spirit's direct and plenary force, his "own imediate power above the power which . . . the word hath of it self." And in that respect Cotton emphasized for a Thursday audience, "I call it *immediate.*"[39]

From this course of reflections upon the seal even more directly spiritist deductions were to emerge. By accentuating Scripture's vehicular, dependent

---

38. *AC,* 126 ("word of God"); *TCG,* 166 *("medium"),* 172 ("couples"), 178 ("clear up"). For Towne, see *AC,* 32.

39. *AC,* 80 ("power"); *TCG,* 191 *("immediate").*

character and making the Spirit the dynamic and dominant partner in the Lord's communications, Cotton tilted the Reformed balance of Word and Spirit, but he made two even more portentous moves. First, he suggested that a gift of assurance so transcendent and direct must be recognized forthrightly as a type of revelation itself. Second, he stretched the category of revelation, thus understood, beyond the realm of assurance and the seal, suggesting that men and women who have "already . . . been sealed" may receive additional revelations "needful for us to know in this our age." Accordingly, and probably at the very time when spiritist doctrines were being explored among the more radical Hutchinsonians, he urged a Boston audience "not to be afraid of the word *Revelation:* . . . let not men be afraid, and say, That we have no *revelation* but the *word:* for I . . . affirme, that if there were no revelation but the word, there would be no spiritual grace revealed to the soul."[40]

As he uttered these words, Cotton knew that he was treading treacherous ground. He hastened to enjoin caution upon his listeners, reminding them that the Spirit speaks only through Scripture, that no "other matter besides the *word*" should be expected, and that it was all too easy to mistake human fancies for genuine revelation.[41] But there is no denying that he had injected incipient spiritist notes into the mix of ideas in the Bay and lent them his authority—and this at a time of volatile religious excitement and dispute. When, indeed, he was called to comment upon Anne Hutchinson's "Revelations" before the General Court in November 1637, he responded evasively but seemed to defend them on the grounds that she consistently linked them to a scriptural text. "Though the word revelation be rare . . . [and] uncouth in our ordinary expressions," yet, when Scripture is read, revelations may come "flying upon the wings of the spirit." In that sense, he concluded, "I think they are . . . lawful." Albeit in relatively modest form, such words reflect the same close relation between a stress on the divine immediacy and an interest in revelatory communications that often typified spiritist circles of the Radical Reformation.[42]

40. *TCG,* 166, 168, 177–178. Access to revelations, he added tellingly, is not limited to Christians of renown but is given to "all ordinary Christians," a category in which many ordinary members of First Church, and almost certainly women, might have placed themselves. *TCG,* 166.

41. *TCG,* 178, and see 177.

42. Ibid.; *AC,* 340, and cf. Winthrop's briefer account at 273. In a lecture delivered late 1638 or early 1639 Cotton expounded a semispiritist doctrine that correlates with his hesitance to condemn Hutchinson's controversial revelations in her trial before the General Court in November 1637. George Selement, "John Cotton's Hidden Antinomianism:

As of 1636–1638 Cotton remained outspoken against the literally antinomian rejection of law as a rule for Christians, but the largest purpose of his revisions was the same as that of his antinomian contemporaries: to curtail the Puritan obsession with behavior. To him as to them, the current divinity seemed nearly to equate Christianity with active endeavor and "qualifications." It spoke of a confident sainthood grounded in gifts alone, yet then dissolved it in the toil and confusion of efforts to be pure. So Cotton centered his revision upon transcendent operations, adding intimations of an immediate revelation through yet above and beyond the sacred writ for which there was little precedent in English free grace radicalism as of 1636, except in the early ministry of John Traske and among a few extremists of perfectionist persuasion.[43]

I have found little precedent likewise for two of Cotton's most distinctive emphases: the seal and the "created" fallibility of human works. All of the articulate exponents of free grace whose theology is outlined in Chapter 10 affirmed the central importance and easy availability of certitude, but none formulated a separate, dramatic endowment of certitude as a major verity of the faith in its own right. Like Eaton in his sweeping appeal to divine powers and gifts beyond creaturely reason, all drew a sharp line between human and divine agency, but none saw how the scholastic antithesis between the created

His Sermon on Revelation 4:1–2," *New England Historical and Genealogical Register,* CXXIX (1975), 278–294. For spiritism in the Radical Reformation, see George Huntston Williams, *The Radical Reformation,* 3d ed. (Kirksville, Mo., 1992), 1299.

43. Crisp expounded a similar but milder doctrine of the Spirit's immediate and personal gift of assurance in *CA,* II, 465–481, but this may date from later than 1636. A strong spiritist element was present in the ministry of John Traske in the 1610s ("PH," 126–131). Two of the charges against Brierley before the High Commission in 1617 pitted the Spirit against the Word, but none was proven ("Certain erroneous opinions gathered from the mouth of Mr. Bryerley and some of his hearers," 317, MS Rawlinson D. 1347, Bodleian Library, Oxford University; Ronald A. Marchant, *The Puritans and the Church Courts in the Diocese of York, 1560–1642* [London, 1960], 40, 233). Spiritist tendencies might have emerged among the followers of Brierley, Crisp, and other antinomian leaders. About 1630 Thomas Taylor complained of "Antinomists, . . . and Familests" who "pretend the *spirit,* and outbast all men, that they are taught, and led, and moved by the *spirit*" (*RV,* sig. A5, A9). Brierley's later insistence that "the spirit . . . from the word ne're swarves" may be a criticism of disciples who had moved to a spiritist extreme ("Of True Christian LIBERTY," poem appended to *CT,* 45). Cf. the depiction of Brierley as a radical spiritist in Philip F. Gura, *A Glimpse of Sion's Glory: Puritan Radicalism in New England, 1620–1660* (Middletown, Conn., 1984), 252. Contemporary perfectionist patterns, embracing notions of divine inhabitation and illumination, are traced in "PH," 25, 250–262, 274–275, 290–292, 305–312.

and increased might help both to formulate and to reinforce that distinction. On these two points, both crucial for defining his relation to the antinomian rising in Massachusetts, Cotton seems to have worked notably original variations on established themes.

Finally, as with Brierley, Cotton's emphases upon lowness and emptiness remained within the penitential ethos of Puritan tradition. He did not, like Eaton, Traske, or Crisp, seek explicitly to lighten the Christian mood or to transform the Deity from prickly sovereign to kindly father. Taken together, the elements summarized here define an original brand of Protestant dissent, one at once passionately stated and intriguingly equivocal: a semi-antinomian, protospiritist gospel that still claimed a place in the disciplinary Puritan world.

Cotton's aim, of course, was constructive. He thought he had found a way to contain hypocrisy and restore morale to the congregational reformation. But his means proved too extreme for the time and place. To make God the all-sufficient actor, converter, and sealer and hence to redefine the human role as dependent, yielding re-action—this, with spiritist tendencies added, was a semi-antinomian move. It rested uneasily with attachment to primitive and outward ordinances. Although less expressly than Eaton or Crisp, it so focused attention upon individual spirituality as to eclipse the corporate dimension of the gracious covenant with its vital disciplinary mechanisms. Although the invocation of Deuteronomic penalties upon the social collective was an ingrained Puritan reflex in crises, and despite the gravity of the disputes in 1636–1638 and their disruptive impact upon the colony, Cotton found little use for the Israelite paradigm and issued no warnings of imminent divine punishment.

But, most important for our purposes, he aspired to scale back or discard prominent elements of the pietist way and install a new and much less recognizably Puritan piety in the New World. And he trafficked in subtleties and paradoxes that must have been taxing for ordinary people. Intending to heal a religious crisis, he therefore helped to spark another. In ways that partly exceeded his own intention, he became the most powerful single theological and pastoral catalyst of the Antinomian Controversy.

CHAPTER 14

JOHN COTTON
AND THE
AMERICAN
ANTINOMIANS

New England's free grace movement was a varied blend. It was shaped in part by the exceptional religious excitements and freedoms of the early years as well as by the difficulties and uncertainties of the Great Migration and early settlement in a wilderness. Most of the insurgents were members of Boston's First Church. Several—including William Coddington, Atherton Hough, Thomas Leverett, William Dinely, and Oliver Mellows—had been Cotton's parishioners in old Boston, and others had ties of family or neighborhood to the Hutchinson family in Alford, Lincolnshire; but dissidents of First Church stemmed from several English locales. If some, as Thomas Weld and others thought, had arrived already "fraught with many unsound . . . opinions," those opinions cannot be traced to a single personal or geographical source. Probably there were links to beliefs associated with known antinomians in the mother country, and the more extreme tenets that surfaced late in the controversy drew in some measure from the Protestant radical fringe. In New England itself, Anne Hutchinson, John Wheelwright, and probably Henry Vane became important disseminators of free grace views in their own right, and their ideas were by no means interchangeable.[1]

---

1. *AC,* 201. English antinomians and the radical fringe: direct influence has not been proven, but several of the accusations against Brierley and his followers in 1617 and Peter Shaw in 1629 resemble beliefs imputed to the Hutchinson party in 1637–1638. "Certain erroneous opinions gathered from the mouth of Mr. Bryerley and some of his hearers," 317–318, MS Rawlinson D. 1347, Bodleian Library, Oxford University; "PS," 706–712; and cf. *AC,* 202–203, 219–247, 263–265, 278, 301–303, and *JJW,* 193, 204–206, 245–246. See also below, nn. 27, 32.

Cotton the Fountainhead of Dissent

In the uprising of 1636–1638, which we now call the Antinomian Controversy, Cotton's role was not the most colorful, but it was central. No mere interested observer and commentator, he participated at nearly every turn. His biweekly lectures and sermons might have sparked and unquestionably nurtured the upheaval from an early period. He stood at the center of things from the opening cycle of argument with Thomas Shepard in early 1636 through a series of duels with the other ministers and the climactic synodical debates in the fall of 1637. In the spring of 1637 he had attempted to increase immigration of those likely to befriend free grace radicalism and was angered by the alien act of mid-1637, which had the opposite purpose. About the same time, he met with members of the antinomian party, who held that only a minority of Christians were properly "sealed with the Spirit," and approved their position. In April, he joined other members of First Church who refused to attend the ordination of a "legal" minister in Concord, and throughout he remained in close consultation with leading dissidents in the Boston congregation. One of their number later recalled that "of the Priests none but *John Cotton* was with us" during Wheelwright's trial before the General Court and at the time of the Remonstrance (protesting the treatment of Wheelwright), and some felt betrayed by his turn against Hutchinson in the last months of controversy. At the trial, when the other ministers argued that Wheelwright had named them agents of the covenant of works, Cotton pointedly refused to agree; and when they wrote a rebuttal of Wheelwright's sermon, Cotton penned a response. Repeatedly he took Hutchinson's part at her civil trial, and, even in the spring of 1638, when he no longer could overlook her heretical propensities, he continued to describe her as "an Instrument of doing some good" in the Bay as a critic of "duties and performances." This and other evidence shows that Cotton, at a minimum, was an active partisan in the conflict.[2]

2. *AC*, 82, 271 ("Instrument"); *JJW*, 212 ("legal" minister); William Coddington, *A Demonstration of True Love . . .* (London, 1674), 12 ("Priests"). For immigration and the alien act, see *JJW*, 208; *WCC*, 241. For charges of betrayal, see Philip F. Gura, *A Glimpse of Sion's Glory: Puritan Radicalism in New England, 1620–1660* (Middletown, Conn., 1984), 176. Cotton's response to the elders, mentioned in *JJW*, 216, probably is not extant, although it may be the "Conference" document in *AC*, 175–198 (and see 173–174). The claim that Cotton's defense of the insurgents was a conscious "power grab" to delegitimize the other ministers and establish his "supreme charismatic authority" is

In all of this, his theological inputs were uppermost. Giving due to a variety of other personal and ideological sources and in particular to "the originality and personal magnetism of a remarkable woman," this chapter connects the crucial issues and indeed much of the very terminology in dispute in 1636–1638 to the Boston teacher, his commanding presence and his limited but grave challenge to pietist conventions. American antinomian teachings cohere with those of their English predecessors and contemporaries, but they took form under Cotton's preeminent influence. Through most of the period from his installation in October 1633 as teacher in First Church, his was the dominant pulpit in Boston, and the citizens of nearby towns (especially Roxbury and Charlestown) where notable free grace contingents emerged had access to his weekday lectures. On Sabbath days, Wilson preached in the morning, Cotton in the afternoon; but, in addition, Cotton lectured every other Thursday and on many special occasions, and his Thursday series continued through 1636–1638 and beyond. Moreover, during most of Cotton's second year in the Bay, in the very months when Anne Hutchinson began to disseminate her critique of the orthodox faith through weekly meetings in her home, John Wilson was abroad, and Cotton alone conducted the preaching ministry in First Church. Probably it was no accident that the troubles started shortly after Wilson's return, when Hutchinson and others began to notice that his message was different from Cotton's and to make unflattering comparisons. Wilson also was absent from mid-May to early August 1637, serving as chaplain in the Pequot War, and Cotton again held forth alone.[3]

We have no certain record of his earliest teaching in Boston, but his sermons during the time of conflict engaged the major issues in dispute before Hutchinson's move to heterodox extremes in the winter of 1637–1638. As noted in the previous chapter, the sermons blurred the binary focus

---

suggestive but speculative and too baldly stated. Darren Staloff, *The Making of an American Thinking Class: Intellectuals and Intelligentsia in Puritan Massachusetts* (New York, 1998), 42.

3. Stephen Foster, "New England and the Challenge of Heresy, 1630 to 1660: The Puritan Crisis in Transatlantic Perspective," *WMQ*, 3d Ser., XXXVIII (1981), 646. For Cotton's and Wilson's schedule of preaching, see Everett Emerson, *John Cotton*, rev. ed. (Boston, 1990), 63. Wilson sailed for England in October or November 1634 and returned in October 1635 on the same ship with Henry Vane (Robert C. Black III, *The Younger John Winthrop* [New York, 1966], 79, 90–91). For Wilson's chaplaincy, see Robert Charles Anderson, *The Great Migration Begins: Immigrants to New England, 1620–1633* (Boston, 1995), III, 2012.

of Puritan understandings of redemption, featured the Deity as source and mover of all the effects of redemption, challenged the contractual element in federal theology, reduced the value of sanctified behavior, downplayed the customary signs and evidences of a good estate in favor of the divinely imprinted seal as the decisive source of certitude, reconceived Christian practice along quietist lines, and emphasized personal inspiration by the Spirit above and beyond the scriptural letter. In context both of the pietist turn and of the first wave of antinomian backlash in England, it is easy to see how such teaching might have incited or encouraged tendencies of the sort associated with Hutchinson and her followers. As a widely experienced casuist, moreover, and himself a troubled veteran of the spiritual warfare subject to "renewed Feares and Agonyes about mine owne spirituall estate," Cotton could tailor his doctrine to the cases of conscience that the practice of piety in general and the current epidemic of hypocrisy in particular had brought to the fore. We can only presume that his manner in the pulpit was realistic and convincing, but it is clear that his portrait of a religious movement in crisis rang true to many of his auditors and to a large majority of the members of First Church.[4]

Clearly it did so to Henry Vane, who upon his return to England professed to "hold nothinge but what [Cotton] approve[s] of." In their teacher's sermons and counsels, Vane and others must have found both a recognizable account of their own cumulative discomforts within the godly community and an appropriate set of countermeasures. It is not difficult to understand why "multitudes of men and women . . . were eager" for the new doctrines, why those doctrines "spread so fast and prevailed so suddainely," or why Cotton's telltale doctrines

---

4. Cotton to Samuel Stone, Mar. 27, 1638, Ms. Am., 1506, pt. 2, no. 12, Boston Public Library (published in *CJC*, 273–274). On the First Church majority: an extant list of "Propositions of the Church of Boston" records fifteen tenets prepared by some members late in 1636, but no names are affixed, and it is unclear how much of the membership it represented or how many of their concerns it included (*WP*, III, 324–327). Cotton thought that "most of the Church of Boston consented with Mrs. Hutchinson" so long as "she openly held forth no more, than what was publicly taught" (*WCC*, 247). When John Coggeshall and William Aspinwall continued to voice extreme opinions after the synod of 1637, Cotton criticized them for "father[ing them] upon the members of *our* church" and for representing them "in the Churches name, . . . when they differed" widely "fro[m] *our* church in Judgm*e*nt" (Sargent Bush, Jr., "'Revising what we have done amisse': John Cotton and John Wheelwright, 1640," *WMQ*, 3d Ser., XLV [1988], 738). Yet there are many, if often exaggerated, recognizably Cottonian themes among the errors collected by the synod; see *AC*, 219–243, nos. 19, 20, 25, 28, 38, 41, 43, 44, 47, 48, 56, 68, 73, 75, 78.

of the seal, the fallible creatureliness of works, and the like figure prominently among the eighty-two errors reported by the synod of 1637.[5]

Moreover, the tendency of the more enthusiastic members of religious movements to press ideas to extremes is evident in the evolution of English radical religion in our period. Christopher Hill notes that some disciples of Roger Brierley and Tobias Crisp moved well beyond positions sanctioned by their mentors. Since the teaching of both men was suggestive beyond their intent and at times incautiously expressed, it was easy enough to misunderstand or exaggerate or to follow ideas to what they thought logical conclusions. When Cotton in the early years of his ministry at First Church began to disseminate a set of ideas almost as provoking as theirs, he inspired a similar cycle of radicalization. The meetings in Hutchinson's household exhibited the tendency to move from a review of sermons to original commentary already familiar in English Puritan conventicles, and certainly his typically cautious and hedging style invited misconstruction. Indeed, the "Ambiguity and Obscurity" of his rhetoric became an explicit point at issue in his debates with the other clergy in late 1636 and 1637. The ministers complained that "sundry things which you have publickly uttered, were [so] darkly and doubtfully

---

5. William Fiennes to [John Cotton], July 1638, *CJC*, 283; *AC*, 201–202 ("multitudes," "spreads). On Cotton's sermons: see above, Chapter 12, n. 22, and text.

Little is known of Vane's theology before his return to England in August 1637, but he lived in Cotton's house during his stay in the colony, was a member of First Church, presumably was in frequent discussion with his host and teacher, and in later years claimed discipleship in Cotton's ideas. For discipleship, see David Parnham, *Sir Henry Vane, Theologian: A Study in Seventeenth-Century Religious and Political Discourse* (Madison. Wis., 1997), 244–245, 257–258; Fiennes to [Cotton], July 1638, in *CJC*, 283. Thomas Shepard remarked in his autobiography that the Familism "begun by Mistress Hutchinson [was then] raised up to a great height by Mr. Vane" and in a letter to Winthrop called Vane "the prime craftsman of forging all our late nouelties" (*GP*, 65; *WP*, III, 415). Giles Firmin recalled in later years that Vane, "who when Governor, was the great Favourer . . . of these Errors, . . . did animate that faction" and that when John Wilson preached at First Church he primed visitors with provocative questions to raise after the sermon about the relation of justification and the human act of faith (*A Brief Review of Mr. Davi[e]s's Vindication . . .* [London, 1693], sig. A; *Weighty Questions Discussed . . .* [London, 1692], 21–22). In Providence in the spring of 1638, Roger Williams noted the Hutchinsonians' "longings . . . after Mr Vane" and their hope of his appointment as general governor of the New England colonies (Glenn W. LaFantasie, ed., *The Correspondence of Roger Williams* [Providence, R.I., 1988], I, 150). Michael P. Winship gives Vane a star part in First Church's antinomian turn, in *Making Heretics: Militant Protestantism and Free Grace in Massachusetts, 1636–1641* (Princeton, N.J., 2002), 6–7, 49–52, 87–88, 227.

delivered" that more radical voices had been led to "father on you" a host of alarming opinions. Cotton himself recognized that "words uttered in the Pulpit . . . [are] easily . . . mistaken," and in a Thursday lecture shortly after the formal resolution of the controversy he acknowledged his own slowness to see the fault in doctrines "framed . . . so near" to his own. In later years he continued to acknowledge that the progressively radical views of the Hutchinsonians were inflated versions of "what I had taught."[6]

Cotton's teachings, too, had more subversive implications for a disciplinary and text-centered tradition than he allowed. By about 1636 he was gesturing well beyond familiar pietist terrain, and it is easy to imagine that under more favorable circumstances he might, like Eaton, have moved on to a boldly new synthesis; but he did not. He remained double-minded, standing undecided but resolute between opposing tendencies. To lower the status of sanctification but preserve commitment to a Puritan moral and ecclesiological reformation, to magnify the Deity's operations upon and within the individual saint yet stop firmly short of a spiritist extreme, to strike at cherished ideals of the pietist turn while clinging to membership in the clerical network—these were deep equivocations, and his advanced intellectual training (he and Charles Chauncy were the only two Bay leaders of the first generation to hold the bachelor of divinity degree) proved indispensable as he strove to articulate and defend them. As the texts of his debates with the ministers attest, the analytic spirit and technical resources of scholastic theology did much to define his role during the controversy. They disposed him to hold faith with careful reasoning. They helped him to formulate and defend slippery doctrinal balances and yet resist being swept to extremes by insurgent religious passions. So far as the record reveals, among elite New Englanders leaning to the antinomian side he alone possessed the intellectual and temperamental virtuosity to maintain such a difficult poise.[7]

6. Christopher Hill, "Dr. Tobias Crisp, 1600–43," in *The Collected Essays of Christopher Hill* (Brighton, 1986), II, 149, and "Antinomianism in Seventeenth-Century England," 163; *AC*, 59, 62, 119; *JJW*, 273; John Cotton, *A Reply to Mr. Williams* . . . (1645), ed. J. Lewis Diman, in *The Complete Writings of Roger Williams*, II (New York, 1963), 80 (and see *WCC*, 246–247; Cotton to John Davenport, after March 1638, *CJC*, 287). Cf. John Underhill's use of "what Mr. Cotton held" in his efforts to seduce Jane Holmes. George Selement and Bruce C. Woolley, eds., *Thomas Shepard's Confessions*, Colonial Society of Massachusetts, *Publications*, LVIII, *Collections* (1981), 78.

7. Neither during nor after the controversy did Cotton fully admit the iconoclastic message of those "truths." For later reflections, see *WCC*, 223–257, 279–290; Cotton, *Reply*

Yet with all the virtuosity in the world, how could Cotton have conveyed so subtle a theology intact to a congregation of average congregational laity, and especially to those stirred by current excitements? What of those like Mary Dyer, William Coddington, or Henry Vane whose discontent with the pietist way was greater than their teacher's yet who were less held by professional considerations, the dread of established elites for popular movements, or a scholastic orientation? How were they to embrace his severe critique of duties and graces and yet preserve allegiance to congregational disciplinary expectations, or to grasp so suggestive (indeed, explosive) yet shaded a concept as his "immediate" revelation? Understandably, they realized more fully than he the quietist and spiritist potential of his ideas. Taking up his infectious romance with free grace and the Spirit with fewer hesitations and compromises and likely bringing to bear some knowledge of antinomian concepts gleaned in England, they were carried into purer and more disruptive radicalism. Well in excess of his own designs, then, Cotton became a powerful catalyst of the antinomian rising.

In other ways, too, he almost certainly did much to rouse and shape the movement. Very little documentation exists of the state of mind of members of First Church in the mid-1630s, let alone of the many outsiders who visited his weekday lectures; but it is unlikely that many at the outset expected to find their religious convictions unsettled under his ministry. Yet who could listen to the eminent teacher analyze phony sainthood or depress the value of "benefits" and sanctification without some loss of trust in behavior and, above all, its evidencing power? John Stedman of Cambridge for one, who upon his arrival heard "Mr. C[otton] speaking how far a man might go under a covenant of works," developed "great fears that was my condition" and found himself "not sleeping quietly." Cotton's analyses might have echoed the experience of many parishioners, but it is a fair guess that others more attached to time-honored sources of assurance found his message positively unsettling; and that, of course, was the intent. Throughout the sermons in *A Treatise of the Covenant of Grace*, Cotton dwelt upon behavioral evidence for justification as moot already for a fraction of the audience, but he just as plainly had in mind a second audience of persons not yet awakened or sufficiently sensitive to the problem. He spoke to console the already perturbed but, in a clear act of semi-

---

to Mr. Williams, ed. Diman, in *Complete Writings of Roger Williams*, II, 80–81. In *WCC*, 235–237, Cotton did acknowledge that he had mistakenly affirmed justification before faith during the synod of 1637 but promptly recanted.

antinomian evangelism, also to alert the remainder to their danger. In all probability, the result was to increase the number of colonists of antinomian tendency and to flavor their views with his own distinctive concerns.[8]

Furthermore, although the strategy Cotton devised to lessen pietist anxieties seemed simple and perfectly targeted, in several ways it might have been counterproductive. Letting God be and do more and humanity less—in theory, this should disentangle assurance from the practical syllogism, make it far easier to obtain and sustain, and set the truly sainted clearly apart from the false; but it had potential to compound the very confusion and anxiety it aimed to cure. In the longer run, should Cotton's new divinity sway New England, hypocrisy would fade and perhaps the millennium would dawn; but, in the meantime, the Puritan venture was in crisis. Hypocrites enjoyed a virtual golden age, and thus he must continue to help the saints distinguish themselves from nearly perfect counterfeits.

The criterion he offered seemed simple enough: the bond to Christ ratified by the seal and confirmed, if need be, after the fact by transformed behavior. But, to judge by the details of his actual counsel in the mid-1630s, this did not eliminate the need for painstaking introspection, and often enough close judgment was required. Have I joined rightly to Christ? Have I received the seal? Since both experiences can be mimicked, fine distinctions must be made. Typically, for example, hypocrites taint their faith with a sense of personal agency, whereas the real believer knows that faith's total capacity is from beyond, that one "is not president of his own power." For ordinary mortals, it must have been difficult enough to comprehend and meet this psychologically ascetic and counterintuitive demand, let alone to persuade themselves that their stance before God derived wholly from beyond with no remainder of "such strength [as] they find in themselves."[9]

In this setting also the question of sanctification as proof of justification took on greater import than Cotton's theory normally would allow. He restricted the use of behavioral signs to infrequent occasions when the seal seemed to blur, emphasized the creaturely dimness both of the signs themselves and of the saints' power to analyze their own thoughts and deeds, and reckoned a sign valid only when accompanied by an extra concursus of spir-

---

8. Selement and Woolley, eds., *Shepard's Confessions,* 74–75. Looking back on the controversy in the late 1660s, Giles Firmin claimed that the insurgents' infectious fix upon *"their* way" to assurance, disallowing "all assurances that came not this way, . . . unbottom[ed] many serious Christians." *The Real Christian* . . . (London, 1670), 283.

9. *TCG,* 43–44, and see 53. For a vintage example of "Cottonian fineness" in drawing self-analytical distinctions, see *FEW,* 53.

itual illumination. Yet the other clergy challenged every element in this construction. Presumably, too, there were many details to clarify in the treatment of cases in his counseling ministry, and it is a fair guess that more than one client found the highly subjective experience of the seal more difficult to detect and a less decisive cure for doubt than Cotton had promised.

So in his lecture sermons, as in his debates with the clergy, he found it necessary repeatedly to refine behavior's evidential value. He advised that sanctified acts testify to a good estate, yet only "when Justification is not wholly doubted of, but in part." Such acts, furthermore, must meet strict standards of authenticity. Saints may derive hope from good works, but only if they have cast off the normal presumption of competence and sense solely "the Spirit of God carrying them along in . . . waies and duties," and afterward they must hear the Spirit's voice within them (as opposed to their own spirits) testifying "that the works of our Spirits are of God and accepted of him." They must determine as well that the works were performed for God's glory alone, unlike the works of hypocrites who profess the same aim but "secretly wind about to their own glory in the end." As these and many similar counsels show, to affirm the use of signs and still hold them to a strictly accessory role proved a delicate business. The more their use was qualified, the more circuitous the casuistry became, and the heavier too the burden of self-analysis upon the laity. Cotton believed that the difference between true and hypocritical signs was *"discernable to Christians,"* but he immediately added that only an elite *"whose wits are exercised in the wayes of the Spirit and Word"* can reliably make the distinction; and what was this but to admit that, at least in some cases, his proposed cure for doubt had led into fresh mazes of analysis and thus begotten more doubt? By such means as these, he might have exerted a latent but powerful impact upon his admirers, disposing a small but fractious minority to make a sharper break with effort and performance and a more categoric resort to transcendent operations than he desired.[10]

In ways both direct and oblique, then, Cotton played the most seminal role in the breeding of dissent in the mid-1630s. The exertion of influence upon individuals is always conjectural, but it is argued here that the antinomian movement rose upon foundations he had laid. If we set aside for the moment the doctrinal extremes that surfaced late in the conflict and the array of undocumented and often improbable heresies assembled by the synod of 1637, a coherent body of ideas remains that differs from previous varieties of free grace

10. *TCG*, 38 ("Justification"), 51 (italicized quotes, and see 46), 54–55 ("wind about"), 107 ("Spirit"); *AC*, 150 ("our Spirits").

radicalism. There was no trace, for example, of the special esteem for Luther that was a hallmark of early English antinomian faith. Here was a free grace theology with a difference, and the largest factor in that difference was almost certainly Cotton. John Wheelwright, the only member aside from Cotton who left behind an ample record of his views at the time, offers a first index of how remarkably Cottonian the so-called antinomian theology was.

John Wheelwright

John Wheelwright from 1623 to 1633 was vicar of Bilby, a town some twenty-five miles distant from Cotton's charge in Lincolnshire and one mile from the Hutchinson clan with their known ties to Cotton. Indeed, he was linked by marriage to the Hutchinson family. His relation to Cotton at the time is not known; but, given their physical proximity, their common link to the Hutchinsons, the well-documented networking tendencies of Puritan clergy, and Cotton's renown as vicar of a large parish, holder of an advanced theological degree, and famous adjudicator of cases of conscience, Wheelwright probably was acquainted with the Boston pastor and his brand of doctrine. The inference is strengthened by the ready coupling of the two men in Massachusetts and by Wheelwright's esteem for his colleague even in later years as "a learned, judicious, holy man of God."[11]

At all events, in the mid-1630s Wheelwright was likely sounding theological notes similar to Cotton's. The evidence comes from Hanserd Knollys's account of his antinomian conversion. Reflecting about 1690 upon his long career in Puritan, antinomian, and Baptist dissent, Knollys recalled that about 1630 he was a young clergyman immersed in the pietist way. He joined with

11. John Wheelwright, *A Brief, and Plain Apology* (London, 1658), 14 (Sargent Bush, Jr., kindly allowed me to examine his copy of this rare tract). On family ties: Wheelwright was Anne Hutchinson's brother-in-law, and the link of kinship appears to have been strong. Winthrop first took note of Wheelwright shortly after his arrival as "a brother" of Anne Hutchinson's, and in her trial before the General Court Anne spoke of her decision to leave England when Cotton and "my brother Wheelwright" had ceased to preach. In a letter to Cotton in 1640, Wheelwright angrily recalled that in mid-1637 the magistrates had not allowed "my brother Samuel H[utch]inso[n]," a brother of Anne's, permission to settle in the Bay by reason of his antinomian leanings (*JJW*, 194; *AC*, 337; Wheelwright to John Cotton, June 3, 1640, in *CJC*, 317). Wheelwright and Cotton might have been acquainted at Cambridge University, since Cotton had been fellow and candidate for the Bachelor of Divinity degree at Emmanuel College during Wheelwright's years of study at Sidney, Sussex.

"gracious Christians, . . . called *Puritans*" and became "strict in performing Holy Duties" and the usual round of spiritual exercises. Angered by the Laudian campaign to enforce the ceremonies of the Prayer Book, he had resigned his benefice about 1632 and pledged never to preach again unless he received a special commission from Christ through the Spirit. Around 1633 or 1634 a direct message arrived. Not in audible voice or vision, but in "words . . . plainly . . . spoken into my . . . Understanding" the Lord "astonished" him with a personal message: "Go to Mr. Wheelwright, and he shall tell thee . . . how to glorifie God in the Ministry." At least three conversations with Wheelwright ensued, probably near or shortly after the end of his ministry at Bilby in 1633. In the first, Wheelwright bluntly named Knollys's religion a covenant of works, calling him a "legal performer of Holy Duties" numb to the ways of "Free Grace." This was a hard shock, and it persuaded Knollys that under pietist misguidance he "had sought Righteousness . . . by Works of the Law, and got[ten] . . . peace by performing duties, and rested on them." During a second visit, Wheelwright advised Knollys to "wait still upon God in Prayer [that is, avoid striving], and Christ would appear again . . . and shew me . . . how to preach." Twice more indeed the Lord spoke directly to Knollys. He imparted the desired call to resume his ministry, ordered him to preach on Romans 8:1, and even "dictated to me in my sleep, what Doctrine I should preach from that text." All of this was reported again to Wheelwright, who said, "Now my beloved Brother, . . . Christ has given you Authority . . . to preach."[12]

If Knollys's account is reliable, then well before his departure for New England the pastor of Bilby had learned—like and possibly from Cotton—to oppose the solifidian side of Reformed religion to the contractual and performative values of the pietist way; and he was at least tolerant of spiritist tendencies of the sort that Cotton sanctioned and that Anne Hutchinson, perhaps under Cotton's tutelage, is known to have developed by 1634. As with Cotton, again, Wheelwright's was not the expressly antilegal faith of a John Eaton or

12. Hanserd Knollys, *The Life and Death of . . . Mr. Hanserd Knollys . . .* (London, 1692), 4, 10–15. For the Wheelwright-Knollys encounter, see also Winship, *Making Heretics*, 45–47. In his Puritan phase, Knollys had "read and searched the Holy Scriptures, read good Books, got acquaintance with gracious Christians, then called *Puritans,* kept several days of Fasting and Prayer alone, wherein I did humble my soul for my sins, and begg'd Pardon and Grace . . . [,] grew strict in performing Holy Duties, and in Reformation of my own life, examining my self every night, confessing my Sins, and mourning for them" (4). B. R. White estimates that the revelations and visits to Wheelwright took place about 1633–1634, in *Hanserd Knollys and Radical Dissent in the Seventeenth Century* (London, 1977), 5.

John Traske. There is no evidence that at this or any later time he questioned the law's binding force upon the redeemed.[13]

If Wheelwright was already a prophet of free grace when he arrived in Massachusetts in mid-1636, we can see why from the start he mingled primarily with "his kindred" of the Hutchinson family and their circle of friends, why he kept pointedly aloof from the other clergy with the exception of Cotton, why in October some citizens whom Winthrop thought were "of the opinion of Mrs. Hutchinson" tried to arrange his appointment as a third minister in First Church, and why after the failure of that effort he was called to the ministry at Mount Wollaston, where several "ringleaders of the Hutchinson faction" (including Anne's husband) were developing farms. It is true that more than seven months were to pass before his dramatic emergence into the limelight, during which time he and his family no doubt were occupied with adjusting to life in a frontier colony. Yet, during the same period, free grace zealotry spread, and opposition grew. The failure (owing mostly to Winthrop's opposition) of Wheelwright's bid for pastoral appointment in Boston, the rounds of often sharp debate between Cotton and the other clergy, Governor Henry Vane's open espousal of suspect doctrines, the speech by the Reverend John Wilson in the General Court warning of mounting "differences and alienations" that in turn brought forth angry protests from members of First Church—these events all fell within the seven months, and Wheelwright came to share the insurgents' sense of embattlement and their increasing militance. Through most of the period his teaching of free grace appears to have been moderate in tone, but by the peak of winter he was ready to boil over. His great role in the drama was to preach a vehement Fast Day sermon before the assembled leadership on January 19, 1637. There, at length, he articulated both the dissidents' fundamental theological concern and their dangerously mutinous temper. It was a terrible mistake. It evoked the cycle of rigorous countermeasures that would stop the upheaval and effect his own expulsion from Massachusetts the following November.[14]

13. In later reflections upon the causes of his expulsion from the Bay, Wheelwright angrily denounced those who "Stigmatize me [as an] . . . Antinomian [or] Libertine" and repeatedly denounced antinomianism as a "fundamental Errour" (Wheelwright, "To the Christian Reader," in *Plain Apology*, unpag., 8, and see 6, 15, 24). William Bartholomew testified in Anne Hutchinson's civil trial, "My wife hath said that Mr. Wheelwright was not acquainted with this [spiritist] way until that she [Hutchinson] imparted it unto him" (*AC*, 343). Wheelwright emphasized the immediate teaching of the Spirit in a sermon of 1654. Winship, *Making Heretics*, 47–48.

14. *WCC*, 226 ("kindred"); *JJW*, 195 ("opinion"), 203 ("differences"); Emery Battis,

The January sermon's impact flowed as much from its threatening manner as from its theological doctrine, and officially Wheelwright was censured and banished, not for heresy, but for contributing to polarization and disorder and for additional defiant gestures before the General Court. Certainly his mood that Fast Day differed from Cotton's. Speaking to the audience at First Church minutes before Wheelwright's sermon, the teacher characteristically had urged "that it was not a fit worke for a day of Fast, to . . . provoke to contention [but] . . . to labour pacification." But the Mount Wollaston pastor was too angry to listen. Sharing little of Cotton's burden of ambiguity and caution and driven by what he later acknowledged as "distempered passions," he drew a stark line between those "oposite to the wayes of grace" (obviously including the plurality of elected officials and clergy present at the sermon) and the "little flocke" of gracious but persecuted saints, and he called the latter to "prepare for battell and come out against the[ir] enimyes."[15]

Yet, if the strategy was not Cotton's, the theological substance of the infamous sermon largely was. It set forth the common doctrinal base upon which Cotton and Wheelwright stood in their debates with the other clergy and upon which Cotton, in Wheelwright's words, "constantly stood by me, and with me" in the trial before the General Court, arguing, "Our Brother Whelewrights *Doctrine is according to God, in the Points controverted.*" And indeed that doctrine, delivered in the same church in which Cotton had preached (or was still preaching) the sermons later gathered in *A Treatise of the Covenant of Grace*, embraced the essential complaint and the primary set of remedies the teacher already had made familiar. A personal bond to Christ himself is at once the constitutive principle of Christianity and an uncondi-

---

Saints and Sectaries: Anne Hutchinson and the Antinomian Controversy in the Massachusetts Bay Colony (Chapel Hill, N.C., 1962), 123 ("ringleaders"). On kindred: Wheelwright told Cotton after 1638 that, "being but new come into the country, having but little acquaintance but with his kindred, and their friends, (who were many of them leavened this way) he spake some things, which if he had before discerned their Familism, he would not have expressed himself as he did" (*WCC*, 226). For his "strangenesse" from the clergy and refusal to "conferre" with those who "were not of his Judgement," see *AC*, 289–290. In explanation of this behavior, Wheelwright recalled during his trial in March 1636 that he had decided "not to consult with flesh and bloud, about the publishing of that truth which he had received from God" (*AC*, 290–291). On Wheelwright's moderate tone: *AC*, 265.

15. *AC*, 158 ("battell"), 163 ("flocke"), 164 ("oposite"), 291 ("fit worke"); *WP*, IV, 414 ("passions"). For Wheelwright's tendency to "state things in an impassioned, uncompromising way," see Bush, "'Revising what we have done Amisse,'" *WMQ*, 3d Ser., XLV (1988), 745, and see 747, 749.

tional gift of free grace. Justification and all the regenerative powers and benefits of religion flow from, and remain secondary to, the Deity himself and his felt "presence." Yet, as of the winter of 1636–1637, the dominant body of settlers have lapsed into an antireligion, a "covenant of works." It deranges all. Diverting attention from Christ to human deeds and gains, it multiplies hypocrites.[16]

To reverse this train of errors, Wheelwright summoned the remaining corps of Christ-centered saints into ideological battle. Their objective was obvious. Making the message resound that "the Gospell . . . doth hold forth Jesus Christ and nothing but Christ," they must reinstate the critical distinction between the Deity himself and the benefits he bestows, with particular emphasis upon the finite creatureliness of human works and their utter dependence upon him. Accordingly, they must challenge the ascendant party's addiction to signs and evidences of a good estate, make assurance the Deity's direct and unreserved gift, and strive to reshape religious praxis along quietist lines. The work will be completed, and the community reinstated in the gracious covenant, when "all is taken away from the creature, and all given to Christ."[17]

In at least two ways, Wheelwright also thrust beyond Cotton, in each case conforming more closely to English free grace radicalism. Speaking in antinomian tones, he mocked the Puritan godly and their precisianist flair. To him little less than to Eaton or Robert Towne, the spectacle of a self-consciously "wondrous holy people" pursuing a way of life "holy and . . . strict and zealous" smacked more of trust in human righteousness than of a state of passive surren-

---

16. Wheelwright, *Plain Apology*, 14; *AC*, 155 ("presence," and see 156, 169), 158 ("covenant of works," and see 161, 163, 164, 166, 167); on hypocrites: 156, 166, 169. Cotton, Wheelwright, and the other clergy: *JJW*, 194–195, 233.

17. *AC*, 160. For the creaturely emphasis, see also *AC*, 164. Signs and evidences: *AC*, 161–162. Like Cotton, Wheelwright cited hungering and thirsting for Christ and love of the brethren as signs often cited in New England (*AC*, 161, and cf. 96, 183; *TCG*, 143, 150). The Fast Day sermon's brief discussion of assurance does not invoke the Spirit's seal in Cotton's sense, but Wheelwright had affirmed and defended the seal in late 1636 if not earlier and reaffirmed it after the antinomian troubles (*AC*, 63–64; Wheelwright, *Plain Apology*, 9–10). On quietist ethics: *AC*, 160, 162–163, 166–168. In late March 1637, Peter Bulkeley reported "Mr Wheelewrights assertion," presumably in reference to the other ministers' view of human agency as a component of faith, "*that* (To beleeue) should belong to *the* Couent of workes" (Bulkeley to John Cotton, [Mar. 31, 1637], in *CJC*, 255). The quietist note stood in such obvious tension with Wheelwright's exhortations to "battle" that Wheelwright felt compelled to address the apparent contradiction (*AC*, 163). Like Cotton and most English antinomians, he also repudiated literal antilegal implications. *AC*, 168–169.

der to God's gifts and acts. Second, on this solemn Fast Day—and in remarkable accord with the roughly contemporary teaching of Tobias Crisp—he
revised Fast Day theory itself to accord with antinomian priorities. In standard
fashion, his audience had assembled to "pray to the Lord and fast and humble
themselves, [that] . . . the Lord may . . . turne away his wrath"; but Wheelwright, like Crisp, now declared their purpose mistaken. In light of its tendency to inflate the worth of human performances, even assigning them power
to curry favor with God, what is the day of humiliation in its present accepta-
tion but another ruse of the covenant of works? One of the sermon's snidest
comments was to this effect. Those most addicted to works-righteousness are
"usually given most unto fasting." Justified saints have occasion to fast, but with
purpose of self-denial and dependence on God. Precisely as Crisp argued, not
earthly punishment and relief, but the loss and recovery of the Deity's presence
is the focal issue of their fasts. Thus "the only cause of the fasting of true
beleevers" is the felt "absence of Christ," and regaining his presence is the
principal objective.[18]

More expressly than Cotton's doctrine, Wheelwright's critique of Fast Day
ritual also weakened the civic dimension of covenant theory. That theory
made a scrupulously and legally ordered life not merely a condition and fruit of
the gracious compact but also a means to sustain the Lord's favor toward the
larger community and to avoid or deflect his wrath. But such were not Wheelwright's emphases now. He upheld a sense of corporate Protestant purpose;
and, to head off charges that "we are . . . Antinomians," he urged freely graced
saints to public as well as private duties, but his larger tendency was to shrink
the importance of temporal and corporate issues. He demeaned behavior as
creaturely, undercut activist impulses, and reduced Deuteronomic incentives
to cleanse and unify the larger society. In January 1637 his words captured the
mood of riled sectarians in severe tension with the ruling authorities.[19]

With the above formulations, Wheelwright struck deeper than Cotton
both in doctrine and manner and drew a step closer to English antinomian

18. *AC*, 154, 157, 164, 169. Wheelwright did not invoke Deuteronomic curses upon New
England in case the antinomian message was rejected. He also noted that the Pharisees in
the Gospel of Mark "fast often" but "the Disciples of Christ fast not" (*AC*, 154). Human
inputs of prayer, fasting, and self-humiliation, all of which hypocrites can feign, are of
value only as quietist, receptive means of "turning to the Lord" (*AC*, 157, 169, and see 154–
156). For Crisp's near-identical doctrine, see *CA*, I, 270–282.

19. *AC*, 168–169. The issues are analyzed in Amy Schrager Lang, *Prophetic Woman:
Anne Hutchinson and the Problem of Dissent in the Literature of New England* (Berkeley,
Calif., 1987), 31–35.

principles. There was little to choose, for example, between his critique of fasts and Tobias Crisp's assault on the Puritan "miscarriage after so many fasting daies." Yet the difference with Cotton was more in degree than principle. So far as is known, Cotton did not outright define the activist godly as persecuting enemies of grace, censure their going theory of Fast Days, or reduce so evidently their civic commitments; but such moves were plausible advances along the path he had blazed. Although there is no evidence of his immediate reaction to the infamous sermon, it is clear from his support of Wheelwright after January 19 and indeed long after his banishment that he ever considered the Mount Wollaston pastor sound in essentials.[20]

Anne Hutchinson

The same cannot be said of Anne Hutchinson. By the time of her church trial in March 1638, Cotton had come to see her as a heretic and liar. That judgment, however, was late in coming. At some risk to himself, he cautiously had favored Hutchinson through most of the controversy and tried to defend her during the trial before the General Court the preceding November. This in turn was based upon belief that her teachings in the main echoed and reinforced his own. Shortly after her arrival late in 1634, he had been pleased to learn that Hutchinson, an active midwife, was giving expectant mothers not only physical assistance but a virtual short course in Cottonian theology. Following Cotton's footsteps, she not only administered comfort to those already troubled but began with a deliberate effort to provoke insecurity. The aim was to persuade her patients, "and by them their husbands," that their present religious course with its heavy reliance upon personal graces, legal duties, and spiritual exercises was a damning covenant of works. This left them "shaken and humbled" and ripe for Hutchinson's—and Cotton's—deeper message of a free covenant of grace and utter reliance upon the Deity. Such teaching, Cotton appreciated, "suited with [my] public ministry," and he long supposed that the weekly meetings in the Hutchinson home, whose announced design was to review his lectures, did likewise. In all this he was encouraged too by Hutchinson's repeated claim that she "was of Mr. Cottons judgment in all things."[21]

20. In 1640 Cotton wrote to Wheelwright that he approved the sermon's doctrine but not its belligerent "application." Bush, "'Revising what we have done amisse,'" *WMQ*, 3d Ser., XLV (1988), 739.

21. *WCC*, 238, 239. Cotton marked the synod of 1637 (August 30–September 22) as "the

Strictly speaking, this claim was false. It masked differences in emphasis and doctrine that were deeper than Wheelwright's and that, as Cotton himself later came to understand, in part predated her disclosure of manifestly heterodox ideas in the months after her civil trial and conviction. Yet it was faithful to a broader truth and one central to the whole insurgency: from first to last, even through her late heretical spree, Hutchinson's views held anchor in Cotton's special revision of the pietist way. The surviving record of those views is largely indirect and from hostile sources, but the drift of her thought together with several of her specific doctrines can be traced with fair confidence. They are devoid of reference to Luther or to any previous antinomian source but savor strongly of Cotton's distinctive interests. In sweeping reaction against her Puritan and pietist father's faith, she reportedly invoked both Cotton's language of "qualifications" and his theory of finespun hypocrisy to debase the esteemed good works of Congregational saints.[22]

When, sometime in 1637, Giles Firmin and others at supper in the Hutchinson residence questioned a claim that Cotton allowed no difference between "the Graces wrought in a child of God and what was wrought in a Hypocrite," Hutchinson retorted, "Yes . . . , he hath delivered something like it." And, she asked provocatively, "[Does] anybody say there is?" She also was preoccupied with the question of assurance, rejected biblical law as a rule for Christian living, and took a pronouncedly quietist approach to faith and sanctification. She decried the heavy Puritan traffic in signs and evidences, repudiating in particular (with Traske and Wheelwright) the "love [of the] brethren" that Cotton himself in England had affirmed and that long had been a standard

---

first time of my discerning a real . . . difference, between the judgments of our brethren (who leaned to Mrs. Hutchinson) and myself" (*WCC*, 235). The extent to which Hutchinson and her disciples claimed Cotton's direct authority for their teaching is uncertain, but see also *WCC*, 225; *AC*, 62, 207, 269–270, 309, 319–322; *JWWP*, 125; *JJW*, 245. Winthrop spoke acidly of Hutchinson's "method . . . to bring the conscience under a false terror" by demeaning the value of graces. *AC*, 309, and see 263, 305.

22. The transcript of the second session of Hutchinson's church trial incorporates two brief sets of answers to heresy charges that she reportedly "delivered . . . in writing" (*AC*, 305, and, for the answers, 375–376). They provide the sole direct evidence of her opinion. The remaining evidence consists of the statements attributed to her in the transcripts of the civil and church trials and a variety of characterizations by Winthrop, Cotton, Edward Johnson, and other hostile observers. The only other extant writing from Hutchinson is part of a letter written in early 1643 to John Leverett. S[amuel] G[roome], *A Glass for the People of New-England* . . . (n.p., 1676), 10. Qualifications: *AC*, 309. Hypocrisy: *JJW*, 193. Marbury's pietist credentials: above, Chapter 11, n. 22.

sign and a key tenet and the cement of the godly subculture. Less equivocally than Cotton, she revealed the affinity between a stress on the divine immediacy and spiritist tendencies long manifest on the Protestant radical left. She urged an intimate bond with Christ and with the very "person" of the Holy Spirit and linked this in turn to an expanded concept of the Spirit's seal of certitude. In a thrust beyond most earlier antinomian theorists but in accord with the affirmation of *"Prophetical spirits"* in Cotton's old Boston sermons on *Christ the Fountaine,* she claimed to be authoritatively oracular in the power of the Spirit.[23]

Sentenced to banishment for sedition and heresy by the General Court, Hutchinson spent the winter of 1637–1638 under house arrest in Roxbury. This was a loose arrest with visitation privileges, and to the members of her family and others who came to see her she divulged a variety of yet more radical ideas. Some had come to her mind during the long months of confinement, and others might have been adopted earlier, at least in embryo, and held in secret. They circulated rapidly among a few of her followers, sparking fresh controversy. In early 1638, the ministers (now including Cotton) and some of the orthodox laity gathered and documented a list of twenty-nine "new sprung errours." When it was forwarded to First Church, it became the occasion for the first major trial for heresy in American history.[24]

23. Firmin, *Brief Review,* sig. A2; *AC,* 322; *JJW,* 193 ("person," and see *AC,* 263); *CF,* 62. On assurance and evidences: *AC,* 263, 309, 322–323, 376. Cf. J. F. Maclear's view that, "unlike many Puritans, [Hutchinson] was apparently untroubled by the problem of 'assurance,'" in "Anne Hutchinson and the Mortalist Heresy," *NEQ,* LIV (1981), 100. Quietism: *JJW,* 193; *AC,* 264, 302. Love of the brethren: *EGJ,* 329, 331–334; *GV,* 48–49; *AC,* 161 (Wheelwright), 324 (Hutchinson). Law: *AC,* 302, nos. 13, 19, 23. Relation to deity: *JJW,* 193; *AC,* 263, 302–303, 358. The seal: *AC,* 263, 269–271, 321–324, 333–335, 346–347, 376. Spiritism: *WCC,* 240; *AC,* 264, 268, 272–273, 336–339; *JWWP,* 134.

24. *AC,* 301. The list of errors is in *AC,* 301–303 (cf. 351–352, 374–375; *JJW,* 245–246). Hutchinson testified, *"I did not hould any of thease Thinges before my Imprisonment,"* and Battis, Maclear, and Gura agree that the most radical of the new ideas were the product of Anne's "winter of forced idleness" in Roxbury (*AC,* 372, and see 303, 376–377; Battis, *Saints and Sectaries,* 233–234; Maclear, "Anne Hutchinson and the Mortalist Heresy," *NEQ,* LIV [1981], 96–97; Gura, *A Glimpse of Sion's Glory,* 261). Yet the lists of errors alleged against Anne at the church trial include others—as that "union to Christ is not by faith," or that "Sanctification can be no Evidence of a good Estate"—that Anne almost certainly had espoused earlier, possibly in a softer form (*AC,* 302, 352). In a letter of 1640 Cotton told Wheelwright that the more forward sectaries "had run a course of haeresie a long tyme . . . before" John Wilson's controversial speech before the General Court in December 1636, and in 1641 or 1642 he recalled that in his first discussions with her he had found her

Since First Church had been the very seat of the free grace insurgency, this was a startling development. But now a majority of its members, men and women alike, were forced to wonder whether their admired prophetess had pursued her oracular arts recklessly far beyond the orthodox pale, and they must have been shaken when Hutchinson at the start of the trial confessed that she had held and uttered all of the new-sprung tenets and then strove to defend those upon which the church's officers chose to focus the interrogation. However sharply she had challenged Puritan tradition hitherto, she had made no open break with its fundamental dogmas. By and large she had confined her witness to a set of themes that Cotton to some extent had legitimized by his uncommon authority and his teacher's office within the congregational scheme and that Vane and Wheelwright had seconded. Collectively, however, the twenty-nine new opinions swerved audaciously far from Puritan and Reformed standards.[25]

The view, for example, that "we are united to Christ with the same union, that his humanity on earth was with the Deity" (which echoes a reported teaching of Peter Shaw about 1630) or that "sanctification can be no evidence at all of our good estate" went much too far to win Cotton's, or even Wheelwright's, assent. Another opinion deemed Hutchinson's "revelations about future events . . . as infallible as any part of Scripture," and four opinions embraced the literally antinomian conviction that "the Law is no rule of life to a Christian." Others moved wholly outside the mainstream Protestant world, denying both immortality of the soul and bodily resurrection. Not even in his least cautious moments had the Boston teacher knowingly intimated such views. On questions of the body and soul, immortality and resurrection, he remained unquestioningly orthodox. He affirmed biblical law as the rule of Christian life and tied his allowance of personal revelation to the sacred text. Accordingly, during Hutchinson's trial before First Church, he took the leading role in the inquiry into her "groce and fundamentall Errors" and pronounced the official censure.[26]

However thin the evidence of actual connections, any and all of Hutchin-

---

dangerously given to "private meditations, or revelations only" rather than the "public ministry" and "that she clearly discerned her justification . . . but little or nothing at all, her sanctification" (Bush, " 'Revising what we have done amisse,' " *WMQ*, 3d Ser., XLV [1988], 739; *WCC*, 240–241). In *AC*, 301, Winthrop reported an acknowledgment by certain lay elders of First Church that Hutchinson had divulged some of her radical views to them.

25. Hutchinson's confession is in *AC*, 303.

26. *AC*, 301–303, nos. 1–5 (mortality, resurrection), 10 ("united to Christ"), 13 ("no rule," and see nos. 19, 23, 25), 26 ("no evidence"), 27 ("future events"); *AC*, 377.

son's errors might have included borrowings from antinomian, Familist, and other persuasions of the Protestant far left in covert circulation in old and New England, including those of the mysterious "woman of Elis" whom she cited in the church trial. But, if so, what was borrowed did not stand alone or unaltered, for Hutchinson and her followers braided all into a distinctive synthesis for which Cotton had laid much of the groundwork. Clearly, the presumed fit of the upstart ideas with his was an indispensable feature of their appeal, possibly the more so since prevailing rules of gender placed limits upon Hutchinson's effective leadership; and, in fact, every one of the errors was linked logically back to Cotton. The thesis that sanctification cannot attest a justified estate, for instance, reflects a long-familiar conviction of free grace radicalism, but it also connects to Cotton's downgrading of sanctification and the associated attack upon signs and evidences. Likewise, the denial of a regulative function to the law extends his critique of the Puritan fixation upon duties and covenant conditions and his reduction of emphasis upon Christ as lawgiver.[27]

Hutchinson's reconstruals of the soul, body, and resurrection stand in a class

27. *AC,* 380 and n. 18. During her voyage to Massachusetts in 1634, Hutchinson divulged opinions that Zechariah Symmes and others on board found dangerous and reported to the authorities upon arrival; Winthrop agreed that she had "learned her skil in England" (*AC,* 201, 263, 317, 322). For possible radical sources, see *FEW,* 164–169, 233 n. 13. "Elis" probably refers to the Isle of Ely, a known Familist center; the woman of Ely might have been Elizabeth Bancroft (Christopher W. Marsh, *The Family of Love in English Society, 1550–1630* [Cambridge, 1994], 214–218; Gura, *A Glimpse of Sion's Glory,* 242). Anne might have learned too of Anne Fenwick, known from the early 1620s for her "effusive . . . outpourings of the spirit," or of Eleanor Davies or Jane Hawkins, notorious visionaries of the later 1620s; see David R. Como, "Women, Prophecy, and Authority in Early Stuart Puritanism," *Huntington Library Quarterly,* LXI (1999), 207, 222; David D. Hall, *Worlds of Wonder, Days of Judgment: Popular Religious Belief in Early New England* (New York, 1989), 96–97. Such figures "set the stage for other Puritan women by helping to forget a social . . . type—the godly female prophet—that had not previously existed in a coherent form" (Como, "Women, Prophecy, and Authority," 222). Claims that they define an already prominent "mystical" pattern in Puritan religion, or even a "well-developed tradition of female mysticism," rest partly upon Geoffrey F. Nuttall, *The Holy Spirit in Puritan Faith and Experience* (Chicago, 1992), and his tendency to read mid-seventeenth-century emphases back into earlier decades and his untenable arguments that "the centre of reference in Puritan piety was the Holy Spirit," that intellectual illumination was the Spirit's primary function in this context, and that Puritanism accordingly *was* "a movement towards [spiritist] immediacy" (91–92, 145). See James Fulton Maclear, "'The Heart of New England Rent': The Mystical Element in Early Puritan History," *Mississippi Valley Historical Review,* XLII (1955–1956), 621–652; Marilyn J. Westerkamp, "Anne Hutchinson, Sectarian Mysticism, and the Puritan Order," *CH,* LIX (1990), 491–492 (quote at 484).

by themselves. At once the most exotic of the new views and the most flagrantly at odds with Reformed dogma, they may appear entirely alien to Cotton's outlook; and he himself roundly condemned them, finding the denial of the Resurrection, a known Familist belief, sufficient in itself "to rase the very foundation of Religion to the Ground." Yet even at this extreme the Cottonian imprint remained, and to understand it we must revisit the Boston teacher's characteristic belittling of the "creaturely." William K. B. Stoever first drew attention to this theme in the Antinomian Controversy. By the early seventeenth century, he argued, Puritan theology had established a working relationship between nature and grace in which the essential goodness and utility of the created order was affirmed. Puritans honored that relationship when they found beauty in the New World landscape, or promoted "the instrumentality of created things" (like the ordinance of preaching or the human faculties of understanding and choice) for bringing persons into a state of grace and transforming their lives. It was just this positive estimate of the creaturely that the American insurgents challenged, and so the theological arguments of 1636–1638 came to turn upon differing views of the relation of God to his finite creations. Was that relation a dialectic, or an antithesis? Does, as the Reformed held, the Deity in his works of redemption employ means that belong to the created order? Or, as Cotton and the American antinomians held, does he act directly and without regard for created instrumentalities? The central polarity of the controversy, Stoever contended, therefore lay "between created being as such and the increated being of the Trinity."[28]

Applied to Cotton, this approach quickly proves its worth. To exalt the divine and devalue the created: this emergent strategy of his later English years did become in Massachusetts the core of his revisionist program, and all of the doctrinal shifts discussed earlier (Chapters 12, 13) were variations upon it. Nevertheless, in his lexicon the created and the increated had a narrower meaning than Stoever's language suggests. Worldly being as such was not in question in 1636–1638. There were no arguments about the created order per se and certainly not about the goodness or beauty of the New England landscape. What Cotton wished to discredit was, not the creation at large, but the inherited Puritan plan of duties and performances. First at issue was the

---

28. *AC*, 371; *FEW*, 5, 171. In a letter written shortly after the church trial, Cotton denounced "the iniquity of sundry members of our church [who] secretly disseminated such . . . dangerous Opinions, as (like a gangrene) would have corrupted and destroyed Faith and Religion." Cotton to Samuel Stone, Mar. 27, 1638, Ms. Am., 1506, pt. 2, no. 12, Boston Public Library (published in *CJC*, 273–274).

worth, not of being, but of doing, of the pietist absorption in human actions and the accompanying prideful sense of accomplishment and desert: that is what he stigmatized as creaturely. When he deplored the settlers' tendency to find value in "something that is in themselves," he had human acts and active qualities first in mind, and certainly "the fundamental Puritan conviction that one must always be active, forever striving." When he denied all self-subsistence to Christian motives and works, construing all as direct and utterly contingent acts of the Spirit, or when he claimed that infused virtues are mere created blessings, it was not so much human being as human capacity that he wished to devalue. The wrong was to see in men and women an ability apart from the divine concursus to do good and dissolve doubt. Conversely, when he refocused attention upon the divine and increated, the primary object was, not the majestic existence of the Trinity or its "sovereign freedom and . . . purity," but its activity: its dynamic, immediate, and ceaseless operation upon and within human beings.[29]

Decrial of the creaturely was blunter and more extreme among the Hutchinsonians, but Cotton's concern and emphasis were preserved. When Wheelwright declared in his Fast Day sermon that Christ's entry into the soul "maketh the creature nothing," he had in mind, not the very being of the self, but its pretense to autonomous and self-disciplining power. A few of the eighty-two heterodox opinions formulated by the synod of 1637 used stronger language yet. The first, for instance, that "in the conversion of a sinner, . . . the faculties of the soule, and workings thereof, . . . are destroyed," and the thirty-fifth, that "the efficacy of Christs death is to kill all activity of graces in his members, that he might act all in all," strained toward outright obliteration of the self; yet they stopped short. Again, it was, not the being and structure of the self per se, but its active propensity that such views contested. With this in mind, we better can understand and appreciate the shock value of Hutchinson's heretical disclosures at her ecclesiastical trial.[30]

During her confinement at Roxbury, daunted by the rout of her party and her own disgrace and imminent expulsion but with unbroken confidence in her cause, Hutchinson turned again to sacred writ. To her the sacred oracles now spoke fresh messages. Apparently from her own study of select texts in

29. John R. Knott, Jr., *The Sword of the Spirit: Puritan Responses to the Bible* (Chicago, 1980), 12; *TCG*, 150; *FEW*, 11.

30. *AC*, 164, 219, 228. Winthrop regarded "debasing the creature" as a primary aim of the insurgency (*JJW*, 248). The roster of eighty-two opinions was a catchall of reports and rumors. It is not possible to judge their accuracy or to know how many actually were espoused by members of the Hutchinsonian faction. See *JJW*, 232–233.

Ecclesiastes, Luke, John, Romans, and First Corinthians, she drew a coherent set of conclusions. Possibly original in the ensemble, they were certainly unorthodox: the human soul and body are mortal and die forever; resurrection and immortality are reserved to a wholly new "spirit" and body bestowed upon those in union with Christ. Measured by the trend of American free grace theory through most of 1637, these judgments were inordinate. No mere variations upon familiar themes of free grace and the seal, they crossed a theological Rubicon. Cutting ties to dogma inherited from patristic antiquity and affirmed by mainline Protestants and Catholics alike, they mark the moment in the Antinomian Controversy at which the concern became ontological. Now created being itself was negated, with all human instrumentalities expunged outright. Denied even a role as inert media, the natural endowments of human beings per se now were deemed ultimately alien to the Christian redemption. Only the self reconstituted in soul and body, with its whole "naturall Life" sloughed away and given immortal replacement, can rise to eternal bliss.[31]

Yet even here the teacher's original presence was felt, for in one central sense Hutchinson's insights climaxed the revisionist activity he had initiated. By late 1637 she and a few of her followers had moved far beyond him, but it was in part the momentum of *his* drive to deglamorize effort and performance that bore them forward. All of the doctrinal hyperboles that the critique of behavior had generated by late 1637, even the appeals to destroyed faculties and deadened graces, were logical steps down the same path. Yet the path had not led to victory. Gradually, orthodox countermeasures had worn the movement down. Vane had departed, and William Coddington and John Coggeshall were preparing to move to Rhode Island. Wheelwright, William Aspinwall, and finally Hutchinson herself had been been convicted and banished. Painfully aware of her outward defeat and under continuing challenge by Thomas Shepard, John Eliot, and perhaps other members of the clergy who visited her winter confine, she still refused to desist. If the attack upon behavior had not brought the desired effect, perhaps the answer was to broaden the critique, to brand human being itself with the stigma of creatureliness and final nullity.

Possibly, additional influences from the radical left also came into play at this time. Hutchinson might have had knowledge of the mortalist heresy and

31. *AC*, 354, 355. Hutchinson also might have spiritualized the resurrection of believers as a symbol of union with Christ, but her exact view is unclear; see *AC*, 301, no. 5, 351, no. 4, and see also 358, 361, 362–363; and Maclear, "Mortalist Heresy," *NEQ*, XLIV (1981), 87–91. In defense of her beliefs in the church trial, she cited at least ten biblical proof texts. *AC*, 354–361.

the unconventional construals of resurrection long familiar to Familist and other fringe circles in the parent country, or with the belief of John Traske and a few other radicals in "two 'souls'" within the Christian self, one continuing a fleshly and "material" life while the other lives justified and deathless in God's eyes. Under pressure at Roxbury, she might have found such ideas increasingly plausible. Yet, even if this were so, their plausibility owed something to Cotton, whose disciple she still claimed to be. To cancel the saving instrumentality of the created soul and body and to replace them with miraculously given and unearthly equivalents had a recognizably Cottonian objective. Partly, at least, it proceeded from his impulse to make more of God and less of humankind and his special disdain for the creaturely. And, when we recall that "creaturely" in his vocabulary referred primarily to works and graces, signs and evidences, and note that a majority of Hutchinson's twenty-nine opinions continued avidly to devalue them all, we may infer that the negation of body and soul was directed to the same end. For what were they but the constitutive elements of the striving self? And what was it to efface and supplant them but to remove the foundation of human striving and create de novo the resigned, other-directed personality espoused in antinomian philosophy—the self deactivated, the one who draws all being and good from beyond, the one whose acts are performed by Christ, the one who no longer had reason to struggle, to mourn, or to aspire toward personal likeness to the divine?[32]

Cotton might have resented the imputation, but Hutchinson thus spoke with some truth when she claimed fidelity to his teaching. At the same time, she was what Winthrop by 1638 considered her to be: the most potent spirit of the American antinomian movement. Bringing to bear prophetic insight and

---

32. *FEW*, 141, 142; *GV*, 21–23. In his illuminating account of the issue in "Mortalist Heresy," *NEQ*, XLIV (1981), 94–95, 103, Maclear connects Hutchinson's mortalism to her repudiation of "all creaturely preparation or helps" and "utter dependence on God's gracious acts." For mortalism, see also Christopher Hill, "Irreligion in the 'Puritan' Revolution," in J. F. McGregor and B. Reay, eds., *Radical Religion in the English Revolution* (Oxford, 1984), 201–202. Peter Shaw in 1619 was also accused of teaching that "the soule of man is mortall" ("PS," 707). Giles Firmin reported an encounter with an "Antinomian family" in England before 1637 who taught that, "as dyeth the Beast, so dyeth Man, denying a Future State" (*Brief Review*, sig. A). On resurrection: Marsh, *Family of Love*, 20–24. Hutchinson could have become familiar with such doctrines from reading Luther, Tyndale, or Calvin, from contact with Familist sources, or from the high-profile cases of Edward Wightman, Peter Shaw, and others in the early Stuart era. Maclear, "Mortalist Heresy," 92–93; "PS," 707; and see "PH," 270–272.

perhaps ideas from the Protestant far left, she made Cotton's teaching radically suggestive. In it she found deeper, nervier implications than he. Her version of free grace would make New England as much a refuge from the practice of piety as from Catholicizing trends and Laudian tyranny in the Church of England. Indeed, it would found in the New World an outpost of the Radical Reformation. Yet it remained in some degree a branch from Cotton's stock. Even through the winter and early spring of 1637–1638, she remained the Boston teacher's loyal as well as deviant disciple.

CHAPTER 15

THE CONSTRUCTION
OF AMERICAN
ANTINOMIANISM

T he beliefs of John Wheelwright and Anne Hutchinson can be reconstructed in some measure, but much remains obscure. Did, for example, Wheelwright approve of or tolerate his sister-in-law's spiritist tendencies? His encounter with Hanserd Knollys earlier in the decade, at about the time of his entry by marriage into the Hutchinson family, suggests that he would have been so inclined. Yet his Fast Day sermon of 1637, focused upon what he saw as the crucial points then at issue, offers no encouragement or sanction for personal revelations beyond the seal, and in later years he stiffly denied that he ever had favored "enthusiasm" or "Familism."[1]

On this point and many others, evidence is sparse, incomplete, and sometimes contradictory; and the difficulties multiply when we turn to lesser-known figures. We know, for example, that Sir Henry Vane, John Underhill, William Aspinwall, and John Coggeshall agreed passionately with Wheelwright's Fast Day sermon and that the latter two leaned—ambivalently, according to Cotton—toward the most radical current opinions on passive faith, inherent righteousness, evidencing a good estate, and the like. Supporting Cotton in late 1636, Vane reportedly also denied any evidential role to sanctification unaccompanied by a "concurrent sight of . . . justification" but went beyond Cotton's doctrine of union with the Deity to maintain "a personal union with the Holy

---

1. For his denial, see John Wheelwright, *A Brief, and Plain Apology* (London, 1658), 6, 11, 15, 24–25; see also *WCC*, 226; and above, Chapter 14, n. 13. In context of its anticreaturely stand, the Fast Day sermon did espouse the immediacy of relationship to the Deity promoted by English antinomian theorists, Cotton, and Hutchinson but did not press the issue in a spiritist direction. In *Plain Apology*, 8–9, Wheelwright denied complicity with the quietist belief, that "Christ did . . . perform for us . . . the law, repenting, and believing for us," as a "fundamental Errour of the *Antinomians*" and insisted that he had always believed "Sanctification to be a good evidence" of a safe estate. These disclaimers reflect alarm at the surge of radical views in midcentury England.

Ghost." He might also have denied that justification entailed a human act of faith. Henry Bull of Roxbury was excommunicated in early 1638 for maintaining that "faith is no condition of the covenant of Grace," that faith follows justification, and that there is "no Inherent Righteousnesse in a believer."[2]

William Coddington also defended Wheelwright, identified "the way of s[alv]ation and Evidenceing therof" as the essence of his concern at the time, and agreed with Hutchinson that the New England clergy "were in the [unsealed] state of the apostles before the ascension." Stephen Greensmith shared Hutchinson's view that all the ministers save Cotton and Wheelwright taught a covenant of works. Mary Dyer apparently was "much addicted to revelations," and her husband, William, openly maintained that "Christ and the Church together, are the new creature, there is no inherent righteousnesse in Christians, *Adam* was not made after Gods Image, etc." In mid-1636 Edward Johnson encountered an unidentified woman who endorsed Hutchinson's revelations and her promise of full assurance, scorned "legall Professors," and claimed that Christ had abolished the law. The following year one of Wheelwright's admirers affirmed immediate revelations without reference to Scripture, depicted the new creature as "a dead lump" void of inherent righteousness and "not acting at all, but as Christ acts in him," disavowed the Decalogue, and spurned the use of all rituals, including baptism.[3]

2. *JJW*, 200, 204 (and see above, Chapter 14, n. 5); Thomas Weld and John Eliot, "The Causes of Hen. Bull[']s Excommunication . . . ," in "Transcriptions by Edward Holden of documents in the Prince Library, Boston Public Library," 85, in Cotton Family Papers, MHS. On Aspinwall and Coggeshall in defense of Wheelwright: *AC*, 257–261. For their radical opinions, see *WCC*, 234–235; Sargent Bush, " 'Revising what we have done amisse': John Cotton and John Wheelwright, 1640," *WMQ*, 3d Ser., XLV (1988), 738; *AC*, 259. On Underhill: *JJW*, 262–263. He claimed to have received an instantaneous gift of assurance while smoking a pipe, but this appears to have occurred before his immigration (*JJW*, 263). He might have seduced one or more women in Boston by playing upon antinomian concerns to relieve "trouble of mind" and to "knock [people] off from their owne Righteousnesse." *JJW*, 264; Richard D. Pierce, ed., *The Records of the First Church in Boston, 1630–1868*, Colonial Society of Massachusetts *Publications*, XXXIX, *Collections* (1961), 28.

3. *WP*, IV, 278; *AC*, 345, and see 347; *JJW*, 253 (Anne Dyer); *AC*, 278 ("lump), 282 (William Dyer); *JWWP*, 134 ("Professors"). Winthrop described the Dyers as "of the highest forme of our refined Familists," and Giles Firmin recalled in later years that "Mr Dyer . . . *would have* Christ to be the new Creature, and would prove it from the Greek Text, 2 Cor. 5:17," rendering it as "if any man be in Christ, the New Creature" (*AC*, 281; Firmin, *A Brief Review of Mr Davi[e]s's Vindication* . . . [London, 1693], sig. A). For a possible link between William Dyer and Peter Shaw, see above, Chapter 10, n. 1. On Greensmith: *JJW*, 228.

As limited and possibly inaccurate as these sketches are, they represent the bulk of our knowledge of individual antinomian belief apart from Cotton, Wheelwright, and Hutchinson. They belong clearly enough to the family of ideas sprung from pietist discontents canvassed thus far. However, as with Hutchinson and Wheelwright in some degree, in no case can they be more than fragmentary reports of their authors' overall outlook. Barring new and significant archival discoveries, our knowledge of the movement's theology will remain both vaguely general and patchy. We cannot know, for instance, to what extent it presented a united doctrinal front or what variations might have sprung from separate antinomian conventicles at Roxbury, Charlestown, Salem, or other places, how individual convictions changed over time, whether figures like Wheelwright, Vane, and John Underhill fairly may be called Hutchinson's followers, what if any differences the rank and file perceived between Cotton's and Hutchinson's tenets, or what fraction of Hutchinson's following shared her late turn into blatant heterodoxy, and so on.

That brings us to even more troubling features of the accounts. Inflamed feelings and warped perceptions were routine in theological disputes in the period, but by March 1637, spurred on by attendant political disruptions and by war with the Pequots, the emotional temperature in the Bay had risen so high as to resemble the volcanic Arminian controversy in the Dutch Netherlands during the first two decades of the century. Upon his arrival in Boston at the height of the struggle, Giles Firmin "was told, the Heat, the Animosities were so high, that [men] were ready to lay Hands on their Swords." "We were in a heate, and Chafed," a member of the free grace party recalled in later years, as did Wheelwright in an apology for "mine own distempered passions" in 1637 and for the "sharp and vehement contentions" for which he was partially responsible.[4]

Under such conditions, prejudice deepened. When, late in 1636, members of the Boston congregation examined a list of fifteen erroneous tenets charged against them by a committee of the Newtown church, they found it a malicious falsification, and Wheelwright's opinions clearly were distorted in an extant list of errors that the ministers devised in secret and submitted to the General Court to aid his prosecution in 1637. In a few cases, when the more

4. Firmin, *Brief Review*, sig. A; *WP*, IV, 278, 414, and see 209. Winthrop reported "danger of a tumult" at the day of the court of elections at Newtown in May 1637, when some of the free grace party made "fierce speeches, and . . . laid hands on others" (*JJW*, 215). In her church trial, Anne Hutchinson apologized for "Censuringe the Cuntrie" in her civil trial, confessing, "I did it rashly and out of heate of Spirit." *AC*, 376.

forward insurgents were brought into ordeals of interrogation and debate, they were pushed into hyperbolic claims beyond their normal intent, and these in turn colored the authorities' accounts of antinomian and Familist heresy. Wheelwright himself had firsthand knowledge of such a process, reflecting later and ruefully that "in [the] heat of Discourse" during the synod of 1637 "certain [exaggerated] expressions fell from me" that were then "numbred amongst my Errors, and made the chief matter of Dispute by them who took all occasions . . . to make me seem erroneous." Likewise, the transcripts of the civil actions against Wheelwright, Hutchinson, and others and of the examination of Hutchinson before First Church reflect the authorities' stern biases and inquisitorial aims.[5]

Productive Opposition Restored

As the slanted indictments in Wheelwright's Fast Day sermon show, anger warped perception on both sides of the controversy; but, since the victors framed most of the durable record, their representations have weighed the most. Any inventory of them must include scattered commentary in works prepared during and after the events of 1636–1638 by Thomas Hooker, Peter Bulkeley, Richard Mather, and others. But John Winthrop, Thomas Weld, Thomas Shepard, and Edward Johnson prepared fuller, more direct and connected interpretations; and the debate at the synod of 1637 (with its eighty-two errors and nine "unsavoury speeches," each with an official refutation) also supplies a broad overview of what the orthodox made of the insurgents' teaching. It is primarily those five sources that inform the following analysis.[6]

---

5. Wheelwright, *Plain Apology*, 23. The Newtown list is not extant, but First Church's response is in *WP*, III, 324–326. Wheelwright preserved and later published an outline and partial summary of the ministers' compilation, which was titled "The Grounds and Reasons of the Dissent of the Elders . . . , from some things delivered by Mr. Whelewright upon the Fast-day" (*Plain Apology*, 7). Hutchinson's admission of immediate revelations at her civil trial and the extreme doctrinal stands taken by William Dyer in his disciplinary hearing before First Church may reflect a similar process. For Dyer, see above, n. 3. The trial transcripts are published in *AC*, 311–348, 349–388.

6. Scattered comments are found in Thomas Hooker's American magnum opus, published as *The Application of Redemption . . . The First Eight Books* (London, 1656), and *The Application of Redemption . . . The Ninth and Tenth Books* (London, 1657); Hooker, *A Commentarie on Christ's Last Prayer . . .* (London, 1656); Peter Bulkeley, *The Gospel-Covenant; or, The Covenant of Grace Opened* (London, 1646); Richard Mather, *The Summe of Certain Sermons upon Genesis 15:6* (Cambridge, Mass., 1652), sigs. A3–A5; and Mather,

Winthrop, the most thorough journalist of the antinomian episode, was also its greatest antagonist. In his *Journal* and in *A Short Story of the Rise, Reign, and Ruin of the Antinomians, Familists, and Libertines,* he supplied by far the most extensive account and appraisal of the events, principal personalities, and beliefs of the movement. In addition to acid commentary, the *Short Story* included an abbreviated account of Hutchinson's civil trial, which placed her in an unfavorable light, and openly associated Wheelwright with "Familisticall opinions." There Winthrop included as well the roster of errors processed by the synod, and Thomas Weld, who prepared the entire work for publication in the early 1640s, added his own interpretative synopsis, together with a sampler of twenty-nine dubious opinions.[7]

In June 1636, Thomas Shepard began a cycle of sermons at Cambridge on the parable of the ten virgins. Although it probably was no part of the original design, the project was shaped and prolonged in part by a need to counter the theological provocations that quickly emerged. Pursuing the series from June 1636 to May 1640, Shepard took occasion to review and assail free grace ideals explicitly, frequently, and in some detail. In so doing, he created a third portrait of heresy, which deserves inclusion here. Finally, writing some fifteen years after the fact, Johnson prepared a systematic but similarly acerbic account for his *Wonder-Working Providence* (1654), spicing the story with memories of personal encounters with its partisans. In each of these sources, the compilation of errors is an omnium gatherum of reports, rumors, personal recollections, statements extracted from accused persons in official proceedings, and in some cases deductions of what the offenders "really intended" and "what they *ought* to believe" in light of their expressed principles.[8]

"The Summe of Seventie Lectures upon the First Chapter of the Second Epistle of Peter," Mather Family Papers, box 1, folder 8, American Antiquarian Society, Worcester, Mass.

7. *AC,* 279; Stephen Foster, "New England and the Challenge of Heresy, 1630 to 1660: The Puritan Crisis in Transatlantic Perspective," *WMQ,* 3d Ser., XXXVIII (1981), 635. Hutchinson's civil trial: *AC,* 262–276. Roster of errors: *AC,* 219–243. Weld's synopsis and sampler: *AC,* 201–218. Dubious opinions: *AC,* 202–203.

8. Shepard's sermons: *The Parable of the Ten Virgins . . .* (London, 1660). For the dating see *WTS,* II, 8, 526. I omit Shepard's *Theses Sabbaticae . . .* (London, 1649), since its treatment of antinomian heresy blends, often indistinguishably, into a larger consideration of English antinomian, spiritist, and antiformalist doctrines of the 1640s. Shepard also drew two brief synopses of the "opinions of [the] Familists" (*GP,* 65–67; *New Englands Lamentation for Old Englands Present Errours* [London, 1645], 3–4). Johnson's account: *JWWP,* 124–131.

Since the roused passions of 1636–1638 assumed in part the form of a heresy scare, the five sources also mirror long-standing assumptions about the nature of antilegal and spiritist heresies and their theological and social consequences. Those assumptions drew upon stereotypes inherited from the long history of heresy hunting in the West. Conspiratorial secrecy, to take one example, had been linked for centuries to the type, or figure, of the heretic and was believed to be a primary trait of the English Family of Love. Since practiced guile was an established meaning of the Familist tag that quickly came into play in New England, it was natural enough for Winthrop, Weld, and Johnson to see a planned deception behind the antinomian troubles. The dissidents of John- son's account had gone with the Jesuits to "Masking schoole," and Weld told of their plot, as they moved to infect the settlers with their opinions and ultimately to capture and redefine the American congregational project, to lavish kindness upon newcomers to the colony, even offering temporary quar- ters in their homes. Thus, "having gotten them into their Web, they could easily poyson them by degrees." Slyly they injected their poison "a little at once into their followers as they were capable, . . . and then stronger and stronger potions. . . . But if any should . . . see their danger, and professe against the opinions, then [they would] retreat, and say, Nay, mistake me not, for I doe meane even as you doe, . . . and [we] differ only in words." And when the doctrinal potions seemed to savor of historic spiritist, libertine, and antino- mian errors, Winthrop, Weld, Johnson, and delegates to the synod of 1637 could frame the new doctrine in eminently useful ways. Perhaps, above all, they could negate the possibility that it expressed fair grievances against the pietist way. Able neither to credit nor easily refute the Familist program, they could deflate it as a mix of heresies imported from afar, guileful, contagious, and rife with danger to church and state.[9]

9. *JWWP,* 122; *AC,* 204 ("Web"), 206–207 (poison). For the established resonances of Familist, libertine, and spiritist doctrines with an accompanying tendency to dwell upon the antisocial consequences of heresy, see Foster, "Challenge of Heresy," *WMQ,* 3d Ser., XXXVIII (1981), 631–632, 635–637, 643, 647–648, 650–651. On lying: Weld outlined an elaborate plan of deception, which included flagrant lying (*AC,* 204–209; and see *JJW,* 244). Cotton came to believe that Hutchinson deliberately had deceived him and that the sectaries' appeal to his authority had been deceitful (*WCC,* 225, 238, 286–287; Cotton, *A Reply to Mr. Wiiliams* . . . [1645], ed. J. Lewis Diman, in *The Complete Writings of Roger Williams,* II [New York, 1963], 80). He also reported possession of a letter from one of the radicals advising the others to "keepe such opinions private to themselves" and their friends, but when in public and "before . . . witnesses to hold forth noe [m]ore tha]n their

From the orthodox standpoint, this was a highly gainful move. The charge of ideological treason is a proven means by which groups in times of conflict collectively highlight norms and remind their members of who does and who does not belong. To Winthrop and his orthodox colleagues, the brush with heresy gave a valuable object lesson both in the havoc wrought by heterodoxy and in its inevitable fall and ruin. But, most important, a tussle with heresy offered a capital opportunity to reinforce the congregational and pietist venture by profiling it against a fresh opposite.

As we have seen, a well-practiced pose of embattlement had become a Puritan marker long before the Great Migration. At least for the more radical spirits who rebuked sinners and strove to reform and control their communities, the inevitable friction with anti-Puritan elements had a beneficial side. It enabled them to frame their identity in antithesis, casting themselves into heroic relief, etching deeper their image of stiff and watchful rectitude, and, as a bonus, making their critics arraign themselves. In this ironic sense it was well that in the mother country the sources of conflict were many and durable. Remnants of the Catholic Antichrist were ever on hand, but the baptized membership of the Church of England embraced a host of declared enemies, including resentful parish Anglicans devoted to the official liturgy, the many opponents of moral reformation at the local level, and, since the mid-1610s, an unholy crew of antinomian Dissenters that emerged within the godly community itself. Ceremonial elements in the official orders of worship and the fabric of the churches were a source of conflict too, even more so as high church forces rose to power in the 1620s, and the enjoyments and celebrations of traditional village culture were a continuing source of friction. No other rite, not even self-inspection or fasting, had done more than the joust with opposing forces to sustain the godly's morale and identity.[10]

In the new land all of this was changed. For the most part, cost restricted

---

Teacher might goe [alon]g with *them*" (*CJC*, 303). The Eatonists' guile and evasiveness are emphasized in Stephen Denison, *The White Wolfe* . . . (London, 1627), "To the Christian Reader," unpag.; *RV*, 63–64; *LG*, sig. B3, 68.

10. I draw here upon a familiar principle of functionalist sociology well summarized in Kai T. Erikson, *Wayward Puritans: A Study in the Sociology of Deviance* (New York, 1966), 4–13, and see 79–107 for application to the Antinomian Controversy. See also Amy Schrager Lang, *Prophetic Woman: Anne Hutchinson and the Problem of Dissent in the Literature of New England* (Berkeley, Calif., 1987), 53; Philip F. Gura, *A Glimpse of Sion's Glory: Puritan Radicalism in New England, 1620–1660* (Middletown, Conn., 1984), 226–229.

the venture to men and families of at least moderate means, created a socially homogenous population, and all but eliminated the crisis of poverty and the subclasses of beggars and vagabonds that it spawned. The Puritan cast of the colonial project and the early screening measures excluded Catholics, members or agents of the Anglican hierarchy, Arminians or churchly highfliers, most enthusiasts for the Prayer Book, and the great majority of English laity indifferent or hostile to Puritan aims. The Bay Company weeded out as well most of the unreformed and disreputable and guaranteed a godly and well-behaved majority. To a large degree the colony was to effect a Puritan reformation of manners, not by force, but by simple exclusion. There were no swaggering sons of the upper classes, and few early citizens of the Bay haunted alehouses, cursed openly, or railed at the precise. So too had vanished the maypoles, rush-bearings, Christmas and Easter festivities, and numberless other rites and merriments that Puritan forces long had opposed; and drinking establishments were few and strictly supervised. When disorders did arise, they were subject to church discipline as well as to correction by a magistracy united in outlook and with broad support in the citizenry.

When Thomas Weld reported in 1632 that in the Bay colony "our ears are not beaten nor the air filled with oaths, swearers, nor railers, nor our eyes and ears vexed with the unclean conversation of the wicked," he thus recorded not merely an increase of moral regulation but a great reversal of religious and social reality. Far from the parent church, its hostile authorities and courts, the first years of settlement in the Bay colony saw once-despised godly factions transmuted into a stable ruling majority able to impose its standards upon the larger community. Once-exclusive English conventicles at odds with much of the larger culture became churches, normative and respected institutions. The subculture of the regenerate, in which godly comradeship hinged upon strict exclusiveness, became the majority and the ruling order. To put the issue the other way around, the many and powerful forces arrayed against the godly in England shrank into relative insignificance in the New World. This is the focal issue in this chapter. In America, much of the fortifying sense of tension with the unregenerate, the disordered, or the heretical was lost. Worries about French Catholic activities to the north and legal challenges to the Bay charter, conflicts with a resurgent festive culture (complete with a maypole and sexual commerce with native women) in the settlement at Merrymount and with Roger Williams's Separatist enthusiasms, and other troubles of the first years might have helped to fill the vacuum for a time. But it was the Antinomian Controversy, heightened by dangers of the Pequot War, that for a period of

two years and with long-lived aftereffects restored a productive opposite to the
pietist children of God. Orthodox accounts of the event draw the implication
plainly enough.[11]

Johnson found the sectaries resistant to being cast in the opposite's role.
They claimed merely to reaffirm familiar verities like unconditional grace or
justification. But Johnson read such claims as camouflage. To lay errors "cheke
by joule with the most glorious . . . truths" was a planned deception designed
"to dazle the eyes of the beholders" and blind them to the underlying deviance.
Echoing the partiality of his time for forms of thought based upon antithesis,
Johnson saw through the screen of likeness to the "dividing" spirit at the heart
of the heretical program. Its monomaniac fix on the transcendent was lethal to
Reformed theology, rending apart law and gospel and all the other prudent
balances at its core. Winthrop too, with his special interest in the implications
for civil society, made much of heresy's bisecting style. Was not the ringleader
"a woman of . . . fierce carriage" who could "endure [no] stop in her way"? And
were not her doctrines vented with an "impatience of opposition" that led to
angry confrontations and contempt of authority? Had not Wheelwright's aggressive deployment of the covenant of works "heat[ed] peoples affections
against their opposites"? And did he not regale his followers with "examples of
bodily fight and bloody victories," drawing them to the brink of insurrection?[12]

Such performances, true fruits of a polarizing movement, had worked

---

11. Everett Emerson, ed., *Letters from New England: The Massachusetts Bay Colony,
1629–1638* (Amherst, Mass., 1976), 97. Other early reporters on life in the Bay colony
shared Weld's perception (ibid., 72, 111, 232). Andrew Delbanco, John Frederick Martin,
and Michael P. Winship argue that the absence of traditional opponents in early Massachusetts had profound psychological effects. Delbanco, *The Puritan Ordeal* (Cambridge,
Mass., 1989), 39–40; Martin, *Profits in the Wilderness: Entrepreneurship and the Founding of
New England Towns in the Seventeenth Century* (Chapel Hill, N.C., 1991), 114–115; Winship, *Making Heretics: Militant Protestantism and Free Grace in Massachusetts, 1636–1641*
(Princeton, N.J., 2002).

12. *JWWP,* 125 ("dividing"), 172 ("cheke by joule"); *AC,* 263 ("carriage"), 275 ("stop"), 293
("opposites"), 298 ("examples"), 309 ("impatience"). Johnson identified four disruptive
antitheses: gospel/law, Spirit/Word, Christ/graces, and Christ/ordinances. Persuaded
that the second element in each pair had come to suppress the former, the dissidents in his
account merely reversed the error. They suppressed law, Scripture, graces, and ordinances
and refounded redemption upon free grace and the Deity's immediate beneficence (*JWWP,*
124–131). Weld dwelt pointedly upon the tendency of heresy to incite "alienations . . . ,
disturbances, divisions, [and] contentions," noting that in the controversial elections of
May 1637 some of the extremer spirits had been ready "to raise a mutinie." *AC,* 209.

much harm, but ultimately they aided the very cause they tried to destroy. The antipodal ordeal that they brought upon New England proved therapeutic. It provided a surrogate for the unregenerate opposition, the heckling "common enemy" of disciplinary religion that, as Shepard repeatedly emphasized, had "drive[n Dissenters] together" in England and bolstered both their religiosity and their self-image. It tested and toughened the colonial venture and brought out its virtues. It put the deviants' errors of belief and their antisocial behavior in telling contrast with Puritan wisdom, patience, and steadfastness. It vindicated the congregational way at an early and uncertain stage, at a time when much of the Protestant world still looked on askance, and displayed its ability to correct internal disorder. In the end, Shepard and his colleagues came close to saying that the contest with a hostile party had been good for the orthodox. Even as he rued and denounced the "storme" of the mid-1630s, Weld could praise it as a special design of Providence to prevent the colonists, whose congregational system by 1635 was "sweetely settled in Peace," from growing too "secure."[13]

By framing narratives to serve their own designs, colonial Puritans left a checkered legacy for historical research. They forged a record spotty in coverage, laced with resentment yet smugly triumphal and adjusted to preconceptions of heresy. Their sharply dualistic understanding of truth and error encouraged exaggeration of heterodox belief; it led them as well to minimize variations and ambiguities. But, if these features of the record yield a cloudy vision of the world of dissent, they also offer partial compensation. For precisely through their tendency to generalize and to think within a simple biformity, orthodox voices more freely projected their own ideals and fears into the narrative. If they omitted or were little concerned with many doctrinal details of interest to the modern student, they attended more to the beliefs that shook and tested them the most. In the end, with the stigma of error engraved yet deeper through connections with heresy, Winthrop and his associates had constructed an ultimate opposite of pietist faith and spirituality, a decidedly handy other to assail and to confute and against which to define themselves anew. It was perhaps as true an index of their own as of their opponents' mentality.

13. *WTS*, II, 67, and see 170–171; *AC*, 201 ("storm," "sweetely," "settled"). Shepard directly linked decline and conflict within the churches of New England to their seductive "peace and prosperity" in the absence of a bracing opposition. See *WTS*, II, 166, 169–171, 258–259, 373, 584 (quote at 169).

Expunging Human Partnership

Those five sources reveal some intriguing differences among them. Win-throp's accounts, for instance, centered upon Hutchinson as the fomenter of all the troubles and singled out her spiritist doctrine as the great "secret" of her deviance and charisma, and Johnson played up populist resentment against clerical "black-coates that have been at the Ninneversity." But these were minor variations framed by agreement upon essentials, and to understand the agreement we first must grasp what it was not. In attacks upon free grace doctrine published between 1615 and 1631, Peter Gunter, William Hinde, Joseph Bentham, Henry Burton, and Thomas Taylor identified antilegalism—which all saw as an invitation to anarchy—as the heretical core, and Hinde, Bentham, Burton, and Taylor employed the label "antinomian" or "antino-mist" and thereby made it more familiar to Protestant apologetics by the early 1630s. But specifically in New England the antilegal emphasis was less pro-nounced. All of the sources under consideration reported a dismissive attitude toward the law. Two errors in Weld's sampler of twenty-nine, three of the eighty-two spelled out by the synod of 1637, and four in Winthrop's list of Hutchinson's twenty-nine opinions claimed "that those that bee in Christ are not under the Law, and commands of the word." And a "nimble tongued Woman" who accosted Johnson in 1636 complained of the "legall Professors [who] . . . lie poring on the Law which Christ hath abolished."[14]

Yet this dismissal of law took its place amid other teachings of comparable and in some cases larger importance. Although the American interpreters were themselves eyewitnesses of the rising of 1636–1638 and had no apparent motive to underplay antilegal teaching, they did not see the movement as essentially antilegal. They knew that the antinomian label, like Familist or Arminian, carried instant polemical power and advantage but did not deploy it. Even Johnson, who explicitly listed "Antinomians" among the more promi-nent contemporary "Sectaries," did not use the term in his discussion of the American heresy. In his *Parable of the Ten Virgins* of 1636–1640, Shepard

14. *AC*, 220 ("under the Law"), 278 (and see 262–263, 265, 274, 300); *JWWP*, 127 ("black-coates"), 134 ("nimble tongued"). On antilegalism: see also *AC*, 202–203, 227, 302–303; *WTS*, II, 205, 401. Weld reported the opinion, already espoused by Traske, Antinomus Anonymus, and the "Oxford Antinomian," that preaching the law "is of no use at all, to drive a man to Christ" (*AC*, 202, and above, Chapter 10, n. 24, and text). Antinomian, antinomist: William Hinde, *The Office and Use of the Morall Law . . . of God* (London, 1622), 5; *LG*, sig. A2; *RV*, sig. A5, 53; Joseph Bentham, *The Societie of the Saints . . .* (London, 1630?), 183, 193, 243, 248.

likewise made no use of the term, and neither did he or any of his colleagues depict denial of the law as the crux or climax of the larger pattern. At least in part, that honor belongs to the English editor who in 1644 gave the title *Antinomians and Familists Condemned* to the compilation that in a later edition became the *Short Story*, but his usage does not well capture the outlook of Winthrop, Weld, Shepard, Johnson, and the agents of the Newtown synod.[15]

In point of fact, early orthodox interpreters did not settle upon a master label for the Dissenting movement, perhaps because it did not correspond as a whole to any familiar heresy and presented no single conceptual core. Weld and Johnson preferred common invectives. "Seducers," "deluders," and "Opinionists" were Weld's choice, and Johnson spoke of "erronists" and "sectaries." When they did attempt closer analysis, the orthodox drew attention, not to a single, definitive tenet, but to a cluster of interrelated errors. It included the antilegal element but also distinctive views about union with the Deity, free grace, assurance, and immediate revelation. I argue that all of these orbited around a common concern.[16]

First, as in Winthrop's report of Hutchinson's belief "that the person of the Holy Ghost dwells in a justified person," the notion of special conjunction with a Trinitarian Person was an error in its own right; but Puritan commentators were no less alarmed by its proven harm to their tradition of active spirituality. In brief, they found that persons concerned more to obtain and rest in the Deity's inward presence attended less to their own "spiritual action"

15. *JWWP,* 31 ("Antinomians" [and see 203], "Sectaries"). By the early 1640s, worriedly following the surge of heresies in the mother country, Shepard freely used "antinomian" and "familist" labels (*WTS,* III, 70–71, 92–96, 223). It is is not clear whether Weld supplied the title for his revision of Winthrop's compilation, which was published later in 1644 as *A Short Story of the Rise, Reign, and Ruin of the Antinomians, Familists, and Libertines . . .* (London, 1644). In any event, the choice of terminology in 1644 was certainly influenced by the spread of antinomian ideas that followed the lifting of censorship. In 1894 Charles Francis Adams chose the title *Antinomianism in the Colony of Massachusetts Bay, 1636–1638* for the first scholarly collection of source materials, and David D. Hall followed suit in *The Antinomian Controversy, 1636–1638: A Documentary History* in 1968, although he argued that assurance, not the law, was the central issue. *AC,* 12–19.

16. *AC,* 206, 207, 208, 212. Johnson described the dissidents as "erronists" or "erroneous" at least thirteen times in *JWWP* (see, e.g., 124, 125, 129). He also spoke of "infectious persons," "new Gospellers," and the like (*JWWP,* 126, 131). Focusing upon heretical ideas, Shepard developed no distinctive terminology in the *Ten Virgins* for their human agents. In *Gospel-Covenant,* 293, Bulkeley argued that Anne Hutchinson had learned her heresies "in the Schoole of the Familists"; Hooker spoke of "Familists," "false Teachers," "Kites and Buzzards," "subtil Foxes," and the like. *AR, 1–8,* 133, and see 44; *AR, 9–10,* 581.

and ceased to cultivate their personal dispositions and duties. In the synod's phrase, they *"seeke not for graces, but for Christ."*[17]

Second, according to orthodox report, colonists who believed in divine inhabitation were persuaded equally that union with the Deity is effected and sustained by "free grace," already a term of some infamy for those familiar with the Eatonist and Grindletonian disputes and the London controversies around 1630. Whether in their capacity as "friends of Christ and Free-grace" or as critics of ministers who did not "hold forth a Covenant of free Grace," the sectaries invested it with their own discontents. Positively, it meant quick and final pardon and the seal of the Spirit, but these were above all free. And freedom in this context was defined primarily by opposition. It meant release from all the wealth of practical divinity's disciplinary gains. With one stroke of free grace, all of the penitential moods and deeds, all the close observance of covenantal conditions, all the devoted struggles of holy walking and the watch were whisked away.[18]

Third, once aglow with free grace, the "new Gospellers" bragged of satisfactions unknown to the pietist rank and file, and among them assurance sealed by the spirit ranked foremost. In its own realm the seal was omnipotent, blessing men and women with "such a setled peace that they . . . never doubt more." Some of the sectaries, Shepard recalled, claimed an "inward witness, 'Thy sins are forgiven'; and hence such liberty and joy that they are ready to leap up and down the chamber." But here again the erronists seemed to negate with greater force than they affirmed, now aiming their fire at the practical syllogism and the auxiliary scheme of signs and evidences. It was precisely to undercut them that they pressed the question "whether sanctification be any evidence of justification," making it the primary point in dispute before the exposure late in the game of Hutchinson's extreme fancies. As Edward Johnson learned in his exchange with a female disciple of Hutchinson, the sectaries' answer to the question was a brashly unqualified no. In the blink of an eye, the seal made superfluous all obedience to the divine commands, any "increase in . . . Graces," the passion to be *"diligent"* in the use of ordinances and spiritual exercises, the "deepe sorrow" for sin, and other signs of a gracious

17. *JJW,* 193 ("person," "spiritual"); *AC,* 246 ("seek"). See also *AC,* 220–229, nos. 2, 7, 18, 38. Weld's rendering is similar in *AC,* 202–203, nos. 2, 3, 4, 16, 17.

18. *AC,* 254, 270. Hooker noted the sectaries' tendency to "run away with" the expressions "Pardon, Mercy," dubbing them "false Teachers" who "go under pretence of Free Grace." Hooker, *AR, 1–8,* 50; *AR, 9–10,* 581. See also Bulkeley, *Gospel-Covenant,* 96.

state. Indeed, in the more extreme formulations, these became a positive hindrance to souls in search of security.[19]

Fourth, authoritative voices scored "Familist" belief as the most worrisome and harmful of all. This term, familiar since the drive against the Family of Love around 1580 and a commonplace of contra-antinomian polemic since Peter Gunter's attack on Eaton about 1615, was confusingly multivocal; but most of the time in New England it pointed to spiritist belief, and as such it became the commonest label (save for free grace) in orthodox accounts. There Familism was seen to originate with the seal of the Spirit, to expand into claims for new and authoritative revelations and otherworldly voices and visions, to draw women into assertive behavior beyond their station, and thus to become at once the sectaries' gravest theological aberration and the source and warrant of many others. Winthrop, for whom the pretense to revelation was Hutchinson's "master-piece" and the "fountaine . . . of all our distempers," reserved the label of "Familistical opinions" for those derived from immediate revelation. Johnson too made "rare Revelations" the Familist essence, having the seal of the Spirit obviously in mind when he spoke of "Familists, who . . . make men depend upon strong Revelations, for the knowledge of Gods Electing Love towards them."[20]

---

19. *JWWP,* 126 ("new Gospellers"), 134–135 ("increase," *"diligent"* [emphasis mine], "deepe"), and see 126; *AC,* 205 ("setled peace"), 290 ("sanctification"); *WTS,* II, 313 ("inward witness"). On primary point of dispute, see also *JJW,* 193; *GP,* 65; *WCC,* 242; *AC,* 322. Shepard likewise lamented the sectaries' belief that "the utmost perfection of a Christian [is found] in the seal of the Spirit, not in the mighty [transformative, empowering] actings of the Spirit" upon and within the self (*WTS,* II, 134, and see 78, 133). All commentators except Johnson observed that spiritist inwardness produced indifference or hostility to the Sabbath, the liturgical forms, and other primitive "ordinances" or "means" of the congregational way, but it is their status in the pietist program of duties that I emphasize here. See *JWWP,* 129; *WTS,* II, 58, 171, 176; *AC,* 234, 238; *JJW,* 245.

20. *AC,* 265, 275, 279 (and see *JJW,* 253, 257); *JWWP,* 31, 50. Familist doctrine, thought Winthrop, made "such revelations as *Abraham* had to kill his Son" or Paul's ecstatic experience of the third heaven into "ordinary" Christian fare (*AC,* 278). Winthrop's concept of Familism may reflect that of John Knewstub, Puritan pastor at Cockfield, Sussex, a long-standing friend of the Winthrop family and a prominent literary antagonist of the Family of Love; see Francis J. Bremer, "The Heritage of John Winthrop: Religion along the Stour Valley, 1548–1630," *NEQ,* LXX (1997), 534. For Shepard on Familism, see *WTS,* II, 500. In his later *Theses Sabbaticae,* the Familist label takes on an additional range of meanings; and in his *Autobiography,* written in the late 1640s, it became a compendious term for the heresy "begun by Mistress Hutchinson" (*WTS,* III, 70, 73, 96, 223; *GP,* 38).

Once again, the doctrine was brazenly opposite to the pietist way. Assuredly, the immediate Familist offense was the claim to knowledge neither
conveyed nor controlled by the Word, but what was the Word in a Puritan
sense but precise demand and rule? And what, then, was American Familism
but another artifice of the sectaries' antipietist plot? In league with all their
other moves, it was a means to break clear of the maze of controls that the
fraternity had constructed from sacred writ. Inevitably, where the Word's
constraining rule was replaced by free impulses, some Familist settlers grew
"very loose and degenerate in their practises . . . As no prayer in their families,
no Sabbath, [and] . . . frequent and hideous lying." Before they were brought
to heel, the worst of them—like Hutchinson or Underhill before the General
Court, or those who were inspired by a "sudden motion or revelation" to
prepare an unlawful protest against Wheelwright's conviction for sedition in
March 1637, or the several women, including Hutchinson, who defied male
authority—were verging toward willful disorder.[21]

Despite their different arcs of attack, all the above errors aimed at a common foe. They struck at axioms widely shared throughout the mainline Protestant world, but their special quarry was all striving to mobilize, order, purify,
and thereby inflate the worth of human agency and behavior. No master term
emerged to name it, and no New Englander of the period provided an exact
conceptualization. Weld and Johnson posited a "naked Christ" as the sectaries'
primary message, and that was an epitome of sorts. It meant that the Savior in
all his uplifting presence, with his full array of earthly and heavenly benefits,
now was given without the mediation of human efforts and duties. Consider
the upstarts' magnification of hypocrisy to the point that "the graces of Saints
and Hypocrites differ not." This in effect defines all human acts, including
those of sealed saints and even those of Adam before the Fall, as hypocritical
and therefore valueless. And what was one to make of the demand of some in
the Boston congregation that "in the Church, hee that will not renounce his
sanctification, . . . cannot bee admitted" or that those seeking assurance must
"renounce all the work of grace in them" and merely await the seal? What of

---

Thomas Hooker applied the Familist label both to spiritist belief and to the "vain conceit"
that "a man may sit still and do nothing." *AR, 1–8,* 44, 133.

21. *AC,* 216, 277. In a purge of antinomians from the church at Roxbury in 1638, Henry
Bull was excommunicated for "gross sins of lying" associated with "familisme." Boston,
Record Commissioners, [Sixth Report], *A Report of the Record Commissioners Containing
the Roxbury Land and Church Records,* 2d ed. (Boston, 1884), 81; Weld and Eliot, "The
Causes of Hen. Bull[']s Excommunication." For Underhill's sexual aberrations, see above,
n. 2.

the sectaries' disdain for created graces and works and indeed for any and all "gifts or graces, or inherent qualifications"? And why did they, or the most radical among them, unleash against godly behavior a provocateur's flair for the outrageous, claiming that "all a believer's activity is onely to act sinne" or that "to take delight in the holy service of God, is to go a whoring from God"?[22]

Examples could be multiplied, but without appreciable change in the implication. At all points, the radical program was custom-made to expunge human partnership from the Christian redemption. To perceive this grand design, moreover, offered many advantages. It exposed the erring gospel's head-on threat to the pietist way and its treasury of means for building identity, and it supplied an easy key to both the comprehension and the rebuttal of a large and sometimes exotic mix of doctrines. But it also brought to mind another helpful strategy of historic struggles against heresy. Perhaps nothing better illumines the mentality of Winthrop and his colleagues than their interest in imagining the ultimate consequences of a course of error. Had the erronists achieved their end, were existing incentives and controls discarded, and only immediate inspiration left to guide the actions of men and women, what would result? Two outcomes seemed probable, and neither church nor society could survive them.

The first, most predictable outcome was anarchy. Perhaps by 1636 the material well-being and sense of common purpose in the New England settlements had softened the dread of disorder that long had weighed upon social elites, but the ensuing cycle of conflict stoked it anew. According to the Lord's "orthodox servants," radical theory raised the prospect of social disintegration, and radical actions began to realize it. Hutchinson's and Wheelwright's imperious division of community into parties of grace and of works fostered a spirit of resistance to authority, bred "disturbances, divisions, contentions"

22. *AC*, 203 ("Saints and Hypocrites" [and see 222, 223; *JJW*, 193; *JWWP*, 126–127; *WTS*, II, 204], "act sinne" [and see 228]), 205 ("naked Christ"), 234 ("delight"), 253 ("renounce . . . sanctification"), 263 ("renounce . . . grace"), 264 ("qualifications"); *JWWP*, 134 ("naked Christ"). To Shepard, the denial of "created graces" was "a delusion digged and hatched out of the steam of the lowest sink of hell," and he wished to "let that opinion, that the graces of saints are fading and mortal, rot and die" (*WTS*, II, 275, 354). See also the defense of "created spiritual gifts and graces" and "qualityes" in Richard Mather, "Seventie Lectures," 105–107. In sermons delivered at Hartford in 1638–1639, Hooker explicitly strove to rehabilitate the terms "disposition" and "qualification" (*AR*, *1–8*, 29–54, 159). Two of the charges against Peter Shaw in 1629 had described sanctified behavior as a positive hindrance to salvation. "PS," 708–709.

galore, "miserably interrupt[ed] the civill Peace," and at times approached outright "mutinie."[23] Such difficulties were heightened by a philosophy that swallowed up all moral distinctions in the category of hypocrisy and so far devalued moral behavior that even "hainous sinnnes" like murder or incest ceased to jeopardize one's standing before God. They were compounded further by spiritist pretensions that are "not subject to controll" and "cannot stand with the peace of any State." Ultimately they might lead to revolutionary violence, as in the "Tragedy of M[ü]nster" in Germany a century before.[24]

The second outcome was a form of disintegration too, and equally revolutionary, but it was far less colorful. Yet, more than any other element outlined in this chapter, it reveals what the orthodox ultimately abhorred and strove to extinguish in the heresy they made of "free grace." Not disregard of law per se, uncontrolled revelation, or even the threat of a violent rising was the most compendious opposite to the pietist way, but the simple, final arrest of human endeavor itself. In their rebuttal of claims to be led by the Spirit and enjoy a "meerly passive" blessedness, earlier rebuttals of antinomian teaching had laid groundwork for this perception, but the first full conceptualization of a subjectless, actless heresy was a New England work.[25]

If virtually every error cited by Winthrop, Weld, and the Newtown synod shortened the checklist of duties, three of the more radical ones threatened a deeper subversion. Taken together, they showed that saints who pursue the spiritual warfare not only go a-whoring from God but also traffic in sheer illusion. Graces, meant in the traditional sense as implanted tendencies to

23. *JWWP*, 52; *AC*, 209, 213. Some cases in point were the "tumult" that broke out at the elections of May 1637, the Boston authorities' subsequent withdrawal of support for the Pequot War, and the "tumultuous course, and divers insolent speeches" made in the Court at Wheelwright's trial (*JJW*, 215, 217; *AC*, 253–254). In *WP*, 133, Johnson spoke of a "floud of errors violently beating against the bankes of Church and civill Government."

24. *AC*, 224 (and see 202), 274, 275. For Münster, see also *JWWP*, 132. See also Winthrop's report of a woman given to "revelations" directing her to commit murder and suicide and the implications of a "Communitie of Weomen," in probable reference to polygamous practices at Münster, which Winthrop and three clergy including Cotton drew at Hutchinson's church trial (*JJW*, 271–272; *AC*, 362–363, 372). A member of First Church reported that Underhill during the Antinomian crisis "told me of a Revelation . . . he had" that a woman he desired would lose her husband and marry him. This was the same woman with whom he was under "suspicion of incontinency" in 1638. Helle M. Alpert, "Robert Keayne: Notes of Sermons by John Cotton and Proceedings of the First Church of Boston from 23 November 1639 to 1 June 1640" (Ph.D. diss., Tufts University, 1974), 316; *JJW*, 264; and see above, n. 2.

25. *RV*, 72.

godly behavior, became a term of abuse among the sectaries; for, in the first of the errors, they made God the sole disposer of action. One might speak of graces still, but only to transfer their operative power to the Deity: "Graces are not in the soules of beleevers, but in Christ only." With a push to the limit of theocentric logic, this proposal made God the actual working "Subject" of Christian behavior. No virtuous deed is done by William or Jane. It is not they who believe or love, but "Christ [who] beleeves, . . . [or] loves, etc" in them. Or, more sweepingly, it is the "Holy Ghost [who] . . . doth all the works of [human] natures"; it is "Christ [who] . . . transacts us him selfe." One of the eighty-two errors refuted in 1637 went so far as to recast the apostle's eschatological hope that God will be all in all as a wish that he *"act* all in all."[26]

Yet if God be the sole agent in Christianity, and thus no one can "bee exhorted to any duty, because hee hath no power to do it," what part was left for the individual? And indeed what was left of the individual? From the perspective of a Winthrop or Weld, the radicals' answer to these questions— the second and third errors—laid the human subject supine and inert. It drained sainthood of dynamic qualities and stopped the dialectic of divine initiative and responsible human agency. From a monocausal premise a sharply altered estimate of Christian action itself had emerged. In truth, "my" faith, love, devotions, or virtues are not mine. They are a divine handiwork visited upon me, an extrinsic process that overtakes my faculties. Even the belief that the soul "goe[s] out to Christ" for power to act or that "wee act in the strength of Christ" overrates human capacity. The human part is to lie patient, to move only as moved, to be "acted by the Spirit inhabiting"; the saint does not act at all.[27]

Were these purely negative pronouncements? The orthodox understood them so. They found no verbal import in the radicals' call to *"doe* nothing, [but] onley . . . stand still and waite for Christ to doe all." They did not grasp,

26. *AC,* 203 ("Subject," "beleeves"), 220 ("Holy Ghost"), 223 ("Graces"), 228 (*"act"* [emphasis mine]), 378 ("transacts us," and see 278).

27. *AC,* 233, 235. In one passage in the *Ten Virgins,* Shepard spoke of those who "put a Christian in such an estate of sanctification as that he is a mere patient, in next disposition to move if he be moved. Like a weathercock." This echoed Cotton's portrait of the sealed Christian who, "as a Mill moved by the breath of the wind," has "no further motion . . . but as Christ moves him" (*WTS,* II, 332; above, Chapter 11, n. 25, and text). In a sermon at Charlestown in 1644, Thomas Allen pointedly emphasized that the regenerate "soul is Active, and an Agent: and not a mere Patient" ("Sermons by Thomas Shepard and Thomas Allen, 1644," in Shepard Family Papers, folder 2, p. 43, American Antiquarian Society).

or found no reason to remark, that to urge a person "to *see* [that] I have no grace [operative capacity] in me" was to authorize self-analysis and self-mobilization of a sort. Likewise, the Newtown synod understood the claim that "the Spirit acts most in the Saints, when they *indevour least*" as a brief for idleness, not as a call to feats of abnegation. No one noted the admonitory force of such expressions or their movement in a logical circle that called for deliberate effort to halt effort and also hailed the religiously potent effects of the effortless state. No one saw resemblances between that state and the *Gelassenheit* ("abandonment") that was sometimes commended in Catholic mystical and Radical Reformation theologies. An ironic analysis would distract from the real peril—the conviction growing in New England that the highest means to heaven was to stand still and do nothing.[28]

Mere calls to inaction, however, did not go far enough. The radicals of orthodox report saw the invasive whirl of works as symptomatic of a yet deeper evil, a molding of the settlers' very selves to serve the religion of exercises. What was the final product of regeneration Puritan-style? A befitting type of personality, a compulsive striver—a religious *homo operosus*. The covenant of works had no stronger hold in New England than this, and it was too entrenched to yield to a counsel of inaction alone. An effective counterstrategy therefore must have two further objectives. It must directly engage the question of selfhood, asking every pietist would-be saint to reconsider, "Who am I?" At the same time, it must recognize that a self so malformed is beyond cure. The freely graced man or woman who draws being from "not acting at all" is the fruit, not of therapy or reform, but of an act of extinction. Rightly grasped, free grace did not simply freeze the self's own motions; it administered a deathblow. That was the sense of Hutchinson's thesis that "the soule remain[s] always as a dead Organ" and a follower's reported view that "every new creature is as a dead lump." It illumined the erronists' rendering of poverty of spirit as the "sight of nothing in a man's self" and the claims refuted at Newtown that "in the conversion of a sinner . . . the faculties of the soule . . . are destroyed and made to cease" and that Christ "kill[s] all activity of graces" and "workes in the regenerate, as in those that are dead." It explained too their project to replace the voided human agent with God as the worker of Christian behavior, as in their claim that all active graces are "in Christ as in the Subject, and none in us" or that "Christ *is* the new Creature." Such doctrine,

---

28. *AC,* 203, 204, 231, all emphases mine. On the radicals' tendency "to sit idle and dream of the Spirit," see also *WTS,* II, 58, 78 (quote), 318. *Gelassenheit:* see above, Chapter 10, n. 29, and text.

Shepard thought, flatly extinguished the self. It obliged the Lord to make his earthly "music without any [human] strings."[29]

Such proposals had a double shock value. By putting them on display, the orthodox could make their audiences cringe before heresy's wild extremes, but they also meant to expose its brazen eloquence, its feel for the jarring rhetoric needed to propel a people into deviant paths. And the paths of radical theory were foreign indeed. To make the Deity not only a killer of graces but the very subject of human action blotted out the self. The dissidents' actual behavior, it is true, gave a different impression. Hutchinson and other leading radicals of orthodox report were, not poor in spirit, but swollen with self-importance. Their demands were unnegotiable, their manner was pushy to the point of insubordination, and their movement bristled with intimations of power and even violence. Yet the contradiction eluded the orthodox. The beliefs and acts they damned were in perfect rapport. All came from a single plan: to disengage the grindingly busy self that had come to the fore in Puritan faith, and that plan cut almost unimaginably deep. It challenged the going system of reality itself. It intended the end of man, the annihilation of the driven penitent and controller acclaimed in Puritan philosophy. In place of this figure a different order of saint would arise, cut to a minimalist design. By Puritan lights it was no recognizable self at all. Its distinction lay in what it lacked and could and did not do. Devoid of operational capacity, the freely graced saint generates "no act of his owne done by him." Moreover, since passive traits now reigned, the accustomed busy flow of action must shrink to a trickle. Not even a private or family prayer would be said "unless the Spirit stirre us up"—and that was an unscheduled, situational, and perhaps infrequent event. Should this ideal prevail in New England, the careful, linear, and protracted walk of pietist religion would become a leisurely ramble. Saints would be loafers by Puritan lights, and Christianity a bone-idle art.[30]

Here, and once more crisply opposite to Puritan principle, lay also the major key to heresy's mushroom growth. To Winthrop it was "a wonder upon what a sudden the whole Church of *Boston* (some few excepted) were . . . infected with [Hutchinson's] opinions," together with many from neighboring

29. *AC,* 203 ("Subject," "Creature" [emphasis mine], and see the second and eighth errors cited in *AC,* 220 and 221; and *WTS,* II, 277, 287, 332–333), 219 ("conversion"), 223 ("the regenerate"), 228 ("activity"), 264 ("Organ"), 278 ("not acting," "lump"); *WTS,* II, 203 ("nothing"), 332 ("music"). Coggeshall apparently described the "New-creature . . . as a New-nothing." *CJC,* 304.

30. *AC,* 203–204, 232. The Newtown synod condemned the view that "it is legal to say, *wee act* in the strength of Christ." *AC,* 233, emphasis mine.

congregations. It "hath not beene knowne in former ages," he added, "that ever so many wise, sober, and well grounded Christians, should so suddenly be seduced." Weld too marveled that the new opinions "should [have] spread so fast and suddenly amongst a people so religious and well taught." Yet, however startling it might be, the rampant spread of error was easy to understand. Part of the explanation was found in the nature of heresy itself, which American (like European) analysts conceived as an infectious plague; and the effect was enhanced when, as in the Bay colony, the infection was further enhanced by conspiratorial planning and execution.[31]

But infection and conspiracy could work only if fitted to a human context. A crafty duper like Hutchinson succeeded by knowing her intended victims and targeting her ideology to their special vulnerabilities. What special allure, then, had the opinionists devised? Clever enough to recognize that the settlers' discontents were many, they formed a multifaceted appeal. The seal of the Spirit met a need for clear assurance; and, when expanded into a doctrine of personal revelations, it satisfied desires for firm and indubitable guidance, for devotional rapture, and for personal esteem and power. Yet all these appeals were secondary to another. Winthrop and Weld expressly singled out the promise of a relaxed style of life as the core attraction, and Johnson's account and the list of errors condemned at Newtown did so implicitly. As Winthrop saw it, the insurgency grew so fast because it offered "a very easie, . . . way to heaven," and Weld agreed. He too found the key in "the nature of the Opinions themselves, which open [an] . . . easie way to Heaven." Since the way "was made easie, . . . no marvell so many like[d] of it." Here was heresy's prettiest lure. In defiance of every Puritan instinct and catering directly to humanity's natural aversion to ascetic regimentation, it made the route to heaven a path of least resistance.[32]

A penchant for ease also had underlain the struggles against Puritan reform in English parishes since about 1570, but the analogy is limited. The American rebels were, not conservative villagers, but disenchanted Puritan insiders.

31. *AC,* 203 (Weld), 264, 276.

32. *AC,* 203, 264. For the disease metaphor, see *AC,* 203, 212; C. H. Firth, ed., "Thomas Shepard to Hugh Peter, [Dec. 27,] 1645," *American Historical Review,* IV (1898–1899), 106; *JWWP,* 131–132. Shepard saw aversion to the "difficulty" of the pietist way as the root of antinomian belittling of sanctification's evidential value (*WTS,* II, 402). In his election sermon of May 8, 1638, Shepard attributed the insurgency to "a spirit of discontent w[hich] usually ariseth in a people under the strict government of god: . . . [who want] more liberty." "Thomas Shepard's Election Sermon in 1638," *New England Historical and Genealogical Register,* XXIV (1870), 363.

They had first tried and then forsaken the course of bridled conduct. And what was the bridle but the immensely exacting, clerically directed praxis once delivered to the saints by Richard Greenham, Richard Rogers, and William Perkins and enhanced to the utmost under New England conditions? By defining most of the clergy as agents of the covenant of works, the erring tenets damned all their pulpit rites of humiliation and preparation, all their legal and disciplinary exhortation, and all their finespun casuistry. They brought under fire the whole work of the Greenham era, the entire art and lore of pietist spiritual direction.

Further, they disqualified all of the spiritual exercises implicitly and many by name. Weld noted a discontinuance of daily family prayers and Sabbath duties in infected households, and Shepard rued the insurgent view that, "if a man fasts, prays, watches against his distempers, mourns . . . , and follows God hard here, he is a legal Christian." Johnson recorded denunciations of "legall duties and performances" such as "preparation worke," "poring on the Law," keeping the Sabbath, gathering signs and evidences of a good estate, "hearing of Sermons, observing duty Morning and Evening, and many such like matters"; he, with Shepard and Weld, found a marked hostility to the fixation upon sins and the penitential atmosphere that stood central in the practice of piety. In the synod's litany of errors, the saints were bidden not to be concerned with the "frequency or length of holy duties or trouble of conscience for neglect thereof." They must cease pouring energy into *"meditation and duties"* and searching the Scriptures. No longer (in another blow at likeness to God) should one dwell upon Christ's life as a "patterne according to which men ought to act" or review the "former experience of God[']s grace in mee" as an introspective means to strengthen faith and comfort conscience.[33]

That procedure alone, of course, the deletion of one rite or another or even the whole round, could not bring the pietist drill to full stop. When he marked Wheelwright's scorn for colonists "exceeding[ly] holy and strict in their way" or when he growled that "most of [Hutchinson's] new tenents tended to slothfulnesse, and quench all indevour," Winthrop knew that the sectaries had seen through the lines of Sabbath observance or self-analysis to the underlying

---

33. *WTS*, II, 58 ("distempers"); *JWWP*, 125 ("preparation"), 126 ("legall duties," "Sermons"), 134 ("Law"); *AC*, 220 ("patterne"), 234 ("former experience"), 238 ("holy duties"), 246 (*"meditation,"* and, for poring over Scriptures, 229). Weld on prayers and Sabbath duties: *AC*, 216. Johnson on Sabbath and signs: *JWWP*, 126, 186. Shepard and Weld on sins and repentance: *JWWP*, 126, 134; *AC*, 203, 204; *WTS*, II, 204.

performative drive. Accordingly, their critique of duties one by one dovetailed with the move (described above) to contest and finally to evacuate the acting human subject itself. Should this twofold tactic succeed, should it prove possible to exorcise both the pietist rites and the busy "indevour" which drove them, then at long last would the way to heaven be eased.[34]

Sugary Bounties

To be sure, the construct of heresy we are surveying embraced more than a set of negations. As it served no orthodox purpose to advertise heresy's pleasures, Winthrop and company gave them skimpy and always disdainful attention. Nevertheless, they made the attractions clear. The most obvious delights were three: unmediated union with God, imperturbable certitude, and personal revelations. These made the benefits known to more ordinary folk seem petty indeed. They swept beyond all the customary gifts and graces, beyond the whole tainted realm of exactions and hypocrisies, beyond all that was uncertain, "mortall and fading." Although no explicitly millennial conception appears, they rose above limits of finite existence itself as that was defined by Puritan faith. Putting behind them both the stark realism of Reformed theology and the orchestrated postponement of gratifications that was the pietist private liturgy, the benefits proposed arrival and fulfillment here and now. Saints lifted this high could fatten at will upon "the sweetnesse of *Free Grace*." At one with the Lord, they were granted a "brighter," "cleerer" sense of pardon, enabled "more clearly [to] see Christ," and had the exhilarating sense of being actuated by him in all their ways. Through the "hot inflamation of their owne conceited Revelations" they entered a spiritist lotusland, savoring the seal of assurance together with knowledge so full that clerical instruction no longer was needed, with "rare Revelations of things to come," with an inerrant ability to judge others' spiritual estates, and with other luxurious favors. And what less than "ravishing joy" could such gifts evoke? What could one do, when the Spirit so moved, but erupt in "soule-ravishing expressions and affections"? Merely to list these sugary bounties was to show how far the sectaries had drifted from earthly reality, from reality as known in pietist faith with its shifting mix of fulfillment and deferral.[35]

On balance, too, a few of the authorities had to admit that the sectaries'

---

34. *AC*, 264, 287.

35. *AC*, 205 ("sweetnesse," "expressions"), 224 ("mortal"), 240 ("brighter," "see Christ"), 264 ("cleerer"); *JWWP*, 127 ("rare Revelations"), 132 ("inflamation"), 134 ("Joy").

theology contained some creative elements. Hutchinson reportedly worked out an entire revision of covenant doctrine. She found the covenant of works first manifest by *"Cain,"* then "ratified at Mount *Sinai,"* and later "carried on in the Letter of the Scripture" to culminate finally in the New Testament pact of free justification and the seal. It was equally clear that her mortalist teachings had sweepingly revisionist implications. All the more provocative as female constructs, they mandated a sweeping redraft of Christian redemption and eschatology. Working toward a large-scale conceptual shift, they conveyed the whole "mystery of [a] new Religion." "Surely had this Sect gone on awhile," Johnson supposed, "they would have made a new Bible" from their skein of revelations.[36]

Yet, no matter how positive the appearance of the radicals' gifts, affections, and conceptual proposals, their power stemmed from negation. They were largely reactive, part of the bid to slip the Puritan harness, and they proceeded from explicit acts of denial. Free grace and its entitlements were a means of exodus from the whole business of "frequency or length of holy duties or trouble of conscience for neglect thereof." The seal conquered doubt precisely as it was disconnected from "fruits of sanctification," from "any conclusion by a [practical] Syllogisme," and from the charge to bend all motions of the human heart and body to the rule of the Book. Within the freely gracious covenant a saint could "know I am Christ[']s, not because I doe crucifie . . . lusts . . . , but because I doe not crucifie them." Again, unconditional promises gave peace to troubled souls, but only upon realization that "no comfort can be had from any conditionall promise," and one of the errors gathered by Weld stated bluntly, "To see I have no grace [implanted graces] in me, will give me comfort." In Johnson's report, the highest radical gaieties were a reflex of escape from "deepe sorrow," the programmed self-loathing that darkened Puritan spirituality. Real joy flowed from "casting of[f] all godly sorrow for sin" or from the realization, "I should never have cause to be sorry for sinne." Through their common premise that the Lord loves and pleasures a saint "never the better for any holinesse in him," these and a host of comparable assertions exploded the pietist system's capital delusion and opened access to heady fulfillments, but they rooted those fulfillments in negation. Sheer relief from pietist burdens was the primal pleasure, and the ground of all others.[37]

36. *AC*, 206 ("mystery"), 264–265 (*"Cain,"* "ratified," "carried"); *JWWP*, 129 ("new Bible").

37. *AC*, 202 ("no comfort"), 203 ("no grace," "holinesse"), 232 ("Syllogisme"), 238

To an even greater extent, then, than the "antinomist" heresy described by Henry Burton or Thomas Taylor, what colonial critics saw and described in the troubles of 1636–1638 was therefore a counterreligion. Strictly speaking, since the use of sanctification as an evidence seems to have been the most frequently debated point, assurance might be designated the central issue in the controversy from the orthodox standpoint. But beneath it, beneath all the points explicitly in dispute, lay a more fundamental concern: to maintain, in all its heroic rigor, the variant of ascetic Christianity that had crested in the pietist turn. Read against this background, the New England meaning of free grace and kindred slogans was clear. Despite their committed and idealistic pose, the sectaries proposed an abandoned way of life. They invited people not merely to do less but to "do" nothing. So they became agents of the first American *Gelassenheit*, of a capitulation to sheer impulse and to carefree ease. Here was the most inexplicable and fearful prospect of all. It obliterated visible sainthood. It promised rest and ease, but opened the door to whimsy and ultimately to anarchy. Could there be a more completely imagined and exploitable antipode to the pietist way?

We cannot know how closely the construct tallied with the actual beliefs of Hutchinson and her coinsurgents, although Winthrop found them claiming a "difference betweene them and us . . . as wide as between Heaven and Hell," but its repugnant alienness resonated with the orthodox in helpful ways. In particular it renewed opportunity to reap gain from the clash of opposites. Contemporaries did not put the matter in such terms, of course, but they sensed that their identity both individually and corporately fed upon aversion and opposition and that the present crisis was therefore opportune. By showing, as Winthrop put it, that free grace induces a state of lax misrule with "all things . . . turned upside down," it aimed to cast the ideal of ardently ordered life into flattering relief and to heighten orthodox distinctiveness and solidarity. A scrap with heresy was unnerving, but it refreshed the psychology of identity-by-antithesis, proving again that saints fare best against resistance. For a time the older sectarian demand to "shun the society of corrupt and erroneous persons," whose force had been dimmed within the rising congregational establishment before 1636, could dispel dreams of ease and call

---

("frequency," and see 203: "Trouble in conscience for . . . neglect of duties, shewes a man to be under a Covenant of workes"), 239 ("fruits"), 246 ("I am Christ[']s"); *JWWP*, 134 ("deepe sorrow," "godly sorrow," "to be sorry"). For the seal disconnected from Scripture, see *AC*, 202, 230, 238.

wavering spirits back to bracingly difficult religion. If within two years the insurgency was put down, the Antinomian Controversy had served a good turn in New England's "complex adjustment to being unopposed."[38]

38. *AC,* 253, 254 (see also Wheelwright's remarks quoted in Bush, "'Revising what we have done amisse,'" *WMQ,* 3d Ser., XLV [1988], 745); Mather, *Sermons upon Genesis,* sig. A4; Alan Heimert and Andrew Delbanco, eds., *The Puritans in America: A Narrative Anthology* (Cambridge, Mass., 1985), 15.

REFLECTIONS

This study has approached the first antinomian wave, and more particularly the American Antinomian Controversy of the mid-1630s, as an outcome of choices made and directions taken over the course of a century. Around 1615 scattered agitations arose against the Puritan pietistic faith, the dominant force in English spirituality of the time. The crux of its offense was a zest for control and purity so strict as to evoke the epithet "precise." Perpetuating in Protestant guise the ancient mystique of Christian asceticism and contemptus mundi, building upon the strongly ethical bent of the earlier English Reformation and of Reformed Protestantism abroad, and linking sola fides to covenant conditions and to Deuteronomic law and justice, it surfaced first in presbyterian circles of the mid-Elizabethan years. It rose to maturity, however, upon the most impressive surge of religious creativity in its time. The achievement of later Elizabethan and early Stuart Puritans, this owed most initially to Richard Greenham and the program of piety and control he outlined in the quarter-century after about 1570. In time it embraced the first extensive practical theology, the first Sabbatarianism, the first programmatic concentration upon "conversion," the first surge of religious anxiety, the first systematic science of casuistry, the first large complex of spiritual exercises, and many other conceptual and practical achievements in context of the late Reformation. So potent a complex deserves recognition as the first full-scale pietism in the Protestant mainstream, and certainly it deepened the emotional resources of the Puritan movement, but of crucial interest within this study is its great expansion of means for the tighter regulation of life.

Becoming the specialty of the spiritual brotherhood of mainstream Puritan clergy, the pietist way was put into practice in a host of households, conventicles, parishes, and towns in the decades around 1600 and beyond and was borne to New England in the migrations of the 1630s. By the second decade of the century it had reached the levels of grinding demand that evoked Eatonist, Grindletonian, and other reactions. Endeavoring to reconstruct Protestant Christianity as a non-, even contradisciplinary venture, they forged pietist Puritanism's defining heresy.

Albeit with many individual variations, both the early English agitations for free grace and the New England surge of 1636–1638 turned on a simple diagnosis of the Puritan fault. The practice of piety was struggle and fear again. It imposed heavy costs and delayed rewards. It made life a long, embattled journey of remorseful mood and frequently uncertain destination. Accordingly, a battery of critics, from John Eaton to Anne Hutchinson, redefined the inherited faith. Freed from the false charisma of holy walking and its evidential worth, they minimized or sifted away all demand and denial, eased or canceled the tiresome journey, and made the rewards immediate. Reimagining the Christian course as a relaxed, even desultory way of life under divine promptings, they contested the very concept of religion as a disciplinary system. In theory, at least, the result was to make the gospel a horn of plenty. It dispensed easy, quick, and lasting satisfactions and fittingly happy moods and freedoms. In a word, religious faith antinomian-style was Puritanism's ideal "other," its almost perfectly configured opposite. It was at once a dissenting presence within the Puritan community and a charter for *post*-Puritan, postdisciplinary Christianity.

Puritan commentators judged the charter dizzily utopian. They stood for spiritual realpolitik. Life within history, even the higher life of the elect, was subject to tight restraints. While the Old Man (with Satan's assistance) remained at large within the saints and spiritual warfare with all its ups and downs was their daily lot, they were locked in imperfection, in what Greenham termed a "purgatorie in this present life." Theirs was a world of limits, of an ever-pressing dread of disorder, of struggles for self-mastery, of force and punishment, of fluctuations and uncertainties. Within that world they could survive, and some could flourish, but their best works were flawed and their enjoyments inconstant. Until the end of history, they must live by an interim strategy of patience and deferral. To saints thus resigned to "cares, anguishes and vexations," antinomian teaching seemed a crude burst of impatience. Confounding earthly with heavenly possibilities, it gushed romantic wishes for freedom and plenitude. Fulfillment now! was its essential creed. In unconsidered haste to wait and delay no longer, it spoke of a tamed self, of release from law, duty, punishment, and perhaps from "ordinances," of unmediated contact with the divine and perhaps of spiritist revelations, of full and stable certitude, and of an amiable deity smiling over all. This was a fine string of promises, or rather of "imaginary golden dreaming fancies," for one and all they left hard and inexpugnable realities out of account.[1]

---

1. *WRG*, 59; Robert Cawdray, *A Treasurie or Store-house of Similes* (London, 1600), 499 (and see 430); Joseph Bentham, *The Societie of the Saints . . .* (London, 1630?), 185. Thomas Shepard spoke similarly of antinomian "golden dreams of grace." *WTS*, II, 377.

Those who spoke for free grace found the pietist way equally unrealistic. Stiffened to the utmost by a zeal to be precise, its disciplinary program was an elite venture, a monasticism in all but name that overbore ordinary people, and it was this excess that antinomian agents sought to curb. Marking a path to quick fulfillment that neutralized or bypassed human efforts, it made the break with ascetic and ritual-heavy religion, which Puritans, for all their showy anti-Catholicism, had failed to achieve. Most important, it brought Christian practice back within the range of human competence.

And how better to do so than by making God more and the human creature less? This was the defining strategy of the first antinomian wave, and, although it rejected pietist ideals, it remained intriguingly dependent upon them. It not only embraced but also radicalized the mistrust of the self fostered by Puritan penitential divinity, depth psychology, and the whole complex of doubt and evidences—not to mention the primitivist critique of "human invention." As distrustful of man as any structuralist or postmodern antihumanist of the twentieth century, antinomians from Eaton to Hutchinson reconstructed the Christian redemption along two lines. First, they belittled or, most markedly in Hutchinson's late visions, vacated the activist self, locating all agency within an engulfing divine process. That alone would halt the ever-spinning cycles of pietist striving and regimentation.[2]

Second, however, they recuperated selfhood in a new form. Upon the demise of the Puritan activist heavy with skills, duties, and doubts, an opposite self arose whose cardinal skill was *not* to mobilize or manipulate. Since redemption is a process that claims the self, over which one has no control, the saint's métier was an effortless letting go. But this conception too fed upon Puritan ideals. Letting go was, not loafing, but a focused skill and ritual of a sort, a revised art of preparation. However framed in contrast to the Puritan spiritual war, it lived by contrast with its opposite, in unintended symbiosis.

Puritan ideals and accomplishments also underlay another frequent antinomian supposition: that the pardoned self is tamed and can be trusted to behave. Obviously, those gripped by this conviction were speaking from experience. Their quarrel was not with conventional moral standards; and, unlike

2. Neglect of this element weakens Louise A. Breen's argument linking American antinomianism to the interests of "risk-takers, adventurers, and men of action" like John Underhill. She suggestively correlates their culture of honor with the spiritist themes of 1636–1638 but does not explain how their "fractious behavior" comports with a theology that also deprecated human agency and accomplishment and favored yielding over self-assertive attitudes. *Transgressing the Bounds: Subversive Enterprises among the Puritan Elite in Massachusetts, 1630–1692* (Oxford, 2001), 70–71.

the Dionysian Ranters of a later day, once forgiven and assured they felt in themselves no hedonist release. They did not consider the possibility that their own self-control was a learned pattern, a hard-won and tenuous product of socialization both in the larger English culture and in the Puritan subculture. Their belief that morality would take care of itself was plausible in part because Puritan disciplinary instruction had succeeded so well. So, invisible and unacknowledged, the hated controls of the pietist way underwrote the cause of its bitterest detractors.

Nevertheless, the insurgency's overt design was to ease the Christian journey. Or, to push the metaphor further, it was to supply a lasting oasis of rest and refreshment that removed the need for further exertion and hardship. This has bearing upon the familiar suggestion that antinomian theology had special appeal to certain social groups. Knowledge about the early English antinomians is skimpy, with a few indications of substantial female involvement, but women, tradesmen, and artisans did play a large role in the American movement. Perhaps to make *in*action the religiously effectual state, to reduce the pressure to perform religious duties, had special pertinence to commercially active settlers scrambling to develop their farms, homes, and businesses in the initial phase of settlement. The belief that grace is free removed a burden of conscience, freed more time and energy for secular activity, and required no conscious sense of disloyalty to the religious cause. These connections are plausible, if unprovable.

Yet other elements of the antinomian witness point in a contrary direction. At least in theory, its strong bias away from religious work, struggle, and self-denial, its preference for an improvisational praxis under the Spirit's unforeseeable visitations, and its Platonizing aversion to the creaturely do not seem to mark paths toward a commercial business mentality. The difficulty diminishes when one recalls that antinomian teaching tended to separate the creaturely and the religious, that merchants and artisan members of the American antinomian party belonged to a transitional phase of economic development that commingled the secular and spiritual, that tensions between religious and secular vocation were common among devoutly Christian men of business in the seventeenth century, and that mechanisms of selective perception might have been at work. Nevertheless, the business implications of antinomian teaching remain intriguingly mixed.

So do the implications for gender. At one level, antinomian ideology challenged the primacy of male (active, assertive) qualities. By urging men, not to act, but to react it invited them, at least in their dealings with the sacred, to become more womanly; and its sanction of female (yielding) traits offered women a new source of self-worth. Yet a claim to direct personal contact with the sacred could legitimize assertive and obstinate behavior. When antinomian men and women argued their cause, and especially when they met resistance, the ethic of self-abnegation and *in*action was little in evidence. Eaton's reported "particularitie in carriage, his . . . shew of zeale, his vehement deliverie, [and] his vociferations" stand in some tension with his quietist ideal. His published works as well as those of John Traske, Robert Towne, and other early figures are righteous, embattled, and testy. Their dogmatic sureness equaled that of their opponents, and their demands were no less hard and unnegotiable. Defining a sole and imperative path to redemption, they evinced male qualities after all.[3]

The pattern is most apparent in New England. There, in the time of crisis, antinomian behavior savored little of *Gelassenheit,* but much of spiritual battle. Hardly the work of a womanly man, John Wheelwright's Fast Day sermon of early 1637 exudes more belligerent machismo than any other recorded speech from seventeenth-century English America. Henry Vane stoutly defended its assertion that preaching the gospel of free grace must break the colony's peace and spoke of "turneing the world upside downe." In Wheelwright's trial in late 1637, William Aspinwall "turned his backe upon the Court, and used menacing speeches." By John Cotton's report, Aspinwall and John Coggeshall reacted furiously to the decisions of the synod of 1637, styled their opponents "enemyes," and "high-handedly" urged others to ignore the legalist ministers and refuse customary respect to the orthodox magistrates. Facing excommunication in 1638 for his part in the insurgency, Henry Bull of Dorchester displayed "Impudent and contemptuous behavior, in the Assembly" of the church.[4]

3. *HP,* 6.

4. Sir Henry Vane, "A Brief Answer to a Certain Declaration . . . ," in *Hutchinson Papers,* Prince Society, Publications (Albany, N.Y., 1865), I, 82 [94]; *AC,* 258; Sargent Bush, Jr., " 'Revising what we have done amisse': John Cotton and John Wheelwright, 1640," *WMQ,* 3d Ser., XLV (1988), 738 (Cotton's report); Thomas Weld and John Eliot, "The Causes of Hen. Bull[']s Excommunication . . . ," in "Transcriptions by Edward Holden of documents in the Prince Library, Boston Public Library," 85, in Cotton Family Papers, MHS. Wheelwright felt the need to address the apparent contradiction between meekness and combat (*AC,* 164–165). Roger Williams remarked the "rigid and censorious" manner of the newly arrived Hutchinsonians in Providence in the spring of 1638 (Glenn W. LaFantasie, ed., *The Correspondence of Roger Williams* [Providence, R.I., 1988], I, 149). "In their speech, [was] nought but self-deniall," said Robert Baillie of the American antinomians, but "their malice towards all that dissented from them, was . . . extreme" (*A*

John Winthrop noted Anne Hutchinson's "fierce carriage," her "fierce speech and countenance" in her embattled hours. Not only a dominating tone but a certain grandiosity crept into her reported spiritist deliverances, as in her claim unerringly to distinguish "between the voice of my beloved and the voice of Moses" in the pulpit, her assertion "that if she had but one halfe houres talke with a man, she would tell whether he were elect or not," and to her expectation that her weekly audiences receive her message "not . . . as it comes from me, but as it comes from the Lord Jesus Christ." This and other evidence suggests that exertive and domineering urges still ran strong within the Dissenting party and indeed moved to the fore in 1637–1638. When the crunch was on, allegiance to "free grace" seemed to make the human creature more, not less.[5]

Deliberately, I have approached the first wave of antidisciplinary religion from about 1615 on its own terms so far as possible and not as a foreshadow of later developments. Yet the developments traced above laid important groundwork for the midcentury sectarian splurge. Several ways out of the pietist way had been blazed. Eatonist, Grindletonian, Hutchinsonian, and other strategies were available to make religion less restrictive and more enjoyable. Unconditional pardon and certainty, divine immediacy and benevolence, slackened reverence for law as well as for creaturely "forms" and mediations— in varying degrees these familiar themes of English radical religion around midcentury had been formulated and put into practice well beforehand under the aegis of free grace. And, in faraway Massachusetts, Anne Hutchinson, with no small help from Cotton, had lifted antidisciplinary religion to a new level by joining it to an oracular spiritism, mortalism, and other themes of the Radical Reformation. So too had critiques by Peter Gunter, William Hinde, and others provided initial antinomian constructs as well as models of ortho-

---

Dissuasive from the Errours of the Time . . . [London, 1645], 62). In *Prophetic Woman: Anne Hutchinson and the Problem of Dissent in the Literature of New England* (Berkeley, Calif., 1987), 8, 42, Amy Schrager Lang discusses antinomianism's paradoxical mix of passivity and assertiveness. See also her remarks on "the arrogance of the antinomians," in "Antinomianism and the 'Americanization' of Doctrine," *NEQ*, LIV (1981), 225.

5. *AC*, 263 ("carriage"), 269 ("Lord Jesus"), 275 ("speech"), 308 ("talke"), 337 ("my beloved"). Delivering the disciplinary admonition to Anne in the church trial, Cotton censured her for "the highth of your Spirit and being puft up with your owne parts" (*AC*, 372). In *WCC*, 241, he recalled her tendency to be "sharply censorious of other men's spiritual estates." See also the account of Hutchinson's "manlike arrogance" as "gender reversal" in Michael G. Ditmore, "A Prophetess in Her Own Country: An Exegesis of Anne Hutchinson's 'Immediate Revelation,'" *WMQ*, 3d Ser., LVII (2000), 374–375.

dox counterattack upon which midcentury heresiographers could draw, just as they exploited the American *Short Story of the Rise, Reign, and Ruine of the Antinomians, Familists, and Libertines* when it appeared in 1644. There are possible connections to the more distant future too, to the celebrations of human happiness and divine benevolence within the religion of the Enlightenment, to the antinomian currents that played around the fringes of later evangelical awakenings, to the eighteenth- and nineteenth-century arguments about the role of human and divine instrumentality in revivals, and much more.

Were, finally, ideals of piety, strictness, and exactitude in Puritan America measurably affected in the immediate aftermath of the antidisciplinary revolt? Many historians discern an overall "hardening" effect. The trauma forced restrictive adjustments of the congregational system and reinforced orthodox teaching. The former claim is challenged by findings of no oppressive trend in congregational practice in the following years, but the doctrinal impact is far more difficult to assess.[6]

Cotton's course after Hutchinson's banishment is a case in point. In the mid-1630s he was concerned above all to redress a crisis of hypocrisy and doubt by urging a major reversal of course, a tilt away from human behavior and toward the Deity's gifts and works. Major issues of that time continued to occupy him thereafter. He continued to stress human corruption and incapacity as well as the Deity's animating work, to urge the all-sufficiency of Christ or the divine covenant of grace, and to grant sanctified behavior a strictly auxiliary place in evidencing the saints' status before God. Yet not one of his numerous later works, not even *The Covenant of Gods Free Grace Applied to a Disquieted Soul,* assumes a crisis of hypocrisy in the Bay or aims a broad challenge at the going scheme of redemption. Reconciled now with most of his fellow ministers, Cotton hailed the "strict Laws and holy commandments" of the congregational way. He urged his charges to "Kepe close to the Ordinances of God, and the . . . Rule of the word" as well as to "private holie duties" and spoke less reservedly of the value of conditional promises. Possibly with a copy of John Preston's sermon "Exact Walking" before him, or John Ball's paraphrase of the same, he warned Bostonians about 1640 to "walke more exactly, and more accurately" under threat of Deuteronomic punishments.

6. For an example of the "hardening" thesis, see Andrew Delbanco, *The Puritan Ordeal* (Cambridge, Mass., 1989), 159, and see 176, 179. The thesis is challenged by James F. Cooper, Jr., *Tenacious of Their Liberties: The Congregationalists in Colonial Massachusetts* (New York, 1999), 46–59.

More remarkably, he now allowed both a correct grasp and practice of apostolic polity and the performance of religious duties a role in assurance. Gradually he ceased to stress the Spirit's work above and beyond the Word, made the agency of the seal less singular and decisive, and featured spiritual troubles as normal and recurrent. Moreover, if these adjustments constitute a 'hardening, they were more than a reaction to the defeats of 1637 and 1638. Reflecting alarm at extreme views in Rhode Island and the great contemporary surge of radical theologies in the parent country, including those "written under the glorious and fallacious styles of free grace," they addressed transatlantic concerns.[7]

Hardening trends were evident too among the frontline theologians who had opposed Cotton and the free grace insurgency in the 1630s, and again more than colonial issues were at stake. During the 1640s and 1650s and well beyond, defenders of the faith repeatedly dissected and damned the errors associated with Hutchinson and reaffirmed the pietist dialectic of pardon *and*

---

7. John Cotton, *A Brief Exposition . . . upon the whole Book of Canticles* (London, 1655), 26 ("Laws"), 141 ("holy duties"); Helle M. Alpert, ed., "Robert Keayne: Notes of Sermons by John Cotton and Proceedings of the First Church of Boston from 23 November 1639 to 1 June 1640" (Ph.D. diss., Tufts University, 1974), 221 ("Kepe close"); John Cotton, *An Exposition upon the Thirteenth Chapter of the Revelation* (London, 1655), 44 ("more exactly"); *WCC*, 271 ("free grace"). For Preston and Ball, see above, Introduction, n. 4, and text. On corruption and incapacity: Alpert, ed., "Notes of Sermons by John Cotton," 340–341; Robert Keayne, "Notebook, 1643–1646," transcription of MS in MHS by Merja Kyoto, 17 (Kyoto kindly allowed me to examine her transcription). On all-sufficiency: Cotton, *Exposition upon Revelation*, 153, 160–187; Cotton, *The Covenant of Gods Free Grace . . .* (London, 1645), 11–16; 1644 is the probable date of composition (Everett Emerson, *John Cotton*, rev. ed. [Boston, 1990], 141). Assurance: Cotton, *Exposition upon Revelation*, 21; Cotton, *Gods Free Grace*, 10, 20, 24. Conditional promises: Alpert, ed., "Notes of Sermons by John Cotton," 265–268; Keayne, "Notebook, 1643–1646," 9. Spirit's work: in a lecture of late 1638 or early 1639 Cotton affirmed revelations of future events. A set of notes on the lecture was published in George Selement, "John Cotton's Hidden Antinomianism: His Sermon on Revelation 4:1–2," *New England Historical and Genealogic Register,* CXXIX (1975), 283–294. In *The Powring out of the Seven Vials . . .* (London, 1642), 8, Cotton affirmed divine communications in meditation and prayer but censured "private revelations without the Word." Rebutting "familist" and Seeker challenges later in the 1640s, he testified that "the greatest light that I expect is not above the Word, much lesse against it" (Cotton, *A Reply to Mr. Williams . . .* [1645], ed. J. Lewis Diman, in *The Complete Writings of Roger Williams,* II [New York, 1963], 28). The seal: *Exposition upon Revelation,* 151, 153, 175, 182; Cotton, *God's Free Grace,* 16; Cotton, *Canticles,* 4. Spiritual troubles: Cotton, *Gods Free Grace,* 4–11, 17; Cotton, *Canticles,* 39–42, 127–128, 131–137. Alarm at radicalism: Cotton, *Canticles,* 59; Cotton, *A Reply to Mr. Williams,* 15–17, 23; *WCC,* 223, 305; *CJC,* 449–450, 502, 528–533.

of the holy walk. Inevitably, the procedure cast legal and disciplinary values in stronger relief, but its exact effects are elusive. Not only Cotton but all American congregational theologians by the early 1640s were engaged by the momentous turn of events in the mother country. There a fresh round of heresies had emerged, and in them many of the errors enumerated by the synod of 1637 seemed to live again and to imperil the great and perhaps millennial work of reformation that the English godly had begun. In this context midcentury theological adjustments in the New World cannot be explained in parochial terms. They belong to the larger story of mainstream godly defense of the pietist way, ever embattled and with all its precisianist spin, in both Englands.[8]

8. Yet contrary tendencies also appeared. Calls to "betake [your] selves to God alone, and cast [your] selves wholly upon him," or acknowledgment that saints properly disposed "melt into Christ . . . destroy themselves and make Christ all; [and have] . . . no wills but [are] melted into Christ's will," may owe something to free grace radicalism (Peter Bulkeley, *The Gospel-Covenant; or, The Covenant of Grace Opened* [London, 1651], 211; *GP,* 224). Shepard developed this train of thought "when I was hearing Mr. Cotton at Boston" late in 1643 (*GP,* 224). Further research may show that the Antinomian Controversy contributed to a selective enhancement of both poles of the Puritan-Reformed ellipse.